Gift and Grit

In 1998, Bill Clinton hosted a town hall on race and sports. "If you've got a special gift," the president said of athletes, "you owe more back." *Gift and Grit* shows how the sports industry has incubated racial ideas about advantage and social debt since the civil rights era by sorting athletes into two broad categories. The gifted athlete received something for nothing, we're told, and owes the team, the fan, the city, God, nation. The gritty athlete received nothing and owes no one. The distinction between gift and grit is racial, but also, Joseph Darda reveals, racializing: It has structured new racial categories and redrawn racial lines. Sports, built on an image of fairness, inform how we talk about advantage and deservedness in other domains, including immigration, crime, education, and labor. *Gift and Grit* tells the stories of Roger Bannister, Roberto Clemente, Martina Navratilova, Florence Griffith Joyner, and LeBron James – and the story their stories tell about the shifting meaning of race in America.

Joseph Darda is an associate professor of English at Michigan State University. He is the author of three previous books, including, most recently, *The Strange Career of Racial Liberalism*.

Gift and Grit

Race, Sports, and the Construction of Social Debt

JOSEPH DARDA
Michigan State University

Shaftesbury Road, Cambridge CB2 8EA, United Kingdom

One Liberty Plaza, 20th Floor, New York, NY 10006, USA

477 Williamstown Road, Port Melbourne, VIC 3207, Australia

314–321, 3rd Floor, Plot 3, Splendor Forum, Jasola District Centre, New Delhi – 110025, India

103 Penang Road, #05–06/07, Visioncrest Commercial, Singapore 238467

Cambridge University Press is part of Cambridge University Press & Assessment, a department of the University of Cambridge.

We share the University's mission to contribute to society through the pursuit of education, learning and research at the highest international levels of excellence.

www.cambridge.org
Information on this title: www.cambridge.org/9781009584081

DOI: 10.1017/9781009584074

© Joseph Darda 2025

This publication is in copyright. Subject to statutory exception and to the provisions of relevant collective licensing agreements, no reproduction of any part may take place without the written permission of Cambridge University Press & Assessment.

When citing this work, please include a reference to the
DOI 10.1017/9781009584074

First published 2025

A catalogue record for this publication is available from the British Library

Library of Congress Cataloging-in-Publication Data
NAMES: Darda, Joseph, author.
TITLE: Gift and grit : race, sports, and the construction of social debt / Joseph Darda.
DESCRIPTION: Cambridge, United Kingdom ; New York, NY : Cambridge University Press, 2025. | Includes bibliographical references and index.
IDENTIFIERS: LCCN 2024055270 | ISBN 9781009584081 (hardback) | ISBN 9781009584074 (ebook)
SUBJECTS: LCSH: Sports – Social aspects – United States. | Athletic ability – Social aspects – United States. | Racism in sports – United States. | Racism – United States. | African American athletes – Public opinion.
CLASSIFICATION: LCC GV706.5 .D364 2025 |
DDC 306.4/830973–dc23/eng/20250311
LC record available at https://lccn.loc.gov/2024055270

ISBN 978-1-009-58408-1 Hardback
ISBN 978-1-009-58406-7 Paperback

Cambridge University Press & Assessment has no responsibility for the persistence or accuracy of URLs for external or third-party internet websites referred to in this publication and does not guarantee that any content on such websites is, or will remain, accurate or appropriate.

For my brothers

I think anybody with a special gift has a special responsibility. ... If you have a special gift, if God gave you something that other people don't normally have, and no matter how hard they work they can't get there, then you owe more back.
—President Bill Clinton, ESPN Town Meeting on Race and Sports, April 14, 1998

You simply don't deserve this kind of cowardly betrayal. You have given so much and deserve so much more.
—Dan Gilbert, open letter to Cleveland Cavaliers fans after LeBron James announces his departure from the team, July 8, 2010

Contents

	Introduction: The Natural's Bouquets	1
1	The Mismeasure of Sport	23
2	Roberto Clemente on the Black/Brown Color Line	54
3	Black on Black	85
4	How the Student-Athlete Subsidizes the Amateur	116
5	Color Commentary	152
6	Draft Capital	182
	Epilogue: Sports Norming	212
Acknowledgments		223
Notes		225
Bibliography		275
Index		305

Introduction

The Natural's Bouquets

A thirty-four-year-old rookie walks into the dugout of the worst team in Major League Baseball. He carries a battered valise and a bassoon case containing a near-magical bat with "Wonderboy" branded on the barrel. He wears a dark beard and a grimace and comes bearing a short-term, minimum contract. The cantankerous manager looks him up and down and exclaims, "Oh, my eight-foot uncle, what have we got here, the Salvation Army band?"[1]

What the manager has, he learns, is a natural. The rookie, arriving from some rural nowhere, hits the cover off balls. He smacks home runs for sick children. He breaks record after record. He leads the club from last to first and into a tight pennant race. Sportswriters marvel at the rookie's feats. He resembles, they write, "the burly boys of the eighties and nineties more than the streamlined kids" of the 1940s. "He was a throwback to a time of true heroes," they tell one another, "a natural not seen in a dog's age, and weren't they the lucky ones he had appeared here and now to work his wonders before them?"[2]

Bernard Malamud discovered the muse for his classic baseball novel, *The Natural*, in 1947, when he watched Jackie Robinson take the field for the author's hometown Brooklyn Dodgers. Robinson's debut had, Malamud's biographer writes, restored his "youthful interest" in the game and given him some of the raw material for his protagonist and the natural of the title, Roy Hobbs.[3] Malamud, then a high school English teacher with literary ambitions, scrapped a wandering autobiographical novel titled "The Light Sleeper" – six publishers rejected it, and Malamud burned the manuscript – and made the first notes toward a baseball novel that wedded Arthurian legend to the folklore and cornball clichés of the national pastime.

Malamud had watched Robinson break the color barrier at twenty-eight, old for a rookie, if not as old as Roy (or Malamud, a thirty-eight-year-old first-time novelist). He had listened as sportswriters declared Robinson, with a .297 batting average and twenty-nine stolen bases in his first season, a natural. The *New York Times* hailed Malamud's 1952 debut as the first "serious novel" about baseball.[4] The critic Leslie Fiedler celebrated the "lovely, absurd madness" of the story, describing it as "Ring Lardner by T. S. Eliot."[5] No one mentioned that Malamud had, at the dawn of the Black athlete, written a novel about a white natural, summoning him from a receding racial past, a time of burly boys and true heroes.

By the time Robert Redford rounded the bases in the 1984 film adaptation, most Americans, including the filmmakers, had ceased to believe that a white athlete could ever be a natural. Redford's Roy Hobbs is more supernatural than natural. Ahmad Rashad, the broadcaster and former NFL wide receiver, observed in his 1988 memoir that he could close his eyes and listen to a football game and know right away which player was Black and which white. "When [a commentator] says that somebody is a 'natural,' so fluid and graceful, you know he's talking about a black performer," he wrote. "When you hear that this other guy's a hard worker, or that he comes to play every day on the strength of guts and intelligence, you know that the player in question is white. Just open your eyes."[6] Rashad could see, as others had argued before and have argued since, that attributing athletic success to natural talent meant discounting other factors: intelligence, dedication, teamwork. "It is a wise warrior," the sociologist Harry Edwards once wrote, "who proceeds with caution and discretion when an enemy tosses bouquets in his direction."[7]

Malamud, born in 1914 to Russian Jewish immigrant parents, could recall a time when the natural's bouquets landed at the feet of a near-white working class: the immigrant from the streets of New York (Lou Gehrig, Hank Greenberg), the farm boy from the sticks (Ty Cobb, Shoeless Joe Jackson). Indigenous athletes once received them (Jim Thorpe, Lewis Tewanima) and sometimes still do (the Kalenjin of East Africa, the Tarahumara of northern Mexico). The natural is a form of anti-Blackness, as Rashad and Edwards said, and it is something else and something more.

Introduction: The Natural's Bouquets

This book tells the story of the athletic gift since Roy Hobbs left the field. It is a book not about elite athletes but about how the way we imagine elite athletes affects the rest of us. It offers a theory of athletic racialization that, while concentrating on the nation's long-running but ever-shifting investment in Black athleticism, suggests what a future after the Black natural might look like and whose interests it might serve.

Racialization makes inequality appear fair. Capitalism requires inequality, and racialization allows us to excuse emerging forms of inequality as deserved. New socioeconomic conditions create new categories of winners and losers, and racialization, adapting past categories, enshrines them as natural, permissible, intractable. The color line bends and blurs. Racialization lets us live with inequality. It hides it. It justifies it. And perhaps most of all, it encourages us to throw up our hands and say, This is how it is, and it can't be helped.[8]

Sports are built on the appearance of fairness, and they inform how we talk about equality in other domains. The ideology of the level playing field can, as the historian Amy Bass writes, be "smoothly extended as a metaphor for racial and national equality," and it is, all the time.[9] The odd thing about the level playing field is that no one buys it. We all recognize that sports aren't about equality but competing inequalities – inequalities of size, preparation, equipment, facilities, access, coaching, diet, health. The dominant ideology of sports is not the level playing field but the unequal playing field that the public accepts as fair. Which advantages do we deem legitimate? And which illegitimate? Where do we draw the line? May Roy use his strange bat? May Branch Rickey sign Robinson?

Athletic racialization sorts athletes into two broad categories: the gifted and the gritty. The gifted athlete is the recipient of God-given talent. The gritty athlete receives nothing. The gifted athlete owes the team, the coach, the fan, God, nation. The gritty athlete owes no one. Athletic racialization is a form of ontological accounting. A gift, as Jacques Derrida wrote, establishes a relation of giver and recipient that, even when entered into without conditions, presupposes that the recipient owes something in return. The giver establishes a "hold on" the recipient that makes a genuine gift, a gift without debt, all but impossible.[10] Giftedness is a gift with an ambiguous donor. It carries a free-floating debt that others, who may have no relation to the gifted athlete at all, can claim. When LeBron James left the Cleveland Cavaliers in 2010 to sign with the Miami Heat, Cavs owner Dan Gilbert, a cofounder of Quicken Loans, published an open letter to Clevelanders. "You simply don't deserve this kind of cowardly betrayal," he wrote on the NBA's website. "You have given so much and deserve so much more."[11] LeBron was gifted, and Gilbert and Cavs fans had claimed the debt and expected a return on investment. LeBron would, as he announced on an ESPN special that summer, be taking his talents to South Beach, and Clevelanders demanded a percentage back. LeBron owed them.

Most theorists of race attribute racialization not to organizations – MLB, the NBA, the Cleveland Cavaliers – but to the state. In the first edition of their classic *Racial Formation in the United States*, Michael Omi and Howard Winant, writing amid the civil rights rollback of the Reagan administration, defined racialization as "the extension of racial meaning to a previously racially unclassified relationship, social practice, or group." The sociologists observed that new racial knowledge had been "most definitively institutionalized by the state," and they dedicated much of that edition, and have dedicated much of every edition since, to the "racial state."[12] Others have followed their lead. The geographer Ruth Wilson Gilmore compares the state's management of racial categories to how it maintains roads, electrical grids, and other forms of infrastructure: They need to be "updated, upgraded, and modernized," or they will crumble.[13] The historian Nikhil Singh defines racialization as the state's ongoing differentiation between "zones of protection from and vulnerability" to state-sanctioned harm.[14] The cultural theorist Lisa Lowe describes it as the violence through which the state constructs the boundaries of the universal human.[15] (I'm also a card-carrying Omi-and-Winantian, having written books about how the state has made race by defining who may act in self-defense, who may claim the entitled status of veteran, and who must wait on freedom and for how long.)[16]

Most theories of racialization do not attend to the individual. The reason is obvious: Other than a few world leaders, the individual is not making or moving racial boundaries. We act, it seems, in the long shadow of the racial state. But, as Gilmore writes, we do, all of us, "make places, things, and selves, although not under conditions of our own choosing."[17] We make them within a social structure. Racial knowledge does not trickle down from the state to the individual but gets formed, from above and below, at the intermediate level of the organization, where state and individual interests collide. This is where sports come in, where Dan Gilbert and Cavs fans get their say. Sports leagues and franchises, their owners encourage us to believe, belong to us – our national pastime, America's game. But they don't. Gilbert owns the Cavs, not Cleveland. The sports organization acts as a public good when it suits its interests and as a business when it doesn't. It functions as a structural go-between, facilitating the transfer of racial meaning from the state to the individual and from the individual – owner, administrator, coach, athlete, writer, fan – to the state.

I'm far from the first to ask how sports form racial knowledge. The sociologist Ben Carrington theorizes, with a nod to Omi and Winant, what he calls "sporting racial projects," in which, as he writes, "sport helps to make race make sense and sport then," having given racial categories a veneer of observable common sense, "works to reshape race."[18] Bass shows how sports science has long sustained a waning but, it seems, unkillable commitment to race as biological difference and how Black athletes have seized the belief in their own athleticism as a resource to transform the nation and themselves.[19] The sociologist Douglas Hartmann defines sports as "contested racial terrain," a terrain that can, as one of our biggest cultural stages, "transform racial formations."[20] Carrington builds his argument outward from Jack Johnson's 1908 ascent to the heavyweight boxing title, Bass and Hartmann theirs from Tommie Smith and John Carlos's 1968 Black-gloved salute in Mexico City. This book investigates not the big swings in the racial life of sports – the birth of the Black athlete, the rise and decline and rise again of the political Black athlete – but smaller, more subtle shifts in athletic racial knowledge since the civil rights era. Working at the more modest scale of the racial shift, I aim to illuminate the mechanism through which sports make race, what I call giftedness, with the hope that sports might allow us to see race not as it was but as it forms, live, on the field and in the stands. I sketch the architecture of what could be called a social "pre-emergence" or "structure of feeling."[21] This is a book about sports that asks whether we can, if we catch the right line of sight, peer around the racial corner.

The athletic gift took on new meaning after civil rights. The ascendent countermovements of the 1970s succeeded in casting the most modest forms of racial redistribution – affirmative action, busing, the enforcement of voting rights – as state-issued gifts to communities of color, and a rising class of free-market ideologues reframed all human relations in terms of creditors and debtors, givers and takers. Black athletes, who made small fortunes and achieved greater fame, found themselves caught between backlash and financialization, celebrated and derided as paradigmatic gift recipients. The athletic gift structured how the public talked about civil rights and social debts. It furnished a language – gift and grit, talent and hustle – through which Americans encountered genetics, immigration reform, crime, college admissions, media, and finance. There's nothing natural about the natural. The assignment of giftedness reflects time-bound interests. It will change as they do.

Athletes we'd now call white once bore the burden of the gift. Roy Hobbs was "a natural," his bench coach tells the manager, "though somewhat less than perfect because he sometimes hit at bad [pitches]."[22] The manager frowns. "I mistrust a bad ball hitter," he says. "They sometimes make some harmful mistakes."[23] The foreshadowing is not subtle. Roy makes one harmful mistake after another, on the field and off. The novel ends with him chasing a bad ball. (In the movie, he hits a towering, slow-motion home run.) When the franchise's crooked owner refuses to negotiate a new contract, the fans organize "Roy Hobbs Day" and shower the natural with gifts: two TV sets, six crates of lemons, a frozen side of hog, a four-burner electric range, a deed to a lot in Florida, twelve pairs of monogrammed shorts, a bearskin rug, a Chris-Craft motorboat, and a white underslung Mercedes-Benz, which Roy drives around the outfield, waving to his benefactors.[24] He owes them, he knows, not for the TVs and car but for his athletic gift, the debt to which they have staked a claim. He must either settle the debt, with a pennant, or live the rest of his life as someone who wasted a gift, who failed when success had been handed to him.

The novel ends with the greatest debt collector cornering the natural. "Say it ain't true, Roy," a boy on the street, thrusting a newspaper at him, asks.[25] The headline alleges that Roy had thrown the final game of the season. The boy, reenacting a story, untrue but enduring, about Shoeless Joe and the Black Sox scandal, had invested his innocence in the natural, and Roy had let him down and will, the reader knows, die a social debtor. Gilbert told the same story about LeBron in 2010. "This shocking act of disloyalty from our homegrown 'chosen one,'" the Cavaliers owner wrote, "sends the exact opposite lesson of what we would want our children to learn."[26] The natural, the chosen one, the shoeless South Carolina mill hand with the swing you couldn't teach – they all owed us, and owed our children.

The debt of giftedness weighs on athletes but heavier on the communities for which they act as cultural substitutes. But Malamud's natural no longer carries the debt of others. Roy, making his big-league debut in the 1940s, succeeds and fails as an individual, not as the athletic stand-in for a race. The Immigration Act of 1924, which curtailed the flow of immigrants from eastern and southern Europe, severing ties to ancestral homelands, and the first Great Migration, in which millions of Black

Southerners relocated to northern cities, transformed the white races into a white race of confederated "ethnicities" made legible through a contrast with Blackness.[27] The immigrant natural and rural natural turned into white athletes who, vanishing into the norm of white male embodiment, shed their gifts. Roy, the white natural, straddles two racial worlds, looking back to a time of disaggregated whiteness and forward to the age of the Black athlete, whose arrival instilled the new consolidated whiteness with a no-duh common sense.

The athletic color line shifts. It fractures. It crosses other lines of difference. It serves one interest and then another. This book follows the athletic gift as it moves through track and field, baseball, boxing, football, and basketball, and into conversations about science, language, law, affirmative action, entertainment, and gambling. The gift carries a debt and the open secret of how sports make race in America. We need to know the natural's bouquets before we can pick them up and throw them back.

The athletic gift is not discovered but constituted through the search. In the quarterfinals of the 100 meters at the 1988 US Olympic Track and Field Trials in Indianapolis, Florence Griffith Joyner – lane 5, one-legged purple speed suit – lowered herself into the blocks and ripped off the fastest time ever recorded in the event: 10.49 seconds. She had lopped more than a quarter second off the world record. (She would run faster than the former record in all four rounds that week, three times with legal wind readings of below 2 meters per second.) The broadcasters did not react at first. She couldn't have run that fast. It had to be an issue with the stadium scoreboard or the wind gauge, which registered 0.0 meters per second. "It cannot be. No one can run that fast," one said. "The heat here must be doing something to the electronics."[28] It had to be the weather.

It wasn't the weather. Officials determined that the clock hadn't malfunctioned and that the wind reading would stand. There must be something wrong, others decided, with the sprinter herself. "Florence, in 1984, you could see an extremely feminine person," the Brazilian middle-distance runner Joaquim Cruz said in a TV interview that summer. "But today she looks more like a man than a woman."[29] Pat Connolly, who had coached Evelyn Ashford, the woman whose record Griffith Joyner had broken, observed that the sprinter's face had changed "almost overnight," hardening "along with the muscles that now bulged as if she had been born with a barbell in her crib." Connolly wondered whether Griffith Joyner had "found herself an East German

Florence Griffith Joyner at the 1988 Summer Olympics.
Photograph by Lennox McClendon. From AP Photo.

coach."[30] The sprinter's critics had no evidence that she had taken performance-enhancing drugs. She hadn't failed a test. But something was off, they decided, about how she embodied her gender. She was too masculine, too muscular. She bore an excess, a gift of some kind, whether received (talent) or taken (performance-enhancing drugs). If it wasn't the clock or the wind, it had to be something. No one can run that fast.

Griffith Joyner's critics felt that she owed them an answer. She had run too fast for a woman. How? Judith Butler, then an assistant professor at George Washington University completing a book – you've heard of it – in which they claimed that we don't have genders but perform them into being, thought that women's sports could transform the gender categories we inhabit. Butler, a tennis fan, had followed the career of Martina Navratilova since the late 1970s, when she won the first of her record nine Wimbledon singles titles. The sport had received the young Navratilova, twenty-one when she first rose to world number one, as a threat to the gender ideal of the women's game. She was muscular. She was aggressive on the court. She lifted weights. She showed her frustration

Introduction: The Natural's Bouquets 9

with officials. She dated women. But broadcasters and tennis writers celebrated the older Navratilova, who won her final Wimbledon title in 1990, as the new ideal, a model for Steffi Graf, Conchita Martínez, and other emerging stars. Women's sports had "the power to press the boundaries of gender ideals," Butler wrote in 1998, reflecting on an unusual collaboration between Stanford's Department of Comparative Literature and its Department of Athletics, Physical Education, and Recreation. Navratilova's career had, Butler thought, established women's sports as a "distinctively public way" in which we reencountered "woman" as "a limit to surpass."[31] Butler did not see Navratilova's transformation from threat to ideal as evidence of degendering or a return to some lost state of nature but as one sign of a crisis of knowledge through which gender categories could change. The sport had reimagined Navratilova's gift as grit, her threat to a gender ideal as the ideal. She had earned her muscles and her titles. She didn't owe tennis a thing, not a cut or an explanation. (Navratilova has since taken a lead in the campaign to bar trans women and girls from competitive sports, policing the categories she once challenged. I would guess that she has lost Butler as a fan.)

Griffith Joyner never shook her debt. The sprinter died in 1998, at thirty-eight, after suffering a seizure in the middle of the night and suffocating in her bed. The coroner attributed her death to an undiagnosed cavernous hemangioma, a congenital condition with no known association with steroid use. Her husband, the triple jumper Al Joyner, called the coroner's investigation his wife's "final, ultimate drug test."[32] Some of her critics relented. Others didn't care what the coroner said; they had seen what they'd seen. "In 1987, [Griffith Joyner] looked like a normal woman athlete," one wrote in the *Times* after her death. "By the following year, almost miraculously, her body was strong and rippling."[33]

Tennis learned to love Navratilova's muscles. Track and field never forgave Griffith Joyner for hers. Why? Navratilova, who fled her native Czechoslovakia at eighteen, underwent a second transformation that Butler did not acknowledge: The tennis star entered the 1980s as an Eastern Bloc émigré – a status then associated with state-sponsored Soviet and East German doping – and exited the decade as an American athlete who, during the Reagan administration's reescalation of the Cold War, could be counted on to condemn the communist government of her homeland. Griffith Joyner, a young Black woman, achieved fame and moderate fortune at the height of another war on drugs and as the president defended cuts to social services by telling stories about Black female welfare cheats wearing furs and driving Cadillacs. The tennis player's social debt shrank, and the sprinter's grew. Giftedness offers a shorthand for talking about human value – whom we owe and who owes us, whom a norm must accommodate and who must accommodate it. Navratilova could not have become tennis's new ideal without a natural. She needed someone else's more salient gift to turn her own into grit. Navratilova troubled gender. Gender troubled Griffith Joyner.

Take American football. It once constituted an ideal form of masculine athleticism. But the sport's image changed as the athletes who turned out and made the cut did. Now almost no white liberal middle-class parents would, white liberal middle-class parents declare, let their sons take the field because football is violent, dangerous, militaristic, racist. It is too much. The masculine norm had moved on. I'm not defending Roger Goodell's NFL or condoning the perpetuation of an epidemic of brain trauma, but the ease with which we now dismiss football as an aberrant masculine culture follows a pattern. "Masculinity," the gender theorist Jack Halberstam writes, "becomes legible as masculinity where and when it leaves the white middle-class body," and giftedness is what we call that legible gender in sports.[34]

Athletic racialization is as unstable as what Butler called athletic genders. It assimilates ideological racialization (Navratilova's anticommunism and the "whitening" of the former Eastern Bloc) and gendered racialization (Griffith Joyner's criminal muscles).[35] It does not conform to a rigid color line. It reuses old racial categories but is not a "new plantation." It changes because it has to; it has to stay ahead of an also evolving but ever-lagging dominant antiracism. (Describing college football programs as plantations, as some do, is a strategic overstatement, not a historical argument. It serves a purpose but perhaps at the cost of seeing the racial present as it is.)[36] Athletic racialization lets us believe that the fastest woman in the world owes us something for all that she's been given. The gift is an excess that we claim as our rightful cut of athletic capital.[37]

Marcel Mauss did not see the gift as an instrument of capital. In his 1925 *Essai sur le don*, published in English as *The Gift*, the anthropologist argued that the persistence of gift giving under capitalism signaled the limits and perhaps the inevitable failure of the market. People desired forms of reciprocation that did not begin and end with the exchange of goods and labor, and Mauss found evidence of the gift's presence all around him. He identified the rise of state social services as the return of a "group morality" that he believed Indigenous peoples of the Pacific Northwest and Pacific Islands observed in their gift-giving practices.[38]

Introduction: The Natural's Bouquets

But Mauss did not see the state as the gift giver but the indebted recipient. The worker "feels now as he has always felt – but this time he feels it more acutely – that he is giving something of himself, his time and his life," he wrote. "Thus he wants recompense, however modest, for this gift."[39] Workers offered the gift of their labor – a gift constituted of surplus value as well as, for Mauss, "a part of oneself" – and the state ought to compensate workers for what they gave to the nation it governed.[40] W. E. B. Du Bois agreed, enumerating in *The Gift of Black Folk* all that Black people had contributed to the United States – and all, he implied, that the United States owed in return.[41] Griffith Joyner was not, for Mauss and Du Bois, the recipient but the gift giver. She had shared her athletic labor with the public. It owed her.

Derrida thought that Mauss had, in a book titled *The Gift*, managed to write about "everything but the gift."[42] If a gift demanded reciprocation, as Mauss said it did, then was it a gift at all? Was the practice of gift giving that the anthropologist regarded as a counterweight to the market nothing more than an act of exchange with a moral facade? Derrida thought that the gift, if it gave at all, gave time, time for the recipient to reciprocate – time that also bound the recipient in a debt relation. Mauss regarded the social bonds formed through gift giving as the foundation of human relations of care, Derrida as conditions for coercion. The anthropologist David Graeber, a champion of Mauss's thought, dismissed Derrida's critique of the gift as pretentious and predictable. "Those who like to think of themselves as engaged in cutting-edge critical theory," he wrote in 2001, now engage with Mauss through Derrida, who examines the "concept of the gift to discover – surprise! – that gifts, being acts of pure disinterested generosity, are logically impossible."[43] Derrida published his most thorough engagement with Mauss, *Donner le temps*, in 1991, and it landed for some, including Graeber, as an overfamiliar trick. But perhaps we should see the difference between Mauss's gift and Derrida's not as a transhistorical philosophical disagreement but as measuring the distance from 1925 to 1991. "*Homo economicus* is not behind us, but before us," Mauss wrote.[44] At the height of Derrida's fame, it was us.

Neither Mauss nor Derrida wrote about giftedness. Who gives it? Whom does the gifted person owe? You'd think the answer would be God or no one. But the athlete identified as gifted owes the team, the coach, the fan, Dan Gilbert, the boy who asks his hero to "say it ain't true" – all make claims on the athlete's unearned talent. The assignment of giftedness burdens the athlete with a free-floating debt, and another word for free-floating debt, after civil war and civil rights, is race. "Emancipation instituted indebtedness," Saidiya Hartman writes. The "gift of freedom," as freedmen's manuals and other Reconstruction-era literature described the Thirteenth Amendment, defined the terms of a new, related form of unfreedom, a servitude more durable than the last because it was cast as liberation, a gift that could never be forgiven.[45] Refugees in the Global North have suffered under their own version of that gift, which obliges them, as Mimi Nguyen observes, to show thanks to a state that may have razed their homeland and which binds them to a "colonial order of things."[46] Griffith Joyner did not live in servitude, and she had not lost her homeland. But she did make a comfortable living as an athlete after civil rights, and some thought that the state had, with the Civil Rights and Voting Rights Acts and Title IX, given her something, that it and the nation it governed had contributed to her success. Others on the left thought that she, as a Black athlete, had an obligation to speak out against injustice and carry on the legacy of what the journalist Howard Bryant calls "the Heritage."[47] Du Bois's gift of Black people and Mauss's gift of workers had been reversed, and the athletic gift – a gift as enigmatic as freedom – taught the public how to measure the debt.

The criticism may have bothered Griffith Joyner, but she had a good life. She won three gold medals at the Olympics in Seoul, where she twice broke the world record in the 200 meters. She returned to endorsement deals that netted her an estimated $4 million in 1988. She modeled athletic wear and high heels. She wore a milk mustache for the Got Milk? campaign. She sold nail accessories and a doll – the Flo Jo Doll; tagline: "let your dreams run free." Advertisers could not, one writer observed, get enough of her "exotic beauty."[48] (The gender excess her critics assigned to her did not have to be a masculine excess. Some found her too feminine. She couldn't win.) But advertising executives grumbled about her and her manager's demands, telling the *Times* that they had nicknamed her "Cash Flo" for the high cost of doing business with the sprinter.[49] The executives also complained that she hadn't returned their calls in the first week after Seoul, when her name recognition would have been highest. She owed them a discount and a call, they thought. Her fifteen minutes were almost over, and they were doing her a favor. Where was her gratitude?

Griffith Joyner had grown up in public housing in the Watts neighborhood of Los Angeles and died in a big house that she had bought for herself and her husband in a tree-lined, oceanside Orange County suburb. She had made it, and she would return business calls when she wanted, if she wanted. But the debt of giftedness is shared. It informs how we think about difference and deservedness and human value. We might call it the "burden of over-representation" or "symbolic labor" or a "racialized form of consumerism."[50] But the accounting is the same. The gift died with the last breath of the fastest woman ever, but the debt lived on, unforgiven.

Flo Jo returned from Seoul as Cash Flo because of a man in an office building in downtown Cleveland. Mark McCormack founded International Management Group in 1960 with one client, the golfer Arnold Palmer. There was, at first, nothing international about it. Palmer was from the steel mill town of Latrobe, Pennsylvania, and, as one of the biggest stars on the PGA Tour, his total annual income, including tournament winnings and endorsements, amounted to less than $60,000.[51] His contract with Heinz earned him $500 and all the ketchup he could eat.[52] But McCormack, an amateur golfer who had competed against Palmer in college, had big plans. He thought that athletes could be "more popular, better commercial vehicles for companies to sell their products," and he turned Palmer into one of the most saleable brands in sports – signature clubs, Wheaties boxes, ads for auto insurance and watches and cigarettes and later Nicorette.[53] He also, like Griffith Joyner, had a doll ("ages 4 to 104," "fully posable figure!").

McCormack took his cut and expanded. He moved into other sports and then into fashion and music. He bought events and stadiums and training academies. He took on corporate clients. He added a broadcasting division and offered financial management services. He signed Jack Nicklaus and Pele and Venus and Serena Williams and Tiger Woods and Gisele Bündchen. *Golf Digest* named him "the most powerful man in golf." *Tennis Magazine* called him "the most powerful man in tennis."[54] *Sports Illustrated* declared him, in an issue with Michael Jordan on the cover, "the most powerful man in sports." IMG had, it wrote, "tentacles that reach into the backwaters where sport and the dollar meet."[55]

McCormack invented the commercial athlete. Adolf Dassler, the founder of Adidas, may have been the first to use athletes as brand ambassadors. Jesse Owens wore a shoe of Dassler's design at the 1936 Berlin Olympics after the German cobbler visited him in the athletes' village. But McCormack recognized that athletes could be made into lucrative brands themselves. What did Arnie know about lawnmowers or photocopiers? Nothing. How often did he and O. J. Simpson rent cars at a Hertz desk? Never. Did it matter? McCormack thought it didn't, and he was right. He was "the first to realize that sportsmen could be marketed like soap powder or Cornflakes," the *Economist* wrote in a critical assessment that wouldn't have bothered McCormack.[56] He liked to introduce himself not as the most powerful man in sports but, writing the script for all future agents, as the facilitator of others' fortunes. "I am probably better known as 'the guy who made Arnold Palmer all those millions' than I am by my own name," he liked to say.[57] Some have celebrated McCormack as the athlete's liberator. Matthew Futterman, of the *New York Times*, has credited him with freeing athletes from the "grand old men" of sports, and a direct line can be drawn from McCormack to LeBron's agent, Rich Paul, and the athlete empowerment movement of the 2010s.[58] The athlete got rich, and all that McCormack asked was a cut of the take.

But McCormack, who died in 2003, contributed something else to the business of sports. In selling the athlete as a brand, he also invented the modern fan, the customer for his client, and he offered himself as a model. McCormack may have been best known, as he claimed, for his association with Palmer, but millions knew him as one of the best-selling authors of business advice books at a moment when, in the first flush of neoliberalism, the genre was reaching new heights. This was the time of *In Search of Excellence*, *The Art of the Deal*, and *The Seven Habits of Highly Effective People*. In *What They Don't Teach You at Harvard Business School*, which topped the *New York Times* Best Seller list for twenty-one consecutive weeks in 1984 and 1985, McCormack introduced a formula that writers like Malcolm Gladwell and Michael Lewis would later ride to the airport book rack: He used sports as a delivery mechanism for simple business lessons. He acknowledged that signing Palmer, Nicklaus, and Gary Player (golf's "Big Three" of the 1960s) as his first clients was "like winning a lottery."[59] But he couldn't bank on luck, he wrote, because athletes were the riskiest kind of investment. Athletes got hurt, got old, retired young, attracted scandal. He had mitigated that risk, he explained, with a client list of more than a thousand. If one client's career didn't pan out, he had another who could sell Buicks and Michelob Ultra. "Björn Borg can break a leg," he liked to tell his vice presidents. "Wimbledon cannot."[60] The smart investor was in the Wimbledon business, not the Borg business. Borg, an IMG client, was McCormack's favorite example because he had retired from tennis, without warning, at twenty-six. *What They Don't Teach You at Harvard Business School* used sports to illustrate business advice, but it also used business to illustrate sports advice. Fans should think like investors, McCormack believed. You couldn't count on one athlete. You

Introduction: The Natural's Bouquets 15

had to hedge one's career against the other. Don't get attached. Get out of the Borg business and into the Wimbledon business.

The most powerful man in sports turned the athlete into a brand and urged the fan to become an investor. McCormack boasted that the margins in his business could be as high as 60 percent. The athlete had a gift, an excess, and the smart fan, acting as an investor, claimed it as a debt and expected a profit. McCormack had not, as he and Futterman claimed, liberated the athlete. He had liberated himself and the fan, whom he advised in business and sports, from the risk of being an athlete. Michael Jordan needed Michael Jordan to succeed. Mark McCormack didn't. Why be like Mike when you can be like Mark?[61]

McCormack thought the fan should be an investor. Theodor Adorno thought the fan might be a fascist. The philosopher could see trouble ahead when, at the end of his life, he delivered a radio lecture about what kind of education, for children and adults, could guard against another Holocaust, and whether sports fueled or mitigated mass violence. Football could, he allowed, "have an anti-barbaric and anti-sadistic effect by means of fair play, a spirit of chivalry, and consideration for the weak." But it could also "promote aggression, brutality, and sadism."[62] He worried most not about athletes but about the people in the stands, who "do not expose themselves to the exertion and discipline required by sports but instead merely watch." The fan, whose behavior reminded Adorno of the "good old authoritarian personality," ought to be "analyzed systematically."[63]

C. L. R. James shared some of Adorno's concerns. But James, who credited cricket with much of his early political education, did not condemn fans as a class. He was troubled by one kind of fan above all others: the American fan. When the Trinidadian intellectual moved to the United States in the late 1930s and attended a baseball game – he had been told that it was like his beloved cricket – he could not believe the "howls of anger and rage and denunciation" that fans "hurled at the players as a matter of course."[64] It was like nothing he'd seen before, and it disturbed him.

James wrote his book on cricket. Adorno never wrote his on the fan. He died three years after the radio address. What might he have said? Adorno had moved to the United States around the same time as James, fleeing Nazi Germany. His time there, in what Thomas Mann called "German California," informed his and fellow Frankfurt school émigré Max Horkheimer's theory of the "culture industry," which manufactured not mass culture but a mass audience deluded by a belief in the freedom of consumer choice. In the early 1940s, Adorno and Horkheimer had radio, magazines, and most of all film – they were in Southern California, after all – on their minds. Perhaps the older Adorno would have included sports in his definition. Perhaps he would have seen, as still too few do, sports as culture – and as the kind of mass culture through which "the whole world is made to pass through."[65] Adorno was unsure about the athlete. He feared the fan.

McCormack did not. He sought to monetize the kind of fervor that worried Adorno, and he thought he could do it best with a certain kind of athlete. Though McCormack had built IMG through the white country-club sports of golf and tennis – he didn't think athletes in team sports had the same reach, and he didn't want to deal with franchise owners and general managers – McCormack had long sought a Black star. In the 1970s, he wrote to tournament organizers in Europe, urging them to invite the Black American golfer Jim Dent, the longest driver on the PGA Tour. "I have a very interesting suggestion insofar as a black player is concerned," he wrote one. "He is receiving a lot of attention and a lot of publicity."[66] In *What They Don't Teach You at Harvard Business School*, McCormack mourned the endorsement earnings that Muhammad Ali had left on the table. He could have made a king's ransom, McCormack thought, had Ali cultivated a more "positive, wholesome, 'nonboxer' image."[67] In 1990, McCormack circulated an article about a ten-year-old Venus Williams to his vice presidents.[68] He later met with Don King, who promised he could "deliver" Venus to IMG.[69] McCormack did sign Venus and her sister Serena and, after years of carefully orchestrated overtures, a golfer out of Stanford named Tiger Woods.

McCormack never articulated why he thought a Black star would be good for IMG. But he did, it seems, see value in Blackness itself; I can't think of much more that Ali and Woods have in common. Perhaps he thought that the Williams sisters and Woods could sell their sports to a wider audience. Or perhaps he thought they would let tennis and golf fans believe that their sports weren't all that elitist after all, or at least not racist. He sold Dent's services to golf pros as a bargain, charging one-fifth of what he did for his bigger-name clients, but the Williams sisters and Woods were among the best compensated athletes in the world. What was McCormack selling to advertisers? And what were they selling to consumers? McCormack the business advice author determined that the strongest form of relation between the athlete and the consumer was the investment. The consumer must, like an amateur agent, invest in the athlete, and the best kind of investment was the one with the biggest return.

Perhaps McCormack knew that a fan would feel entitled to more from some athletes than from others. "With fame and fortune comes responsibility," the Augusta National chairman said in 2010, after revelations of Woods's extramarital affairs. "It is not simply the degree of his conduct that is so egregious here. It is the fact that he disappointed all of us, and more importantly, our kids and our grandkids."[70] With fame and fortune comes, for the gifted athlete, an unforgiveable debt.

Sports Illustrated recognized McCormack for having "built an entire industry." But the magazine deserves some credit. In 1960, Time Inc. founder Henry Luce installed André Laguerre as managing editor, and Laguerre, a former *Time* Paris bureau chief who had hobnobbed with Albert Camus and other French intellectuals and artists after the war, refashioned *SI* as a new kind of sports magazine – sophisticated, self-knowing, investigative, a *New Yorker* for the man in the stands. He introduced the long-form "bonus piece" and recruited novelists and cultural critics as contributors. Sales surged as Ali rose to fame, and Laguerre assigned more features on race and athletes' involvement in the social movements of the time, including Jack Olsen's celebrated 1968 series "The Black Athlete."[71] The sportswriter, long derided as a hack, authored long meditations on Ali and other Black athletes and reemerged as a man of letters. Frank Deford, whom Laguerre hired out of Princeton in 1962, acknowledged that the staff was then limited to his "own kind: the male WASP" and that he couldn't have timed his arrival in the profession better.[72] ESPN followed with men in suits sitting at Cronkite desks, and before long sports talk overshadowed sports. Fans – immersed in never-ending discussions of draft busts, bad trades, exorbitant contracts, and drug cheats – needed time to assess their investments.

Harvard Business School teaches students about IMG. It recognizes McCormack for having "invented the field of sports management."[73] But he did more than invent a field. He established sports management as the dominant way to be a fan.

McCormack thought athletes could sell lawnmowers and Buicks. Bill Clinton hoped they could sell his agenda. He named Griffith Joyner the cochair of the President's Council on Physical Fitness and ran four miles with her and her husband and a staff photographer along the Potomac River. (Al dropped out after three. "They're in pretty good shape," he said of his wife and the president.)[74] In 1998, Clinton made ESPN a stop on his fifteen-month "national conversation on race," with network anchor Bob Ley moderating a roundtable that included

Jim Brown, Georgetown basketball coach John Thompson, and Griffith Joyner's sister-in-law, Jackie Joyner-Kersee. "Rightly or wrongly, America is a sports crazy country," Clinton said in his opening remarks at the thousand-seat Cullen Theater in downtown Houston, "and we often see games as a metaphor or a symbol of what we are as a people."[75] The president, then embroiled in the scandal over his affair with a White House intern, handed things over to Ley and receded into the background. He may have been thinking about the hundred reporters massed at the back of the theater, all waiting for a chance to ask him about Monica Lewinsky. The administration had added the event, Clinton's communications director said, because sports hold "the imagination of a very large sector of the American public, including people who are not otherwise engaged in issues of public policy, let alone race."[76] The initiative's executive director said that the White House aspired to reach one elusive demographic with the event: "men who are sports fans."[77]

But President Clinton struggled to articulate what sports had to do with race. It had something to do with fairness, he suggested. Or it was about teamwork? Perseverance? He didn't know. But his first thanks went to ESPN, a cable network that could not hope to reach the audience of the big four networks and that prohibited ABC, CBS, NBC, and Fox from airing more than four minutes of the ninety-minute event. Clinton knew, as McCormack did, that sports ran through the organization – MLB, the NBA, Wimbledon, the self-declared worldwide leader in sports. The state looked to ESPN to have a national conversation about race.

The sociologist Victor Ray sees the organization as the missing link in how social scientists theorize race. Most organizational theorists, he observes, discount race, seeing it as "in" but not "of" the organization. Most race theorists discount the organization, seeing it as subordinate to the state. Ray identifies what he calls "racialized organizations" as structures that "consolidate resources along racial lines" and "limit the personal agency and collective efficacy of subordinate racial groups while magnifying the agency of the dominant racial group."[78] He offers segregation in the civil rights era as an example. The racial state acted through the organization, authorizing the segregation of restaurants and local public transportation, as did the individual, choosing to enforce or subvert the color line. We remember the legislation and heroic (or infamous) individual but struggle to see the mediating structures that hold things in place and through which change occurs. The sports organization is a racialized organization with an audience. Most of the organizations that Ray investigates do not interest people enough to sustain a TV network

Introduction: The Natural's Bouquets 19

Keyshawn Johnson (*left*), President Bill Clinton (*center*), and Jim Brown (*right*) at an ESPN-hosted town meeting on race in 1998. Photograph by Stephen Jaffe. From Getty Images.

of around-the-clock channels devoted to their every move. Most people don't wear shirts with their homeowner association president's name on the back or tailgate shareholders' meetings. The sports organization is a racializing organization. It consolidates resources along racial lines, as Ray suggests, but it also offers a model for other organizations. It draws the lines. The sports organization establishes the parameters of what Pierre Bourdieu called the "sporting field," and the sporting field has offered a ready metaphor for other fields, from law to education to finance.[79] Bourdieu himself often relied on sports metaphors to articulate his theory of the social field.[80] People want to see the org chart of World Athletics, Major League Baseball, the sports magazine, the college athletic department, ESPN, and the National Football League. The Clinton administration's ESPN "town hall" wasn't a break from the serious business of government. It was the racial state in action.[81]

A half hour into the ESPN event, the discussion turned to the natural. An audience member, a high school student whose question the network had vetted beforehand, asked whether the belief that Black athletes are "physically equipped better" than white athletes constituted a form of antiwhite discrimination. We're "really not getting to the point," Brown responded. Thompson asked if he could swear on the live program. Another high school student, conflating affirmative action with college athlete recruitment, asked why "minority athletes" should be admitted to competitive universities and colleges over white students with better grades and test scores. Thompson, running out of patience, pointed out that most recruited athletes weren't students of color and that there were a lot of other more consequential preferences worth considering. "Our society is about special preferences," he said.[82]

Clinton ducked the questions about Black athleticism and college admissions. But when Ley next turned to him, the president seemed to answer them. "Do you think athletes have a special responsibility," the ESPN anchor asked the president, "or is that unfair?" "No, I don't think that's unfair. I think anybody with a special gift has a special responsibility," Clinton said. "If you have a special gift, if God gave you something that other people don't normally have, and no matter how hard they work they can't get there, then you owe more back."[83] The answer earned him one of the biggest ovations of the evening. President Clinton wouldn't say whether he thought Black athletes had a gift or whether a college's decision to admit athletes of color constituted a gift, but he didn't hesitate to say what he thought about gifted athletes: They owed us. God had given them an advantage, something others don't have, and it was fair for the public to demand something in return. The president of the United States was calling in the athlete's debt.

I must have been listening.

I was ten years old at the time. When adults asked me what I wanted to do when I got older, I would tell them that I wanted to be like my dad, a baseball fan. I achieved my career ambitions early, in the summer before third grade, when my team, the Seattle Mariners, made an improbable run to a division title and then defeated the New York Yankees in a thrilling American League division series. The team's (and the league's) biggest star was centerfielder Ken Griffey Jr., whom the Mariners had drafted first overall a week before I was born, in June 1987. Griffey hit home runs and stole bases. He wore his hat backward. He rocked back and forth in the batter's box, as if he couldn't wait for the action to resume. He was a daring fielder, sometimes to his own detriment. (He missed three months of the 1995 season with a broken wrist, after chasing a ball into the outfield wall. But he caught it and held on, his gloved hand dangling from his forearm.) He made cameos on *The Simpsons* and *The Fresh Prince of Bel-Air* and in the movie *Little Big League*.

Nintendo, which owned the Mariners, released *Ken Griffey Jr. Presents Major League Baseball* and *Ken Griffey Jr.'s Winning Run* for Super Nintendo and then *Major League Baseball Featuring Ken Griffey Jr.* for Nintendo 64. Adults called him "The Kid." Kids called him "Junior." The Mariners roster included other stars and future Hall of Famers – Randy Johnson, Edgar Martinez, a young Alex Rodriguez – but, for a Northwest kid in the 1990s, Major League Baseball was the Griffey show. We shushed our parents when he was batting. We held our bladders and our breath.

I was a fan. I had done it. I listened to the Mariners games on the radio in the evening and checked the box score in the morning. I rocked Griffey's first signature shoe, the Nike Air Griffey Max 1, until the soles fell off and wore a T-shirt that announced him as a candidate for the White House: "Griffey in '96." I don't think I got the joke. Had I been old enough to vote and he old enough to run, I would have cast my ballot for the candidate with the beautiful swing. And I wore my too-big Mariners hat every day – backward, of course.

I thought Ken and I had an understanding. But in 2000, after eleven seasons with the Mariners, he left. Griffey signed with his father's former team, the Cincinnati Reds. He wanted to live closer to his family, he said, and he wanted to honor his father. He switched his number from 24 to Senior's number 30. He had attended high school in Cincinnati and watched his father win two World Series with the Big Red Machine. "I'm finally home," Griffey said in his first news conference as a Red.[84] The Mariners had offered him a larger contract (an eight-year, $148 million extension compared with a nine-year, $116.5 million deal), but he turned it down. He had other priorities – his wife, his kids, the dreams of his younger self.

I hope now, at thirty-seven, that I would have the confidence to make the same kind of decision that he had. But at twelve, I felt cheated. Didn't Griffey owe me something? Didn't he owe Seattle? The Mariners? Hadn't we given him something that entitled us to his signature on that extension? I had learned the language of American fandom, the language that the president himself – the man who defeated Bob Dole and the Mariners centerfielder in the 1996 election – endorsed. Griffey had a gift from God, and we could ask more of him.

I was a fan of Mark McCormack's design. I had bought the merch. I had invested in Griffey, I thought, and held an imagined debt. What made me, a white middle-class kid from central Washington, think that a young Black man from Cincinnati, whom I'd never met, owed me? I had been a recipient of the gift of Griffey's athletic labor, but I couldn't see that then. This book is, among other things, an investigation of my ugly feelings on that day in 2000 when Ken Griffey Jr. signed with the Cincinnati Reds.

What, C. L. R. James asked himself amid the turmoil of a second world war, do people live by? What, beside food and shelter, sustains them, allows them to go on? One thing people wanted, he realized, was sports, and they wanted them "greedily, passionately."[85] His observation held in the United States, but there, he discovered, they wanted something more: a return on investment. Fans tossed bouquets wrapped in debt-collection letters. He was horrified. Couldn't they see that they were the lucky ones that the athletes on the field had appeared here and now to work their wonders before them?

I

The Mismeasure of Sport

On September 13, 1995, at the annual meeting of the British Association for the Advancement of Science, Roger Bannister stood and addressed his colleagues as a man of science. "As a scientist and not a sociologist," he said, "I am prepared to risk political incorrectness by drawing attention to the seemingly obvious but understressed fact that black sprinters and black athletes in general all seem to have certain anatomical advantages."[1] Bannister, the first man to break the four-minute barrier in the mile, then sixty-six and a semi-retired neurologist, was not an anatomist. He had devoted his medical career to autonomic disorders. The evidence for his claim? He had watched that summer's World Athletics Championships, in which Black North American athletes had dominated the shortest races and East Africans the longest. The winner of the 1,500 meters, the Algerian Noureddine Morceli, had lowered the mile world record, the record that Bannister once held, to 3:44.39 at the end of the 1993 season. (The barrier-breaking Bannister of 1954 would have just been entering the homestretch, 100 meters back, when Morceli crossed the finish line.) Something, Bannister thought, had to account for the absence of white athletes from the medal stand.

Bannister had not done his homework. At the gathering in Newcastle, the 156th meeting of the BAAS, he cited his own common sense. "It is perfectly obvious when you see an all-black sprint final that there must be something rather special about their anatomy or physiology which produces these outstanding successes – and indeed there may be, but we don't know quite what it is," he said.[2] He wondered whether Black athletes might have longer Achilles tendons or more fast-twitch muscle fibers. He mused about altitude and warm climates and the resulting genetic inheritances of East and West Africans. He didn't know. He had watched a track meet, traveled to Newcastle, walked onstage, and speculated about why a Jamaican Canadian had won the 100, why a Black American had won the 200 and 400, and why an Ethiopian had broken the meet record in the 10,000. He was not a sociologist. He was the man at a bar who, after a few beers, thought he'd share his thoughts about the Black people on TV.

Bannister might have regretted his remarks, which made international headlines, but he knew that he'd face criticism when he made them. That's why he shielded himself with his medical degree ("as a scientist") and rallied culture warriors to his defense ("I am prepared to risk political incorrectness") before he'd said a thing. Ben Carrington, then a graduate student at Leeds Metropolitan University, wrote a letter to the editors of the *Independent* reminding them, their readers, and Sir Roger that "biologically distinct 'races' do not exist."[3] A columnist for the *Tampa Bay Times* observed that by Bannister's logic the disproportionate number of white doctors must result from some anatomical advantage (larger brain stems?) – a direct route to the "Nazi game plan."[4] But most British and American media covered without condemning Bannister's comments. His chief antagonist seems to have been the one he imagined for himself. *Sports Illustrated* staff writers Jack McCallum and Kostya Kennedy allowed that Bannister had failed to acknowledge "environmental conditions" but commended the man their magazine had named the 1954 Sportsman of the Year for showing "gumption by introducing an anatomical theory to explain the seemingly high number of athletically successful blacks" and giving "us something worth thinking about."[5] Bannister had given his critics two choices. Either you were for science or you were for ignorance. Either you confronted the world as it was or you stuck your head in the sand and ignored the evidence, racing around the track, measured to the hundredth of a second, in front of you.[6]

The 1995 BAAS meeting was not the first time Bannister had floated theories about an innate Black athleticism, and it wouldn't be the last. After Filbert Bayi of Tanzania broke the mile world record in 1975, making him the first African record holder in the event, Bannister had noted the "advantages of Africans dwelling at high altitude" and suggested that the International Olympic Committee might need to regulate altitude training in the future. "A wise athlete of the future will choose African parents to gain this environmental advantage!" he wrote at the time.[7] (He did not mention the advantages of Europeans dwelling at high altitude.)[8] In an interview ahead of the 2012 London Summer Olympics, Bannister, then eighty-three, mused about Usain Bolt's "slave genes." "The West Africans, of course, have an inbuilt advantage," he told the interviewer. "Having been transported to the West Indies, only the toughest endured. They have astonishing muscle composition with those fast fibers and superior genes." He then added that British athletes remained most successful in the middle distances, including the mile, because middle-distance events demand "mental as much as physical expertise."[9] Bayi broke the world record in the mile because he was born 6,000 feet above sea level. Bolt broke the world records in the 100 and 200 because his ancestors had survived the Middle Passage. Bannister had broken the four-minute mile because he had grit. That's what he concluded, as a scientist.[10]

Bannister was nothing if not consistent. What he said in 1995 was what he had said in the 1970s and what he would say again in 2012. But his remarks elicited almost no reaction in the 1970s and 2010s. What made 1995 different? News of Bannister's comments at the BAAS meeting arrived in the United States at a time when the dominance of some Black athletes in some leagues and events had led scientists and science writers to search for answers in their culture, environment, and, with increasing insistence, in their genes. Americans had, by the time Bannister made his stand, watched the NBC *Nightly News* documentary *Black Athletes: Fact and Fiction*, read the *USA Today* series "Race and Sports: Myths and Realities," and encountered every conceivable twist on the title of the 1992 movie *White Men Can't Jump*. Bannister had his defenders in England. He found an audience in the United States.

The debate into which Bannister inserted himself was a tired one. Nature or nurture? commentators asked and asked again. Did East Africans win marathons because of their genes or because of a running tradition or, as in the kinesiologist Robert Malina's "biocultural approach," some combination of and interaction between genetics and culture?[11] The disagreement between the two sides hid a larger consensus: that the Black athlete constitutes a coherent scientific classification, a classification that, in a society that values the natural above the social sciences (and all sciences above the humanities), enters the collective consciousness in biological form. The science of race and sports is the science of giftedness. Bannister had run a 3:59.4 mile in leather shoes and on a cinder track after training fewer than thirty miles a week. But he and others asked what gift God had given Noureddine Morceli.

Bannister wanted the members of the British Association for the Advancement of Science to know that he wasn't a sociologist, and sociologists wanted him to know that they agreed. Brett St. Louis condemned Bannister and the research to which he referred as trafficking in a "naïve inductivist approach" that authorized "palatable racisms" among non-scientists.[12] "It seems," Carrington and Ian McDonald wrote in 2001, "that one of the basics of scientific statistical methodology – that all first-year undergraduates know only too well – namely that correlation does not prove causation, is lost on many of those working within university sport science departments."[13] Few words carry more weight than "as a scientist," and Bannister wasn't alone in using them to validate racial athleticism in the 1990s. If he had, as he claimed, risked censure to defend science, then whom did that science serve? What made this the hill that the first sub-four-minute miler and a growing number of writers would die on?

Theories of athletic racial difference tend to surface at moments of social change. Amy Bass, citing the 1936 Berlin Olympics and the activism of Black athletes in the late 1960s, suggests that scientists and consumers of science writing may be seeking comfort in theories that validate a weakening social order.[14] We want to believe that things are the way they are for a reason, and we seek evidence that reassures us, backed by measurements and times. The anthropologist John MacAloon once observed that the modern social sciences and international athletic contests arose at the end of the nineteenth century out of a shared fascination with the divisions of human life. Each asked, MacAloon writes, "Is there such a thing as Man or are there only men?" He described the modern Olympic Games as a "performance system" that reflects but also constitutes how we inhabit the world and the behaviors that we consecrate as tradition.[15] MacAloon had in mind the ceremonial dimensions of the Games: the lighting of the torch, the medal stand, the flags, the anthems. But international games have also been occasions for another kind of "performance system": the theater of science. When Bannister delivered his remarks in Newcastle, he was an actor on one of the biggest scientific stages, and he knew it. He hadn't done the research. He wasn't a geneticist. But there was the stage, and he had an audience waiting.[16]

Sir Roger assumed a hard line between Black and white that anatomists had long ago discarded as unscientific. But science writers had found a way to restore it. "Blacks are like boys. Whites are like girls," Malcolm Gladwell wrote in 1997, distilling the research of the geneticist Kenneth Kidd and echoing other science writers.[17] He cited a study of standardized math test results that showed that male and female students had similar scores on average but that the distribution was wider (more high scorers and more low scorers) among male students. If you acknowledged a male/female gender binary and that male students had greater variation in math skills than female students, then it wasn't a stretch, Gladwell argued, that a Black/white racial binary also existed and had some bearing on athleticism. Female math students and white athletes clustered around the mean; male math students and Black athletes ranged. He grafted race onto gender, using the latter to naturalize the former.

We have witnessed the reverse in the ongoing movement to bar trans girls from high school sports. When the conservative Christian legal advocacy group Alliance Defending Freedom filed a federal lawsuit against the Connecticut Interscholastic Athletic Conference for allowing two Black trans girls to compete in track and field meets, it chose a white cisgender sprinter to lead the suit, casting her as the embodiment of a threatened women's division. The inclusion of "those two biological male athletes," she testified, denies us "our right – a woman's right – to win."[18] Her message found an audience with track and field fans on the right and some on the left because it echoed the long-standing conviction that white sprinters didn't have a chance, that Black sprinters had a biological advantage that denied their white competitors a real shot at the medal stand. ADF grafted gender onto race.[19]

Bannister assumed that African middle- and long-distance runners had been blessed with some sort of gift – a genetic gift, the gift of being born at elevation. He, a white Brit, had not. He had earned his four-minute mile. They owed a debt, while we all, as the fawning writers of the time claimed, owed Bannister for pushing the limits of human stamina and will. The gift converts racial debt (the Black athlete with a self-evident racial advantage) into gender debt (the female athlete with a self-evident gender advantage) and gender debt into racial debt. When the International Association of Athletics Federations (now World Athletics) announced new sex-verification testing for women athletes in 2011, some critics asked, Why not men? Shouldn't men also be testing for genetic advantages that created "an unlevel playing field for some male athletes over other male athletes"?[20] In the name of fairness, the IAAF had introduced sex-verification testing that was itself unfair to all women athletes. But most critics of the new testing regime overlooked how some male athletes had been accused of, and even tested for, genetic advantages that officials, athletes, fans, and a retired neurologist considered out of bounds, illegitimate. The gift is the mechanism that transforms illicit racial advantages into illicit gender advantages, and back, while obscuring how one sustains the other. The regulation of elite athletes' bodies is not about naturalness but about which advantages we deem fair and earned and which unfair and unearned – who has grit and who bears a gift from the genetic gods.[21]

The science journalist Jon Entine believed then that genetics research was on the verge of revealing unassailable racial truths. When he visited Bannister at his home in Cambridge, England, in the late 1990s, he found a man he described as "tired and worn," shuffling from a "tattered" chair to his bookcase to retrieve his 1955 memoir *First Four Minutes*, "the only visible evidence in the entire room that he was once a world-class athlete."[22] Accusations of racism had, Entine suggested, brought Bannister low, left him wandering in the wilderness, a lone voice for science and reason. Entine knew which word had gotten the doctor in trouble, and he had traveled to Cambridge to defend the doctor's right to use it. Sir Roger had, he writes, "come to regret using the 'N' word – natural."[23]

Dean Cromwell would have agreed with Bannister. Cromwell, the head track coach at the University of Southern California from 1909 to 1948, guided Jesse Owens to four gold medals at the 1936 Berlin Games – a blow, in American lore, to Nazi racial theories. But Cromwell, a member of the isolationist America First Committee who had authorized the removal of two Jewish members of the 4 × 100 meter relay team on which Owens starred, had other ideas about his most famous athlete's achievements. "The international competition of the Olympic games in recent years has shown how racial history and racial physical characteristics contribute to track and field ability," he wrote in his 1941 coaching manual *Championship Technique in Track and Field*. "The Negro excels in the events he does because he is closer to the primitive than the white man. It was not so long ago that his ability to sprint and jump was a life-and-death matter to him in the jungle. His muscles are pliable, and his easy-going disposition is a valuable aid to the mental and physical relaxation that a runner and jumper must have."[24] Cromwell believed that Owens's victories had come "relatively easy" to him because of the innate "bounce" that he shared with other Black athletes.[25] He credited East Asian success in the triple jump to "sturdy legs" resulting from centuries of crouching and Finnish dominance in the distance events to the "hardy" constitution of a forest-dwelling people.[26] Like Bannister, he thought that American and British athletes had their best shot in the middle distances because "no natural physical qualifications are needed."

Americans and Brits found success in the mile, he wrote, because it "put a premium on strong-willed determination" and commitment to "training and technique."[27] Cromwell didn't consider race marginal to athletic achievement. He didn't stick his musings about Owen's natural bounce at the back of his book. He launched into his racial theories right away, in the introduction, on page 5, before he'd said a thing about training.

Cromwell issued his training manual as American anthropologists sought to distance themselves from Nazism. "Anthropology in many countries is being conscripted and its data distorted and misinterpreted to serve the cause of an unscientific racialism," members of the American Anthropological Association wrote in a statement at the end of 1938. "Race involves the inheritance of similar physical variations by large groups of mankind, but its psychological and cultural connotations, if they exist, have not been ascertained by science."[28] Franz Boas, a founder of the association and mentor to a generation of anthropologists that included Ruth Benedict, Melville Herskovits, Zora Neale Hurston, and Margaret Mead, had devoted much of his career to debunking the idea that race governed behavior. Behavior arose not from "racial

Left to right: Dean Cromwell and sprinters Malvin G. Whitfield, Barney Ewell, Harrison Dillard, and Mel Patton aboard the SS *America* en route to London for the 1948 Summer Olympics. From AP Photo.

affiliation," he had argued in 1925, and not for the first time, but from the family and "cultural environment."[29] Race offered no indication of how someone would act. Their family, their culture might. With a second world war looming, Boas, then in his eighties and retired from Columbia University, continued to make his case. Racial discrimination, he wrote at the time, rests on "the unproved assumption that the differences in culture which we observe among peoples of different type are primarily due to biological causes."[30] But for all that he argued against racial determinism, Boas refused to let go of race science, of the racial biological division of the human, seeing it, in fact, as the first line of defense against the scientific racism of Nazi Germany and of men like Cromwell.[31]

Benedict continued her mentor's work. In 1939, at Boas's urging, she, his former student and now colleague at Columbia, devoted a semester-long sabbatical to writing a short, general-audience book on what she called, establishing the term's modern usage, *racism*. "Confusion between the facts of race and the claims of racism is universal in the modern world," Benedict wrote in the foreword to *Race: Science and Politics*, "and this volume is arranged to show that they are polls apart."[32] She organized the book into two sections, the first on race (the facts, the science) and the second on racism (the claims, the politics). Benedict shared Boas's belief that the former could counteract the latter and devoted herself to educating the nation on what she held to be the legitimate biological science of race. "We must know the facts first of Race," she told her readers, "and then of this doctrine that has made use of them. For Racism is an *ism* to which everyone today is exposed."[33]

The Boasians are often credited with moving race from the domain of the natural to the social sciences, from race as fact to race as construct. But they did not abandon biological theories of race but used them as the base on which they built their study of culture. With her colleague Gene Weltfish, another former student of Boas, Benedict turned *Race: Science and Politics* into an all-ages illustrated booklet, *The Races of Mankind*, which reached more than a million readers at the height of the war. The army issued it to officers. School districts assigned it to students. The Detroit Cranbrook Institute of Science modeled a traveling exhibit after it. The United Auto Workers commissioned an animated film version to distribute to local unions in the South. The Boasians had hit the mainstream. In *The Races of Mankind*, Benedict and Weltfish identified three racial categories or "stocks" (Caucasoid, Mongoloid, Negroid) but, as their mentor had before them, disassociated racial belonging from behavior. "One race is not 'born' equipped to build skyscrapers and put plumbing in their houses and another to run flimsy shelters and carry their water from the river," the anthropologists wrote. "All these things are 'learned behavior.'"[34] One illustration shows two members of each race, one tall and one short, above a caption noting, "There are tall ones and short ones in all colors."[35] The Black and Asian figures wear loincloths. The white figures wear business suits. Benedict and Weltfish insisted that culture, not race, determined behavior but then sorted cultures (skyscrapers and flimsy shelters, business suits and loincloths) into racial biological categories. The educational booklet might have seemed to readers then like a refutation of Cromwell's Black natural athlete, but it echoed the coach's belief in stable racial divisions from which arose, in the Boasian model, distinct cultures.

Benedict and Weltfish defended the scientific standing of some forms of difference but not others. They and their circle recognized three (and sometimes four) racial categories. Other human divisions constituted what they called ethnicities, a term to which, amid the war, they gave new meaning. "Aryans, Jews, Italians are *not* races," Benedict and Weltfish wrote in *The Races of Mankind*, distinguishing language, faith, and nation from the natural science of race. "Jews are people who acknowledge the Jewish religion. They are of all races, even Negro and Mongolian."[36] Ethnicity had once meant race; the Boasians defined it against race. They wanted to combat the antisemitism of Nazi racial theories, but the distinction between race and ethnicity to which they contributed had the inadvertent effect of consolidating whiteness and further naturalizing the divisions between Asian, Black, and white.[37] Ethnicity made the Jewish American, the Irish American, the Italian American whiter and the African American Blacker.

A million Americans read *The Races of Mankind*. A lot more followed Cromwell's athletes. In distinguishing anti-Blackness from antisemitism, Frantz Fanon asked readers to imagine that "four fifteen-year-old boys, all more or less athletic, are doing the high jump." One of the boys, all of whom are white, bests the others with a mark of four feet ten inches. Then a fifth boy, a Black boy, arrives, sets the bar a half-inch higher and clears it. The difference is trivial, but the four white boys, Fanon wrote, "experience a destruction."[38] What differentiated anti-Blackness from antisemitism? Anti-Blackness registered, for Fanon, at "the level of the body."[39] It surfaced at the track, where the slightest difference between a Black athlete and non-Black athletes could launch a thousand scientific studies. How had he done it? How had he cleared that last half-inch? There must be an answer. The difference must mean something. "With the Negro," Fanon wrote in 1952, "the cycle of the *biological* begins."[40]

The Boasians remade the idea of biological racial difference for an age of civil rights and antiracism. The success of a few Black athletes made it seem like common sense and feel, for some, like a destruction.

Cromwell had wondered about the innate abilities of Finns in distance races and Germans in the weight events. The interventions of the Boasians had voided his theories about different white "races," recategorizing them as ethnicities, cultural units belonging to a broader white race. If Finns ran faster than Germans, if Germans threw further than Finns, then we now attributed it to culture – to a national tradition, a training regimen, heart, guts. But if a Black athlete broke a world record, then *Championship Technique in Track and Field* read like breaking news. "Negroes are not supposed to have great stamina," an unnamed "baseball authority" told Charles Maher of the *Los Angeles Times* in 1968, when asked why MLB starting pitchers remained almost all white. "They have great power and speed but not as much endurance as whites."[41] Bert Nelson, the longtime editor of *Track and Field News*, attributed the dominance of Black American athletes at shorter distances to their "great inherent ability to relax." Most white sprinters "tied up" at the end of races, he told Maher, echoing Cromwell, whose book he cited.[42] "I think Negroes are more naturally endowed," Vince Lombardi, the legendary coach of the Green Bay Packers, said.[43] Maher, who devoted a weeklong series to the subject, cast doubt on some of the more outlandish racial theories but remained committed to chasing a biological answer for Black athletic success. "It has not been scientifically established that there are innate differences between whites and blacks," he wrote, summarizing the feeling among the scientists he interviewed. But "there is also no absolute proof that such differences do NOT exist."[44] A good enough reason, it seems, for Maher's editors to assign him more than 10,000 words.

In 1971, Martin Kane, a senior editor at *Sports Illustrated*, decided to add more theories to the pile. Citing a British endocrinologist who had measured the bodies of track and field athletes and other unnamed "researchers," Kane informed a subscriber base of more than two million that the average Black American had a shorter torso, narrower waists, longer arms and legs, and more muscled arms and calves than the average white American. "There is reason to believe that his fat distribution is patterned differently from the white man" as well, he added, and a "trifle" of evidence that Black Americans have larger adrenal glands.[45] Kane recited Cromwell's relaxation theory. He attributed the lack of Black swimmers at international events to the "greater density of their bone and muscle."⁴⁶ He wondered about Achilles tendon length. But he devoted most of his feature to the "slave genes" theory that Bannister recited in 2012. "For every two condemned to slavery, only one [survived the Middle Passage] to labor in the New World. The majority were warriors captured from other tribes, therefore physically superior," he wrote. "The traders, naturally, dickered for the fittest."⁴⁷ Black Americans had been, in the words of one of Kane's interviewees, a Black 400-meter world record holder, "bred" for the kind of strength that sports reward.⁴⁸

Harry Edwards, the sociologist and activist, wrote a rebuttal in the *Black Scholar*, taking Kane to task for his and his sources' bogus science. He broke down and refuted Kane's theories one by one but also issued a warning to the Black athletes who had agreed to interviews with the writer and endorsed some of his racial claims. "This admission [of Black athletic superiority] has not been put forth grudgingly," he wrote. "Rather it has been enthusiastically presented and echoed, even by sports commentators and coaches, usually considered conservative or right-wing in their orientation toward the thrust for black dignity in sports."⁴⁹ Why? he asked. What made white coaches and writers willing and eager to cede ground to Black athletes that they had once guarded with every trick of law and science? Edwards had his own theories. He recognized that the idea of athletic giftedness discounted every other ingredient that contributed to an individual athlete's or team's success. A white man who coached or wrote about athletes for a living had much to gain from declaring Black athletes gifted. He had all the more to gain from it, Edwards knew, as more athletes began to challenge the structure of their leagues and teams and the governing bodies that regulated how they conducted themselves.

But Edwards faced a more daunting challenge than refuting Kane's bad science. How could he fire back without endorsing an alternative race science? How could he answer without countering a biological theory of difference with a cultural theory that Franz Boas and his followers had built on a biological foundation of Caucasoid, Mongoloid, and Negroid races? Arguing nurture over nature, as Boas taught us, would not put the natural to rest.⁵⁰

Amby Burfoot never forgot the Kane–Edwards debate. The editor in chief of *Runner's World* magazine could see why Edwards had criticized Kane. He knew that the title of Kane's essay, "An Assessment of 'Black Is Best,'" invited a second, silent assessment. But Burfoot, the winner of the 1968 Boston Marathon, wasn't satisfied. He thought that accusations of racism had chilled a legitimate scientific discussion and left racist ideas to simmer out of sight, at the bar and in fans' minds, unchecked. He had tuned in to the NBC *Nightly News* documentary *Black Athletes: Fact and Fiction*, to which Edwards contributed, and heard Brooks Johnson, the Black head track coach at Stanford, tell Tom Brokaw that he intended to find a white Carl Lewis. "You're going to find a white Carl Lewis?" an incredulous Brokaw asked. "They're all over the place," Johnson answered. "Well, where are they?" "A lot of them are doing other things."[51] Burfoot couldn't imagine a white Lewis, so he decided to ask scientists whether they thought a white athlete could ever run like Lewis, who in 1991 had set a new 100-meter world record of 9.86 seconds. Burfoot had contacts. He made calls. No thanks, they said. "Go ahead and hang yourself," one told him, "but you're not going to hang me with you."[52]

Burfoot would not be dissuaded. A "genetics revolution" was coming, he thought, whether Americans wanted to hear it or not, and he had a job to do.[53] He found a few scientists willing to speak with him, including Malina of the University of Texas and Claude Bouchard of Laval University in Quebec. (Malina and Bouchard also contributed to the NBC doc and almost every other story about race and sports for years; either no one else would agree to an interview or reporters weren't looking far for sources.) Burfoot distilled Malina's and Bouchard's research into a 1992 essay titled – and the title says it all – "White Men Can't Run," which his magazine ran ahead of that summer's Barcelona Olympics. "Track and field is the perfect laboratory sport," he wrote.[54] We had the results, and the results showed that athletes of West African heritage were the fastest humans over short distances and that athletes of East African heritage were the fastest over long distances. Frank Deford selected Burfoot's essay for the 1993 edition of *Best American Sports Writing*, declaring it a "conclusive treatment" of race and running and a bold investigation of a taboo subject.[55] "White Men Can't Run" did not incite a backlash. Edwards didn't write a rebuttal accusing Burfoot of veiled racism. The most incensed mail he received came from white athletes affronted by his title: I can to run! Some of this has to do with the messenger. Burfoot was a better writer and much better versed in the scientific literature than Kane ever was. But the times had also changed. The Human Genome Project had launched to much fanfare, and Michael Jordan was leading the Dream Team in Barcelona, inaugurating a new age of Black athletic celebrity. White men can't run? Well, of course they can't.

The Mismeasure of Sport

Runner's World, August 1992. Reproduced by permission from Hearst Magazine Media.

The work of a science writer is to take a dense literature by and for scientists and make it understandable and relevant to nonscientists. Analogies are among the science writer's most reliable tricks, and Burfoot found his in gender. "Women excel in law school, medical practice, architectural design and the business world, but they never win at sports. They don't even want to compete side by side with men," he wrote. "Why not? Because sports success stems from certain physical strengths that women simply don't have. We all acknowledge this."[56] If you acknowledge a gender division between men and women in which the best male athletes are faster and stronger than the best female athletes, then why not, Burfoot reasoned, as Gladwell later would, acknowledge that there may be a racial division between Black and white in which the best Black athletes are faster and stronger than the best white athletes. He used a naturalized male/female binary to naturalize a Black/white racial binary, and he cited as evidence the track and the clock, a laboratory of gender and racial differentiation. He wouldn't be the last.

Burfoot did not otherwise address women's running. He left that to Linda Villarosa, who contributed a companion essay titled "The Other

Kenyans." Villarosa, a senior editor at *Essence*, told the stories of East African women runners who had not yet achieved the success and fame of their male teammates. "It is almost inconceivable that the same fertile ground hasn't produced a female superstar," Villarosa wrote, noting that no Kenyan woman had ever won an Olympic medal.[57] She recounted the thwarted careers of Rose Thomson, an eleven-time All-American at the University of Wisconsin, and Mary Chemweno, a national record holder in the 800 meters, and interviewed rising stars Susan Sirma and Delilah Asiago about their ambitions. Villarosa, the rare Black contributor to *Runner's World* at the time, did not extract from their stories some broader racial truth. She did not write about their genes or their anatomy. She did not turn Thomson, Chemweno, Sirma, and Asiago into stand-ins for East Africa. She granted that their lives, as elite athletes, had been unusual, indicative of nothing other than life as an elite Kenyan athlete. Deford didn't choose "The Other Kenyans" for *Best American*. He must have assumed what writers had long assumed: that the measure of man resided in men.

East African runners first arrived on the international stage in the 1950s. Kenya sent a team to the 1954 British Empire and Commonwealth Games in Vancouver, where Nyandika Maiyoro, an early national star, finished fourth in the three mile, an event won by the Brit Chris Chataway, who had led his friend Bannister through 1,300 meters in the first sub-four-minute mile. At the 1960 Rome Olympics, Abebe Bikila won the marathon, barefoot on cobblestones, and set a new world record, becoming the first gold medalist from the continent. He defended his title in 1964 and again broke the world record. The rise of East African distance running culminated at the 1968 Games, where, 7,000 feet above sea level in Mexico City, Africans won every distance event, including the 1,500 meters, in which Kipchoge "Kip" Keino trounced the American star Jim Ryun. It was, for Bannister, the end of an era. It had to be the altitude, or something.

Keino, it turned out, belonged to the Nandi, one of the Kalenjin tribes indigenous to the highlands of the Great Rift Valley. After the Kenyan team's dominant showing in Mexico, it didn't take long for Western writers to begin wondering whether something was in the water. In 1975, *Runner's World* commissioned a book investigating the roots of East African distance running success, *The African Running Revolution*. "What accounts for the tremendous success of these runners?" the editor asked in his foreword. He highlighted two contributions: one from the famed coach Jack Daniels, the other from an unknown writer named

John Manners. The editor urged readers to turn to Manners's essay, "In Search of an Explanation," which offered, he wrote, "a number of possible anthropological and cultural explanations" for what track fans had witnessed in 1968.[58]

Manners was not himself an anthropologist, but he had other credentials. He was the son of the anthropologist Robert Manners, who had studied with Benedict and other Boasians at Columbia in the 1940s and built a distinguished career of his own at Brandeis. When John was twelve, his father had moved the family to Kenya to conduct fieldwork among the highland tribes, and John, fascinated with the region, had returned in his twenties as a Peace Corps volunteer. He found much of the talk about East African runners in the West distasteful. "Amateur physiological theorizing is rife," he wrote.[59] He warned against unfounded arguments about leg length and Achilles tendon function but did, with some hesitation, float a few cultural theories. Almost all of Kenya's medal winners and world record holders hailed from the eleven Kalenjin tribes. Manners had lived with villagers belonging to the largest of them, the Kipsigis, as a twelve-year-old. He observed that cattle raiding – running down and corralling cattle on the land of neighboring tribes – had long been a feature of life in the highlands. In a footnote, Manners wondered whether the most successful cattle raiders would have had more wives and children than others and whether cattle raiding could have then "acted as a powerful genetic selection mechanism, favoring strong runners."[60] He also cited ritual adolescent circumcision as evidence of a culture that valued the kind of stoicism that might facilitate success in endurance sports.

Manners didn't seem convinced of his own theories. He later told David Epstein, the author of *The Sports Gene*, that he hadn't given them much thought.[61] Others did. *Sports Illustrated* staff writer Kenny Moore, who had finished fourteenth in the hot, humid, thin-aired marathon at the Mexico City Olympics, consulted Manner's essay for his own about the East African running tradition. "In the rest of the world, sport serves as an initiation, as a true test. In East Africa, initiation is the initiation," he wrote in 1990, reciting the cattle raiding and circumcision theories. "Sport is a pale shadow of the competitive life that has gone on forever across this high, fierce, first continent. Is it any wonder that frail European varieties feel threatened?"[62] Moore did not attribute East African running success to genetic or anatomical advantages. He identified culture (cattle raiding, stoicism) as the driving force behind all the medals and records. He did not want to go where some scientists and writers had in framing East African distance runners as biological outliers, gifted athletes who had an edge on other runners by the sheer fact of their Africanness. He was a liberal, a culturalist, a Boasian.

But Moore's racial culturalism did nothing to check others' racial biologism. It gave consumers of science writing the choice of seeing East African distance runners as one or another kind of racial puzzle. "Quite frankly," Malina acknowledged in 1988, outlining his biocultural model, "biological and cultural homogeneity overlap."[63] The nature-versus-nurture debate was never much of a debate. Both sides agreed that, when we tuned in to an international track meet, we were witnessing the drama of coherent human divisions set against one another, some, the results revealed, with greater talent than others. A racial debate, in which Malina seemed like the wise man in the middle, was, all along, a racial consensus that assumed the scientific coherence of the Black athlete.[64]

The growing fascination in the Global North with the East African highland tribes merged Black athletic racialization with long-held beliefs about Indigenous difference. Anti-Blackness tended to, as Fanon observed, elevate the biological above the cultural; settler fantasies about Indigenous life, the cultural above the biological. The former surfaced in writer's observations about East African runners' slight frames, high waists, and thin calf muscles, the latter in their theories about East Africans' high-altitude living, communal training, and diet. Two gifts, scientists and science writers determined – one that couldn't be emulated and one that could. Aileen Moreton-Robinson observes that what she calls "possessive logics" structure settler colonial thought, casting Indigenous peoples and their lands as "always predisposed to being possessed and exploited."[65] A white American runner could move to Iten (or Flagstaff), live and train in a collective arrangement with other runners, and eat Ugali. The Indigenous gift could be taken, should be taken. The Black gift couldn't. It had to be regulated, tested. One motivated theft, the other fear.

Other athletes motivated empathic concern. Some writers, searching for an angle in a crowded field, turned to the dilemma of the white athlete. The 1991 *USA Today* series "Race and Sports: Myths and Realities" included the story of a white running back at Tennessee State. The first line: "Chad McCollam isn't supposed to be a running back."[66] In 1992, Peter King of *Sports Illustrated* wrote about Ricky Proehl, one of a shrinking number of white wide receivers in the NFL. "Now I can understand how a black guy feels when he walks into a bar and everyone stares at him because he's the only black guy in the place," Proehl told King.[67] The magazine ran King's story under the headline "White Guys Can't Run," confirming, if nothing else, that white guys can't write original titles. *SI* returned to the issue in 1997 with the cover story "Whatever Happened to the White Athlete?," in which S. L. Price recounted white sprinter Kevin Little's struggle with racial self-doubt. Little, who had competed for the United States at that summer's World Championships, making it to the semifinals in the 200 meters, observed fewer white entrants in his events every year and wondered whether he might be among the last white sprinters. "Whites have in some respects become sports' second-class citizens," Price wrote. "In a surreal inversion of [Jackie] Robinson's era, white athletes are frequently tagged by the stereotypes of skin color."[68]

Neither King nor Price attributed the lack of white athletes at wide receiver, cornerback, and in some track and field events to genetics. (Price suggested that the rise of skateboarding and other alternative sports – the X Games debuted in 1995 – could account for some of the diminished interest among white kids in football, basketball, and track.) But their stories suggested that white athletes suffered some kind of disadvantage and that their absence had undermined faith in a meritocratic ideal – but, in a bizarre reversal, not because of the advantages of being white, male, and affluent but because of advantages now believed to be inherent in Blackness. "Now I know how a black guy feels."[69]

Stories about the disappearing white athlete coincided with increased concern over and testing for anabolic steroids and EPO (erythropoietin), which led, at the end of the decade, to the formation of the World Anti-Doping Agency. Every new world record in track and field, most set by Black athletes, stirred doubts and accusations. (Hicham El Guerrouj of Morocco set long-standing mile and 1,500-meter world records in the late 1990s, right before the introduction of the first test for EPO, and some observers remain convinced that he couldn't have done it without a tall drug cocktail.) The convergence of athletic racial theories and antidrug evangelism made it seem like Blackness was a kind of drug, something that needed regulating. Was Carl Lewis on drugs? Or was he the drug?

Malcolm Gladwell had an answer. The science journalist, still a few years from ruling the TED Talk circuit, thought that the accusations had gotten out of hand. In 1997, he reviewed John Hoberman's *Darwin's Athletes*. He didn't like it, but not because Hoberman blamed Black communities for encouraging a harmful "sports fixation" among Black children, for which others criticized him.[70] Gladwell thought Hoberman was inflating the significance of athletes in national culture and looking for someone or something to call racist. "Sometimes a baseball player is just a baseball player," he wrote of Hoberman's critical take on the legend of Jackie Robinson, "and sometimes an observation about racial difference is just an observation about racial difference."[71] The trouble with all the talk about racial difference in sports, Gladwell thought, was that it often confused differences in variation with differences on average. He cited the research of Kenneth Kidd, the geneticist, who had found that some Central African tribes boasted greater genetic variation than all humans outside Africa combined, the theory being that when bands of migrants first left the continent tens or hundreds of thousands of years ago, they took a small subset of human genetic variations with them, forming more homogeneous communities that we would later define as Arab, Asian, white. From this, Gladwell surmised that the fastest and the slowest runners in the world would be found among Africans and people of recent African descent. Africa contained the greatest genetic variation. We noticed that the fastest runners were Black. If we held a race to crown the slowest human, the winner, he assumed, would be Black, too.

To land his argument, Gladwell turned to gender. Studies had shown that female math students scored as well as male students on average but that more male students landed on the far ends of the distribution. Gladwell noted that almost every individual winner of the Putnam Mathematical Competition had been male. Male math students weren't better than female students on average, but they had more variation; they were the best and the worst. He tied his two stories together with a bow: "Blacks are like boys. Whites are like girls."[72] Gladwell, the son of a white English father and a Black Jamaican mother, cited the male/female binary as evidence of a Black/white binary. Women are from Venus, men are from … Africa? Robert E. Park had once, to the irritation of a young Ralph Ellison, described Black people as "the lady among the races," a formulation that Burfoot and Gladwell reversed.[73] Gender difference, in their writing, validated racial difference. Park, Burfoot, and Gladwell recruited it as an instrument of racialization, of race making. Sometimes Black people were ladies. Sometimes white people were girls.

Others assumed that science writers wouldn't need analogies for long. "The issue of whether there are meaningful differences between populations *has all but been resolved*," Jon Entine wrote in his 2000 book *Taboo: Why Black Athletes Dominate Sports and Why We're Afraid to Talk about It.* "Soon we will have maps pinpointing the genes responsible for many traits."[74] Entine, a genetics true believer, thought that "self-censorship" and "postmodernist reasoning" had made writers scared to state the obvious and that genetics research would free them, if they'd let it.⁷⁵ He wrote *Taboo* because he thought sports offered an ideal forum – an "access point," a "perfect laboratory" – for reckoning with racial difference, neglecting how, as Gladwell at least acknowledged, studies of Black and white elite athletes reveal almost nothing about the rest of us joggers in the broad human middle.⁷⁶

Entine knew why his critics were on high alert. He devoted an entire section of his book to the history of race science and the eugenics movement. But he remained convinced that the solution was not to abandon race science but, in the tradition of Boas, to improve it. Not all scientists agreed with him. "'Black' isn't really a category that a biologist can recognize," Stephen Jay Gould, the author of *The Mismeasure of Man*, said.⁷⁷ The kinesiologist David Hunter, a regular interviewee in stories about race and sports in the mid-1990s, had grown disillusioned with the field and the chatter around it by the end of the decade. "Canadians are good at ice hockey," he told the *Baltimore Sun*. "But nobody says that we should look to see if they are born with especially strong ankles."⁷⁸ The anthropologist Jonathan Marks accused Entine and others of a self-serving "genohype."⁷⁹ He considered it no coincidence that Entine later joined the American Enterprise Institute, home of Charles Murray, coauthor of *The Bell Curve*.⁸⁰ Entine and others charged on, defending science, whether science needed defending or not. The genetics revolution would, they believed, vindicate them.

The "taboo" of Entine's title was a racial taboo. He devoted the book's final section to women athletes ("What about Women?"), but he didn't see gender as controversial. He considered the male/female binary settled science. Who could doubt it? Had Entine read Judith Butler, he would have dismissed them, using his favorite insult, as an antiscience "postmodernist." But things were about to change.

"In case you don't know, I didn't win the race tonight," Pierre Weiss, a sixty-two-year-old Frenchman with a gray mustache and loose tie, said from a rostrum inside the 75,000-seat stadium. "I'm just replacing Semenya." Weiss, the general secretary of the International Association of Athletics Federations, sat beside Janeth Jepkosgei of Kenya, the silver medalist in that evening's women's 800 meters, and Jenny Meadows of Great Britain, the bronze medalist. The winner of the event, the eighteen-year-old South African Caster Semenya, had torn away from Jepkosgei, Meadows, and the rest of the field over the final 200 meters to win by more than two seconds in a new national record of 1:55.45. On the IAAF's recommendation, she did not attend the news conference.

Semenya had not cheated, Weiss told the room. But the IAAF had, he admitted, confirming rumors circulating around the stadium and in the tabloids, ordered doctors in Berlin and South Africa to investigate Semenya's gender status. "If at the end of this investigation it is proven that this athlete is not a female," Weiss said, "we will [remove] her name from the results of the competition today" and redistribute the medals.[81] Semenya had not cheated, but she was also, the IAAF general secretary's remarks suggested, not innocent.

Others didn't wait for the results of the investigation. "These kinds of people should not run with us," Elisa Cusma of Italy, who finished sixth, said after the race. "For me, she's not a woman. She's a man." Mariya Savinova of Russia, who finished fifth, told Russian media that the IAAF didn't need doctors to determine Semenya's gender: "Just look at her."[82] (Savinova, who won the 2011 world title in the event and the gold medal at the 2012 London Olympics, defeating Semenya, later admitted to using steroids and received a four-year ban.) Cusma, Savinova, and others at Worlds received the South African's success as Bannister had received East Africans' in the distance events: It was a threat to them, and they would call in the scientists.

Semenya, born and raised in a rural village in northern South Africa, had burst onto the scene that summer when she ran a head-turning

Caster Semenya in the 800-meter final at the 2009 World Athletics Championships. Photograph by Michael Sohn. From AP Photo.

1:56.72 in Mauritius, knocking more than seven seconds off her best time from the season before and setting the national record that she would break a few weeks later in Berlin. The result had, we later learned, raised alarms at the IAAF, which reached out to Athletics South Africa, the national governing body for track and field, and urged it to administer sex-verification testing. Athletics South Africa brought Semenya in for testing the week before Worlds, telling her that it was a routine drug screening.[83] She then flew with her coach to Berlin, where more tests awaited her. Nick Davies, the communications director for the IAAF, told the *New York Times* that the federation's investigation would be thorough and scientific. "There is chromosome testing, gynecological investigation, all manner of things, organs, X-rays, scans," he said. "It's very, very comprehensive."[84] Man or woman? Science had the answer. Give it time.

The IAAF first instituted sex testing in 1966. The success of Soviet women at international meets motivated rumors in the West that the USSR had been binding male athletes' genitals and entering them in women's events. The association, determining that it could no longer trust national governing bodies to test their women athletes, began conducting genital checks. It discovered no bound members. Protests over the invasive tests – the "nude parade," critics called it – led the IAAF and the International Olympic Committee to switch to chromosome testing (administered with a cheek swab) for the 1968 Mexico City Games. After banning and then reinstating Spanish hurdler Maria Martínez-Patiño, an XY woman with a rare condition that made her cells insensitive to androgens, including testosterone, the IAAF switched again in 1991 to PCR testing for the SRY gene (the sex-determining region Y gene). It abandoned sex-verification testing altogether ahead of the 2000 Sydney Olympics while granting itself the latitude to test athletes who raised "suspicion."[85]

Semenya's performance in Berlin, the IAAF decided, met that low bar. "Two things triggered this investigation," Davies wrote to the *New Yorker* in an email. "Firstly, the incredible improvement in this athlete's performance ... and more bluntly, the fact that SOUTH AFRICAN sports Web sites were alleging that she was a hermaphrodite athlete."[86] The IAAF had investigated because some websites claimed that Semenya had run too fast for a woman – that was the best that the association's communications director could do. The sociologists Cheryl Cooky and Shari Dworkin write that sex-verification testing is founded on an "underlying belief that all biological males are stronger, bigger, faster, and thus superior athletes when compared to all biological women competing in the same sport."[87] Far from defending women athletes, sex testing, they observe, reinforces a belief in the inferior status of women. It assumes that any characteristic associated with men could be the source of an unfair advantage, that maleness is a kind of drug. Readers of Cromwell and Kane and Burfoot and Entine had heard this before. Semenya had attracted the IAAF's testing regime as a masculine woman but also as an African. The association had deemed her not unnatural but too natural. With Semenya, the natural athlete had reached the end of a long road, transforming from the occasion for a foot race or a game to the ruin of it. Semenya's gift, the federation decided, was too great. It would have to be taken from her.

Semenya retained her title, but the IAAF wouldn't let her back on the track until the next summer, after she'd undergone treatments to lower her androgen levels. Genital checks had failed. Chromosome testing had failed. The SRY gene didn't have the answer. The IAAF decided to try again: Ah, it must be testosterone. Butler commended the initial decision on the *London Review of Books* website. They observed that the IAAF had negotiated an agreement that distinguished eligibility from identity. "It is important to keep in mind," Butler wrote, "that we can invoke certain standards for admission to compete under a particular gender category without deciding whether or not the person unequivocally 'is' that category."[88] The IAAF had never said that Semenya wasn't a woman, Butler observed. It had investigated whether she could race in the athletic category of woman, a category that it and the IOC negotiated and defined. But Butler's comment, which they titled "Wise Distinctions," skated over how the athletic categories of man and woman inform how we define ourselves and others off the track. Elite athletes serve what the criminologist Kathryn Henne describes as a "biopedagogical function," modeling the kind of body that we should all, through exercise and diet, seek to emulate.[89] Barring Semenya from international track and field unless she lowered her androgen levels sent the message that, while a masculine woman might be a woman, she could not inhabit the elevated status of an elite athlete. She was a woman, but, the association suggested, we should not want to be like her.[90]

The gifted athlete is in a bind: She must be a role model, and she is forbidden from being one. In 2007, Marion Jones, who had won three gold medals for the United States in Sydney, received a six-month prison sentence after admitting that she had lied to federal agents about her use of steroids and about her involvement in a check-counterfeiting scheme.

The next summer, she wrote a letter to President George W. Bush from her cell, asking that he commute her sentence. Doug Logan, the chief executive of USA Track and Field, decided to write his own letter to the president, which he released on the USATF website. "If you have athletic talent or money or fame, the law is applied much differently than if you are slow or poor or an average American trying to get by," he wrote. "To reduce Ms. Jones's sentence or pardon her would send a horrible message to young people who idolized her, reinforcing the notion that you can cheat and get away with it." USATF should have known all along that Jones was too good to be true, Logan added. It was time to "right the ship" that she had "nearly run aground."[91] Jones's gift had made her a role model, and it shouldn't have, he suggested. It should have triggered more testing, greater distrust. She had owed the young fan something for her athletic talent, and USTAF should have called in the debt a long time ago. Others had cheated. Others had taken drugs. But something about Jones, a Black woman who had been the face of Team USA, had, according to Logan, cost us all.

In the 1990s, Burfoot and Gladwell had cited the gender binary as evidence of a Black/white racial binary. In the 2000s, the IAAF and USATF did the reverse, using the well-worn grooves of race science to authorize an athletic gender science. Writers had been suggesting for years that Black athletes had anatomical advantages that had left white athletes unable to compete. Now, as the IAAF sought to reconstitute the gender binary through the regulation of testosterone, athletes and fans did not need a lot of convincing to believe that Black women were fast because they were Black women and that, if they were fast enough, they might not belong in the women's division at all. Gendered racialization had transformed into racialized gendering. The scientists and science historians Rebecca Jordan-Young and Katrina Karkazis describe testosterone as a "synecdoche for masculinity." Talk of testosterone, they write, "weaves folklore into science," authorizing "cultural beliefs about the structure of masculinity and the 'natural' relationship between women and men."[92] Testosterone was the latest in a long line of racializing and gendering tools that have defined Blackness as an excess of athleticism, a gift, and femaleness as a lack, a deficit – definitions that collide in the figure of the Black woman athlete. In Logan's letter to President Bush, there was almost a sense of relief, it seemed to me, in his recounting of Jones's steroid use. It made sense to him. He should have known. No woman can run that fast.

Others, including a new generation of science writers, agreed. In his search for a "sports gene," David Epstein determined that most women didn't have it. "Insofar as there is an 'athleticism gene,'" he wrote, recounting the banning and reinstatement of Martínez-Patiño, "the SRY gene is it." The sex-determining region Y gene is the gene that triggers the formation of testicles and the cells located inside the testes that release testosterone. "The SRY gene is a DNA skeleton key that selectively activates genes that make the man," he wrote in his 2013 book *The Sports Gene*.[93] It was as close as he came to naming what his title teased. The sports gene wasn't a gene at all; it was, for him, a gender.

Epstein, a former collegiate middle-distance runner, had decided to dust off the debates of the 1990s, which had receded after Entine's *Taboo*. "Did Eli and Peyton Manning inherit Archie's quarterback genes, or did they grow up to be Super Bowl MVPs because they were raised with a football in hand?" he asked in the introduction. "Did Ken Griffey Sr. gift his boy with baseball batter DNA?"[94] Nature or nurture? The old material sold better than ever, and the book climbed to number nine on the *New York Times* Best Seller list.

Epstein built his argument against one of the catchiest social theories of the time, Gladwell's 10,000 hours rule. Investigating the careers of high achievers in business, finance, law, music, and science, Gladwell had suggested that, in addition to good timing, one thing united them all: 10,000 hours of grindingly hard work. "Researchers," Gladwell wrote in his 2008 megahit *Outliers*, "have settled on what they believe is the magic number for true expertise."[95] He cited the psychologist Anders Ericsson, who studied violinists and identified the number of hours devoted to the instrument as the best indicator of who would ascend to the status of world-class soloist and who would make their careers as teachers of the craft. (Ericsson later accused Gladwell of overgeneralizing his research, which, of course, Gladwell had.)[96] Epstein thought Gladwell had overstated what hard work could do. Most of us didn't have the base talent to make the NBA, he argued. We could train for 10,000 hours and still not come close. We succeeded and failed according to what he called the "10,000 hours plus or minus 10,000 hours" rule.[97] Epstein noted theories about the sickle cell gene variant common among people of sub-Saharan West African descent and the ACTN3 gene ("a gene for speed") common among all Africans and people of recent African descent. To make his case, he told what he called "a tale of two jumpers": the Swede Stefan Holm, who finished fourth in the high jump at Worlds in 2007 after a lifetime of single-minded training, and the Bahamian Donald Thomas, who won gold a little more than a year after entering the event for the first time, untrained and wearing basketball sneakers. A research team examined Thomas and determined that he was, in Epstein's words, "gifted with a giant's Achilles tendon."[98] Holm needed a lot more than 10,000 hours to make a World final. Thomas needed almost none at all.

The stories Epstein told about Black athletes tended to end with anatomical and genetic theories about Africans and people of African descent. The stories he told about white athletes tended to end with them: individual case studies, genetic freaks. He closed his book with Eero Mäntyranta, the Finnish cross-country skier who won gold in the 15- and 30-kilometer events at the 1964 Winter Games in Austria. Mäntyranta had a rare genetic mutation that led to an elevated red blood cell count. It also gave the skier's skin a color that Epstein, who visited Mäntyranta in northern Finland, likened to "the red paint that comes from [the] region's iron-rich soil." The geneticist who discovered Mäntyranta's gene mutation in the 1990s, long after his retirement from racing, determined that it had given Mäntyranta an edge, a natural lift. Science, Epstein concluded, had given us a richer understanding of the Finn's feats of endurance: "100 percent nurture and 100 percent nature."[99] Scientists and science writers did not see Holm or Mäntyranta as stand-ins for white men or for northern Europeans. Holm, a social outlier, had dedicated his entire life to his event. Mäntyranta, a biological outlier, had a rare genetic mutation. But Thomas's success must, they thought, tell us something about the West Indies, about Africa, about the Middle Passage, about slavery. What has the long search for a sports gene been other than a search for Blackness?

Gladwell reviewed *The Sports Gene* for the *New Yorker* and asked the question that it circled but never stated: Did talent constitute an unfair advantage? He thought that Epstein's book ought to be read alongside a new memoir by the cyclist Tyler Hamilton, one of Lance Armstrong's US Postal Service teammates, in which Hamilton shared details about his and Armstrong's use of EPO, growth hormone treatments, blood transfusions, and masking agents. Hamilton's memoir, Gladwell wrote, "describes the flip side of the question that Epstein explores. What if you aren't Eero Mäntyranta?" He observed that Hamilton and Armstrong had used "science, intelligence, and sheer will to conquer natural difference" and didn't see why we celebrated Mäntyranta, with his rare genetic mutation, but not Hamilton and Armstrong, with their stashed vials of EPO.[100]

Gladwell contrasted a white Finnish athlete with two white American athletes. But he knew that when commentators and fans talked about gifted athletes, most didn't have a Finnish skier in mind. Bannister had wondered whether East African runners had an unfair advantage in the thin air of Mexico City. Did athletic governing bodies need to regulate altitude training? Others wondered whether a masculine South African woman had an illicit edge at the World Athletics Championships in Berlin. Should the IAAF ban her or force her to undergo hormone treatments? No one asked about the Finnish skier with a rare genetic mutation. Gladwell thought that we should, or, if not, that we should let Lance shoot EPO to his heart's content, that we should let him use "science, intelligence, and sheer will to conquer natural difference."[101] If white men can't run, then why not let them turn themselves into others whom we assume can? The real drug was talent.

Some gifts couldn't be emulated. Others could. In the summer of 2006, the cover of *Men's Health* magazine declared that, for a mere $4.50, a reader could learn the "amazing secrets of the men who live forever."[102] Christopher McDougall, a contributing editor, had traveled to the Copper Canyon of southwestern Chihuahua, Mexico, to live among the Tarahumara (or Rarámuri) people famed for their long-distance running and returned with health advice for the American man. "When it comes to the top 10 health risks facing American men," he wrote, "the Tarahumara are practically immortal: their incidence rate is at or near zero in just about every category, including diabetes, vascular disease, and colorectal cancer."[103] McDougall, a six-foot-four, 230-pound writer in his mid-forties (not built for marathoning, he acknowledged), decided to train like a Tarahumara: eating their lighter, vegetarian diet and running thousands of miles in traditional Tarahumara sandals (leather thongs tied around the calf). He lost weight. He felt more relaxed. A sore foot healed. He could run longer than before and without pain. The article's sidebars showed readers how to emulate Tarahumara running form, detailed an Indigenous "botanical balm" (geranium), and offered capsule reviews of minimalist trainers (Nike Free, Vibram FiveFingers).[104]

Publishers took note, and McDougall received a reported mid-six-figure advance for a book-length investigation of Tarahumara running. The resulting *Born to Run: A Hidden Tribe, Superathletes, and the Greatest Race the World Has Never Seen* sold more than three million copies, making it, by a wide margin, the best-selling running book of all time. The marketing materials touted more secrets: The tribe's "superhuman talent is matched by uncanny health and serenity, leaving the Tarahumara immune to the diseases and strife that plague modern existence."[105] The idea of the Indigenous natural athlete, which dates back to at least the turn of the twentieth century, had never taken the biological form of the Black natural, allowing McDougall to sell it to non-Indigenous readers as a bundle of health tricks they could add to their fitness routines: eat light, take geranium, lose your shoes. The Tarahumaras' gift for running could be commodified. It was consumable in a way that Black athletes' giftedness, conceived as a biological endowment, could not.

In the 1990s, teams of Tarahumara had traveled to the Leadville 100, a 100-mile race through the Colorado Rockies, to run against some of the best ultramarathoners in the world. Tarahumara runners won back-to-back titles in 1993 and 1994. Victoriano Churro won the 1993 race, in a little over twenty hours, at age fifty-two. McDougall decided to go looking for scientists who could account for Churro's resilience – how could he run like that in his fifties? why didn't he get hurt or burned out? – and he found the biologists Dennis Bramble and Daniel Lieberman. Bramble and Lieberman had coauthored a 2004 article in which they'd challenged the scientific consensus that endurance running emerged in the genus *Homo* as "merely the by-product of enhanced walking capabilities." The biologists studied the mechanics of human locomotion and the fossil record (the latter suggesting that running evolved long after and without immediate relation to walking) and offered an alternative theory: that humans, seeking calorie-rich food sources through either scavenging or hunting, had evolved to run. "Today," Bramble and Lieberman wrote, "[endurance running] is primarily a form of exercise and recreation, but its roots may be as ancient as the origin of the human genus."[106] McDougall, who visited Bramble at the University of Utah and Lieberman at Harvard, cast the Tarahumara as closer to that origin and a reminder to the inhabitants of the Global North of their nature. "Running was the superpower that made us human," he wrote in *Born to Run*, giving the biologists' research a self-help twist, "which means it's a superpower all humans possess."[107] Running constituted a birthright but also something that had to be mined from the cliffs of the Copper Canyon.

McDougall imagined the Tarahumara as belonging to another time. After watching children organize a game that involved trail running while dribbling a wooden ball, he mused that he felt as if he'd "discovered the Future of American Running, living five hundred years in the past."[108] In *Men's Health*, he described *Born to Run* as the story of "an average American man" (himself) who "adapted himself to the secrets of this unbreakable, unbeatable, nearly immortal tribe and turned himself into a 21st-century Tarahumara."[109] (Do not actual Tarahumara live in the twenty-first century?) Of the book's climactic race, in which American ultramarathoner Scott Jurek goes head-to-head with Tarahumara runners on their home turf, McDougall wrote that Jurek had agreed to the race because he had wanted to test himself against not the best in the world but "the best of all time," "the immortals," Bramble and Lieberman's ancient running man.[110]

McDougall wasn't the first to see the mountains of Chihuahua as a medicinal time machine. An Oklahoma City cardiologist named Dale Groom had visited Tarahumara villages in the late 1960s to discover whether high-volume endurance training did, as some doctors thought then, cause an enlargement of the heart. He found that Tarahumara runners had excellent cardiovascular health, the best, he claimed, since ancient Greece, before "the human brain supplanted muscle as man's dominant means of conquest."[111] Groom found among the Tarahumara lessons in medicine and health that he could bring back to the United States, combining ancient muscle with modern science. McDougall delivered Groom's vision to the masses, selling Tarahumara culture as the secret to a slimmer waist, a better night's rest, a longer life.

McDougall wrote *Born to Run* in the shadow of Franz Boas. Though he treated the Tarahumara as alien to modern life, he suggested that,

Scott Jurek (*left*) and Arnulfo Quimare Gutiérrez (*right*) in the mountains of southwestern Chihuahua. Photograph by Luis Escobar. Reproduced by permission from Hearst Magazine Media.

culture being learned, an American man like himself could assume their traditions as his own and realize the health benefits. William Willis, a Black anthropologist who had studied at Columbia under Benedict and others, leveled a famous criticism of the Boasian model later in his career in which he argued that his discipline had used the "diversity [of societies of the Global South] to show that sociocultural change was feasible in white societies." Anthropologists acted as "'penny' imperialists," he wrote, gathering knowledge from Black people, Indigenous people, and people of color and then offering their findings as lessons to the Global North.[112] McDougall, who made a small fortune from his venture in Indigenous Mexico, didn't write a book for or about the Tarahumara. The heroes of his book were three white men who trained and ate like them: Jurek, himself, and a seeker from Colorado named Micah True, who moved to the Copper Canyon in midlife and took on the alias Caballo Blanco, or white horse. The long American tradition of "playing Indian," the historian Philip Deloria once observed, "rests on the ability to wield power against Indians – social, military, economic, and political – while simultaneously drawing power from them."[113] McDougall wanted his readers to see what going Native could do for their health and their marathon times. It had done wonders for him.

In the final race, a Tarahumara runner, Arnulfo Quimare Gutiérrez, outduels Jurek for the win. McDougall finishes hours later, staggering across the finish line, exhausted, after twelve hours of suffering, which he recounts in excruciating detail. In the conclusion of *Female Masculinity*, Jack Halberstam reflects on filmmakers' fascination with the aging white male boxer and suggests that it may tell us something about white masculinity itself: "Although the battered white male boxer takes massive amounts of abuse in the ring, he also manages to emerge triumphant every time."[114] It may be, above all, the image of abuse – working at it, earning it – that has shielded the white male athlete from the nebulous debt of giftedness. The Indigenous runner flies through the mountains; the white runner toughs it out. I follow a running website on which the editors often refer to athletes who may have run slower times in high school or attended a Division III school or who may work a regular job or do high-volume training or all of the above as "blue-collar runners." The term doesn't refer to income or wealth but a talent class.

The success of *Born to Run* gave others, including the British journalist Adharanand Finn, a model for athletic travel writing. Finn, after reading McDougall's book, decided to move to the Great Rift Valley in search of the secret to East African dominance on the track and the roads. "If I find their secret," he told his wife, "I can bottle it and make a fortune."[115] In *Running with the Kenyans*, he chronicles his six months in East Africa, during which he maintains a list of possible "secrets" to African distance-running success in his notebook. Finn, more self-aware than McDougall, acknowledges the error in his mission. "You people come to find the secret, but you know what the secret is?" Colm O'Connell, an Irish missionary and longtime high-school running coach in Iten, Kenya, asked him. "That you think there's a secret. There is no secret."[116] Finn had to agree. He had moved to the Rift Valley chasing a secret that Western scientists and science writers had created in the act of seeking it.

Others had gone looking for the secrets that Finn sought – Dean Cromwell, Amby Burfoot, Malcolm Gladwell, Jon Entine, David Epstein, the IAAF, the IOC. Where had the brave young Bannisters gone? scientists and science journalists asked. And what would it take to restore them to the top of the medal stand?

In the spring of 2023, I went for a walk and had dinner with Burfoot. He emailed me after the Boston Marathon, which we'd both run (he at seventy-six!), when I was living a short drive from his home on the Connecticut coast. My mom had subscribed to *Runner's World* when I was a kid, and I can remember reading his columns before I'd ever run more than a PE mile. I had an article forthcoming in the feminist theory journal *differences* in which I discussed "White Men Can't Run," and I had recently revisited some of his writing about Caster Semenya. We had a lot to talk about.

In 2018, the IAAF had announced new rules for athletes with what it described as "differences of sex development." Semenya would need to undergo hormone treatments if she wished to compete in the 400-, 800-, and 1,500-meter events. (She was then the two-time defending Olympic gold medalist in the 800.) Semenya fought the decision, and, the next spring, the Swiss-based Court of Arbitration for Sport ruled against her. In a 2–1 decision, the court determined that the IAAF's rules "are discriminatory" but that "such discrimination is a necessary, reasonable and proportionate means of achieving the IAAF's aims of preserving the integrity of female athletics."[117] After the decision, Burfoot acknowledged in a column on the website LetsRun.com that news of the ruling, for which he had advocated, had not come as a relief. It left him, someone who had devoted his career to celebrating what running could do for the fastest and the slowest among us, with a feeling of "heaviness." Did we, he seemed to ask, want a sport in which discrimination was deemed necessary? Could that be a sport with integrity? "Track and field could use a global, unifying story," Burfoot wrote, "and Caster Semenya could be it."[118] It wasn't the story that the sport's governing bodies decided to tell, but, walking along the water with the 1968 Boston Marathon champion, I was glad that we could agree that it was a much better story than the one the sport had been telling.

2

Roberto Clemente on the Black/Brown Color Line

Monte Irvin saved Roberto Clemente for last. On August 6, 1973, Irvin, who first made his name as a versatile left fielder for the Newark Eagles at the twilight of the Black leagues, stood before a podium in Cooperstown, New York, and acknowledged his fellow Hall of Fame inductees: George "High Pockets" Kelly, Warren Spahn, and, "of course, my real good friend Roberto Clemente."[1] Clemente had died that winter in a plane crash off the coast of Puerto Rico, and Irvin glanced at his friend's widow, Vera, seated on stage, as he spoke. He had met Clemente a long time ago in San Juan, he said. Irvin reflected on his playing days there and in Cuba, Venezuela, and Mexico before breaking into Major League Baseball, at thirty, twelve years into his professional career. His Hall of Fame plaque – "Negro Leagues 1937–1948, New York N.L., Chicago N.L., 1949–1956" – didn't acknowledge his time in the Caribbean and Mexican leagues. Irvin had been, for the Hall and in that week's news, an icon of civil rights and integration, a man who took his talents from the Black leagues to the big leagues and showed a wider public what he could do.

Clemente, his late friend, an Afro–Puerto Rican as Black as Irvin, received a different kind of tribute. The *New York Times* declared that his induction, in an unprecedented special election that spring, had made him "the first Latin-American player picked for the museum at Cooperstown."[2] The *Atlanta Daily World*, the long-running Black newspaper, agreed: Clemente's stood as "the first induction of a Latin American player."[3] The Baseball Hall of Fame had, that August day, celebrated two men for breaking new ground in the game – one Black, the other, in the emerging language of the time, Latin.

Clemente had idolized Irvin as a child in the mid-1940s. On weekends, he would take the bus from his home in Carolina, east of San Juan, to Sixto Escobar Stadium to see Irvin roam the outfield for the Senadores. "He not only was a good hitter but had a very good arm," he recalled of his childhood hero. "Even my friends called me Monte Irvin as a nickname."[4] Clemente waited outside the stadium before games, hoping to catch a glimpse of Irvin, who, like other African American stars of the time, cobbled together a living with income from the Black leagues, winter ball in the Caribbean or Mexico, and barnstorming in between. Irvin noticed the local kid milling around the entrance and invited him to walk in with him. Clemente saved fifteen cents and gained a mentor. "I taught Roberto how to throw," Irvin said. "Of course, he later surpassed me."[5]

Clemente could see himself in Irvin, Irvin in Clemente – an Afro-Puerto Rican and an African American who lived for baseball. No one noticed the resemblance in 1973. Irvin's career had been domesticated. Clemente's had been disassociated from Black baseball. The two men who had first met outside a stadium in San Juan arrived, thirty years later, on opposite sides of a Black/brown color line.

C. L. R. James had encountered that line as a young cricketer on colonial Trinidad. In his first year out of school, he had played for a club he remembered as a "motley racial crew" of Black and brown cricketers and one white man, "a Portuguese of local birth, which did not count exactly as white (unless very wealthy)."[6] When it disbanded, the young James had a decision to make. He received invitations from the club of the brown middle class, his elite education compensating for his dark skin, and from the club of the Black lower middle class. He chose to follow his light-skinned friends from boarding school to the brown club, a decision he came to regret. It had, he thought, taken him "to the right" and suspended his "political development for years."[7] Club cricket had forced him, a defensive batsman with a nascent anticolonial consciousness, to take a side in the island's racial struggle, a struggle not limited, he discovered, to color.

James leapt the line that later separated Irvin from Clemente. But the line didn't serve the young Trinidadian. It left him with a sense of loss. He had cut himself off from something that he couldn't then name. "Between the brown-skinned middle class and the black," he later wrote in *The Life of Captain Cipriani*, his first book, "there is a continual rivalry, distrust and ill-feeling, which, skillfully played upon by the European peoples, poisons the life of the community."[8] The color line governed race on the island, but it often bent, blurred, shifted. It gave rise to other lines and categories of difference. A white Portuguese without an inheritance could sink below whiteness. A Black cricketer who delivered lectures on Wordsworth and Longfellow at local salons, as James did, could rise above Blackness. But the bending, blurring, and shifting did not destabilize but strengthen the color line. It obscured white dominance behind a young cricketer's decision between Black and brown and an Afro–Puerto Rican star's transformation into the first Latino Hall of Famer.

Clemente debuted with the Pittsburgh Pirates in 1955, eight years after Jackie Robinson took the field for the Dodgers, as Black. White sportswriters insisted, no matter how many times Clemente corrected them, on calling him Bob. Black sportswriters welcomed him as one of their own, hoping that he might return the National League Rookie of the Year Award to MLB's Black fraternity, after a white player, Wally Moon, won it in 1954, ending a seven-year streak.[9] (He didn't, but Frank Robinson won the award in 1956.) Historians have challenged the story that the integration of the game unfolded in two waves: first the Black wave of Jackie Robinson, Irvin, Willie Mays, and Hank Aaron, then the Latino wave of Minnie Miñoso, Clemente, and Juan Marichal and later Fernando Valenzuela and thousands more. The waves didn't come one after the other. Before Robinson, general managers looking for an edge but unwilling to break the game's racial code sometimes turned to Latinos, including Afro-Latinos, who carved out careers in the Black leagues (as African Americans did in the Caribbean and Mexican leagues), to give their rosters a boost. Latinos "acted as test subjects in a battle over the color line's exclusionary point," Adrian Burgos writes.[10] Cubans had been "a gauge for how 'white' a black player could be," Lisa Brock and Bijan Bayne observe.[11] The Clemente of 1955, while he might have once acted as a test subject or gauge, belonged to a ballfield diaspora. He was Black.

At the Hall, Irvin remembered the Clemente of the diaspora. Few others did. The baseball card manufacturer Topps dropped Bob for Roberto in 1970 – not out of respect for the man, it seems, but because of a new, more rigid line forming between Black and Latino. He would be remembered as, in the words of the late historian Peter Bjarkman, "Latin America's first true baseball hero."[12] The Clemente of 1973, while he might have entered the big leagues as a Black prospect, belonged to the Latin game. He was brown.

Major League Baseball institutionalized the Black/brown color line. In 1965, it followed the NFL and NBA by introducing an amateur draft. It was a cost-saving measure. Competitive bidding had led to large signing bonuses for the most promising young prospects. MLB excluded foreign-born Latinos as well as Puerto Ricans from participating in the draft. The draft regulated the domestic market and turned the Caribbean, where scouts could sign prospects at sixteen, into the wild west of talent recruitment.[13] It reinforced a growing sense that African Americans and Latin Americans were locked in a zero-sum struggle for resources. When Afro-Dominican pitcher Juan Marichal swung his bat at African American catcher John Roseboro during a game that summer, baseball writers interpreted it as a sign of interracial antagonism. Black and Latino players, they determined, belonged to separate, competing racial groups that hated each other. For Afro-Latinos, like Clemente, their language had superseded their Blackness. Latinos "who first came to the United States to play baseball had a double obstacle to face," Orlando Cepeda remembered. "We were black. But even worse, we could not speak the language."[14] In 2007, the outfielder Gary Sheffield, then at the end of his playing career, attributed the decline in African Americans in baseball to the rise in Latin Americans. MLB is "able to control [Latin Americans]," he said. "So if [an African American] is equally as good as this Latin player, guess who's going to get sent home?"[15] Cepeda set himself apart from his African American teammates, Sheffield from his Latin American teammates. Their "overlapping diasporas" of the Black Caribbean and Black America now constituted competing diasporas.[16]

The passage of the Immigration and Nationality Act of 1965 transformed the racial demographics of the United States, and of Major League Baseball. The act abolished the National Origins Formula, which had restricted immigration from the Eastern Hemisphere, and imposed limits on immigration from the Americas. Latin American immigrants kept coming, but, due to the act's restrictions, more and more arrived undocumented, structuring Latino racialization in the United States. Historians of Latino life see the Immigration Act as a critical moment in the formation of a state-recognized panethnic Latino demographic. The addition of the "Spanish/Hispanic origin" question to the census followed in 1980 (after a trial run in 1970). The association of Latinos with immigration and "origin," the legal historian Laura Gómez writes, encouraged Latinos to see themselves as distant from African Americans – as belonging to an ethnic rather than racial class, "striving 'immigrants'" on their way to whiteness.[17]

The rise of Latinos in baseball would seem to stem from the wider changes instigated by legislation and economic conditions.[18] In *Making Hispanics*, the sociologist G. Cristina Mora argues that racial and ethnic classifications form in three stages: first, the state responds to and co-opts the demands of racial or ethnic leaders, then it negotiates the boundaries and meaning of the new classification with group leaders, then the state and group leaders undertake the "collaborative marketing" of the classification.[19] Culture, including sports, falls into the third stage, as marketing – Latino night at the ballpark. The state makes race, and national culture absorbs and perpetuates it. First law, then sports. I would have assumed the same of Latino racialization and baseball – that the state led and sports followed. But I kept encountering evidence of the reverse: that Major League Baseball had institutionalized a Black/brown color line and familiarized fans of the national pastime with it before Congress or the census did. Stage three, then stage one. Marketing, then co-optation. Sports, then law.

Clemente and other Afro-Latinos' reracialization as Latin can be tracked through a word. The Puerto Rican outfielder was, the *New York Times* declared after his death, "proud," "sullen," and, above all, "superbly gifted."[20] He and other Latin Americans arrived, it seemed to mainland observers, out of nowhere, with skills that had to be God-given, raw gifts that MLB managers and coaches could hone into greatness. The idea of the gifted Latino athlete was not new – mainlanders had been referring to Cubans as naturals since the late nineteenth century – and it borrowed from the script of the Black athlete. But a new set of racial attributes recategorized Clemente, the Afro–Puerto Rican, as Latin. He embodied, writers and broadcasters decided, a Latin brand of showboating; he was, to use the term that irritated Clemente most, a "hot dog." He was too proud. He showed too much emotion. He was a whiner, a malingerer. He sat when others would have taken the field. He relied on his talent. Clemente encountered what the ethnic studies scholar Yomaira Figueroa-Vásquez identifies as an ever-shifting "relational cartography of racialization." Scholars must, she writes, consider how modes of racialization "diverge and overlap" if we are to "better understand the forms of anti-Blackness endemic to modernity."[21]

From his 1955 MLB debut to his 1973 induction into the Hall of Fame, Clemente endured a racial fracturing. After civil rights, his embodiment of Blackness became less legible to most Americans, as his first language took on new racial significance. His Blackness receded as writers, ignoring his status as a citizen of the United States, dwelled on

Clemente's foreignness. Writers ascribed to the older Clemente not the gift of talent – as they did to his African American teammates – but the gift of the developed world, a shot at the good life. The Black/brown color line encouraged baseball fans to see the civil rights reforms and the Immigration Act as two competing forms of state gift-giving that carried distinct racial debts. The front office, coach, and fan felt entitled to make demands on Black and Latino big leaguers and to leverage one debt against the other. This wasn't lost on Clemente. He described himself as "between the wall."[22] Major League Baseball had cast him as the bearer of one gift and then another.

The Black/white color line has never been total. It became less so after 1965. Afro-Latino big leaguers faced a suffocating in-betweenness, legible within neither a racialized Blackness nor an ethnicized Latinoness.[23] Perhaps because of his place as the first Latino Hall of Famer or because he died on an aid mission to Nicaragua, Clemente underwent a more complete recategorization as Latino. But he is not often remembered as

Left to right: Roberto Clemente, Willie Stargell, and Donn Clendenon at Forbes Field in Pittsburgh in 1965. Photograph by Charles "Teenie" Harris. Reproduced by permission from the Carnegie Museum of Art.

Black, as an integrator who made his major-league debut at the onset of the civil rights movement's most commemorated decade. The political scientist Claire Jean Kim argues that the racial order is governed not by one binary, Black/white, but two, white/nonwhite and Black/non-Black. For Asian Americans (Kim's subject) and Latinos, white dominance and anti-Blackness act together as a ceiling and a floor. Non-Black people of color are denied the privileges of whiteness but rewarded for participating in anti-Blackness.[24] In the 1960s, Major League Baseball modeled a third binary. White owners, general managers, and sportswriters took accounts of conflicts between Black and Latino teammates and opponents as evidence that African Americans and Latinos belonged to separate clubhouse blocs that couldn't get along. The story of the 1960s wasn't Black/white but Black/nonwhite, and they, the white mediators, were here to help.

The Black/brown color line divided a diaspora. The transnational circuit of the Black leagues and the Caribbean and Mexican leagues brought African diasporic peoples into close contact, serving as, historians note, a "site of exchange" and a source of "racial pride and politics."[25] It facilitated what Frank Andre Guridy calls "diaspora-making," a bond formed through not "roots" but "routes."[26] The invention of Latin ball, of a Latin American baseball culture separate and apart from Black ball, obscured a diaspora that summoned the histories of the transatlantic slave trade and waves of colonialism in the Caribbean and that offered an alternative to national belonging (the form favored by states as well as the liberationist groups of the 1960s). A new generation of revisionist baseball historians framed the Black leagues as one long movement toward integration into the national pastime, with the Caribbean a mere way station for the Black-league prospect on his way to the big leagues. Clemente and other Afro-Latinos' ethnicization as Latin took the diaspora out of Black baseball. It recast them as pioneers of another game from another place. Irvin and Clemente, thirty years after they met outside Sixto Escobar Stadium, landed in different wings of the Hall of Fame.[27]

The baseball writers of the 1960s couldn't imagine Irvin and Clemente as friends. Black and Latino players didn't, they determined, like one another. In the months before the 1960 season, Robert Boyle, an early *Sports Illustrated* staff writer, undertook an investigation of, as his eventual title announced, "The Private World of the Negro Ballplayer." In the lengthy feature, he told a story not of Black life in a white business, as a reader might have expected, but of a mutual distrust between Black and Latino teammates, all of whom he described as "Negroes." African Americans had "certain reservations" about their "Latin Negro" teammates, he wrote. "Latin Negroes do not willingly mingle with American Negroes off the field." He traced that uneasiness to "the segregation issue" and to "the American Negroes low status in U.S. society in general," suggesting that Latino and Latin American players, including Afro-Latinos, distanced themselves from their non-Latino Black teammates to elevate their own racial status.[28] Alex Pompez, the Cuban American director of international scouting for the San Francisco Giants and a former Black-league club owner, told Boyle that Afro-Latinos often struggled to adapt to the segregation of the South. Afro-Latinos were not, the sportswriter concluded, "Negroes, as least as far as they themselves are concerned."[29] One unnamed African American player confirmed Boyle's thesis. "I'm not any better than they are," he said, "but I'm not any worse, either. They think they're better than the colored guy."[30] Boyle did not interview any active Latino players. Their private world remained private. Thirteen years after Robinson broke the color barrier, Boyle nudged that barrier from Black/white toward Black/brown, recasting Afro-Latinos – by their own choice, he suggested – as Latin.

The belief that Latinos had it better than, and might want to disassociate themselves from, their Black teammates descends from the name of an African American club that formed on Long Island in 1885: the Cuban Giants. Sol White, an infielder with the club and perhaps the first historian of Black baseball, told a reporter in the late 1930s that he and his teammates had "passed as foreigners" by speaking "a gibberish to each other on the field which, they hoped, sounded like Spanish."[31] Historians have since raised doubts about White's account, but the idea that he and other African American athletes of the time identified as Cuban out of a sense of mischief and racial self-interest stuck, lodging itself in Black-league lore. (Boyle recited it in 1960 – "to get games, they called themselves the Cuban Giants" – and the 1976 film *The Bingo Long Traveling All-Stars* turns it into a gag.)[32] Most of the Cubans whom White and the Giants encountered would have been Black themselves and no better off after Reconstruction, not that promoters would have bought the charade that White described, had his team ever tried it. (Pompez later reclaimed the name for his Cuban Stars, a Black-league team of Cubans and other Latin Americans, and his New York Cubans, a club of African Americans and Latinos. His teams' names signaled not interracial theft but acts of diasporic institution building.)[33]

Cubans of the 1880s and '90s traveled the Black baseball circuit and associated the sport with resistance to the Spanish Empire. For them, it stood in contrast, the historian Louis Pérez writes, to bullfighting, the height of sporting achievement in imperial Spain. Baseball was modern, democratic, civilized; bullfighting backward, colonial, barbaric.[34] The tale that early Black clubs called themselves Cuban to receive better treatment, to secure some of the wages of whiteness, transformed a sign of diasporic consciousness – of African Americans seeing themselves in Afro-Cubans and Afro-Cubans seeing themselves in African Americans – into an act of racial deceit, a joke, something that a reader or moviegoer could laugh at. Baseball could be a sign of freedom and an instrument of racial division with which management disciplined difference.

The invention of Latin ball anticipated the rise of *Latino* as a demographic classification. Gómez, Mora, and other historians of the post-1965 racial reordering trace the term to a convergence of social movements (Boricua and Chicano), federal agencies (the Cabinet Committee on Opportunities for Spanish-Speaking People and the Census Bureau), and media organizations (Univision) that responded to the demands of Latino leaders and detected political and commercial opportunities in drawing together heterogeneous Spanish-speaking communities. The Census Bureau tested the origin question ("Is this person of Spanish/Hispanic origin or descent? Fill one circle.") in 1970 and added it to the short form in 1980 as a supplement to the race question, setting *Latino* apart as an ethnic designation that overlapped with Black, Native, and white. The bureau was concerned that combining them could render past data unusable and lead to decreases in the Black, Native, and white counts in some regions, thereby reducing government support for other constituencies.

The race/ethnicity distinction created confusion. The bureau maintained that Latinos did not constitute a race but then interpreted the data as if they did, sorting Black, Latino, and white into nonintersecting categories ("non-Hispanic Black," "non-Hispanic white"). "Although technically Hispanics could be any race," Mora writes, "the racial analogies made the Hispanic category seem race-like."[35] The vagueness of the term, Gómez adds, has made Americans reluctant to name anti-Latino racism *as racism* and set Latinos against their Black neighbors in a struggle over resources along the Black/non-Black color line. In *Inventing Latinos*, she identifies the census as the foremost state mechanism of racialization: "The state, via the census, produces race, and race and racism produce the census, in a dialectic feedback loop."[36] The first part of her schema is intuitive, the second ambiguous. A novel form of "race and racism" does not originate at a meeting of the Census Bureau. It must mature elsewhere first, with shifting socioeconomic conditions and the stories told about them. Most Americans didn't then (and don't now) think twice about census data. But many did watch baseball, the national pastime, in which Cubans, Dominicans, Mexicans, Puerto Ricans, and Venezuelans had coalesced into what one historian described as "the most visible Latins in the United States."[37] For the sporting public, the image of a ballclub divided into Black, brown, and white smoothed over the incoherence of a new racial classification that the state would come to recognize during the 1970s. The 1980s could not have been "The Decade for Hispanics," as the civil rights leader Raul Yzaguirre declared it, if the 1960s had not first been the decade of Latin ball.[38]

Social scientists have wondered as well about the coherence of an ever more heterogeneous Black population in the United States. The 1965 Immigration Act brought more immigrants from Africa as well as the Caribbean, where, despite restrictions on immigration from the Western Hemisphere, tens of thousands of future citizens received visas through labor certification and family reunification programs. Post-1965 Black immigrants often achieved "greater social and economic status than black Americans," the demographer Tod Hamilton observes, because they arrived "at a time of expanding opportunities for minorities and for women" and because of "selectivity in migration" (wealth, education, ambition).[39] Hamilton worries that ignorance of the patterns of Black immigration gives the public the false impression that African Americans have made dramatic economic gains since civil rights, when a closer look at the data reveals a more sobering truth. Few studies, he notes, account for the differences between a descendant of people enslaved in the American South and a first-generation Nigerian American.

The sense of intraracial difference can erupt into the kind of suspicion that Boyle's interviewees voiced. The political scientist Christina Greer, confirming their fears, suggests that many Black immigrants to the United States cultivate an "elevated minority status," wherein Africans and Afro-Latinos seek to remain "perpetual outsiders and forever foreign so as not to ever fully incorporate themselves into the black American populace" – "an extension of the model minority," she calls it.[40] Greer's model casts Black immigrants as the authors and beneficiaries of that differentiation, as having observed the anti-Blackness around them and elected to distance themselves from native-born Black Americans, reaching for the other side of the Black/non-Black divide. Perhaps. But the foremost authors and beneficiaries of the Black/brown color line in baseball were the decision-makers in front offices (almost all white men) and high-profile sportswriters (almost all white men), who defined the boundaries of Blackness not to elevate Afro-Caribbeans over African Americans but themselves over athletic labor. Major League Baseball functioned as a national network of racializing organizations that institutionalized a rigid Black/Latino line and then, 162 games a year, taught it to the fan sitting in the bleachers, watching from home, or reading the morning paper.

MLB general managers had once tested the color line with Latinos, but Afro-Latinos could not, they decided, be integrators. Afro-Latinos embodied the wrong kind of Blackness, a Blackness that, in the evolving logic of civil rights–era baseball, was turning into something else. The Afro–Puerto Rican first basemen Vic Power, a future six-time All-Star, languished in the minor leagues from 1951 to 1953, waiting for Yankees general manager George Weiss to call him up. He hit .331 for the club's top minor-league affiliate in 1952 and then led the AAA league in batting in 1953. "The Yankees never have been averse to having a Negro player," Weiss said, when a reporter asked him about Power. "Our attitude has been that when a Negro comes along who can play good enough baseball to win a place on the Yankees, we will be glad to have him, but not just for exploitation." He added, without using Power's name, that "the first Negro to appear in a Yankee uniform must be worth having been waited for."[41] The other two New York teams, the Dodgers and the Giants, had integrated their rosters, and Weiss had to explain why his club hadn't. He blamed Power, the Yankees' top Black prospect, for being the wrong kind of Black player. Power didn't conform to Weiss's conservative standards – the Puerto Rican had little patience for mainland racial mores, often dating white women and lighter-skinned Latinas – but the general manager also wanted the kind of press that Branch Rickey had received for signing Robinson. He didn't think he'd get it for promoting an Afro–Puerto Rican to the big leagues, so he never did, trading Power to the Philadelphia Athletics before the 1954 season.

The hollowing out of the Black and Caribbean leagues through unidirectional integration had rendered African Americans and Latinos pure labor, with no controlling stake in the future of the game.[42] The division of the new talent pool into Black and brown gave white owners and managers an additional lever of power. Pompez, who, compared with most of his peers in the Black leagues, made a smooth transition to the majors, still found himself working as a scout for an organization that could dismiss him on a whim, as Weiss did Power.

Jim Bouton, who pitched for Weiss's Yankees, the Seattle Pilots, and the Houston Astros in the 1960s, described MLB clubhouses as a hostile environment for Latinos in his 1970 memoir *Ball Four*. He had seen anti-Latino racism get uglier during his nine seasons. He remembered a white teammate telling an injured Dominican catcher to "talk English! You're in America now" – a common complaint in New York, Seattle, and Houston, Bouton acknowledged. Cepeda recalled walking into the Dodgers clubhouse on the first day of spring training and seeing the same message on a sign: "Speak English. You are in America."[43] Bouton singled out general managers and coaches as the worst offenders. Joe Schultz, the manager of the short-lived Pilots, referred to all Latinos on his team as "Chico." Spec Richardson, the general manager of the hapless Houston Astros, once climbed onto a team bus and stared at five Latinos speaking Spanish to one another. "He stood listening for a while, his eyes shifting back and forth, as if he understood what they were saying," Bouton remembered. "Finally he said, 'Abbadabba dab-badabba.'"[44] Richardson controlled their contracts and could trade them whenever he wished.

Bouton's Latino teammates, who may have been from different countries, found themselves lumped together through an emerging racialization of language. Bouton does not mention whether they have dark or light skin; their salient characteristic is their first language. Sportswriters described them as gifted, as they had Robinson and his generation of African American major leaguers, but with a difference. Their gifts arose, writers implied, from their foreignness. They had come, it seemed, out of nowhere, as Roy Hobbs once had out of the rural West. Latinos had received an unearned athletic gift, and they owed the game a debt. Spanish marked their gift, their debt, and distinguished it from the one that Robinson and his generation of African American stars had brought to the big leagues in the late 1940s. The Black natural was familiar and indebted to the heroic general manager who gave him a shot. The Latino natural was foreign and indebted to the benevolent nation that took him in. Their white teammate, all grit, owed no one; he, with no longer the faintest relation to Bernard Malamud's natural, had paid his debts to the baseball gods with sweat and sacrifice.

Latinos needed a "bill of rights," Felipe Alou, the San Francisco Giants outfielder, decided in 1963. MLB commissioner Ford Frick had hit him and other Dominicans with a $250 fine for taking the field in a series of exhibition games against a team of Cuban all-stars in Alou's hometown of Santo Domingo. Alou, furious, accused the commissioner of a willful ignorance of Dominicans' and other Latinos' situations. The games had been goodwill exhibitions for a nation enduring political turbulence after the assassination of the dictator Rafael Trujillo, and most Dominican major leaguers, who tended to have lower salaries than their mainland teammates and fewer offseason endorsement deals, needed the income from winter ball. "We had to play the Cuban series," Alou wrote that fall. "You have to know all this before you can understand why I was so angered by the action of Mr. Frick."[45]

Cubans, Puerto Ricans, and Venezuelans had their own histories and grievances with the league, but Frick and the owners had, in reprimanding them as one, as Latins, united them. Alou observed that his immigrant status made earning a living in the United States more difficult but that being a citizen hadn't shielded his Puerto Rican teammate José Pagán from anti-Latino racism. "[Pagán] is treated the same way as any Latin who is not an American citizen," Alou wrote. "This means that the Puerto Ricans find themselves closer to other Latins than to other Stateside players. It makes foreigners out of a country's citizens."[46] Their manager, the notorious Alvin Dark, had banned Spanish in the clubhouse in 1962, and Alou, Pagán, and other Latinos resolved to answer as a racial coalition. Raced as Latin, they turned around and demanded rights for that race.

Alou, an Afro-Dominican, could see his foreignness overriding his Blackness. When the Giants signed him in 1956 and sent him to a Class D affiliate in Lake Charles, Louisiana, he, new to the United States, roomed with a Black teammate from Harlem. Most of the team and most of the people in the town identified him as Black, not Dominican or Latin. That changed in the big leagues, where he experienced a kind of racial reshuffling, first raced Black, then "Black Latin," then just Latin, a classification analogous to but, he discovered, disassociated from Blackness. His coaches assigned different negative attributes to African Americans and Latinos. African Americans "choked." Latinos didn't hustle or had "no guts."[47] Their anti-Black and anti-Latino beliefs shared a lineage – ideas about weak work ethic and cowardice belong to a long tradition of anti-Black thought – but they functioned in the 1960s, Alou noticed, to distance Blackness from brownness while freeing whiteness, unnoticed, from the racial scrum. He and other Latinos sought to repurpose their reracialization to their own ends – to turn it into an international coalition through which to make demands on management – but ran into a media narrative that cast them against not the commissioner or the owner but their own teammates.[48]

A flashpoint in MLB's racial reordering came on August 22, 1965, when Giants Afro-Dominican ace Juan Marichal swung his bat at the Dodgers Black catcher John Roseboro. Roseboro had grazed Marichal with the ball as retaliation for the Giants pitcher having beaned two Dodgers earlier in the game, and Marichal went after him, striking him over the head and setting off a dugout-clearing brawl. Marichal received an eight-game suspension and a $1,750 fine. Most sportswriters framed the incident as evidence of a growing rift between African Americans and Latinos. "The true problem is that the American Negroes and the Latin Negroes do not like each other – not even a little bit," Dick Young of the New York *Daily News* wrote of the Marichal–Roseboro incident. "They are on the opposite sides even when they wear the same uniform."[49] Bob Broeg, the sports editor for the *St. Louis Post-Dispatch*, described Marichal's actions as characteristic of "a tendency of Latin American ball players to fight with weapons other than their fists," which he condemned as "dangerous and despicable" and as setting a poor example for the "hero-worshipping small fry."[50] Willie Mays of the Giants had shielded his friend Roseboro during the fight, leading Young, Broeg,

Juan Marichal (27), John Roseboro (*center*), and Sandy Koufax (*right*) at Candlestick Park in San Francisco in 1965. Photograph by Robert H. Houston. From AP Photo.

and others to conclude that Mays had identified Marichal's actions as racial, an attack on all non-Latino African Americans in the game. Most sportswriters, while they had different takes on the details of the incident, agreed on a basic fact: The fight was the manifestation of long-simmering resentments between Black and Latino athletes – and the Black and Latino communities for which they stood. They lacked other evidence. But theirs was a rule of one: One example makes a trend.

Joe Black, the former Black-league pitcher who had signed with Robinson's Dodgers in 1952, couldn't believe what he heard. He dismissed the idea that African Americans and Latin Americans didn't get along as a "ridiculous theory," reminding readers of the *New York Amsterdam News*, then the largest Black newspaper, of the diasporic routes that had, in his time, connected the domestic Black leagues with the Caribbean and Mexican leagues.[51] But Black found himself swimming against a current of white baseball men agreeing with one another that something called Latin ball now stood against Black ball, one forever swinging a bat at the other.

Clemente, once hailed as the next great Black outfielder, died as the face of Latin ball. "I'm Puerto Rican. I'm Black. And I'm between the wall," he told Sam Nover of the Pittsburgh NBC affiliate WIIC-TV in 1972.[52] Sportswriters, with whom he often clashed, never had the patience to hear him out, he said. He was Black, Latino, and Puerto Rican, a citizen of the United States, and writers wanted one thing at a time, a story they could tell in fifteen column inches. Over his long career, they had told one story and then another, recategorizing him, an Afro–Puerto Rican raised in the shadow of the island's sugar cane plantations, as Latin. They had stuck him between the wall.

Clemente, whose career coincided with the rise and reversal of civil rights – he signed his first contract in the year of the *Brown v. Board* decision and entered the Hall of Fame in the summer that the Nixon administration formed the Drug Enforcement Administration – had watched Major League Baseball build the wall. In 1960, his Pirates had faced the Yankees in the World Series. *Life* magazine, with a circulation of more than five million, enlisted Jim Brosnan to break down the Pittsburgh roster. The editors introduced Brosnan, an undistinguished relief pitcher for the Cincinnati Reds, as a "highly literate man," and he framed his scouting report as "my book on the Pirates." Of the Pirates right fielder, he wrote, "Clemente features a Latin-American variety of showboating. 'Look at *número uno*,' he seems to be saying." Brosnan recounted how Clemente had earned a reputation as "hard-headed" when, while running from first to second, he had taken a ball between the eyes and "didn't even blink."⁵³ The Reds relief man, who a few years earlier might have identified Clemente as Black, described his athleticism and behavior as signs of his Latinoness. He threw, caught, and hit like a Latino. Brosnan, contributing to the athletic reracialization of Afro-Latinos and the consolidation of *Latino* as an intermediate racial/ethnic classification, offered the Yankees bullpen a racial scouting report: Pitch to Clemente as you would any Latin American batter. (Clemente had once hit a walk-off, inside-the-park grand slam off Brosnan, so the Reds pitcher may not have been the man to ask.)

Brosnan, who managed sixty-eight saves over ten years with four teams, modeled a new role for the white athlete in integrated times. He was an intellectual. Or at least he adopted the persona of one. In 1958, *Sports Illustrated* published excerpts from his diary – "the uninhibited diary of a professional ballplayer" – with a photograph of the pitcher, then with the St. Louis Cardinals, in suit and tie, grinning, an unlit pipe between his teeth. "The pleasant young fellow on the left looks like a professor," an editorial note read. "He wears glasses, smokes a pipe, reads good books and welcomes conversation on any subject from religion to real estate." The note introduced Brosnan as the "antithesis" of Jack Keefe, the uneducated, headstrong protagonist of Ring Lardner's dead ball–era baseball stories.⁵⁴ He didn't have the strongest arm, but Brosnan, the editors said, compensated for it with a one-of-a-kind mind; he was an eccentric genius among jocks. His 1960 book *The Long Season*, a recounting of a full season through diary entries, landed him on the bestseller list, establishing a way for Bouton and other white journeymen to distinguish themselves (and make a buck) off the field, as a growing number of Black and Latino major leaguers outmaneuvered them on it.

Brosnan, who had attended Xavier University for a year, never graduating, fashioned himself as a student of race. In *The Long Season*, he recalled a conversation with Brooks Lawrence, a Black teammate on the Reds, in which he had surprised Lawrence with his knowledge of jazz. "I didn't know you like jazz, Brosnan," Lawrence remarked. "What do you dig? Basie? Progressive? Dixieland?" "I try to make every scene, man," Brosnan told him. When he noticed that all of Lawrence's favorite musicians were Black, he offered an aside to the reader: "This was the first time I'd talked seriously to Lawrence. Best to find out if he was stuffy about being a Negro. Some of them are. Why they feel they have to be better than us I don't know."⁵⁵ Brosnan framed his book as an "inside chronicle" of the MLB clubhouse, which turned into an amateur investigation of the sport's Black and Latino cultures. "It's a Negro term, isn't it?" he asks some Black teammates of an Italian anti-Black slur he hears them using. A glossary of baseball terms in the front matter included the entry "Bean Bandit: A Latin-American ballplayer."[56]

The pitcher's next book, *Pennant Race*, another season-long diary, turned to what he called the "lobby of Latins" forming in the big leagues. "As a minority group in a Caucasian world, they stand out with hand gestures hypnotic and lip movements unintelligible," Brosnan wrote of finding himself, the white athlete as anthropologist, "en conclave" among Latino teammates gathered behind the batting cage.[57] The sociologist Roderick Ferguson argues that white liberals sustained their racial dominance after civil rights through a "certain investment in minority difference" by which they established themselves as administrators of an antiredistributive multiculturalism.[58] Brosnan and other white benchwarmers, staring down their own obsolescence, made the move to administration early, distinguishing themselves from their Black and Latino teammates as clubhouse intellectuals, defining and sorting the bodies around them.

The changing racial demographics of the national pastime caught the attention of a first generation of sociologists of sport. In 1967, Harold Charnofsky, an assistant professor at Cal State Dominguez Hills and a former minor-league infielder, delivered a paper at the annual meeting of the American Sociological Association in which he argued that "racial and ethnic equality in baseball is still a matter of expedience with respect to the dollar."[59] The local and then national press took note. The *Los Angeles Times*: "Whites, Negroes Keep 'Social Distance.'" The Associated Press: "Social Gap Seen between Races in Big Leagues." Charnofsky had conducted seventy-three interviews and one marathon "bull session" with active major leaguers (fifty-eight white, nine Black, six Latin American) and found that few associated off the field with teammates of other backgrounds and that many of the white interviewees thought their Black teammates benefited from "favoritism" and considered their Latino teammates "temperamental."[60] The sociologist concluded that, while the league might have curbed overt forms of discrimination out of economic self-interest, racism endured "in a variety of subtle ways."[61]

But Charnofsky's paper, which he had distilled from his then-unfinished dissertation, did more than observe racial differences in Major League Baseball. It, with the weight of science behind it, created them. It naturalized the idea that Black, white, and Latino constituted discrete racial categories to be studied one at a time, compared, and contrasted. One appeared favored, another temperamental. His Latino interviewees were no longer, as they had been in the early 1960s, Black Latin. They were now Latin, a third wing of the racial clubhouse, neither Black nor white. When Charnofsky filed his dissertation, he included a footnote acknowledging that Latinos and Latin Americans could also be, and often were, Black. Their "development is a sociological story that merits separate attention beyond the more general discussion presented here," he admitted.[62] But he, Brosnan, and others hadn't waited to tell the story of Latin ball, with or without letters after their names.

Clemente did not care for sportswriters. He thought that they didn't listen and that, by quoting him as speaking an almost incomprehensible English, discounted his intelligence. After a 1961 game, the Associated Press boiled an interview down to one infamous sentence: "I get heet and Willie scores and I feel better than good."[63] The *Pittsburgh Post-Gazette* ran the article under the headline "I Get Heet, I Feel Good." Les Biederman of the *Pittsburgh Press* once had Clemente discussing the weather as a three-year-old might: "Me like hot weather, veree hot. I no run fast cold weather. No get warm in cold. Not get warm, no play gut."[64] Clemente accused Biederman of creating "propaganda" against him and later told United Press International that he blamed writers for casting Latinos as "something different entirely from the white players" and "inferior in our station of life."[65] He could see that white baseball men had resecured their dominance of the sport, a sport with a growing number of Black and Latino stars, through the administration of difference, which often involved first inventing and then hierarchizing it. While critics then and now dwell on the lack of Black and Latino owners and coaches, Clemente implicated the white world of sportswriting as an agent of the racial status quo in Major League Baseball. The league administered the written rules, but the writer, he argued, enforced the silent ones.

Although Clemente admitted, in his 1972 interview with Nover, that he disliked "lots of writers," not all of them raised his ire.[66] Howard Cohn acknowledged that other sportswriters exaggerated Clemente's accent, a custom that wouldn't, he wrote in a 1962 profile for *Sport*, "be duplicated here."[67] Cohn observed that Clemente and other Afro-Caribbeans faced obstacles in Major League Baseball that few owners or managers had bothered to address and that his colleagues sometimes magnified. "Because they speak Spanish among themselves, they are set off as a minority within a minority," he wrote. Generalizations about

Afro-Caribbeans "fall apart easily enough, of course, when individual skills and personalities are considered. But some people don't, or won't, consider them."[68] In 1965, Arnold Hano, author of the acclaimed *A Day in the Bleachers*, asked how a star of Clemente's caliber – a World Series champion, a four-time All-Star, a two-time batting champ – could be the recipient of almost no endorsement deals. The answer: language and race. Salaried at $50,000, the Pirates right fielder did not, Hano wrote, earn "too much extra, because Clemente is Latin and Clemente is dark-skinned, and somehow advertising agencies think that there's nothing quite like running a stainless blade over the pink cheek and fuzzy skin of a young white lad from Peoria."[69] Cohn and Hano heard Clemente out. Baseball reporters had, he showed them, wedded race to language and language to national belonging, imagining an intermediate race of Spanish speakers who must hail from somewhere else, foreigners to the national pastime. The 1930 census had included "Mexican" as a race, and the bureau had for a time used Spanish surnames to count Mexican Americans, a method that managed to both over- and undercount the intended population.[70] Clemente was encountering the next racialization of language, a racialization that had superseded his Blackness and that would soon, with the 1965 Immigration Act, widen.

But the Pirates star found something he could use in sportswriters' broad generalizations about Latinos. A beloved veteran by the mid-1960s, Clemente mentored the next generation of Latinos then entering the league. He made headlines in 1966, when he told the Associated Press that MLB shortchanged Latin Americans, offering them smaller contracts than their mainland teammates and never inviting them to off-season events or introducing them to the league's corporate partners. "I am an American citizen. I live 250 miles from Miami," he said. "But some people act like they think I live in the jungle some place. To the people here we are outsiders, foreigners." He told the AP, which described him as "brooding" and "intense," that he had been organizing gatherings of Latinos to talk about their concerns.[71] Some teams admitted that they looked at scouting in the Caribbean as a cost-saving measure. A promising Dominican player might sign for $1,500, one team official told the *New York Times*, whereas a white American high school or college prospect could demand as much as $60,000. MLB clubs recovered the escalating cost for white prospects – checked the "dollar drain," as the *Times* put it – by extracting more for less from Latin American athletic labor.[72] Clemente thought the term *Latin* elided his and others' heterogeneous identities and histories with the United States, but he also recognized, as

Felipe Alou did, that Latinos needed to organize. The name on the banner mattered less than the alignment of interests.

When the 1971 Pirates – lauded for fielding the first all-Black and Latino starting lineup – won the World Series, sportswriters, fans, and the Pirates themselves described the team in the language of difference that had emerged over their longtime star's career. "You had a Latino player in Clemente, a black guy [in] Willie Stargell and you got a white guy in [Bill] Mazeroski," Steve Blass, who pitched in Game 7 for the Pirates, later told the Clemente biographer Bruce Markusen. "We had the whole program covered. They were leaders. All three of them."[73] Never before, Markusen writes, had MLB fielded a team "assembled purely on available talent with no consideration of skin color." The Pirates had "changed baseball."[74] Brosnan, Charnofsky, and Blass had come to think of the league in new racial terms: not of Black and white but of Black, white, and brown. Clemente, Stargell, and Mazeroski might have together led the '71 Pirates, but they also, Blass suggested, headed discrete racial cohorts in the clubhouse. Clemente over here, Stargell over there.

Clemente had, in Kim's model, landed between twin racial binaries, situated below whiteness but above mainland Blackness. Earlier in her career, the political scientist described the racial order not as hierarchical (A over B over C) but as constructed on two axes: superior/inferior and insider/foreigner. On the superior/inferior axis, Asian Americans (and Latinos) were superior to Black and inferior to white. On the insider/foreigner axis, they were "apart" from Black and white as unassimilable.[75] Afro-Caribbean immigrants would, in Kim's model, be inferior and foreign, below and apart. But the racial order sustains itself on rivalries between inferior and foreigner, Black and nonwhite. Thrust across one color line, Afro-Caribbeans reemerged as Latino. The invention of Latin ball in the years before and after the Immigration Act tested a Black/nonwhite color line that would inform a rising multiculturalism. White baseball men moved Clemente from Black to nonwhite but also removed themselves from the racial scene, obscuring white dominance while attributing anti-Blackness to Latinos and anti-Latino racism to African Americans. Clemente entered the Hall of Fame in 1973 as a Latin trailblazer, Stargell in 1988 as a Black icon. The Veterans Committee inducted Mazeroski in 2001 as a Pittsburgh Pirate.

Clemente might have found himself caught between racial binaries – "between the wall," as he put it to Nover – but he lived in Black

Pittsburgh.[76] In 1955, Pirates pitcher Bob Friend introduced the Puerto Rican rookie to Phil Dorsey, a Black postman with whom Friend had served in the Army Reserve. Clemente had been living in a cramped downtown hotel room, and Dorsey set him up with his friends Stanley and Mamie Garland, a Black couple with a spare room in Schenley Heights, a hub for Black culture in the city's Hill District. Dorsey, Clemente's first and best friend in Pittsburgh, took the newest Pirate to the Crawford Grill, the renowned jazz club where John Coltrane, Miles Davis, and Charles Mingus played. Gus Greenlee, owner of the Pittsburgh Crawfords of the Black leagues, had founded the club in the 1930s, and it remained a hangout for visiting Black athletes into the 1950s. Jackie Robinson and Roy Campanella could be found there whenever the Dodgers came to town. Dorsey and Clemente shot pool at the local Y and at a bar that Dorsey's brother owned in Homewood, another of the city's Black neighborhoods. The press knew Dorsey as Clemente's constant companion and protector, nicknaming him "Pittsburgh Phil." Dorsey, who liked the nickname, had mock business cards printed up: "Pittsburgh Phil, representing Roberto Clemente."[77] The young outfielder ate every night with the Garlands, whom he referred to in later years as his American parents. Black players from the States showed him and other players from the islands how to navigate mainland segregation. "'Wait a minute,'" Joe Black, the Dodgers pitcher, remembers telling one of his Puerto Rican teammates who wanted to go clothes shopping, "Let somebody go with you cause you can't just walk in all these stores."[78] Clemente wasn't Latin in 1950s Pittsburgh. He was Black.

But memories change. Bill Nuun Jr., a sportswriter and editor with the *Pittsburgh Courier* who lived four blocks from the Garlands, later told an interviewer that Clemente had been an outsider in Schenley Heights. "I think it was always tough for Clemente," he said. "For years in the black community there was a little tension with blacks from other countries. There were no Puerto Ricans to speak of, not like in New York. The thing here was steel mills, which didn't draw workers from the Caribbean."[79] African Americans and Afro-Caribbeans didn't get along, he suggested, and that had left Clemente on the outside of the Schenley Heights and Homewood communities. But Nuun, who later rose to managing editor at the *Courier* and served as a scout for the Pittsburgh Steelers, might have been transposing later beliefs about Black–Latino antagonism onto the 1950s. How, after all, could there be tension between African Americans and Puerto Ricans if there weren't any Puerto Ricans in Pittsburgh? Black and white Pittsburghers would

Roberto Clemente and Phil Dorsey in 1971. Photograph from AP Photo.

have identified Clemente as Black in 1955. Major League Baseball had not yet institutionalized a Black/brown color line.

Nuun himself had once written of the Pirates right fielder as a native son. Every spring, the *Courier*, headquartered a short walk from the neighborhood in which he and Clemente lived, ran a list of active Black major leaguers that didn't differentiate between African Americans and Afro-Latinos. Nuun, the longtime author of the list, had never failed to include Clemente in the 1950s as one of the league's brightest "tan stars."[80] (Nuun had also been the one to promote the young Puerto Rican as Black baseball's best shot at reclaiming the National League Rookie of the Year honors in 1955.)[81] One of Nuun's colleagues, William Webster, had asked in a 1954 column, "How Democratic Is Baseball?" His answer: very – for white men. MLB owners and general managers had kept costs down by bringing African Americans and Afro-Caribbeans into the league on barebones contracts, building a white "baseball democracy" through the co-optation and exploitation of a once-independent transnational circuit of Black athletic labor.[82]

Clemente had worked with Nuun in the fight to integrate hotels and restaurants in Fort Myers, Florida, where the Pirates held spring training. "I am against segregation in any form," Clemente told him, describing how he and other Black Pirates couldn't room, eat, or travel with their white teammates in southwest Florida. "We are members of the Pirates. As such, we should be given the same privileges as all the rest of the players."[83] No one, least of all Nuun, doubted the young Puerto Rican's Black bona fides in his first years with the team.

But the doubts did come. Rumors swirled during the 1960 season that Clemente considered himself above African Americans. A note in the *Courier* stated that the Afro–Puerto Rican "didn't want to be recognized as a Negro." Clemente had told a reporter that he didn't like how white people in the States treated Black people, including himself. The reporter interpreted him as meaning that he didn't like being treated as a Black person. Some readers then took the reporter's paraphrase as an admission that Clemente didn't like being Black, that he had disavowed his Blackness and other Black people. Clemente rushed down to the paper's offices on Centre Avenue to "nail that lie."[84] Nuun interviewed him and ran their conversation as a guest column. It appeared in the phonetic spelling that, Clemente knew, further distanced him from non-Latino Black Pittsburghers, undercutting his argument that he identified with them. "Som' co-lored people I understand saying Clemente, he not like co-lored people. This is not the truth at all. Look at me, I am not of the white people," he said, in Nuun's rendering of the interview. "Thees' people tell me that I don't like co-lored people. Well, I use this time to tell deeferent. I like myself, so I also like the people who are like me."[85] No one would ever mistake him for a white man, Clemente stressed, and neither Black Puerto Ricans nor Black mainlanders would benefit from a division between them. But he could never shake the rumor that he didn't consider himself Black – that he must be Latin, a racial buffer between his Black and white teammates, Black Pittsburgh and white Pittsburgh.

Other Black newspapers split on the racial status of the Afro-Caribbeans making their major-league debuts in the 1960s. Older baseball writers, some of whom had played with Afro-Cubans and Afro–Puerto Ricans in the Black leagues and on the islands, tended to see Clemente and other Afro-Caribbeans as Black and situate them within the unfolding civil rights struggle. Sheep Jackson of the Cleveland *Call and Post* celebrated "the rise of the Latin Negroes," recalling how African Americans, Afro-Cubans, and Afro–Puerto Ricans had toiled together in the interwar years, bouncing from the Black leagues to the Caribbean and Mexican leagues and barnstorming together. "In those days the games were played on open diamonds mostly, where the old tin-pans were passed among the spectators," he wrote in 1965, a day before the Marichal–Roseboro incident ignited talk of a rift between Black and Latino major leaguers.[86] He remembered a world not of Black and Latin but of a diaspora of athletes who had cobbled livings together in the shadows of empire and Jim Crow.

Jackie Robinson, who had done a short stint with the Kansas City Monarchs before signing with the Dodgers, recognized that Black and Latino players, while coming from different backgrounds, shared common enemies. When Giants manager Alvin Dark, who had banned the speaking of Spanish in the San Francisco clubhouse, told a *Newsday* columnist that his team had struggled because it had "so many Negro and Spanish-speaking players" who lacked the "mental alertness" of their white teammates, Robinson redirected the blame back at Dark.[87] How can the team's African American and Latino players perform their best, he asked, when they "have to work with a man who has strange cobwebs in his mind about people of color?"[88] Robinson admitted that he had been shocked by Dark's contribution to a 1964 volume he had coedited on the integration of baseball in which the manager, a Louisiana native, had suggested that white southern coaches "take care" of Black athletes better than northern coaches.[89] Robinson and his coeditor had titled the volume *Baseball Has Done It*. Dark got fired and then hired and then fired and hired again. He titled his 1980 autobiography *When in Doubt, Fire the Manager*.

A younger generation of Black sportswriters, not sharing Jackson's memories of transnational Black ball, identified Latinos, Black and white, as belonging to a third, nonintersecting racial bucket. After Hank Aaron rebuked an Atlanta broadcaster for naming Clemente, not him, the best right fielder in the game, the *Courier* ran a column titled "J. Robinson-Mays Age Dying: The Latins, Whites Take Over Baseball." The unnamed columnist observed that the paper's own list of "standouts" for the 1967 season – one player per position, plus three pitchers – included "only one non-white American," Tigers ace Earl Wilson. Afro–Puerto Ricans Cepeda and Clemente, two nonwhite American citizens, had made the list, but the columnist, not counting them or other Afro-Latinos, concluded that Major League Baseball had "applied brakes to the brigade of U.S. tanskins to compensate for their inescapably devastating triumphs in boxing, basketball, and football." The columnist identified the awarding of the 1965 American League MVP to Afro-Cuban shortstop Zoilo Versalles as a crisis for Black baseball, marking "the first time a tan import had been chosen."[90] Versalles's MVP would have once been heralded as a Black achievement, a continuation of a tradition that

Robinson and Mays (and the Afro-Cuban Miñoso) inaugurated. Now it marked the end of that tradition. The *Courier* had once hailed Cepeda and Clemente as belonging to a "record crop of 41 Negro stars" in the league.[91] Now it counted them among the "tan imports" undermining Black ball.[92]

Even Sheep Jackson changed his mind. Two years after reminding his readers of a sporting diaspora that bound African Americans and Afro-Latinos, he worried that the former's "colored brethren are taking the spotlight [from them], whether they want to admit it or not."[93] His attitude toward Latinos had changed. In 1965, he wrote that the time in which they huddled together in the clubhouse had "gone forever." In 1967, reversing course, he wrote that Latinos "stick together in the majors" and that it would "take time for them to mix more with both the white and colored Americans."[94] Latinos were, in his column, integrated and then self-segregated, "Black Latins" and then Latins. When Clemente died, *Ebony* ran a tribute that dwelled on how "nothing quite bugged him like the comparison of his playing to that of" Willie Mays. "I am not Weelie," he had, according to *Ebony*, once said. The tribute let readers believe that Clemente had disliked the association not because he wished to be seen on his own terms but because he didn't want to be identified with a Black man.[95] The Afro–Puerto Rican who had lived in Schenley Heights and caught shows at the Crawford Grill no longer belonged in Black Pittsburgh.

Clemente's career coincided with the transformation of Robinson, who retired in 1956, from hero to legend. Doc Young of the *Chicago Defender* chronicled Robinson and his generation across the 1950s and then memorialized them in books and columns. In his 1953 volume *Great Negro Stars and How They Made the Major Leagues*, Young situated Robinson among a host of other Black athletes making their way in a once-segregated league, including Miñoso, the Afro-Cuban outfielder and Black league star who made his MLB debut in 1949, two years after Robinson. Young described theirs as "the era of Jackie Robinson, Minnie Miñoso, et al."[96] But his 1963 book, *Negro Firsts in Sports*, a rough sequel to *Great Negro Stars*, elevated Robinson and his general manager, Branch Rickey, above the rest. "Seldom before in history has so vastly important a change in a racial group's fortunes been as directly traceable to one person," he wrote of Robinson. "To Jackie, also, can be attributed the broadening of opportunity for colored players from such Latin American areas as Santo Domingo, Cuba, Puerto Rico, South America."[97] Though he continued to celebrate Miñoso, Young had shifted from an account in which Robinson and Miñoso had struggled together against Jim Crow into one in which Robinson led a wave of African Americans into the major leagues, creating the conditions for a later Latin American wave. Miñoso retained his status as Black, but younger Afro-Caribbeans didn't make the racial cut. Players who entered the majors before 1955 (Miñoso, Vic Power) were Black. Players who entered after (Alou, Cepeda, Clemente) were Latin.

Young might have contributed to the racial reshuffling, but he knew who had the strongest interest in drawing a line between Black and brown. "Invariably, it's the Caucasian," he wrote after Marichal struck Roseboro with his bat in 1965, "who screams the loudest."[98]

Doc Young never forgot the Black leagues of his youth, but others had to recover them. "Negro baseball was at once heroic and tawdry, a gladsome thing and a blot on America's consciousness," Robert Peterson wrote in his 1970 book *Only the Ball Was White*, the first of a wave of revisionist histories of the Black leagues. Peterson, a freelance writer who had once witnessed Josh Gibson smack "the longest home run ever struck" in his western Pennsylvania hometown, recounted the rise and decline of the Black leagues as a tale of American sin and striving that culminated, of course, with Robinson's heroic stoicism and Rickey's gruff idealism.[99] He and the historians who followed him – William Brashler, John Holway, Donn Rogosin, Jules Tygiel – bent over backward to stress Black baseball's Americanness, a national framing that didn't leave much room for the diasporic intimacies that the Black leagues had fostered throughout the Americas.

Tygiel, a Brooklyn native who taught for years in the history department at San Francisco State, introduced his 1983 classic *Baseball's Great Experiment* with a nod to Gunnar Myrdal. "The main trend in [the nation's] history," the Swedish sociologist, who set the tone for a generation of racial liberals, had written in 1944, "is the gradual realization of the American Creed" of "freedom and equality for all."[100] The United States had good bones, the Swede thought, and he urged his American readers to trust in time. Tygiel, following Myrdal's lead, declared Robinson's integration of the Dodgers "a symbol of imminent racial change and a direct agent of change" that looked ahead to *Brown v. Board* and the modern civil rights movement.[101] Peterson's and Tygiel's books, which motivated a generation of baseball historians to research the Black leagues and advocate for belated Hall of Fame inductions and record-book corrections, arrived with some of the first histories of Latin American athletes in the United States, including Jerry Izenberg's

1976 *Great Latin Sports Figures: The Proud People*, in which Izenberg, a longtime writer for the *Newark Star-Ledger*, celebrated Clemente as "the proudest of The Proud People."[102] The new revisionist historians, all liberal, all diving into the archives with the best of intentions, Americanized Black baseball, distancing it from the Caribbean, and Latinized Afro-Caribbeans, distancing them from Blackness.[103]

That's not to say that historians of Black baseball ignored the Caribbean and Mexican leagues. In his 1983 book *Invisible Men*, the historian and documentarian Donn Rogosin, who in 1981 organized the Smithsonian's first exhibit dedicated to Black baseball, acknowledged that "the impact of Latin American baseball on the Negro leagues is the missing link in black baseball history."[104] (Burgos, the historian of Latino baseball, remembers reading Rogosin's reference to a Latin American "missing link" as the moment that kickstarted his own career.)[105] In his 1975 oral history, John Holway, a prolific historian of the game, published a series of interviews in which former Black league players recounted their international adventures. Newt Allen of the Monarchs: "I've played in almost every state in the Union, in Canada, Mexico, Puerto Rico, Cuba, Venezuela, Japan, China and the Philippines." Willie Wells, the shortstop who, according to legend, taught Robinson how to turn a double play: "I played in Cuba, Mexico, Puerto Rico – thirteen years in Cuba, five years in Mexico." Othello Renfroe of the Monarchs, Cleveland Buckeyes, and Indianapolis Clowns: "I played ten years of professional baseball – all the islands, Venezuela, Puerto Rico, Mexico."[106] But American historians' interest in the Caribbean and Mexican leagues remained bound to the struggle for integration in the United States. Peterson observed that the "raids that took players out of the country" put pressure on Black teams to pay their players better and on MLB teams to integrate, lest the integrated Mexican League of wealthy businessman Jorge Pasquel surpass their own in talent and profit.[107] Rogosin argued that "it was in Latin America that the critical groundwork for integration occurred."[108] The Caribbean and Mexico offered, in their telling, auxiliary venues for an American story of racial progress.

Early Black-league historians imagined Latin America as the integrated antithesis to a segregated United States. "The most important thing about winter *beisbol*," Brashler, the novelist and journalist, wrote, "was the absence of a color line. Whites played with blacks, Puerto Ricans, Mexicans, and Cubans in front of Latin crowds."[109] In Brashler's *The Story of Negro League Baseball*, an accessible distillation of his years of research, the transnational circuit offered not emergent forms of diasporic belonging or institutions worth preserving for their own sake but a laboratory for mainland integration. Of the Cuban League, Rogosin remarked that it "became a traditional and important conduit of baseball information between white and black American players." For African Americans, Cuba functioned as "an escape valve from repressive racism" where the "status hierarchy of American baseball was forgotten." For white Americans, it delivered a lesson in Black life and revealed that "outstanding Negro-leaguers were perfectly capable of playing major-league baseball without incident, animosity, or undue emotional trauma."[110] Brashler, Rogosin, and others characterized the Caribbean as color blind to contrast it with the mainland United States and condemn Jim Crow as a singular horror.

Roberto Clemente and C. L. R. James knew a different Caribbean, a Caribbean in which white dominance and anti-Blackness also, if better disguised than in the American South, governed the racial order. "Every country you go into, you're going to have to pay," William "Sug" Cornelius of the Chicago American Giants told Holway. "You take the white Mexican, he's the same way toward the black Mexican. You know some Mexicans are darker than I am. And some Cubans are darker than I am, and it's the same way."[111] In a Black Mexican and a Black Cuban, Cornelius did not see Latins but himself.

Peterson had not, he acknowledged in the first pages of *Only the Ball Was White*, been first. In 1907, Sol White, the onetime Cuban Giant, had published a 128-page pamphlet titled *History of Colored Base Ball* that Peterson described as "an invaluable though sketchy picture of early teams and players."[112] The pamphlet included a chapter on Cuban players, whom White described as lacking "the baseball nerve" of African Americans. He did not address the origin of the name Cuban Giants, which he set in quotation marks, as if to suggest some significance to or irony in the name.[113] Not until a 1938 interview with *Esquire* did he claim that he and his teammates called themselves Cuban to "conceal the fact that they were just American Negro hotel waiters," a story that he, not having joined the Cuban Giants until four years into the team's existence, admitted "came to him" from other players.[114]

Most of the historians of the 1970s and '80s accepted White's account as fact. The Cuban Giants "talked gibberish on the field, hoping to pass themselves off as Cubans," Holway wrote in *Voices from the Great Black Baseball Leagues*.[115] "The players chattered gibberish on the field to pass as Cubans," Tygiel wrote, echoing Holway, in *Baseball's Great Experiment*.[116] The liberal historians latched onto the story of Black men passing as Cuban because it revealed the color line as arbitrary, something that a player could transgress with a name and some bad Spanish. But passing, as scholars of the phenomenon have long argued, reifies racial boundaries as much as it subverts them. The story of African Americans passing as Cuban to book games against white teams destabilized the Black/white binary by first stabilizing a Black/brown binary. Holway and Tygiel recycled White's 1938 anecdote about the Cuban Giants speaking mock Spanish as baseball writers recast Clemente and a rising generation of Afro-Caribbean pros as Latin.

The Black-to-Cuban passing narrative reached a wider audience with Brashler's 1973 novel *The Bingo Long Traveling All-Stars and Motor Kings* and the 1976 film adaptation starring Billy Dee Williams, James Earl Jones, and Richard Pryor. Brashler got the idea for the novel, which tells the story of an independent Black baseball club barnstorming across the Midwest in the late 1930s, while attending the Iowa Writers' Workshop. He read Peterson's book and decided to conduct his own research, traveling to St. Louis to interview James "Cool Papa" Bell and gathering materials, he later wrote, on "the language and the life-styles, the times and the social conditions, as avidly as if I were a historian."[117] The novel ends on the cusp of integration, and the protagonist Bingo Long, a veteran catcher too old to have a shot at the big leagues, complains of the MLB scouts who for years had told him, "Bingo, if we could only prove you was one of them Puerto Ricans we could sign you up."[118] He plans instead to go play ball in Cuba or Mexico – in Brashler's novel, the no man's lands of the sport.

The filmmakers who adapted *Bingo Long* took Brashler's mention of Black-to-Latino passing and ran with it. In the big-screen version, Pryor's character, Charlie Snow, tries to break into white baseball by passing first as Cuban under the name "Carlos Nevada" and then as Indigenous under the name "Chief Takahoma." "They've got Cubans down in Cuba blacker than you," he tells the other all-stars, "and they still ain't no Negroes."[119] The film consolidated the post–civil rights reracialization of Afro-Latinos as Latins, who "ain't no Negroes," and carried it backward into the Jim Crow era, taking the diaspora out of Black baseball. The traveling all-stars never left the Midwest. Carlos Nevada had never been Black. Major League Baseball imposed a new racial structure on the sport through which the public processed the demographic changes that followed the passage of the 1965 Immigration Act as well as the recovery of a Black sporting history that never had such clean lines.[120]

Some remembered another Black ball. In his 1984 autobiography, Amiri Baraka looked back on the Newark Eagles of his youth, where he had felt a sense of belonging not bound to the United States. "Those other Yankees and Giants and Dodgers we followed just to keep up with being in America," he wrote. "But for the black teams, and for us Newarkers, the Newark Eagles was pure *love*." He mocked Major League Baseball's relentless celebrations of Jackie Robinson and integration as the fulfillment of an American creed, asking, "Is that what the cry was on those Afric' shores when the European capitalists and African feudal lords got together and palmed our future[?] 'WE'RE GOING TO THE BIG LEAGUES!'"[121] At Ruppert Stadium in Newark's Ironbound neighborhood, he had once, at the urging of his father, introduced himself to the team's left fielder and Clemente's idol, Monte Irvin, who bent down and shook his small hand. The integration of Major League Baseball propelled Irvin to a bigger stage and a World Series title, but it came at the cost of a league in which a Black ballplayer could be more than valuable athletic labor. For Baraka, integration and the resulting dissolution of the Black leagues stood not as a national triumph but as a diasporic loss, the alienation of Black people from the pure love of the Newark Eagles, a team he remembered as "being in America" but of something larger. The Eagles of his boyhood belonged to a circuit of Black ball that bound the American South to the Caribbean, Central America, and Mexico, uniting African Americans with the people who would become, in the racial shift of the 1960s and '70s, Latin.

Walter O'Malley, the chief legal counsel to the Brooklyn Dodgers at the time of integration, later admitted to the sportswriter Roger Kahn that Branch Rickey had chosen Robinson over the Afro-Cuban Silvio García because he could sell "an American boy who had gone to war" as American first and Black second.[122] He couldn't sell García as the former, and before long, he wouldn't have been able to sell him as the latter either.

Baseball has transformed since Irvin and Clemente's time into a sport with a reputation as white and rural. One recovering baseball fan after another has bemoaned, in national media, the vanishing Black baseball star, citing statistics suggesting that the proportion of Black players in the majors has dropped from 18 percent in the 1980s to 7 percent in the 2020s.[123] (Chris Rock, a lifelong fan of the New York Mets, on most African Americans' thoughts on the team in 2015: "What the fuck's a Met?")[124] But it all depends on how you count. The sport is, from another angle, Blacker than ever. Afro-Caribbeans dominate the league, but their Blackness has grown less legible since the Immigration Act and the state's recognition of a freestanding panethnic Latino demographic.

Athletic racialization divided a diaspora. It separated Blackness from Latinoness and then set them against one another. Burgos and Guridy note that suspicions surrounding a 2001 Little League World Series team from the Bronx – investigators later found that star pitcher Danny Almonte's father had manipulated his birth certificate – distilled a wider racialization of Dominicans and Puerto Ricans at the turn of the century. Baseball, they write, has been a "laboratory for the testing of new understandings of race."[125] Another way to describe parents' and sports media's suspicion of Almonte is that they had labeled him gifted. He possessed an excess of some kind. Was he too old? Was he taking performance-enhancing drugs? Whatever it was, they decided, someone ought to investigate. Major League Baseball had built an institutional structure for the reception of Almonte and others as possessing a gift, but of a different kind than Irvin or Gary Sheffield or his own African American teammates.

The reracialization of Afro-Latinos as Latin had shrouded diasporic intimacies, hiding them behind emergent lines of difference. But the traces of other forms of athletic belonging remained. Monte Irvin found them in San Juan, C. L. R. James on Trinidad, Amiri Baraka at a Newark Eagles game, Roberto Clemente in Pittsburgh's Hill District. Their pastime – crisscrossed with lines, barriers, binaries – was never as small as a bronze plaque in Cooperstown, New York.

3

Black on Black

On the night in 1935 that a twenty-one-year-old Joe Louis knocked out Max Baer, Richard Wright witnessed a second fight on the Chicago streets. The future author of *Native Son*, then twenty-seven and seeking a publisher for a novel titled "Cesspool" (he never found one), crammed into an overflowing South Side tavern to listen to the fight on the radio. When Louis caught Baer with an overhand right and a left hook in the fourth round, sending the white former champ to his knees, Wright and a throng of revelers rushed into the street to celebrate, shouting and dancing, halting traffic, "joy-mad and moving to they didn't know where." The next month, in the communist-affiliated *New Masses*, Wright reflected on the events of that night. Louis's win had, he thought, shaken something loose on the South Side. His Black neighbors had discovered "a feeling of unity, of oneness," he wrote. "And it had happened so confoundingly sudden that the whites in the neighborhood were dumb with fear." He couldn't say what had changed, but he knew what Louis meant to the people raising their fists and shadowboxing in the street: "Joe was the concentrated essence of black triumph over white."[1]

Young men climbed onto the running boards of big Chevies rolling down 47th Street, asking the crowds as they rode by, "Who ye fur – Baer or Louis?" Trollies couldn't get through, and their conductors, surrendering to the masses, abandoned them. Then, Wright remembered, the police arrived. But the commissioner hadn't sent white officers, he noticed. "Oh, no, black cops, but trusted black cops and plenty tough. Cops who knew their business, how to handle delicate situations. They piled out of patrols, swinging clubs."² A night that had begun with a Black man knocking out a white man in the ring ended with Black people clubbing Black people in the street. Though Wright's editors claimed, in a long note, that the Louis–Baer fight had revealed that Black people, if they directed their energies against their "real enemies" (fascists, the ruling class), "will be valuable in the common struggles of all oppressed [people], black and white," Wright concluded on a more ambivalent note. "The spell," he wrote, remembering the second fight of the night, "was broken."³

For others, it held. Maya Angelou remembered listening to Louis fights at her grandmother's store in Arkansas as a child. "My race groaned," she wrote, whenever Louis looked like he might go down. When he won, more often than not with a knockout, the men, women, and children gathered around the radio would celebrate with Cokes and moonshine, Louis having "proved that we were the strongest people in the world."⁴ The biographer Randy Roberts describes him as Babe Ruth, Lou Gehrig, and Joe DiMaggio rolled into one and, as a patriotic Black champion in an age of Jim Crow and world war, a "moral compass during a turbulent

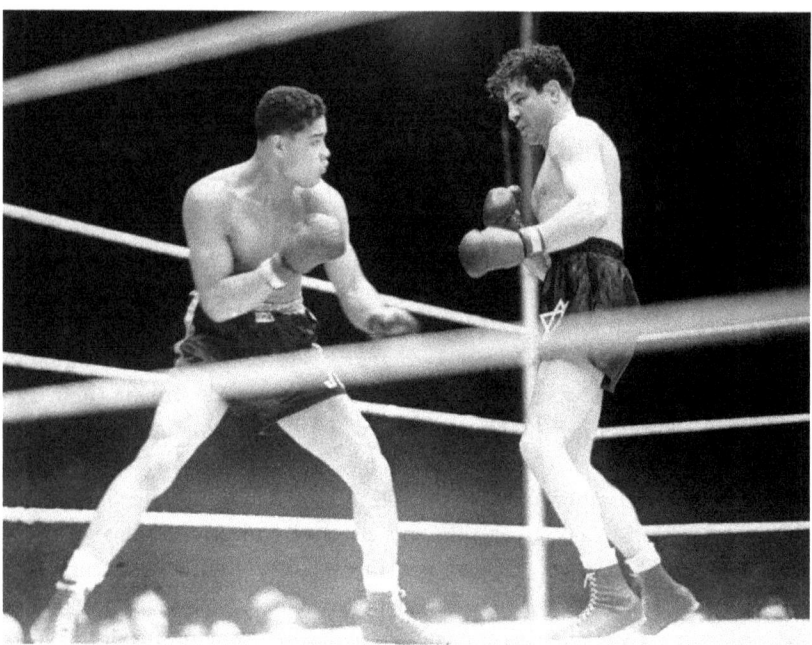

Joe Louis and Max Baer at Yankee Stadium in 1935. Photograph by Stanley Weston. Reproduced courtesy of the Stanley Weston Archive.

era."[5] In 1940, the sociologist E. Franklin Frazier interviewed Black high school students about Louis. One said that he wanted to be like Louis because of "the pleasure there must be at knocking hell out of a white man who thinks he is your superior."[6] Frazier concluded that young Black people of all classes identified with the fighter's "conquests of whites."[7] His fellow sociologists St. Clair Drake and Horace Cayton Jr. attributed the fascination with Louis to a growing desire for "beating the white man at his own game" and discovered that the *Chicago Defender* dedicated more headlines to Louis in the 1930s than to any other "race hero." (Haile Selassie came in a distant second.) Cataloging the most significant events for Black families, they listed Christmas, Easter, Thanksgiving, and "a Joe Louis victory."[8]

The fight that Wright heard on the radio had overshadowed the one he'd seen on the street. Louis ushered in the second era of the great white hope, and the hopes weren't much of a match. Louis ascended to world heavyweight champion in 1937 and defended his title twenty-five times – a record for all weight classes. Fans grew accustomed to watching Louis turn back one white challenger after another, inducting them into what boxing writers took to calling his bum-of-the-month club. (He and his management chose white opponents because they thought it was what fight fans wanted and what they'd shell out a few dollars to see.)[9] But Wright, who died in 1960, the year a young Cassius Clay returned from Rome with a gold medal around his neck, had foreseen another, more distant future for the sweet science. The spell of Black over white had been broken by the arrival of Black on Black, one, under orders from the commissioner, swinging clubs at the other.

Boxing was, on at least one score, ahead of the civil rights curve. Louis's reign in the ring coincided with the reign of Jim Crow in other sports, and after 1956, when Rocky Marciano retired, Black fighters ruled the heavyweight division – Floyd Patterson, Sonny Liston, Muhammad Ali, Ernie Terrell, Joe Frazier, Jimmy Ellis, George Foreman, Leon Spinks, Ken Norton, Larry Holmes, and on and on. Only the Swede Ingemar Johansson interrupted the parade of Black champs that culminated in "the heavyweight boom of the 1970s."[10]

The great white hope had left the ring, and the sport needed a new story to tell. The historian Elliott Gorn once observed that boxing lends itself to a structure of "antithesis." It converts, he wrote, "a conflict of values into a palpable physical struggle."[11] Black fighters received one of two scripts, the historian Andrew Kaye notes. Writers cast them as either "virtuous and loyal" (Louis) or the "threatening doppelgänger"

(Jack Johnson).[12] The art historian Nicole Fleetwood identifies the iconic Black athlete's two available "frameworks" as what she calls "representational politics" (she cites Jackie Robinson) and "racial achievement" (Paul Robeson).[13] Athletes who don't conform to either framework are often forgotten or, in time, retrofitted to one or the other. Louis cultivated an image as the anti-Johnson. Robinson testified against Robeson before the House Un-American Activities Committee. The end of the great white hope set the stage for a more immediate clash between contrasted embodiments of Black athleticism: Louis versus Johnson, Robinson versus Robeson.

When two Black fighters touched gloves, it felt to some like the direction of a movement was on the line. Of the 1962 Patterson–Liston title fight, James Baldwin, who sat ringside with Norman Mailer, wrote, "I felt terribly ambivalent, as many Negroes do these days, since we are all trying to decide, in one way or another, which attitude, in our terrible American dilemma, is the most effective." He didn't want to choose between two Black men. He longed for the time of Joe Louis, whom he called "the last great fighter for me."[14] Mailer did not share Baldwin's ambivalence. He rooted for Patterson.[15]

Baldwin claimed to know almost nothing about boxing. Mailer claimed to know it all. The short-lived men's magazine *Nugget* had sent Baldwin to Chicago for the fight. *Esquire* had allotted Mailer, in the early stages of his transition to nonfiction, 20,000 words for a fight that lasted two minutes and six seconds. It was a time of rising subscriptions and expense-account martinis for the American magazine, and in the absence of Baer and the white bums-of-the-month, the sportswriter, with an awful lot of column inches to fill, sought a sociological take for an age of civil rights. Patterson–Liston had to mean *something*. Leave it to A. J. Liebling, Red Smith, W. C. Heinz, and the two men on assignment seated ringside at Patterson–Liston.

"Sportswriting was still something of a netherworld when I chanced upon it," Frank Deford remembered of that time. "I'm convinced that the Golden Age of Writing about Sports began just about the time that I, The Kid, providentially strode into the vestibule."[16] André Laguerre, the urbane managing editor of *Sports Illustrated*, had hired Deford out of Princeton in 1962 as Laguerre set about imbuing the magazine with a middlebrow aesthetic – more thoughtful than the sports page but never demanding, the home of long-form cultural criticism (his "bonus piece") as well as – another Laguerre invention, the Swimsuit Issue. (Deford's Princeton degree would have appealed to Laguerre, the son of a French diplomat educated at an elite English boarding school.) A generation later, a *Chicago Tribune* columnist could declare, with a straight face, that "a century from now, when scholars want to learn how Americans lived in our time, they'll turn to *Sports Illustrated*."[17] Not bad, Deford had to admit, for a bunch of former hacks.

Deford's generation, writing for a growing college-educated middle class, taught the fan to find more subtle racial meaning in a fight between two Black men. It drew a new color line – a color line tailormade for a time of ascendent liberalism and civil rights – through the middle of Blackness, replacing a desire to see the white hope redeem the race with a desire to see the right kind of Black athlete win. Writers and fans assumed, as they had once assumed of Irish and other near-white immigrant pugilists, that Black men had a gift for the fight game, but they sorted the gifted Black fighter into two subcategories of giftedness: the grateful and the ungrateful, the athlete who acknowledged a debt to God and nation and the one who didn't – and who deserved to be laid out. Mailer could couch his condemnation of one embodiment of Black athleticism in his support for another. The story of Black on Black that he and others told showed the public how anti-Blackness could survive civil rights: It had to come wrapped in pro-Blackness.

Baldwin was right to be worried about how Mailer and others encountered Patterson–Liston. The direction of a movement wasn't on the line, but the direction of a countermovement might have been. In the early 1970s, as Ali lost and then reclaimed his title, the Black press raised an alarm over "Black-on-Black crime." At a 1970 news conference, Jesse Jackson, then directing the Southern Christian Leadership Conference's Operation Breadbasket out of Chicago, denounced local government, the Chicago Police Department, and the white press for "their silence and ineffectiveness in dealing with the present black-on-black crime crisis." The *Chicago Defender* declared it "an indictment against silence."[18] Alvin Poussaint, a medical doctor who studied the effects of racism on mental health, contributed an article to *Ebony* titled "Why Blacks Kill Blacks" ("Psychiatrist Finds Ghetto Violence against Its Own Residence Poses Major Threat") and authored a book of the same name, with an introduction from Jackson.[19] In 1973, *Jet* ran a cover with a Black man aiming a gun at the reader above the headline "BLACK ON BLACK CRIME." John H. Johnson, the publisher of *Ebony* and *Jet*, considered crime within Black communities an existential threat to Black life in the United States and made a hard distinction, in one issue after another, between "decent law-abiding people" and "perpetrators of Black on Black crime," who, condemned to "lives of frustration and rage and emptiness," see no other way.[20] (Black people did and do commit crimes against one another, as do white people. Most crime occurs between neighbors, and residential segregation was and remains a feature of American life.)[21]

The story of Black-on-Black crime resurfaced in the white press, where it took the form that magazine accounts of Patterson–Liston, Liston–Ali, Ali–Patterson, Ali–Frazier had: The right kind of Black person needed defending from the wrong kind. Some Black people, columnists determined, acknowledged the "gift of freedom" that the civil rights legislation constituted; others took advantage of it.[22] The idea of Black-on-Black crime sold liberals, including Black liberals, on the wars on crime and drugs that would put millions of Black and brown people behind bars. There was something excessive, boxing writers and fans had decided, about Black fighters that accounted for their dominance in the ring. A gift for fighting was fine in the right hands but a menace in the wrong ones. The act of valuing someone (the law-abiding, say) is "fundamentally relational," the late cultural theorist Lindon Barrett observed. It is a subtle "impeachment of the other," including another who may seem to be, at first glance, the same.[23] The law-abiding Patterson needed defending from the criminal Liston. He deserved the gift; Liston had abused his.

Athletes noticed the shift. In 1991, the sportswriter Jack Newfield interviewed two-time heavyweight champion Tim Witherspoon for a book about his former promoter Don King, whom Witherspoon had sued for fraud, restraint of trade, and racketeering. "Don's specialty is black-on-black crime," he told Newfield. "I'm black and he robbed me, so I know this is true."[24] In 2005, Philadelphia Eagles wide receiver Terrell Owens suggested that the team would be better off with Brett Favre than with the Eagles' current starting quarterback, Donovan McNabb, under center. McNabb called the comment a "black-on-black crime."[25] In 2010, the mixed martial artists Quinton "Rampage" Jackson and Rashad Evans faced off at UFC 114, marking the first time that two Black fighters had headlined an Ultimate Fighting Championship event. Jackson promised fans "some more black-on-black crime."[26] (He lost, in a unanimous decision, to Evans.) Witherspoon, McNabb, and Jackson and the talking heads who discussed their remarks thought that they had used a police metaphor to say something about sports, but the metaphor ran the other way. The people who spoke of Black-on-Black crime in the 1970s had used a sports metaphor to call for more policing, harsher sentences, more prisons. The story had traveled from the ring to the local news and on to the statehouse and Congress.[27]

The boxing historian Jeffrey Sammons once observed that the sport reflects and distills historical change. "Boxing *is* history," he wrote.[28] But sports can also prepare the ground for historical change. Sometimes boxing is prehistory.

Boxing writers, the men who had encouraged the search for a white hope in Jack Johnson's time, decided, after World War II, that it had all been a joke. Jack London instigated that search in 1908, when, after Johnson won the heavyweight title, the novelist called on the retired Jim Jeffries to return to the ring and set things right. "Jeff, it's up to you," London wrote, declaring himself with the white man "all the way."[29] His 1913 novel *The Abysmal Brute* follows the rise of a contender from Northern California described as "the hope of the white race."[30] Jeffries didn't redeem the race, but London's fictional fighter does.

In the late 1940s, John Lardner, son of the baseball writer Ring Lardner, revisited that time and recast London's white hopes as laughable dopes. "In the heat of the search," he wrote, in a nostalgic *New Yorker* series titled "That Was Pugilism," "well-muscled white boys more than six feet two inches tall weren't safe out of their mothers' sight."[31] He described boxing tournaments in which one white fighter after another attracted an excited audience of managers and trainers, who thought, for a fleeting moment, that they'd discovered Johnson's next challenger and then watched as the man landed on his back and "had to carry his own pail to the dressing room when he came to."[32] Lardner found Jess Willard, the man who beat Johnson in 1915 (Johnson maintained that he took a dive in exchange for favorable treatment from the government, which had convicted him under the Mann Act), the silliest of all. He recounted how the six-foot-six Willard had once, out of fear, hid behind a referee. After winning the title, the towering Pottawatomie Giant organized his own Buffalo Bill show and demonstrated, Lardner thought, greater talent as a "showman in cowboy roles" than he ever had as a boxer. "The big man was no better qualified to fight for the title than the average spermaceti whale."[33]

The reserved Louis had, Lardner suggested, made the idea of the white hope all the more ridiculous. He dismissed talk of white hopes during Louis's career as nothing more than a "good example of a reflex." Louis, unlike Johnson, "had wide popularity with the press and public," he observed.[34] A. J. Liebling, Lardner's colleague at the *New Yorker* and the author of *The Sweet Science*, one of the great works of boxing literature, agreed. Covering one of Louis's final fights in 1951, against Lee Savold, Liebling remarked that no one, Black or white, wanted the white Savold to defeat the Brown Bomber: "I wouldn't have liked to see Louis beaten by a good young fighter, but it would have been awful to see him beaten by a clown."[35] Liebling went further in 1960, when Floyd Patterson sought to win his title back from Johansson at the Polo Grounds. When the crowd stood and cheered for the Black challenger, he described feeling "a warm glow of gratification – we were a solid *patrie*, where American citizenship meant more than race or color." The nation had left London's white hopes behind. All Americans could celebrate as Johansson went down, Liebling, never an economic writer, added, "like a double portion of Swedish pancakes with lingonberries and sour cream."[36] Jeffries, Willard, Savold, and Johansson turned out to be, in Lardner's and Liebling's telling, a bunch of whales, clowns, and lingonberries. Now a united nation rooted for Louis and Patterson.

Lardner achieved something that his famous father, who died in 1933, couldn't have imagined for a locker-room scribbler: prestige. Ring Lardner had traveled in distinguished circles. His editor was Maxwell Perkins, who had nurtured the talents of F. Scott Fitzgerald, Ernest Hemingway, Thomas Wolfe, and others. (Hemingway, who read Ring's column in the *Chicago Tribune* as a boy, wrote for his high school newspaper under the pen name Ring Lardner Jr. – before Ring named his third son Ring Jr.) But the older Lardner was, in his lifetime, knocked for writing about baseball. Fitzgerald, a close friend, lamented after Lardner's death that he, a "magnificent" talent, had "moved in the company of a few dozen illiterates playing a boy's game," leaving him with a cake that "however deeply Ring might cut into it" had "the diameter of [Cubs first baseman and manager] Frank Chance's diamond."[37] Leslie Fiedler, who believed that most American authors devoted their careers to a single childlike obsession, acknowledged that some chose a varied, rich obsession and achieved canonical status (Melville on seafaring) and others, like Lardner, "whose essential subject was baseball," didn't and suffered for it.[38] Ring was later lionized for his baseball stories – his *You Know Me Al* is now taught in college classrooms, including my own – but his son didn't have to wait for posterity to receive his flowers.

John Lardner, Liebling, and others benefited from a growing market for middlebrow magazines that, catering to a growing college-educated middle class, invested in long-form reporting that transformed what it meant to write about a baseball game or a title fight. Liebling bemoaned how the introduction of television changed boxing – he called it a "poor substitute for being there" – but his own medium, the magazine, was also remaking the sport.[39] For Liebling and his colleagues, the old story of Black versus white, of the great white hope, felt crude. It belonged to another time. The *New Yorker* men would leave it for the movies and the hacks.[40]

The magazine writer's white fighter was neither a champion nor a challenger but a figure of comic relief, a clown. What made some white men eager to sacrifice their former hopes, to turn Willard and Savold into buffoons? Ben Carrington suggests that Jack Johnson's career marked a shift in how white men imagined their racial and gender dominance. Whereas they had once claimed to belong to the smartest and strongest race, white men after Johnson, Carrington writes, embraced a belief in an "inherent black physical advantage" that indicated not a greater intellect, as it had for them, but a "certain limitation of cognitive development."[41] White men, unable to dismiss Johnson's brilliance in the ring, invented the idea of the Black athlete to secure the white mind. The writing of Lardner, Liebling, and other boxing men of the 1940s and '50s reveals another character in that racial drama, the Black athlete's foil: the white dope. Lardner and Liebling acknowledged the emerging revisionist consensus that Johnson had not been an outlier but one of at least five Black boxers who could have, if given the chance, beat Jeffries. The white man they beat, or would have beat, earned nicknames like "the Diving Venus," or had a "chin of crystal," or "fell in a straight, pure, Doric line, like a tree crashing in a forest."[42] White men ceded the ring with the idea of the Black athlete and then reinforced that idea, excusing themselves from the fight game, with stories of flat-footed white dopes with weak chins. Boxing writers had, with the white dope, surrendered the sport to the Black fighter. But they would demand something in return.[43]

White boxing men had found new gigs, as Lardner and Liebling knew, among a rising class of sports intellectuals. Though Lardner celebrated Johnson for his achievements in the ring, he did not see the heavyweight champion as a defining figure of the era. He reserved that distinction for the white managers who invented the great white hope and made a fortune off it. "The great-hope crusade did not produce great fighters," Lardner wrote. "However, it teemed with talented managers."[44] His colleague Liebling forged a new kind of sportswriting that often dedicated more words to how the writer took in an event than to the event itself. He identified the boxing ring, with characteristic *New Yorker* self-knowing, as "a great place for adding to your repertory of witty sayings" and for delivering a "running expertise nominally aimed at your companion" but audible to fans in neighboring rows. Lardner and Liebling thought that, as Black men came to dominate boxing, the former racial significance of the sport had faded. When Louis beat Savold, Harlem did not break out in "wild exultation" as it had in 1935, Liebling wrote. When Patterson beat Johansson, the neighborhood "gave no evidence of a celebration."[45] When Louis vacated the title and anointed two Black men, Ezzard Charles and Joe Walcott, as the leading contenders, ensuring that a Black fighter would succeed him, no one batted an eye, and Lardner and Liebling thought it good for boxing – or at least good for the white liberal boxing writer. The color line had not vanished but shifted. Lardner, Liebling, and the onlookers for whom they modeled an emerging form of fandom speculated about the athletic gifts of champion fighters. The gift, conceived as an excess, left something for them to claim – an ontological debt owed.[46]

Prizefighting had been a crime not long before. In 1876, the Massachusetts Supreme Court affirmed the conviction of two fighters on assault charges, ruling that boxing matches "serve no useful purpose, tend to breaches of the peace, and are unlawful even when entered into by agreement and without anger or ill will."[47] The next generation of high-profile boxers would spend as much time defending themselves in courtrooms as fighting each other in the ring.

The crime stuck to some more than others. Social scientists of the time, as the historian Khalil Gibran Muhammad shows, used new statistical evidence to attribute white immigrant crime to class obstacles and Black crime to racial deficits, naturalizing a connection between Blackness and lawbreaking. The idea of Black crime "made" urban America, he writes – and it swelled the ranks of white America and rewrote the rules of anti-Blackness for a post-emancipation age.[48] When two white fighters faced off, it was sport. When two Black fighters entered the ring, it summoned other associations. Would one fighter assault the other? Would one bite the other's ear? Smart fans could, the magazine writer said, let the white fighter off the hook; he was a joke. But they would need to watch the Black fighter.

The era of Black-on-Black title fights reached full bloom with Ali's arrival. Louis, a Black man who held the title from 1937 to 1949, fought his most memorable bouts against white opponents. Marciano, a white man who held the title from 1952 to 1956, won the belt from Walcott and then defended it once against him and twice against Charles.

Ali, though he took on all comers in a too-long sixty-one-fight career, discovered, against the conventional wisdom of the time, that he didn't need a white hope in the challenger's corner to sell tickets. The philosopher Grant Farred describes Ali as the athletic embodiment of what he calls, with a nod to Antonio Gramsci, a "vernacular intellectual": an intellectual emerging from a nonelite social class who remains connected to that class but without the institutional credentials or affiliations of the traditional intellectual.[49] Ali's unwillingness to conform to the established racial decorum of the sport – to be another humble, patriotic champ in the mold of Louis – challenged the mind-body divide through which white men had claimed the mind by forfeiting the body. No wonder the new sports intellectual tracked his every move, sometimes, it seemed, with a sense of doom.

When Ali got his shot at the title in 1964 against Sonny Liston in Miami, boxing writers didn't at first know what to make of the two Black men facing off. The usual fight narratives didn't fit. In the 1962 Patterson–Liston bout, Patterson had been, as Baldwin wrote, the clear "moral favorite" against Liston, an ex-con whose management had ties to the mafia.[50] Of Ali and Liston, sportswriters couldn't decide which fighter they disliked more. In his regular *Los Angeles Times* column, Jim Murray, a future Pulitzer Prize winner, described Ali as an overmatched loudmouth and Liston as an illiterate killer, as most of his ringside colleagues did, and suggested that theirs would be "the most popular fight since Hitler and Stalin – 180 million Americans rooting for a double knockout."[51] Ali heard him, later remarking that the press had cast him and Liston as twin villains. "So naturally," he said, "when we get in the ring, the people they would prefer if it could happen for it to end in a double knockout."[52] If Patterson–Liston had, for most boxing writers, been good versus evil, then Ali–Liston would be evil versus evil, the braggart versus the thug.

But when Ali, then Cassius Clay, arrived in Miami with Malcolm X, writers who had once considered Liston an existential threat to boxing, for his criminal record and for ending fights with first-round knockouts, now migrated to the defending champ's corner. Liston gained still more reluctant white fans when the FBI leaked information to the *New York Herald Tribune* that Ali had attended a Nation of Islam meeting with Malcolm in New York.[53] "Liston used to be a hoodlum," Murray Kempton, another future Pulitzer winner, wrote, "now he was our cop; he was the big Negro we pay to keep the fresh Negroes in line, and he was just waiting until his boss told him it was time to throw this kid out."⁵⁴ Liston didn't throw the kid out. Ali wore him down over six rounds with dancing jabs until Liston, cut and exhausted, refused to rise from his stool. "Eat your words," Ali shouted at the rows of sportswriters. Red Smith, a regular critic of the young fighter, admitted that "the words don't taste good," but he and the men sitting next to him had found a new narrative for the sport.⁵⁵

Ali often accentuated the differences between himself and other Black fighters using racial language that the boxing press then echoed. He declared the heavier, darker-skinned Liston a "big, ugly bear" and arrived at the weigh-in for their first bout wearing a denim jacket with the words "Bear Huntin'" stitched on the back.⁵⁶ Malcolm urged Ali to see himself as distinct, in faith and racial significance, from Liston and Patterson. In Miami, he showed Ali photos of the other fighters meeting with white Christian ministers, their "spiritual advisors." "This fight is the truth," he told him. "It's the Cross and the Crescent fighting in a prize ring – for the first time. It's a modern Crusades."⁵⁷ While baseball, basketball, and football remained absorbed in struggles over integration – the storied University of Alabama football team remained segregated until 1971 – boxing offered an often all-Black arena in which fans received encouragement, from writers, broadcasters, and sometimes the fighters themselves, to construct their own racial identities through an identification with one or another articulation of Black identity.

Boxing writers cast Liston as a real-life Bigger Thomas, a "king of beasts," as a 1964 *Look* magazine headline described him, but he never had much to say about the broader significance of his fights with Ali. Liston didn't see himself as a racial icon. Ali's next challenger, the former champ Patterson, did. Patterson thought that neither Ali, a "Black Muslim," nor Liston, a "criminal," deserved the title. "There's a tremendous responsibility on the champion that Clay and Liston obviously don't understand – to themselves, to the sport and to the public," he observed ahead of Ali–Liston II. He offered himself as an alternative and vowed, if he faced Ali next, to donate his entire winnings to the NAACP. Beating Ali, whom he continued to call Cassius Clay, would be, he wrote, his "small contribution to civil rights."⁵⁸ Ali fired back. In an interview with Alex Haley, with whom Malcolm wrote his *Autobiography*, he called Patterson the "white man's champion" and taunted him for moving into a white neighborhood where he had faced a hostile welcome. "The big shot didn't have no time for his own kind," Ali told Haley. "He was too busy 'integrating.'"⁵⁹

Patterson welcomed his role as a new kind of hope. When he did get his shot at Ali in 1965, he escalated their feud, writing in *Sports*

Illustrated that "Cassius Clay must be beaten and the Black Muslim scourge removed from boxing." He recalled defeating the white Canadian George Chuvalo at Madison Square Garden and hearing the crowd chant his name. "Come on, Floyd. Come on, Floyd." Patterson, a Black man fighting a white man, had been the American hope that day. "It was a wonderful feeling," he remembered.[60] He described Ali as fighting for the Nation of Islam, himself as defending the red, white, and blue. The NOI won. Ali beat Patterson on November 22, 1965, taunting him for twelve rounds until the referee, watching the older man tuck and stagger, halted the fight. Patterson couldn't hear Ali, whose mouthguard muffled his words, but a writer later told him what he'd said: "Come on, American. Come on, white American."[61] If sportswriters hadn't at first known what to do with Ali the Muslim, Ali the critic of integrationism, then the Patterson fight modeled a new reductive narrative of the Black radical versus the Black moderate, W. E. B. Du Bois versus Booker T. Washington, Malcolm X versus Martin Luther King, the criminal versus the law-abiding citizen. White men had left the ring, but they maintained a rooting interest.

The Black Power movement also embraced Ali as an icon of radicalism. His decision to refuse the draft as well as his famous remark that no Viet Cong had ever called him an anti-Black slur established Ali at the forefront of a wave of athlete activism. In 1969, Harry Edwards, the architect of the Olympic Project for Human Rights, which demanded the restoration of Ali's title and culminated with Tommie Smith's and John Carlos's Black Power salute at the Mexico City Games, challenged the image of sports as a "citadel of racial harmony" in which athletes from different backgrounds learn to work together and bond as teammates. "The sports world is not a rose flourishing in the middle of a wasteland," he wrote. "It is part and parcel of the wasteland." Most white athletes, coaches, and owners continue, he added, to see the Black athlete as a "machine." Edwards identified one athlete who had refused that role: Muhammad Ali, "the saint of this revolution in sports."[62] In *Soul on Ice*, Eldridge Cleaver observed that in sports and elsewhere white men cast themselves as the "Omnipotent Administrator" and Black men as the "Supermasculine Menial." Cleaver also singled out Ali, "the first 'free' black champion ever to confront white America," as the one athlete challenging that division.[63] Edwards and Cleaver did not overstate Ali's significance to Black Power, but that significance, built in contrast to other Black men, contained contradictions. It could be radical, subversive, and anti-Black. Ali's biographers – John Cottrell in the 1960s, Thomas

Hauser and David Remnick in the 1990s, Jonathan Eig in 2010s – all construct his character as a negative of the other Black men he met in the ring.[64]

Some thought that the New Left had turned Ali himself into a white hope. In a review of his autobiography *The Greatest*, which Toni Morrison, then an editor at Random House, shepherded to publication, Ishmael Reed noted that "Ali has become not only the Black Hope, but the White Liberal Hope as well, mainly for his stand on the war in Vietnam." He also suggested that Ali trafficked in colorism when he insulted darker-skinned fighters like Liston. "I suspect that when he describes his black opponents as 'bears' and 'King Kongs' he might be invoking the skin privileges of his caste," Reed wrote. "When he refers to himself as 'pretty' [a common boxer's boast referring to an unmarked face] he might mean his Caucasian features."[65] Reed thought that most fans overlooked the nuances of what Ali said about race and the conflicting agendas that writers foisted on him.

Ali had evolved into everybody's protest athlete – a militant Black hope for some, a liberal white hope for others. He might have challenged the idea of the Black athlete as machine or menial, but he also encouraged that idea in how he talked about the Black men in the other corner, encouraging his followers to value his embodiment of Blackness against another class and shade of Black. "There was this nightmarish image I always had of two slaves in the ring," he said in *The Greatest*, recalling the months before his first bout with Joe Frazier, whom he called an Uncle Tom and a gorilla. "Like in the old slave days on the plantation, with two of us big black slaves fighting, almost on the verge of annihilating each other while the masters are smoking big cigars, screaming and urging us on, looking for the blood."[66] Ali had the same nightmare that Richard Wright once had, a nightmare of losing in the act of winning, of a commissioner sending Black police to the South Side to save it from Joe Louis.[67]

Ali may have trafficked in colorism, but he got an assist from the middlebrow magazine, which took a sociological interest in him and other Black fighters. On the night in 1962 that Liston won the heavyweight title, knocking out Patterson with a crushing left hook in the first round, James Baldwin and Norman Mailer sat in the fifth row, an empty seat between them. Neither man said a word to the other. "There had been a chill between us in the last year," Mailer later admitted. "Now we sat with a hundred-pound cake of ice on the empty seat between us."[68]

Mailer had made more than a few enemies, Baldwin among them, with his 1957 essay "The White Negro," in which he described Black men as natural existentialists for living under the constant threat of sudden death. Mailer argued that the Holocaust and the nuclear bomb had made that threat universal and that Black men had much to teach him and other white people about life under totalitarianism. He named the Black man's student in existentialism "the hipster" or "white Negro." The Black man "could rarely afford the sophisticated inhibitions of civilization," he wrote. "He lived in the enormous present, he subsisted for his Saturday night kicks, relinquishing the pleasures of the mind for the more obligatory pleasures of the body." The hipster, sharing in the Black man's kicks, had absorbed his "existentialist synapses."[69] Baldwin, who had first met Mailer and his second wife, Adele, in Paris in the mid-1950s, couldn't believe that his friend had fallen for the tired anti-Black clichés of Jack Kerouac and the Beats, whom Baldwin thought below him.

Mailer drove a further wedge between himself and his former Paris drinking mate when he dismissed Baldwin in *Advertisements for Myself* as "too charming a writer to be major" who "seems incapable of saying 'Fuck you.'"[70] Baldwin answered with his own essay, "The Black Boy Looks at the White Boy," in which he described Mailer as talented but insecure, an artist undergoing the white man's undignified birthright, something in which no Black person could ever afford to indulge: a midlife crisis. Baldwin, it turned out, could deliver a mean "fuck you" when prompted. He recalled seeing Mailer at the Actors Studio in Hell's Kitchen and noticing his stance: "leaning on the table, shoulders hunched, seeming, really, to roll like a boxer's, and his hands moving as if he were dealing with a sparring partner." Baldwin wondered what had led his friend, the author of *The Naked and the Dead, Barbary Shore,* and *The Deer Park*, which he described as exhibiting a "toughness and subtlety of conception and a sense of the danger and complexity of human relationships," to refashion himself as a hipster with a boxer's bearing.[71]

Mailer's and Baldwin's writing on the Patterson–Liston fight reiterated and distilled their disagreement about the hipster's Black fantasies. Though Mailer admitted to being "for" Patterson, he found the defending champ boring – too bourgeois, too inhibited, too white. "He was a liberal's liberal," Mailer wrote. "The worst to be said about Patterson is that he spoke with the same cow's cud as other liberals. Think what happens to a man with Patterson's reflexes when his brain starts to depend on the sounds of" – and here Mailer quotes from the fighter's 1962 autobiography – "'introspective,' 'obligation,' 'responsibility,' 'inspiration,' 'commendation.'"[72] Fans said they wanted Patterson to win, but some, Mailer thought, harbored a secret desire to see Liston, his Black existentialist, take the title. "Liston was the secret hero of every man who had ever given mouth to the final dispositions of the Lord and made a pact with Black Magic," he declared. "Liston was Faust." If boxing was, as Mailer believed it to be, an "existential venture," then Liston had the edge.[73] He lived with death. Patterson, the liberal's liberal, did not. He had moved to the suburbs. He had gone, in Mailer's language, from hip to square.

Baldwin, an admitted outsider to the fight game, did not see in Patterson a white-bread liberal or in Liston a streetwise Kierkegaard. "I know nothing whatever about the Sweet Science or the Cruel Profession or the Poor Boy's Game," he wrote. "But I know a lot about pride, the poor boy's pride, since that's my story and will, in some way, probably, be my end." Baldwin thought that boxing writers, in their desire

Sonny Liston standing over Floyd Patterson at Comiskey Park in 1962.
Photograph from AP Photo.

to contrast Patterson with Liston, overlooked what united them. He suggested that some (Mailer) resented Patterson because he brought to "what is thought of – quite erroneously – as a simple activity a terrible note of complexity."[74] Patterson managed to be tough and vulnerable, outgoing and self-conscious. Baldwin wrote that some (Mailer) called Liston inarticulate because "he has a long tale to tell which no one wants to hear." Baldwin, who found the whole world of prizefighting bizarre and wouldn't write about it again, concluded that "life's far from being as simple as most sportswriters would like to have it."[75] But he also knew that Mailer and most of the other men sitting ringside with him didn't want to reckon with Patterson's contradictions or Liston's long tale. The boxing writer wanted definable Blackness, Black masculinities to draw lines around and between, to borrow, to steal.

It was 1962, and Baldwin couldn't tell the future. But he worried about what Mailer and other observers, including his allies in the civil rights struggle, might see in a fight between two Black men. Mailer found racial significance in every move a Black fighter made. This was how he turned a two-minute bout into 20,000 words. His editors and readers received his long magazine stories as a new way to encounter sports. He had, they said, brought the careful observations of the novelist to the lower art of writing about two men hitting each other in the face. But his was a minor innovation. His account of Patterson–Liston was nothing more than a slight update on Jack London's white hope, with Patterson cast as the agent of racial order, a Jim Jeffries for a liberal age. (The difference was that Mailer welcomed disorder.) Mailer and other boxing writers conducted what amounted to a test run of what would become the ideological foundation of liberal law and order in the 1970s. The law-abiding Black citizen (Patterson) faced a threat not from white people or the state but from one of his own, the Black criminal (Liston). The political scientist Naomi Murakawa argues that the dominant "backlash thesis," which attributes the wars on crime and drugs to a conservative campaign to reverse the gains of the civil rights movement, obscures how liberals had long proposed carceral solutions to civil rights demands. The United States had not faced a "crime problem that was racialized," she writes, but a "race problem that was criminalized."[76] Crime and drug warriors were "policing the crisis" that the movements revealed and of an economic downturn that hit Black communities first and hardest.[77] Calling Liston a criminal and a threat to the sport was not anti-Black, Mailer could say, but pro-Black because it was pro-Patterson. It was a lesson that the diminished liberalism of the 1970s took to heart.

Baldwin left boxing behind after Patterson–Liston. Mailer found a new muse in Muhammad Ali, to whom he gave the title, a title he could have given himself, "America's Greatest Ego."[78] In 1974, Mailer flew to Kinshasa, Zaire, to cover Ali's bout with the undefeated George Foreman. Ali, no longer the nimble kid, entered the fight as a 4–1 underdog. Mailer, no longer the existentialist, had faced intense criticism for "The White Negro" and didn't know where he stood on race after civil rights. He acknowledged that his "love affair with the Black soul, a sentimental orgy at its worst, had been given a drubbing through the seasons of Black Power" and admitted that, as of Ali–Foreman, he didn't know whether he "loved Blacks or secretly disliked them, which had to be the dirtiest secret in his [Mailer's] American life."[79]

In *The Fight*, Mailer, undeterred, introduced a new theory of Black life. At a bookstore in Greenwich Village, he bought a translation of Belgian Franciscan missionary Placide Tempels's 1945 *Bantu Philosophy*, which argued that "the notion of 'force' takes for [Bantu peoples] the notion of 'being' in our [Western] philosophy."[80] In Zaire, Mailer, reading an English translation of a French translation of a Dutch text of a Belgian's account of African thought, determined that, though alienated from that tradition, Black Americans retained the idea that "each man seeks the maximum of force for himself" and that boxing, a contest of force, signified African life in exile. Mailer thought that he had determined the source of Black men's dominance in the ring. "For heavyweight boxing was almost all black, black as Bantu," he wrote. "So boxing had become another key to revelations of Black, one more key to black emotion, black psychology, black love."[81] In the late 1950s, Mailer had identified the jazz musician as the embodiment of Blackness, the model for his hipster. Now he turned to the Black athlete, who couldn't be emulated. He traced the athlete's philosophy back not to Kierkegaard or Sartre but to Africa.

In Zaire, Mailer abandoned the hipster, constructing a more rigid line between Black and white. Though he described Ali and Foreman as geniuses of a kind, he distinguished their intelligence, a "physical genius," from his own. He laughed at what he called Ali's "prophetic boxing doggerel" and mocked other Black boxing men's desire to take up writing, after hearing that Mailer had signed a million-dollar book contract and "did not have to get hit in the head" to receive his check. Whenever Ali defied his new theory of Black force and white being, Mailer resorted to racial contortions that would have made Madison Grant blush, observing that "Ali was not without white blood, not without a lot of it" and

Black on Black

Norman Mailer and Muhammad Ali in San Juan, Puerto Rico, in 1965. Photograph from AP Photo.

envisioning him as a "white actor who had put on too little makeup for the part and so was not wholly convincing as a Black."[82] Mailer, who had once imagined Blackness as another form of being that white people might move toward, now imagined it as something other than being, an almost antibeing, a force, far removed from the white bohemia of the Beats. His Black athlete had killed the hipster. It took Mailer longer than Lardner and Liebling, but he too had ceded the ring, admitting that he had been a dope all along – a dope, he felt the need to remind us, with a million-dollar book contract.

The Fight tells the stories of three men: Ali, Foreman, and, most of all, Norman Mailer. "There is a lot of him in it," George Plimpton, who wrote his own book about the Rumble in the Jungle, once remarked.[83] The bout itself figures as a "collision between two embodiments of divine inspiration," through which Mailer, the onlooker, the fan, defines himself.[84] Mailer made himself through and against Ali and Foreman, but he also made cash off them. He achieved this feat of self-making with an odd kind of doubling, referring to himself in the third person as "Norman," a character in the drama detached from Mailer the omniscient author. Mailer had first introduced the trick in *The Armies of the Night*, his first-hand account of the 1967 March on the Pentagon, for which he won a Pulitzer Prize and a National Book Award. In *The Fight*, he cast himself in relation to the Black fighters in the ring and above them, a white dope and the administrator of the Black hopes. "Norman," he wrote, "would try to observe with two eyes instead of one."[85]

Ishmael Reed had first met Mailer in 1962 at a Village bar. When Reed encountered him again, in 1978 at Ali–Spinks II in New Orleans, he noticed a change. "Gone were the pug breaks and the frantic fast-talking," he observed, noting that Mailer's hair had gone white. He retained the "glint belonging to the Ali true believer" but "seemed at peace." Reed had loathed *The Fighter*, loathed how Mailer wrote about Black men, but decided to revisit it. Underneath Mailer's bald racism, he discovered something that he had missed the first time around: the author's frustration, "frustration that he couldn't be black." Mailer wished he could but knew he didn't belong in Kinshasa and with Ali's entourage. "Maybe one day," Reed mused, "the genetic engineers in their castles rocking from lightning will invent an identity delicatessen where one can obtain identity as easily as buying a new flavored yogurt."[86] Mailer had gotten old. He'd calmed down. He'd surrendered his hipster fantasies. But he might also have discovered that racial delicatessen of the future. Mailer didn't need genetic engineers or blackface. He, the fight writer with the glint of the true believer, could dissociate himself from the racial drama unfolding in the ring and root for Patterson over Liston, Ali over Liston, Ali over Spinks.

The middlebrow magazine imagined a new cast of characters for the sweet science: the white dope, the grateful Black fighter, the ungrateful menace. But old stories die hard. In 1963, *Esquire* asked, "What would happen if champion Sonny Liston fought Rocky Marciano, Joe Louis and Jack Dempsey on the best night those champions ever had?" The illustrator Roger Riger imagined Liston knocking out Marciano in "the most brutal first round ever seen" and then leveling Louis in two. "He's just too big a puncher," the fictional Louis admits after the fight. The main event, Liston versus Dempsey, goes nine rounds. The "tough Irishman" Dempsey, who held the title from 1919 to 1926, withstands Liston's blows as Marciano and Louis couldn't, wearing him down until, connecting with a big right, he sends the Black heavyweight falling "heavily to the floor, his right glove under his face."[87] The referee counts Liston out and declares Dempsey, masculine icon of the white immigrant working class, the greatest of all time.

Amiri Baraka, then Leroi Jones, fired back. "See the white man dream?" he wrote of Riger's fictional fights in the *Nation*. "We erase the mad-bad big black bad guy by going back in time to get him in a dream," assigning the task, as usual, to "the big strong likeable immigrant." Without a fighter of their own in the game, white men, Baraka argued, had turned to fantasies of Black–white bouts, whether imagining Dempsey in the ring with Liston or embracing a Black boxer (he offered Patterson as an example) as a new kind of white hero. If Mailer had his theory of Black men, then Baraka had his own theory of white men after civil rights: "What [they] cannot gain by experience, [they] will gain by *inperience*, the positing of a 'fantasy' event for what is actually the case."[88]

Did white men want to climb back into the ring? Did they want to face Liston? Was that their dream, their wished-for "inperience"? For some, it might have been. But for others, the image of Dempsey fighting Liston in the pages of a men's magazine offered a different kind of reassurance: evidence that the nation had moved forward, out of the shadows of Jim Crow and into the light of civil rights. The cultural return of the great white hope – in the theater, at the movies, in radio simulations and staged exhibitions – delivered a more subtle form of racial wish fulfillment than Baraka thought: It let white people consign anti-Blackness in sports to the past. It let them, amid the rise of Black Power, fight the racism of another time. The image of the white hope in the 1960s, of Liston duking it out with Marciano and Dempsey, left the nation, then confronting the more intractable material structures of white supremacy that civil rights couldn't solve, shadowboxing with Jim Crow.

Riger's imagined tournament of champions ends with an odd kind of teaser. Dempsey's manager, Doc Kearns, announces that his fighter will not agree to a rematch unless Liston first beats "that other guy," another challenger for Dempsey's crown, who turns out to be Jack Johnson.[89] All but forgotten in 1963, an afterthought in Riger's tournament, Johnson would undergo a renaissance in the age of Black Power. Finis Farr's 1964 biography *Black Champion*, which celebrated Johnson as an unofficial American ambassador, a great "master of his trade" who "created respect for his country," introduced a new generation of fight fans to Johnson's tumultuous life and career.[90] Howard Sackler won a Pulitzer Prize for his 1967 play *The Great White Hope*, in which James Earl Jones, then a minor theater actor, starred as "Jack Jefferson." New York publisher Chelsea House reissued Johnson's out-of-print 1927 autobiography *In and Out of the Ring* under the title *Jack Johnson Is a Dandy*. Boxing promoters Jim Jacobs and Bill Cayton collaborated on a 1970 documentary, to which the actor Brock Peters (Tom Robinson in *To Kill a Mockingbird*) contributed voice-overs. Peters can also be heard on Miles Davis's 1971 album *Jack Johnson*, which originated as the soundtrack for the film, intoning on the song "Yesternow," "I'm Jack Johnson, heavyweight champion of the world. I'm Black. [They] ain't never let me forget it. I'm Black, all right. I'll never let them forget it."[91]

The historian and biographer Theresa Runstedtler credits Johnson's cultural resurgence to Ali, who, amid his ban, invited comparisons to the former champ and followed the routes of global diasporic fame that he had forged in a time of empire and Jim Crow.[92] After Jacobs screened the Johnson documentary for him, Ali told his trainers that he'd like to dedicate his comeback fight against Jerry Quarry to Johnson. "Jack, wherever you are, rest easy in your grave," he planned to say. "This White Hope won't get away." His cornermen, Bundini Brown and Angelo Dundee, talked him out of it, but Brown did shout to him during the fight, "Jack Johnson's ghost watching you! Ghost in the house!"[93] Ali later told his biographer Remnick, "I grew to love the Jack Johnson image. I wanted to be rough, tough, arrogant" – the kind of fighter "white folks didn't like."[94]

White folks might not have liked Ali, but they no longer hated Johnson, who had reemerged as an icon of Black Power but also, for some, a sign of white progress. A white fan could read Farr's biography or go see *The Great White Hope* and perceive not the continuities Ali did (a durable, mutating anti-Blackness) but a problem (the anti-Blackness of the 1910s) solved. The Black Power movement discovered one Johnson; moderates found another.[95]

The Great White Hope, which opened at the Arena Stage in Washington, DC, in 1967, before moving to Broadway, invited analogies to Ali, his recent conviction for draft evasion, and Black Power but at a safe historical distance. Jones, who read Farr's biography while in rehearsals, modeled his character after Ali, hired one of his former trainers, and said of Johnson in *Ebony*, "From the day he took the title to the day he lost the title he seemed caught up in the same kind of mania and hysteria that characterized Muhammad Ali's active career."[96] Ali himself attended a performance in 1968. At intermission, after a scene in which the exiled Jefferson/Johnson vows to move to Mexico, stand at the border holding his championship belt, and declare "Here Ah is," Ali delivered his best Jack Johnson at the entrance to the theater. "Here Ah is! Here Ah is! Here Ah is!" he said with his hands held high as if brandishing his own belt.[97] When journalists pressed him about the similarities between his and Johnson's careers, he allowed that "you just change the time, date and details and it's about me."[98] Or, in other words, it wasn't about him at all. It was about Johnson, a man who fought white men and refused to conform to the dictates of Jim Crow, not Ali, a man who fought other Black men and refused to conform to the dictates of the liberal wing of civil rights.

The play and the 1970 film, a faithful adaptation that also starred Jones as Jefferson and Jane Alexander as his tragic white love interest, sets Jefferson against a straw man, the former champion Cap'n Dan. After orchestrating a fight between Jefferson and a young white hope, the Kid (the Willard character), with a defeated white hope, Frank Brady (the Jeffries character), refereeing, Cap'n Dan brags, "The whole world's gonna see [Brady] take [the heavyweight title] in his hands again, and hold it up and pass it on, like the Kid'll pass it [on]." The former champ, the inveterate segregationist, does not hide his intention: "This time we'll keep it in the family!"[99] Few white theater- or moviegoers would have seen themselves in the character of Cap'n Dan, but with the marketing of the play and the film as a statement on Ali and Black Power, he offered white audiences an image of racial animus from which they could disassociate themselves, a racism they could externalize. After state boxing commissions stripped Ali of his title, Ernie Terrell won it, then Joe Frazier, then Jimmy Ellis, then George Foreman – all Black men. Cap'n Dan and the Kid had vanished from the scene a long time ago. Ali received an offer of $400,000 to play Johnson in a movie but turned it down because, he said, "a black hero chasing white women was a role I didn't want to glorify."[100] The federal government had not gone after him for an interracial relationship but for refusing the draft, not for being Black but for what he said about being Black in the United States, not for his "unforgivable Blackness" but for his unforgivable Black dissent.[101] The historical difference between the two boxers does not diminish the significance of seeing Johnson, whose reign led Congress to ban the interstate transport of fight films and contributed to the emergence of Black moviegoing culture and a rise in Black-owned "race theaters," on the big screen.[102] But the conflation of Johnson and Ali to which *The Great White Hope* contributed discouraged audiences from seeing how anti-Blackness had changed, that the differences between the two men's stories revealed as much as their similarities.[103]

The return of the white hope on-screen hid the emergence of a more subtle story in sports magazines and then in the wars on crime and drugs. In a 1979 special issue of *Ebony* titled "Black on Black Crime: The Causes, the Consequences, the Cures," the magazine's Washington bureau chief observed that the most successful Black racketeers, whom he described as role models for disaffected youth, could be found at "championship heavyweight boxing matches," watching one Black fighter pummel another for sport. A rift had opened up, he said, between "Black haves" and "Black havenots" – a rift that the white press would translate into the law-abiding citizen grateful for their freedoms and the ungrateful criminal.[104] It wouldn't be long before other magazines would be declaring it time for Black communities to "develop programs to combat [Black-on-Black crime], rather than blaming the historical racism of American society."[105] This wasn't Jack Johnson's America, or Jack Jefferson's, or even Rocky Balboa's.

At least one white fight fan did more than shadowbox. In 1958, George Plimpton, at the urging of his editor at *Sports Illustrated*, wrote a letter to the light heavyweight champion Archie Moore to see if he might, "in the cause of literature," fight a three-round exhibition with him. Moore agreed, and Plimpton later recounted the bout in *Shadow Box*, his 1977 book about the sport and his vicarious career as an Ali fan. "I am built rather like a bird of the stiltlike, wader variety," Plimpton wrote, casting himself as the ultimate white dope. "Since boyhood my arms have remained sticklike: I can slide my watch up my arm almost to my elbow." In the first round of the exhibition, Moore broke Plimpton's nose, and for the next two rounds Plimpton threw soft jabs with blood and tears running down his face. "Breath, man, breath," Moore, enfolding the writer in a clinch, whispered in his ear.[106]

Plimpton never boxed again. He didn't have to, he discovered. He could fight through Ali, his nose safe from further damage. In *Shadow Box*, Plimpton chronicled his transformation from amateur boxer to professional fan, from his three rounds with Moore at a gym in Midtown Manhattan to the Ali–Foreman fight in Kinshasa, where he and Mailer tried to hire a fetishist or "witch doctor" to give a lift to their man in the ring. When Ali knocked out a tiring Foreman in the eighth round, Plimpton and the other white men of letters who had gathered in Africa for the fight – Maury Allen, Bill Cardoso, Mailer, Hunter S. Thompson, Dick Young – celebrated as if they had won the heavyweight title themselves. Mailer, Plimpton observed, had "bobbed and weaved and ducked" along with Ali throughout the fight as if dodging Foreman's fists himself. "My sense of well-being had been greatly bolstered by what had happened that night," Plimpton admitted, circling back to his one exhibition fight as a young man, "not because I preferred Ali to Foreman but because another issue had been resolved at the same time."[107] He, the author of *Paper Lion*, for which he had tried out for the Detroit Lions – their "last-string quarterback" – had found his place outside the ring, off the field.[108] He had stories to file, books to write, and talk shows to visit. Ali Inc. had given him a handsome living and a straight nose.

Mailer and Plimpton fought through Ali. Others fought through a simulation of him. In 1967, Miami radio producer Murry Woroner staged the greatest boxing tournament of all time, using an NCR 315 computer to determine who would win if John L. Sullivan, long dead, faced Jim Braddock or if Muhammad Ali, then banned, met Max Schmeling. The result, a sixteen-man *All-Time Heavyweight Tournament*, attracted some twelve million listeners and more than $3.5 million in advertising revenue. *Sports Illustrated* declared Woroner, the owner of a closet-sized studio above a bank in suburban Miami, "the broadcasting czar of computerized sports."[109] Some sportswriters criticized the radio tournament, including Don Page of the *Los Angeles Times*, who bemoaned a program that transformed "boxing's flesh and blood warriors of the golden age" into "punch-card robots."[110] But the simulated fights, which culminated with Rocky Marciano (Computer Fighter No. 004) knocking out Jack Dempsey (Computer Fighter No. 002) in the thirteenth round of the final, created a lucrative market, a market that abstracted the Black athletes then dominating the sport, turning them into data. Woroner leaned into the old formula of the great white hope, but in 1967, with Ali fighting Terrell, the radio dramas read as historical fiction.

The stars of the show disputed the results. After listening to the final, Dempsey announced plans to sue the producer for defamation. Woroner told Reuters that he didn't see how Dempsey could challenge the results. He and his team had fed 2,064 variables, including "speed, stamina, punching ability, cunning, susceptibility to cuts, reach, height, weight, age," into the NCR 315.[111] Data, he insisted, don't lie. Ali, incensed that his simulation had lost to the great white hope himself, Jim Jeffries, filed a $1 million lawsuit of his own. In his autobiography, he called Jeffries "history's clumsiest, most slow-footed heavyweight" and observed that "the computer shows that even Joe Louis would go down under the White Hopes of the good old days."[112]

It didn't bother Ali that his simulation had lost. He knew that Woroner's tournament was a gimmick. Jeffries hadn't beat him. He hadn't redeemed his race from the grave. It bothered Ali that fans responded to the simulation as if it were him. His career had coincided with and contributed to the rise of closed-circuit broadcasting, which overtook live events as the sport's principal revenue stream in the mid-1960s.[113] When the promoters of the Ali–Liston rematch, faced with resistance from local politicians, had to move the fight from the Boston Garden to a much smaller venue in Lewiston, Maine, Shirley Povich of the *Washington Post*, citing the anticipated closed-circuit take, asked, "Who cares?"[114] "Liston and Clay would fight in a bathtub before an audience of silverfish," Jim Murray wrote in his column, "as long as the closed circuit cameras were turned on."[115] Few fans witnessed Ali's first-round knockout from inside Lewiston's 4,000-seat arena, which set the wrong kind of attendance record for a title bout. Most watched from their local movie theaters, shelling out five bucks to see Ali–Liston II where a week before they might have seen *Goldfinger* or *The Sound of Music*. Closed-circuit broadcasting had prepared boxing fans to suspend disbelief. Who needed the real thing? After all, Woroner's matches never ended in two minutes and twelve seconds, as the Ali–Liston rematch did, leading some customers to demand refunds.

Ali was right to question the NCR 315's results. Even if Woroner had, as he told *Sports Illustrated*, taken the information "just as it came from the computer," sticking to "logic, statistics and raw research," but the data he entered into the mainframe came from Nat Fleisher, the longtime editor of the *Ring*, and 250 other boxing writers, who rated the sixteen fighters on "factors" ranging from courage to "killer instinct."[116] Their ratings constituted Woroner Production's raw data. (Woroner also altered the computer-generated results to create more dramatic fights.) Ali did not then have a lot of fans among the growing ranks of the sports intelligentsia, who determined how far he would go in the *All-Time Heavyweight Tournament*. In the Ali–Jeffries simulation, the announcer Guy LeBow, whom Woroner hired to call his radio dramas using the NCR 315 data, describes Jeffries as "fair and clean" and "unperturbed with all of the Clay histrionics" and suggests that Ali had never been "subjected to an opponent with the hitting power of Jeffries, unless it was Sonny Liston, who wasn't at all willing to work."[117] Woroner admitted in interviews that "a computer can't program heart or courage," but it could, his factor ratings showed, program anti-Blackness.[118]

Ali, mired in legal expenses from his battle with the Selective Service, struck a deal with Woroner. Settling his suit for a dollar, he agreed to film a staged computer match against the retired Rocky Marciano for a cut of the box office. Ali and Marciano, wearing a toupee and hiking his shorts up to hide a paunch, mock fought seventy one-minute rounds, including seven different endings, unaware of which the NCR 315 (or Woroner) had selected. Marciano had once criticized Ali for creating "a lack of respect for all past champions" and entertained a $4 million offer from a Texas oilman to come out of retirement to "take the title away from the Black Muslims."[119] But he and Ali bonded on set. "The computer is bullshit!" Marciano told the younger man. "This fight will be rigged to come out the way it'll make the most money for the promotors – not us."[120] "Our work is phony," Ali said of his time with the Rock, "but our friendship has become real."[121]

Marciano died in a plane crash a few weeks after the shoot, and business and bullshit demanded one final win for the last of the white hopes. More than a thousand theaters screened what Woroner titled *The Super Fight* on January 20, 1970, with most audiences rooting for the late Marciano, who, in the final cut, knocks out Ali in the thirteenth. A man who, along with seven thousand others, watched the simulation at the Garden told Bud Collins of the *Boston Globe* that the crowd, supporting the Massachusetts native Marciano, "would have torn the place apart if Clay had won." Another Marciano fan compared it to "cheering for John Wayne against the Indians."[122] The editing encouraged audiences to see *The Super Fight* as something more than a movie. "Make no mistake," Woroner announces in the introduction, "you are actually going to see Rocky Marciano and Muhammad Ali at their best because that's the way the computer saw them." Marciano himself bolsters Woroner's claim in a ringside interview in which he remarks, "I'm happy that this fight is taking place on a computer because there'll be no hometown decisions and there'll be no prejudice in this fight." Each round ends with a freeze-frame and, over mechanical noises meant to remind audiences of the advanced computations guiding the match, a readout of the results (points, knockdowns, cuts, injuries) and an assessment of the fighters' condition heading into the next round ("both fighters now below their optimum ability levels").[123]

Ali, who didn't know the outcome beforehand, declared *The Super Fight* racist. "But the computer doesn't know what color you are," Woroner protested. "It acts like it," Ali responded.[124] In interviews after the film's release, he speculated that the NCR 315 had been "made in Alabama."[125] Woroner hit Ali with a $2 million lawsuit, claiming that his remarks had cost his production company future earnings from computer simulation events. The Black press came to Ali's defense, with Doc Young of the *Chicago Defender*, who had also railed against Woroner's *All-Time Heavyweight Tournament*, calling the Ali–Marciano simulation "pure hokum" and "nothing but bull."[126] But the return of the white hope on film had a different, bifurcated appeal for white audiences

Rocky Marciano and Muhammad Ali filming *The Super Fight* in 1969. Photograph from Getty Images.

after civil rights. Racial conservatives could celebrate a simulation of Marciano knocking out Ali as a restoration of white masculine prowess. Racial liberals could watch the spectacle and, measuring the distance from the age of real-life white hopes to their own age of all-Black title fights, see progress, a tale of integration and overcoming. The cinematic white hope let audiences choose their own racial adventure.

Murry Woroner never built the sports simulation empire he had envisioned in 1967, but others carried his dream into the 1970s. "Someone had shown me a tape of Rocky Marciano fighting Ali," Sylvester Stallone, recalling his struggles as an aspiring actor in the mid-1970s, told an Ali biographer. "It was a computer analysis of what would happen. I saw the juxtaposition of styles and contrast, and I was interested." Watching Marciano knock out Ali in *The Super Fight* led Stallone to wonder, "Why not do a story about people who can't fulfill their desires?"[127] Why not, he meant, make a movie about a white American who could hold his own against a Black heavyweight champion, something no one had seen since Marciano retired in 1956? *Rocky*, which he wrote and starred in as an unknown Italian American fighter who goes the distance against the brash Black champ Apollo Creed (Carl Weathers), made more than $100 million on a shoestring budget and won the Academy Award for Best Picture. Most know the journeyman fighter Chuck Wepner, who lasted fifteen rounds with Ali in their 1975 bout, as the inspiration for Stallone's Rocky Balboa. But Stallone also based his script on a computer fight that belonged to the genre of historical fiction, an imagined return to the time of Johnson and Jeffries. (*The Super Fight* also inspired the sixth installment in the franchise, *Rocky Balboa*, in which a computer-simulated match on ESPN inspires a final Rocky comeback.)

The critic Andrew Sarris described *Rocky* as "a clear case of ethnic backlash" against the Black Power movement and contrasted it with Jones's turn as a fictional Jack Johnson. "It is only a few years since we patted ourselves on our liberal toupees for applauding James Earl Jones in *The Great White Hope*, and here we are with Sylvester Stallone's *Rocky* as the most romanticized Great White Hope in screen history."[128] Though the film did, as Sarris observed, align itself with an emerging white ethnic revival that cast white people as minorities in their own right, forming a counterargument to the demands of the civil rights and Black Power movements, it also let white liberal moviegoers pat themselves on their toupees. No fight fan could have mistaken *Rocky* for an accurate reflection of the sport in the mid-1970s. The film itself casts Stallone's Balboa as an anachronism. A poster of Marciano hangs above the mantel in his dingy north Philadelphia apartment. His goldfish, Moby Dick, lives on that mantel, circling his bowl below the white whale of pugilism. Balboa's crusty old trainer, Mickey (Burgess Meredith), seeing the poster, tells him, "You kind of remind me of the Rock, you know that?" explaining, "You move like him, and you got heart like he did."[129] The film suggests that the United States of 1976 had left the white hope behind, in the black-and-white poster above Balboa's mantel.

Stallone merged his role as a white hope with Black-on-Black administration in the third installment of the franchise. Balboa, after defeating Creed in *Rocky II*, faces a new challenge from the brutal Clubber Lang (Mr. T), a character cast in the mold of Sonny Liston, who promises to "torture" and "crucify him real bad." When Balboa loses his title to Lang, a retired Creed offers to train him for the rematch. "We could win it back together," he tells his former rival. If the first two *Rocky* films fulfill the old racial dream of watching a white man go the distance against and then defeat a Black man, the third cloaks it in interracial teamwork, the humbled good Black man encouraging a white man in his battle with the bad Black man. "I can't wait to see this bum fall,"

Creed tells Balboa, watching Lang criticize the two former champions in a TV interview. "Just keep talking, pal."[130] Balboa, once the white hope, reemerges in *Rocky III* as an administrator of Black difference, doing the bidding, Stallone's script suggests, of a reformed Black man (who now appreciates the gift he once possessed) who wishes to see the wrong kind of Black man (who demonstrates no gratitude) taught a lesson. This time, the Italian Stallion, following the lead of the white sports intellectual – of Lardner, Liebling, Mailer, Plimpton – channels one Black man to beat another, committing himself to the cause of antiracist anti-Blackness. MGM and United Artists, which distributed the film, teamed with video game manufacturer Coleco to release *Rocky Super Action Boxing*, ensuring that all kids with parents able to afford the $175 ColecoVision console could knock out Clubber Lang, with Apollo Creed standing in their corner, rooting them on.

Creed, retired and committed to Lang's defeat, sheds his giftedness. Sweating alongside his friend Balboa, he, another self-made American, earns it. He trades his gift for grit, natural athleticism for elbow grease. His moral rehabilitation depends on the presence of another Black contender, the real natural with a taste for violence and a willingness to break the rules. The historian Matthew Frye Jacobson observes that the first *Rocky* films functioned as effective vehicles for white grievance because Balboa is not himself the author of the racial narratives surrounding his climactic fights with Creed. He is not a racist, and he doesn't feel bad for himself. He is uncomplaining, decent. Who could root against him?[131] The third installment further insulates Rocky from criticism, casting him, through his bond with the now hardworking, rule-following Creed, as something more than not racist. He fights against Lang but also for his rival-turned-friend. He is the champion of the former Black champion.

The white hope had found a second life as kitsch. Stallone embodied it. Don King promoted. No one believed that the future of the race was at stake. I mean, have you seen *Rocky III*? The movie's racial B plot was the A plot of the Reagan administration's renewed wars on crime and drugs: Creed versus Lang, Black on Black. Over the course of the franchise's first three films, Balboa trades white ethnic grievance for antiracist anti-Blackness, a defender of one form of Blackness against another. This was nothing new. Stallone had borrowed it from the title bouts of his youth and from the news stories of Black-on-Black crime that followed. You didn't, he discovered, need to be in the ring to win.

Creed's fate anticipated that of the man who inspired his character, Muhammad Ali. Once a threat to the liberal establishment, Ali found himself, fifty-four and shaking from the tremors that accompany Parkinson's disease, lighting the Olympic torch to open the 1996 Atlanta Olympics, with President Bill Clinton and a hundred thousand others standing to acknowledge him as a belated favorite son. Historical distance, it seems, makes the liberal heart grow fonder. One biographer after another told Ali's story, declaring him an "American hero" and an embodiment of the nation – "big, beautiful, fast, loud, romantic, crazy, impulsive."[132] The Greatest, now smaller and quieter, had lost his gift. We could all live with this Ali.

In 1998, Jack Maple, the anticrime strategist for the New York Police Department who pioneered preemptive, data-driven policing, thought of Ali when asked about his former boss William Bratton. Bratton had led the NYPD from 1994 to 1996 and, under Mayor Rudy Giuliani, applied the broken windows theory of law enforcement, making the practice of stop-and-frisk synonymous with the department. Giuliani, feeling outshined by Bratton, whom news media credited for falling crime rates during the mayor's first term, replaced him with Howard Safir, who continued Giuliani's anticrime crusade. "I think Commissioner Safir's doing an excellent job," Maple said, "but he's like Larry Holmes. He's following Muhammad Ali. Holmes was a very good champion, but he was never going to be the greatest." Safir didn't care for the comparison: "He's saying I followed Muhammad Ali? I didn't follow Muhammad Ali. I followed P. T. Barnum."[133] Why did Bratton get to be Ali? Safir wanted to know. I want to be Ali.

Three men who made their names implementing policing tactics that put millions of Black people behind bars cast themselves in the mold of the Black heavyweight champion. Perhaps they had discovered what the Chicago police commissioner had recognized in 1935, when a young Richard Wright watched Black cops break a joy-mad spell on the South Side streets. The great white hope had been vanquished. But someone had to stop Sonny Liston.

4

How the Student-Athlete Subsidizes the Amateur

Ivory Christian didn't feel like a student. The star middle linebacker for the 1988 Permian High School football team of Odessa, Texas, which Buzz Bissinger immortalized in the book *Friday Night Lights*, arrived on the tree-lined, buff-brick campus of Texas Christian University with a full ride and his sights set on a business degree and then graduate school. His high school teammates had dreamed of receiving the call that he had. A Division I program wanted him, and it would cover the costs of his education. Come to TCU.

Christian made the most of his first season. His coaches had planned to redshirt him, but, in a blowout loss to Texas A&M, they turned to the freshman, and he, not yet nineteen, as the broadcasters noted, came through with one big tackle after another for the overmatched Horned Frogs defense. He started the next week against Southern Miss and the next against area rival Southern Methodist. He had established himself as a contributor on the field, but, when Bissinger checked in on him that fall, Christian was second-guessing his decision to follow football to the affluent, suburban Fort Worth campus, three hundred miles east of his West Texas hometown. He, a first-generation Black student, stood out. "When he looked around the campus the only blacks he saw were athletes, and sports seemed to be their only reason for being at the school," Bissinger wrote after visiting Christian at TCU. "And sometimes, it often felt as if he wasn't playing football so much as working at it, getting up every day at six to make study hall, then going to practices and meetings from two in the afternoon to six-thirty in the evening."[1]

Readers of *Friday Night Lights* know Christian as the most "ambivalent" of the Permian High stars. He was reserved, thoughtful – a cocaptain who led by example. He wasn't, some boosters said, "rah-rah enough" for football-mad Odessa. "Let the other players dream their foolish dreams about getting recruited by a big-time school," he thought.[2] Christian didn't fantasize about TCU or the colossal stadiums of the Southwest Conference or the NFL. He wanted to be a minister, he told his father, a truck driver, after dreaming of a "tiny light" at the end of a long, narrow tunnel. He swore off alcohol. He never cursed. He delivered sermons at Rose of Sharon Missionary Baptist, where the minister introduced him as "the reverend Ivory Christian" – words that thrilled the young convert.[3] He read the Bible at his locker before games and at halftime. Ahead of his senior year at Permian, he considered quitting football. He worried that it conflicted with his faith and distracted from his goal of earning a doctorate. He dreamed of congregants addressing him as "Dr. Christian."[4] He consulted the minister, who told him to stick with the sport. "If playing football can get you to college, if playing football can get you an education, then play football," the minister said.[5] Christian took his advice, and TCU came calling.

Football got Christian to college but didn't get him an education. He never earned a degree in business or a doctorate. He hurt his knee in his second season and fell to third string. He butted heads with his position coach and, tired of sitting on the bench, walked off the field and turned in his pads. He'd had enough. Unable to afford TCU tuition, which then ran to more than $11,000 a year, Christian moved home. (His status as a student-athlete made him ineligible to receive need-based aid, which he might have otherwise fallen back on.)[6] Christian, who later earned an associate's degree from Odessa College, had been told that football would facilitate his education. It undermined it. He'd been told that it would be a shortcut to his goals. It was a dead end. "I became a better player, but I paid a steep price for that," the novelist John Edgar Wideman once wrote of his time on the Penn basketball team. "I learned to stake too much of who I was on what I would become."[7] Wideman stuck it out for four years and finished his degree. Christian, who didn't, left with nothing. He had, he discovered, staked it all on the fragile relations of college football. His services no longer needed, TCU showed him the door.

Christian didn't feel like a student at TCU because he wasn't. He was a student-athlete. Historians have long noted the significance of the term, which the National Collegiate Athletic Association introduced in 1956. "Nothing was more important legally and financially to the NCAA and individual institutions participating in athletics," Ronald Smith writes in *The Myth of the Amateur*, "than the use of the term *student-athlete*."[8] In a 2011 *Atlantic* cover story, Taylor Branch, the historian and Pulitzer Prize–winning Martin Luther King biographer, described it as "the NCAA's signature term" – "deliberately ambiguous" and "repeated constantly in and out of courtrooms."[9] Few now use it without a critical aside or an ironic "so-called." The term bound athletic departments to the educational missions of their institutions, shielding them from taxation and demands for workers' rights. Smith, Branch, and others treat the student-athlete as a modification of the NCAA's founding ideal, the amateur. The student-athlete, they suggest, descended from the amateur; the student-athlete is the amateur for a time of heightened commercialization.

But the amateur has thrived since 1956. You can find amateurs on the tennis courts, in the crew house, at your airport gate with matching bags on their shoulders, waiting to board a flight to Des Moines, Tallahassee, Tucson. I ran track for the University of Washington for four years in the mid- to late 2000s. I wasn't a star, even by the standards of a nonrevenue sport, but I received all kinds of benefits: admission assistance, access to exclusive dining facilities and on-call athletic trainers, one-on-one tutoring, early enrollment (I chose my classes ahead of nonathlete seniors as a freshman), vacation-like training excursions to the islands of the Puget Sound, and enough Nike gear to outfit a small village in athleisure (I still haven't, at thirty-seven, gotten rid of it all, and much of it remains unworn). The University of Washington did not make a dollar off my running. I can remember meets in Husky Stadium in which I raced before 72,500 seats, 72,000 of them empty. (UW has since removed the track from the football stadium in a $280 million renovation that included the construction of Husky Track at the head of Union Bay.) You could find me and my team in the athletic department's budget under "expense." The NCAA might have called me a student-athlete, but I wasn't. I was an amateur, and I owed the student-athletes – on the football and basketball teams – for the excesses of my college running career.

The amateur had been a class marker in the age of Jim Crow. The amateur was a gentleman among working-class ringers. The student-athlete did not succeed the amateur but reconstituted it as a racial marker in the age of civil rights. The student-athlete and the amateur have coexisted since, one's uncompensated labor subsidizing the other's idealized commitment to a balanced academic life. The labor of student-athletes on football and basketball teams has, as the historian and former NCAA track and field champion Victoria Jackson observes, funded the nation's and, when considering programs' international recruitment, "the world's Olympic sports development."[10] At TCU, Christian couldn't tell what made him an outsider – his race and class or his status as a student-athlete. Perhaps the answer was both/and. Perhaps the latter was an admissible way to draw the line between the deserving and the undeserving after civil rights.

The mass integration of college sports institutionalized an old idea about the relation between Black athleticism and intelligence. The historian Gail Bederman traces the idea of the dumb jock – that athleticism signals a lack of intelligence – to the turn of the twentieth century, when the ideal form of male embodiment shifted from a restrained Victorian "manliness," which associated strength with intellect, to a virile modern "masculinity," which disassociated one from the other.[11] White middle-class men identified the latter with Black and white working-class men, whom they feared and fetishized. The student-athlete gave institutional form to the gendered and classed athletic racialization that Bederman observes. "Dumb jocks are not born," Harry Edwards wrote of the education of Black college athletes. "They are being systematically created."[12] The structure of NCAA football and basketball, he argued, all but ensured that most Black athletes wouldn't receive the college education they sought. But the revenue their labor generated gave athletes in other sports, most of them white, new standing as amateurs doing it for moral edification and the love of the game.

Edwards identified the student-athlete as an abused class – used for financial gain and brand building and then abandoned, often without a degree. Others imagined student-athletes as abusing a sacred institution, as beneficiaries of a gift that they neither earned nor deserved. At TCU, Christian struggled with the condescension of the Left and the resentment of the Right. Some nonathlete Black students at elite institutions knew how he felt because the battle over affirmative action that first arose in the 1970s borrowed from and intersected with the unending struggle to reform college athletics.

Defenders and critics of affirmative action have turned to the athlete to make their cases. In the 1977 oral argument in *Regents of the University of California v. Bakke*, Justice Harry Blackmun mounted an unsuccessful defense of the UC Davis medical school's allocation of 16 out of 100 total seats for students of color by asking how it differed from athlete admissions. Didn't universities set aside seats for linemen, coxswains, and hammer throwers? he asked. Why not assign a few to Black and Latino medical students?[13] In the judgment of the court, the centrist Justice Lewis Powell redefined affirmative action, which had functioned as a modest form of redistribution (more Black medical students leads to more doctors in Black communities leads to better life chances), as an institution's interest in and right to create a "diverse student body" for the benefit of all students, including white students. He named the athlete as a contributor of diverse skills and quoted, at length, the president of Princeton, who cited "teammates on a basketball squad" as an example of "learning through diversity."[14] When USC came under fire in 1980 for having admitted more than 300 athletes who had not met the minimum GPA and test-score standards for admission, the president who had authorized their enrollment defended it as a "minority access program."[15] The head football coach denounced a call to eliminate athlete admissions as a "racial move."[16]

Others associated affirmative action with athlete admissions as an argument against race-conscious admissions, contending that both violated the meritocratic ideal of higher education. Critics of athlete admissions often construed Black athletes as beneficiaries of unmerited gifts – first the gift of their athleticism, then of their educations. The nonathlete Black students who followed them into the groves of white academe discovered that they were all student-athletes now. (In the 2022 oral argument in *Students for Fair Admissions v. Harvard*, in which the Supreme Court would rule race-based affirmative action unconstitutional, the conservative justices slammed Harvard for the college's admission of "ALDC students" – recruited athletes, legacies, dean's interest list [often donors' children], and children of faculty and staff – with an emphasis on the "A." Where there is debate over affirmative action, there will be talk of athlete admissions.)

Advocates for reforming college sports made things worse. Lawmakers and administrators argued that the commercial interests driving football and basketball contradicted the mission of the institutions that housed them and that the solution to athletic-department scandals was to bring them closer to the uncontaminated, noncommercial core of higher education. James Duderstadt, the president of the University of Michigan from 1988 to 1996, argued that the transformation of Division I football and basketball into big business had isolated athletics from academics. Football and basketball were, he wrote, "where the problems really exist" and "now threaten not only the academic welfare of their participants but the integrity and reputation of the very institutions that conduct them."[17] The historian Murray Sperber introduced his 1990 book *College Sports Inc.* by debunking a series of "myths." The first was that "sports are part of the educational mission of American colleges and universities."[18] He subtitled the book *The Athletic Department vs. the University*. But in dwelling on how the athletic department had changed, he and other advocates for reform failed to see how the university had changed with it. Christopher Newfield, author of *Unmaking the Public University*, writes that since universities moved toward broader racial and gender integration in the 1970s, higher education has become ever more "responsive to market forces and business methods."[19] Football and basketball reflect the educational mission of American higher education. We might not like what they say about it, but they aren't, as Duderstadt suggested, a rogue element. The academic/athletic division that a generation of reformers imagined and bemoaned – with "athletics" naming the two Blackest teams on campus – was about something more than the future of college sports. It was about who deserved a seat at Michigan and TCU and who didn't. It was about the amateur and the student-athlete.[20]

Friday Night Lights didn't follow Christian to TCU and his life as a student-athlete. He had, at the end of the book, made it, at least in the minds of his high school teammates. Some readers of *Friday Night Lights* and fans of the 2004 Peter Berg film may not remember Christian, a minor character in Bissinger's book, at all. But they have not forgotten his teammate Boobie Miles, the star running back of the Permian Panthers who never got his shot. Miles, gregarious and fearless on the field, tore his ACL in a summer scrimmage, and the college recruiters who had been knocking down his door for months vanished. Of the scrimmage that derailed his season, Bissinger recalled student managers removing Miles's pads, stripping him of "all the accoutrements" that made him "look a little like Robo Cop" on the field, until he "looked like what he was – an eighteen-year-old kid who was scared to death."[21] The film elevated the drama further with a scene in which Miles cries on his uncle's shoulder after clearing out his locker: "Now what we gonna do? I can't do nothing else but play football."[22] The rapper Big K.R.I.T. wrote a song about Miles titled "Hometown Hero," and "Boobie" remains a common nickname for running backs. (Miles Sanders of the Carolina Panthers has embraced the name, using it as his Instagram handle.) "Of all the themes raised in the book," Bissinger later wrote, "the tragedy of Boobie Miles is the most important, and the most enduring, one."[23] Miles didn't get his shot. Christian did.

Ivory Christian during a Permian High School game in 1988. Photograph by and reproduced courtesy of Robert Clark.

In a personal email, Bissinger told me that he felt Christian "blew a great opportunity" at TCU with his "tendency to be sour."[24] That may be. But Christian also arrived on campus as a student-athlete, which meant that he was never a student. He was the recipient of a gift, indebted to the institution. He should have been more grateful, the author now thinks.

When Bissinger visited Christian in Odessa in 2015, he discovered that the former football star, then in his mid-forties, maintained a small shrine to his days at Permian, including a framed photograph of himself from the book, seated on the bench and looking out at the field, his helmet off and sweat running down his face. Nowhere in the house did Bissinger find evidence of Christian's brief college career.

"That's it?" Christian asked Bissinger, when the author stood to leave. "That's it."[25]

TCU recruited Christian as a student-athlete. When a leather-helmeted Davey O'Brien led the 1938 Horned Frogs to a national title (and claimed the Heisman for himself), he took the field under a different banner: He was, the NCAA said, an amateur. Founded in 1906 as the Intercollegiate Athletic Association of the United States, the association, amid calls to ban football, advanced "principles of amateur sport" that forbade "inducements" to athletes and sought to establish a "moral tone" for all athletic activities on campus.[26] At the fifth annual meeting of the association, R. Tait McKenzie, a professor of physical education at the University of Pennsylvania and the association's vice president, delivered a "chronicle of the amateur spirit" for the assembled administrators and coaches. He told the story of the rise of athletics in ancient Greece, which, in his version of events, culminated and collapsed in the Roman era with the arrival of "a class of useless professional athletes hippodroming about the country, an unathletic nation, and a degraded sport." Professionalism had corrupted Roman athletics, and perhaps even brought down the Roman Empire, and the association must not, McKenzie counseled, let the fate of the ancients befall the modern campus. It must "restore the sport to those for whom it was designed, the regular student body."[27] It could not have hired hands hippodroming among the better classes.

The football powerhouses of the time, including Penn, nodded in agreement, and then, with the support of deep-pocketed boosters, continued recruiting athletes. McKenzie could preach against the perils of professionalism, but his association lacked the power and the resources to hold member institutions accountable. It subscribed to "home rule," calling on universities and colleges to regulate themselves. Some followed the association's guidelines and most – the schools that wanted to win games and alumni contributions – did not.[28]

The NCAA didn't seek to overturn home rule until 1948. The new national collegiate basketball tournament had furnished it with a source of revenue, and the emboldened association announced new, stricter rules for the conduct of intercollegiate sports that it branded the "sanity code." Universities and colleges belonging to the Southeastern Conference had been offering full rides to recruited athletes since 1935, and their rivals in the Big Ten, which didn't, accused them of abandoning the amateur ideal and exploiting what they deemed an unfair advantage. (Losing football games seemed to be their real concern.) The South must, they told the NCAA, be reined in. "I think there will be cooperation to a very large degree," a confident association president, a Big Ten man out of the University of Iowa, told the *New York Times*. "I doubt that there'll be any deliberate and intentional violation of the code by institutions."[29] The code barred admission assistance for athletes, restricted off-campus recruiting, limited aid to tuition and fees, and forbade boosters from furnishing outside aid to athletes. The reforms didn't last long. Seven schools – five southern universities, as well as Boston College and Villanova, the "sinful seven" – refused. The association failed to muster the votes to ban them, and home rule returned.

Walter Byers had his work cut out for him when, at twenty-nine, the assistant information director for the Big Ten took the helm of the flailing association. (No one with a longer résumé, it seems, wanted the gig.) The young executive director could see the obstacles before him. "To say we were the police is a large exaggeration," he later wrote. "Our task more closely resembled that of study hall monitors maintaining some semblance of order within a rambunctious college family."[30] But he recognized that the association had something going for it: College sports were plagued by scandal, and every scandal strengthened the case for regulation. He caught a break right out of the gate, when news broke that members of the University of Kentucky basketball team, which had won the 1948, 1949, and 1951 NCAA tournaments, had taken bribes from gamblers in exchange for fixing games. Their coach, Adolph Rupp, one of the winningest head coaches of all time, denied it, insisting that gamblers couldn't "reach my boys with a ten-foot pole."[31] But a New York judge admonished him and his team – which, an investigation revealed, received off-the-books cash bonuses – as "the acme of commercialism and over-emphasis." The judge condemned the "athletic scholarship racket as the most fruitful device and scheme yet invented to destroy the amateur code."[32] Byers, seizing the moment, assembled an ad hoc infractions committee and hit UK with a one-year ban. It was, he later acknowledged, a bluff. But he lobbied administrators in Lexington to enforce the ban, and when they did, he had his mandate. The NCAA was, it now seemed, in charge.

Byers served as the executive director of the NCAA from 1951 until his retirement in 1988, as TCU recruited a middle linebacker out of Odessa, Texas, named Ivory Christian. He made his most lasting contribution to college athletics in 1956, when, facing twin threats to the future of college football, he shifted the NCAA's governing ideal from the amateur to the student-athlete. In 1950, Congress introduced the Unrelated Business Income Tax, targeting educational and charitable organizations that engaged in side hustles unrelated to their educational or charitable missions but for which they had not, until then, owed taxes. (The instigating event was the donation of a noodle manufacturing business, C. F. Mueller, to the NYU Law School, which argued that it didn't owe taxes on the income the business generated because it used that income to fund the school's educational activities.) In 1955, the widow of a right guard for the Fort Lewis A&M Aggies of Durango, Colorado, who had died in an on-field collision, filed a claim for death benefits with the Colorado Industrial Commission under the Workmen's Compensation Act. The NCAA executive director had to make the case that athletic departments shouldn't be taxed as businesses – that they belonged under the tax-sheltered educational umbrella of their home institutions – and that the young widow's husband hadn't died on the job. Byer's solution, which he later described as a stroke of evil genius, was the student-athlete. "We crafted the term *student-athlete*, and soon it was embedded in all NCAA rules and interpretations as a mandated substitute for such words as players and athletes," Byers wrote in his 1995 memoir *Unsportsmanlike Conduct*, a too-late confession of the sins of the association under his watch.[33] He amended the NCAA constitution, adding the term sixteen times in the first four pages.[34] Student-athletes were, as he defined them, less than workers (*student*-athletes) but more than students engaged in a bit of extracurricular fun (student-*athletes*). He had, with two contrasted words, saved college football's emerging business model. The IRS never called. The young widow lost her case.[35]

Walter Byers at the NCAA headquarters in Kansas City, Missouri, in 1961. Photograph from AP Photo.

The NCAA invented the student-athlete to situate the athletic department within the university's educational mission. It didn't want the IRS taxing football as an unrelated business or state industrial commissions intervening on athletes' behalf, and it succeeded. But the term meant something else for athletes. It formalized their status as nonstudents, on campus but not of it, the most celebrated and alienated of the young people walking the quad. The student-athlete was not a variation on the theme of amateurism but something new. It acknowledged that some athletes were not amateurs. Amateurism had, as the long-standing ideal of college sports, maintained the fiction of the football recruit as indistinguishable from his nonathlete classmates. The student-athlete, as an institutional defense mechanism, conceded that some college athletes did not belong in the classroom, that they had been given an academic gift (admission into a world not their own) in exchange for the institution's use of their athletic giftedness. The athletic department did not write the football or basketball star a check; it orchestrated the circulation of gifts. In his 1971 book *The Athletic Revolution*, the educator and activist Jack Scott identified two dominant traditions in American college athletics: "the British tradition of sports as a means of inculcating youth with moral character" and "the Spartan tradition with its emphasis on sport as preparation for the military."[36] The amateur, institutionalized through the NCAA as a corrective to the violence of football, embodies the British tradition. The student-athlete, institutionalized through the NCAA as an admission and defense of football as a commercial venture, embodies the Spartan tradition. The distinction was not new in 1956; amateurism had long served as a class marker. But with the student-athlete, the NCAA gave a name to the athletes who didn't conform to the social class of the amateur. It would have to acknowledge them, the Spartans, the hired hands, the ringers, the nonstudents, the gifted.

Student-athletes were, at first, white. Their status was not a racial but a class signifier. The Big Ten had lobbied the NCAA to regulate athletic recruitment in the 1940s because it didn't want to fund athletes' educations, but it also didn't want to see Alabama trounce Michigan. The SEC and the next two largest southern conferences, the Southern and the Southwest Conferences, had fought restrictions on recruiting because they didn't want to integrate. (Their threat to secede from the NCAA amid the debate over the 1948 reforms led more than one writer to summon images of Fort Sumter.)[37] Big Ten schools had begun integrating their rosters, and the southern conferences knew that their refusal to recruit Black athletes left them at a disadvantage. But athletic scholarships, which the NCAA codified with the introduction of the student-athlete, allowed them to incentivize the best white athletes in the North to leave home and suit up for the Georgia Bulldogs or Ole Miss Rebels or the TCU Horned Frogs. "For college students who sought to play varsity sports," the historian of higher education John Thelin writes, it would be "a great decade if you were a White male. All other students encountered a peculiar mix of opportunities and exclusions."[38] From the GI Bill to the gridiron, it was an age of white (and male) affirmative action.[39] At TCU, Christian sometimes wondered whether his teachers and fellow students assumed he was an athlete because he was Black. In the 1950s, they might have assumed the same thing about a big-shouldered white student from out of state – another ringer brought in from the North to throw, catch, tackle, and uphold Jim Crow.[40]

But the amateur lived on at some institutions. In 1945, the leaders of eight of the oldest East Coast universities and colleges signed an agreement that their athletes would "be truly representative of the student body and not composed of a group of specially recruited and trained athletes."[41] In 1952, they signed a second agreement eliminating spring football and ending their involvement in end-of-year bowl games. A third agreement, in 1954, reaffirmed their commitment to forbidding athletic scholarships and extended the restrictions to all intercollegiate sports. It also gave the coalition a name: the Ivy League. The president of Princeton later wrote in a memo to the NCAA, in which he denounced the establishment of national admissions standards for athletes, that Ivy League institutions "do not award athletic scholarships or subscribe to the concept of the 'student athlete.'"[42] Ivy League football and basketball vanished from the national stage after the agreements. Critics have noted that Ivy League universities and colleges still used other forms of aid to recruit athletes, but the formation of the Ivy League from a declared resistance to athletic scholarships institutionalized the idea that academics and big-time sports didn't mix, that to succeed at one meant sacrificing the other. Princeton did not enroll student-athletes because the student-athlete, as a class, lacked the intelligence and academic ambition of the Princeton man. Scholars have contested the assumed divide between academics and athletics. (Thelin argues that A&M now stands not for "Agriculture and Mining" or "Agriculture and Mechanics" but "Athletics and Medicine.")[43] But the image of the dumb jock – an outsider among scholars and students, gifted a seat in another otherwise meritocratic lecture hall – endures.

Southern universities used the student-athlete to maintain the color line, eastern universities to reinforce their elite status. The term functioned to distinguish between the deserving and the undeserving, the merited and the gifted, whether in Tuscaloosa or Harvard Yard. Alabama and Georgia, scouring the North for white talent, recruited the student-athlete. Harvard and Yale, seeing the student-athlete as dumb, a nonstudent, declared their allegiance to the amateur. But the racial meaning of the student-athlete was about to change. A revolt was coming.

The white student-athlete faced the mistrust of some teachers and classmates, the Black student-athlete athlete something worse. In *The Revolt of the Black Athlete*, his 1969 book about the ongoing, far-reaching rebellion of young Black athletes, Edwards wrote that coaches at white institutions recruited Black athletes not as they did their white teammates but as if they were ordering balls, helmets, towels. "Like a piece of equipment," he wrote, "the black athlete is used."[44] Edwards knew of what he wrote. In 1960, he had enrolled at San Jose State, where, as one of the few Black students on campus, he had starred at center for the basketball team and broke the school record in the discus. In 1967, Edwards, then a lecturer at his alma mater, rallied students against the college's subordination of Black student needs. The administration showed no interest in hearing their demands until members of the football team threatened to sit out the opening football game. The college was forced to cancel the game, at a cost of $12,000, and Edwards formed, with San Jose State sprinters Tommie Smith and Lee Evans, the Olympic Project for Human Rights.

Edwards's revolt was, to the NCAA, a riot. "Higher education's critical shortcomings of today," Byers wrote in his memoir, "took root during the riots of the 1960s, when more than a few college presidents surrendered academic and campus social standards to the lowest common denominator among the faculties and students."[45] Edwards led a revolt, and Byers led the counterrevolt, which relied, as counterrevolts do, on the idea of crisis, that what may have begun as warranted discontent had devolved into an infectious chaos.[46] The historians Howard Chudacoff and Michael Oriard both describe the institutional backlash that unfolded from 1967 to 1973 as the moment at which the student-athlete transformed into an "athlete-student."[47] (Even Bear Bryant, the longtime head football coach at Alabama, admitted to James Michener in 1976 that, at the bigger schools, the student-athlete is "really an athlete first and a student second.")[48] It was also when the term shed a residual association with the white working-class natural and landed on the Black athlete. Before the Higher Education Act of 1965 or affirmative action or Title IX could alter college enrollments, the reracialization of the student-athlete framed the struggle over which advantages would count as individual merit and which as institutional gifts.[49]

The white student-athlete might have carried a stigma at Harvard and Yale, but, from 1956 to the mass integration of college football in the late 1960s, when the athletic department remained the almost exclusive domain of white men, he had it good. His athletic scholarship was more valuable than almost all other forms of aid. The NCAA barred universities and colleges from canceling a recruited athlete's aid for failure to turn out or contribute on the field, and some schools guaranteed four years of tuition and housing. The white male student-athlete didn't have to be an athlete. He could turn in his gear, grow out his hair, and, unlike Christian a generation later, continue with his education, a nonathlete indebted to no one.

In 1967, the year that SEC football began a long, slow integration, the NCAA decided to devalue the athletic scholarship. At the association's annual convention at the Sheraton-Lincoln Hotel in Houston, Dick Clausen, the athletic director of the University of Arizona and a former football coach, took the floor to introduce a "new interpretation" of the NCAA constitution that would allow universities to terminate financial aid for athletes who left the teams that recruited them or "misrepresented" their abilities (hid a career-ending ACL injury, for example). Clausen's revision, an acknowledgment that athletes had to continue earning their seats in the classroom on the field until graduation, faced no resistance. The association tallied the votes: 214–13.[50] Byers, who backed Clausen in Houston, argued that the revision had nothing to do with integration. (His critics found the timing more than coincidental.) But "the stepped-up college recruitment of black athletes," he later admitted, "was a sensitive issue that we preferred not to discuss in public."[51] Far easier, it seems, to discuss student-athletes and amateurs. He and Clausen may have been color blind, as they claimed they were, but that didn't change the fact that the moment that athletes of color and women athletes walked in the door, the NCAA began attaching strings to the once unconditional full ride.

One writer decided to ask athletes what they thought, and they had words for the NCAA. In 1968, Jack Olsen, a senior editor at *Sports Illustrated* (an early André Laguerre hire) and the author of one of the first biographies of Muhammad Ali, delivered the five-part series "The Black Athlete." "The cliché that sports has been good to the Negro has been accepted by black and white, liberal and conservative, intellectual and red-neck," he wrote.[52] But his investigation revealed that most Black athletes at white institutions felt isolated and used and that they lived under the constant surveillance of their white coaches, who acted as their academic advisers, dorm monitors, and tightfisted benefactors. When he asked one former college athlete what his football career had given him, the man answered, "Well, let's see ... At the University of New Mexico I got a sweater. At Cameron State College in Oklahoma I got a blanket. At Southwestern State I got a jacket and a blanket."[53] Olsen concluded that, far from the leading edge of the struggle to integrate national life, as some athletic directors and coaches described them, college programs had enlisted Black athletic labor without altering their white "ethics and folkways."[54]

Olsen's series set off alarm bells at the NCAA for how it showcased what he called, a year before Edwards's iconic book, "a revolt by the black athlete against the framework and attitudes of American sport" – and for the sheer number of Black athletes, current and former, willing to criticize administrators and coaches on the record. At the University of Washington, one Black athlete after another told Olsen that what their coaches called "The Husky Way" amounted to "The White Way." "What is a Husky?" one lineman asked, mimicking his coach. "A Husky is a man from a third-string high school squad who can run 100 yards in 11 seconds, who is a robot, and you make an all-American out of him." A Husky had grit. There are a lot of white Huskies, a defensive back and sprinter chimed in. But he'd never heard a UW coach acknowledge a Black Husky.[55] Donnie Shanklin, the star running back at the University of Kansas, told Olsen that his coaches stacked his Black teammates at running back, corner, and on the defensive line to ensure that the number of Black starters on offense never exceeded two or three. One athlete shared a letter in which his coach had described his behavior as an "animal response" and informed him, "I am giving you a scholarship and that is more than plenty, and you still have to prove your worth."[56] The athletic directors and coaches who sat for interviews with Olsen, reciting the usual clichés about not seeing color and instilling an ethic of hard work and determination in young men, looked out of touch at best alongside athletes declaring them bullies and bigots.

The NCAA struck back. At the 1969 convention in downtown Los Angeles, David Swank, legal counsel to the University of Oklahoma, recommended an additional revision of association rules that would allow athletic departments to terminate the financial aid of athletes who committed acts of "manifest disobedience."[57] Charles Henry of historically

Black Grambling College, in northern Louisiana, asked, "Is this legislation the result of articles that appeared in *Sports Illustrated* last summer?" No one answered him. He then asked whether an athlete's choice to wear an Afro could constitute disobedience under the recommended rule change. (It could, he'd later learn. At Oregon State that fall, the head coach would demand that a Black linebacker trim his hair and shave his face if he wished to remain on the team and at the school.) Henry continued: "If the coaches told these boys not to be interviewed is this freedom of speech under the First Amendment or construed to be disruptive action under the interpretation that we are asked to adopt?"[58] Swank again didn't answer but said that athletes could go to the NCAA Council (a council on which Swank sat) to inform the association of abusive behavior. The chairman of the Athletic Council at the University of Louisville cut in to say that it saddened him to see the discussion "degenerate in terms of color and race," and, with Henry outnumbered, the members voted. More than two-thirds of the room backed the measure.[59] The *New York Times* headline the next day stated what Swank and his allies refused to admit: "College Athletes Who Protest to Face Loss of Financial Aid."[60]

The NCAA could live with the revolt of the Black athlete. What it feared was that defiant Black athletes could set off a larger rebellion. Their revolt had risen alongside a wider athletic movement of women, athletes with disabilities, and student antiwar activists. It was the most visible manifestation of what Douglas Hartmann describes as a "gathering storm" of movements seeking to remake college sports. As much as the association avoided discussion of race, it had an interest, Hartmann suggests, in situating the revolt within the "politics of race" because it distracted from what the movement said about the "politics of sport."[61] The former could be contained with the occasional reform; the latter could bring the whole house down.[62]

The revolt against the Black athlete rewrote the rules of college sports. The white working-class student-athlete of 1956 had been a class outsider to higher education. He had translated an athletic talent into an institutional gift. He got the message that his reward was a seat in the classroom that he didn't deserve. Be thankful. But the line between the student-athlete and the amateur was, for him, traversable. He could cross over, leave the team, and continue his studies, a white student among white students. The reracialization of the student-athlete in the late 1960s hardened that line, transforming the lives of Black athletes but also restructuring the governance of the athletic department. Racism,

Stuart Hall wrote, is more than one among many hierarchical ideologies; it transforms "the whole ideological field." The reason, Hall argued, is that race carries an aura that other ideologies do not: "an apparently 'natural' and universal basis in nature itself."[63] Racism naturalizes other hierarchies. The student-athlete, once associated with Blackness, could itself racialize. As a subgenre of racial giftedness, it existed close to what Hall considered the core of race's ideological strength. To ward off a revolt of all athletes, the revolt of the Black athlete would have to be isolated and then, in an act of what the political scientists Daniel HoSang and Joseph Lowndes call "racial transposition," used to undercut the wider movement.[64] The racial remaking of the student-athlete shuffled the social hierarchies of the athletic department and made them seem natural, like it had never been otherwise and never would.

After Olsen's "Black Athlete" series, the athletic department needed a PR department, and it found one in Olsen's colleague John Underwood. Underwood, another Laguerre hire, admired coaches. He never commented on Olsen's headline-grabbing series, but it was clear that he disagreed with his fellow *SI* writer and wanted to give college coaches a second hearing. In his three-part series "The Desperate Coach," he cast them as besieged defenders of self-sacrifice and order on campuses now overrun with self-indulgent bohemians and naive revolutionaries. "In the privacy of their offices, over breakfast in strange towns, wherever two or three coaches get together, they talk about The Problem," Underwood wrote.[65] A basketball coach at a small college in Pittsburgh whose athletes had demanded his firing told him, "It probably originated as a black problem, but today it's not race. It's all types."[66] Integration had instigated a wider athletic rebellion – The Problem, as Underwood called it – and now even the once-obedient white male athlete had read Fanon and declared the rule-setting coach a kind of "neo-fascistic racist."[67]

One coach after another bemoaned how their teams diverged from the masculine ideal of their youth, contrasting the clean-shaven white stars of another time with the sideburned Black stars now giving them hell. The new, integrated generation lacked restraint, the coaches said, telling Underwood how athletes refused to cut their hair, wear a tie, and listen to them. One thought that his athletes indulged in sex and drugs ("half of them have probably tried pot").[68] Black athletes had, the desperate coach suggested, given their white teammates a lesson in gender and sexual unruliness, an unruliness that needed to be reined in. The future of sports as the great teacher of men hung in the balance. Most of the coaches who spoke to Underwood didn't want their name used in the story, Underwood wrote, for fear of retaliation from their athletes. Something, he thought, had to be done.

Underwood recognized the emerging distinction between the student-athlete and the amateur, the running back and the rower. He thought that administrators should acknowledge that members of the football and basketball teams were different from athletes in other sports, that they were workers – entertainers and emissaries "paid in the currency of the 'free ride,' an all-expenses-paid education," the value of which could, if they finished their degrees, be "unlimited." He commended the NCAA for authorizing coaches to cancel the scholarships of defiant athletes, but he wondered whether, without abandoning the whole amateur charade and allowing coaches to act as what they were – managers of labor – it could ever be enough. Out of fear for their jobs, coaches now bent to what Underwood called "the Irritational Act, the Superdemander, the Double Standard."[69] Could a coach still be a coach? he wondered. Had college administrations who had once backed the unbending coach surrendered to the revolt of the Black athlete? Underwood's series encouraged readers to wax nostalgic for an imagined time when athletes followed the rules, held their tongues, and could be counted on to sacrifice their own interests for team and school.[70] At TCU, where I taught for nine years, Ivory Christian would have confronted the words of former head coach Dutch Meyer, who led the Horned Frogs from 1934 to 1952, in the locker room and around campus: "Fight 'em until Hell freezes over. Then fight 'em on the ice!" College athletes weren't what they used to be, the coaches said, letting Underwood's readers fill in the rest.

Underwood didn't think that the NCAA rule changes were sufficient to right college sports, and the association agreed. Coaches still had to accuse athletes of manifest disobedience to terminate their scholarships – a move that few, as Underwood noted in his series, wanted to risk making. It would, they knew, create further distrust between them and their teams. In 1973, the association made things easier on Underwood's desperate coach. At the annual convention, at the Palmer House in Chicago's Loop, Wade Stinson, the athletic director of the University of Kansas, recommended limiting all athletic scholarships to one year, allowing coaches to then renew (or not renew) them after every season. Other ADs had introduced similar amendments as far back as 1965 without success. Allowing athletic departments that kind of discretion, the NCAA knew, would make it difficult to argue that they were at all invested in an athlete's education. If student-athletes could be booted whenever they ceased to contribute tackles or buckets, then had they ever been students? But Stinson's amendment sailed through committee and an all-members vote in Chicago without effort – no discussion, no resistance, a decisive show of hands.[71] "It took less than 90 seconds," Byers later remembered, condemning the rule change, a change that he had endorsed at the time, as a "major extension of NCAA cartel authority."[72] The revision might have benefited the association, but the real winners that day were athletic departments, which could now get rid of athletes without having to cut them. All they had to do was not renew the scholarships of athletes whom they deemed disobedient or decided weren't worth the roster spot. The NCAA had, in three moves, hollowed out the student-athlete's full ride. The NCAA might have "crafted" the term *student-athlete* in 1956, but it reinvented it amid the revolt of the Black athlete.

The fight over the status of the student-athlete was about more than who controlled the future of college sports. It was also about who belonged at the best universities and colleges and who deserved the degree that could, in turbulent economic times, translate into a middle-class income. In 1965, President Lyndon Johnson had, in a commencement address at Howard University, declared that the next stage in the civil rights struggle would be not "just equality as a right and a theory" but "equality as a result."[73] A few months later, he signed Executive Order 11246, mandating that federal contractors take affirmative measures to hire and retain workers of color. The Nixon administration continued where Johnson left off, at least at first, by demanding that federal contractors in Philadelphia meet numerical goals for integrating their workforce. But President Nixon had changed his tune by 1972, when a young adviser named Pat Buchanan added a section to his acceptance speech at the Republican National Convention. The American dream was under threat, it argued, from "the specter of a quota democracy – where men and women are advanced not on the basis of merit or ability, but solely on the basis of race, or sex, or color, or creed."[74] The anti–affirmative action movement had arrived, and it sought to do what athletic governing bodies had long done: to distinguish advantages it deemed legitimate (access to a better school district, the resources to hire an SAT tutor or a college admissions consultant) from those it deemed illegitimate (reserving seats in a medical-school class for students of color). Giftedness had long functioned to delegitimize some athletic advantages as unearned, unmerited, God-given talent for which one owes a sacred debt. The student-athlete was born with it. The amateur earned their achievements. Buchanan, the future presidential candidate, seemed to understand that the best way to devalue and eliminate an advantage was to ground it in divisions that people assumed to be natural ("on the basis of race, or sex, or color, or creed"). He and his allies, learning the lessons of athletic governance, were not interested in achieving fairness but in defining it.

The belief that young Black men were taking over college sports was an illusion. Most college athletes were still white, but most belonged to teams that you wouldn't see on TV or in stories by Jack Olsen and John Underwood. The debates at the NCAA conventions suggest that members did not have those athletes in mind as they rung their hands over the future of their athletic departments. Some white athletes in nonrevenue sports got caught in the web of new restrictions and punishments, but most benefited from the racial shift, as I would, enjoying the perks of the profits brought in by the football and basketball teams – better training and dining facilities, nicer gear, more comfortable travel accommodations – while being celebrated as the true ideal of the scholar athlete. (Critics often connect the enormous salaries of some football and basketball coaches to the uncompensated labor of athletes on their teams, but that surplus value also gets dispersed to nonrevenue sports.) The student-athlete was, for a short time, raced white. With the racialization of the student-athlete as Black, white college athletes from middle-class families were freed to return to an earlier model of campus sporting culture. Eighteen-year-olds like me, an unremarkable member of an unremarkable track team, received favors that we did not need and kudos that felt like shots at other members of the athletic department. The second racialization of the student-athlete had restored the white amateur, now with better swag.[75]

Black athletes were not alone in staging a revolt. Women, athletes with disabilities, and student antiwar activists had launched their own, allied challenges to institutional structures that had sidelined them and their causes. Scott, the educator and activist, believed that their revolts could, with some cross-movement organizing, coalesce into a revolution, into what he called "athletics for athletes." He envisioned a sports culture defined not by the martial fantasies and financial interests of administrators, coaches, and fans but by the needs of athletes. What would this look like? Scott, who would later serve, for a tumultuous eighteen months, as the athletic director at Oberlin College, couldn't say. "A program of athletics for athletes cannot be outlined in specific detail," he wrote, "for the one thing it would not be is a preconceived system established in advance by a single individual."[76] Athletics for athletes would be democratic and malleable so that each new generation of athletes might make of it what they want. The NCAA, athletic conferences, and college administrations didn't want a revolution. Most didn't even want reform. What they were willing to offer was a discussion of reform.

After the NCAA moved to a one-year renewable scholarship model, George Hanford, the executive vice president of the College Board, secured a grant from the Carnegie Corporation to begin that discussion. It furnished him with the funding to conduct not a study of college athletics but, as the title of his 1974 report announced, "an inquiry into the need for and feasibility of a national study of intercollegiate athletics." (He found a study needed and feasible.) Hanford, who had earned all-American honors in lacrosse at Harvard, wasn't convinced that amateurism served most college athletes. "The erstwhile coal mining sons of Pennsylvania and their modern counterparts from the black ghettos of urban America or the ice rinks of Canada can well ask," he wrote, "whether amateurism, a privilege of the well-to-do, is consistent with the principle of equality of opportunity."[77] He enlisted Roscoe Brown, a professor of education at New York University and a former Tuskegee airman, to lead a task force on issues facing Black athletes. Brown's task force found "considerable evidence" of anti-Black discrimination in athletic departments, including "inadequate education programs, lack of tutoring, failure of Black athletes to receive degrees in similar proportion to their white counterparts, inequitable treatment concerning financial aid, summer jobs, and jobs for wives, position stacking, playing quotas, social isolation, limitations on dress, political expression, and dating practice" – and more. In the final report, Hanford directed readers to the appendix containing the task force's findings: "Appendix D should be read in its entirety!"[78] But the American Council on Education, which published the report, circulated it without the appendices, in the interest, it said, of "timeliness and economy."[79] Few ever read Brown's paper, and neither the Carnegie Corporation nor the ACE agreed to fund the study Hanford proposed.

In his appendix, Brown addressed the imminent expansion of women's sports and wondered aloud, as few others had, what it might mean in "the special case of Black women." Would the "more general women's campaign," he asked, meet their needs?[80] In 1972, Congress had enacted Title IX, prohibiting gender-based discrimination in all educational programs receiving federal aid, including – as much as the NCAA and most athletic departments didn't want to admit it – sports. The *Washington Post* declared it a "revolution."[81] Byers called it the "possible doom of intercollegiate sports."[82] Supporters of the law quoted the sociologist David Riesman, who had observed that "the road to the board room leads through the locker room."[83] More opportunities for women in sports could, they hoped, lead to more opportunities in the workplace. But Title IX, as the historian Amira Rose Davis and others have documented, served some more than others. The implementation of the law undercut women's programs at historically Black colleges and universities, including the celebrated track and field teams at Tennessee State and the Tuskegee Institute, which had long awarded athletic scholarships to women. White institutions recruited the best Black athletes while, as Brown had feared, leaving Black administrators and coaches behind.[84] Once "the torchbearers for women's sports," in Davis's words, HBCUs struggled to compete, and Black women athletes who enrolled at predominantly white universities encountered athletic departments that had, in the wake of integration, hollowed out the athletic scholarship and placed constraints on athletes' speech.[85] The revolt against the Black athlete had stifled their revolution.

The architects of Title IX borrowed the law's framework from the Civil Rights Act of 1964, using the struggle against racial discrimination as a model for combating gender discrimination. Some had, in fact, made a case for amending Title VI of the Civil Rights Act to include "sex" rather than addressing gender in a separate section.[86] The law launched a thousand analogies. Of the 1973 tennis match between Billie Jean King and Bobby Riggs, one educator remarked, "I think women felt about Billie Jean beating Riggs the way blacks felt after Joe Louis beat Jim Braddock."[87] Analogies to race facilitated Title IX, situating the law in a tradition of legible discrimination and redress, but also obscured how gender interacted with race, suggesting that the former was "like" the latter, not entangled with it. If the NCAA imagined the Black athlete as male, Congress imagined the female athlete as white.

Analogies between gender and race set a course for women's sports in which the commercial reach of men's football and basketball would be the ultimate measure of success. It can be debated whether men's revenue sports were the right model for women's programs – or for men's nonrevenue sports, which have also followed their lead – but it had the observable effect of setting men's and women's programs against one another in what has often seemed a zero-sum struggle for resources and airtime. The NCAA, athletic conferences, and universities built a multibillion-dollar business through the uncompensated labor of young men on football and basketball teams. Flush with cash, they added more nonrevenue sports, including more women's programs – all of which, in time, learned to fashion themselves after football, the darling of the athletic department. Their costs increased, but no revenue followed. Track and field was not football. The result: Athletic departments made more than ever and, as their programs multiplied and sprawled, spent even more. Calls to compensate men's football and basketball teams collided with calls to run women's teams more like them, and all demands faced an athletic department budget that had, like the budgets of their academic neighbors, drifted into the red.

But most reformers didn't see women's sports as integral to the athletic departments they sought to change. Their concern remained with Division I men's football and basketball, where, as James Duderstadt later wrote, "the problems really exist."[88] But no college leader wanted to forfeit surging TV revenue or cross football-obsessed alumni, so most reform efforts got redirected from the conditions of athletic labor to the regulation of athlete admissions. After declining to fund Hanford's study in 1974, the American Council on Education got back into the reform game in 1982, forming a committee on intercollegiate sports that urged the NCAA to establish minimum high school grades and standardized test scores for first-year athletes. The association agreed, adopting the committee's recommendations at the 1983 convention.

Leaders of historically Black colleges and universities, whom the ACE committee had neither included nor consulted, called the move "discriminatory and patently racist."[89] One HBCU president observed that establishing "arbitrary SAT and ACT cutoff scores" targeted "low-income and minority-group families" for which access to higher education was constrained enough. He didn't see why the NCAA needed to add more barriers.[90] The chancellor of North Carolina A&T State was even more frank: "The bottom line ultimately is apparently one of the color of a majority of the kids who take the floor as a 'final four' or the omnipotency of the combatants in the Cotton Bowl."[91] Was the association seeking to strengthen the academic standing of athletic departments? he asked. Or was it seeking to control and perhaps reduce the number of Black athletes dominating the most visible and lucrative events? Integration had diminished once-great HBCU football programs around which had formed what the historian Derrick White calls "sporting congregations" – communities formed in the shadow of Jim Crow for which football was the occasion but that had a greater social function.[92] The HBCU leaders had, they said, heard it before. The association had cut them out, erected new obstacles for Black athletes, and framed it all as the inevitable cost of integration.

The NCAA's defense of the rule changes can be distilled into one word: crisis. It was facing a crisis – of cheating, of academic failure, of boosters recruiting off the books with cash and cars – and it had to do something. Crisis had been good for the NCAA. It had been born out of crisis – "the recent crisis in football plainly indicates that [rules] committees, governed by some responsibility such as ours, are necessary," the association's first president declared at an early convention – and strengthened by it.[93] The historian of college football John Watterson once reflected in amazement at the number of scandals that the game had weathered. "Looking back as a historian at a century of football crises, I am astounded at football's ability to survive and grow," he wrote in 2000. "Each of its three major upheavals [in the 1900s, 1950s, and 1980s] has been a prelude to a growth spurt or came in the midst of a boom on the college gridiron."[94] But perhaps college football has grown not despite but because of crisis, real or imagined, with every new scandal swelling the ranks of an administrative class charged with regulating the lives of college athletes as well as cutting TV and merchandising deals. Newfield, the historian of higher education, describes universities' embrace of market-oriented managerial strategies since 1980 as higher education's "devolutionary cycle."[95] Private-sector reforms, he observes, shift resources away from education while raising rather than, as promised, containing costs. Increasing costs trigger additional budget crises, which renew calls for private-sector reform. Football has led the devolution of American higher education, showing how stories about a crisis of undeserving, entitled student-athletes could facilitate commercial interests. Athletic administrators increased revenue and awarded themselves with larger salaries. The amateur received new facilities and acclaim from all sides as a true scholar, and the student-athlete bore the cost.

The NCAA heard the criticism of HBCU leaders, commissioned some studies, and then further tightened the screws on Black athletes. The 1983 rule changes had allowed "partial qualifiers" (athletes who met either the GPA or test-score minimum but not both) to enter college on an athletic scholarship and take an "academic redshirt" that would allow them time to devote to their studies. In 1989, the association voted to bar partial qualifiers from receiving financial aid. (Boobie Miles, had he not hurt his knee before the Permian Panthers 1988 season, would have been one of the recruits affected.) Georgetown basketball coach John Thompson, the first Black head coach to lead a team to a Division I basketball title, walked off the floor before a game against Boston College and said he would not coach again until the association agreed to reconsider the change. What the rule did "was accept [the] inequality [in the education system] and compound it," he later said. "By imposing a centralized test on kids who did not receive a centralized education, the NCAA judged disadvantaged kids by the results of the privileged."[96] This time, the NCAA backed down, but it would continue to redirect blame for one scandal after another from itself and conference and university administrations to athletes with bad grades and low scores.

The NCAA sought to reform athlete admissions on the heels of its 1981 decision to host women's championships. It was an about-face for the association, which had lobbied Congress to create a Title IX carve-out for men's football and basketball and, failing, fought the enactment of the law in court. For years, Byers, a seasoned Washington warrior by then, had described Title IX as an existential threat to college sports. The football and men's basketball teams you love, he would say in interviews, could not survive it. In 1981, he reversed course, calling the association's decision to host women's championships "a historic commitment by the NCAA to enhance opportunities for women."[97] He commissioned the writer Jack Falla to write a book commemorating the association's first seventy-five years, *NCAA: The Voice of College Sports*, which suggested that the NCAA had been ahead of the law in fighting for women's athletics. ("The first notable action [by the NCAA] actually takes place *before* passage of Title IX" with the creation of a special committee on women's sports, Falla wrote. The committee had been chaired by David Swank, the driving force behind the association's "manifest disobedience" rule.)[98]

Had the executive director changed his mind about women's sports? Or had he read the writing on the wall and moved to manage what he could no longer block? He did, it seems, harbor some concern about the Association for Intercollegiate Athletics for Women, which had governed women's sports in the NCAA's absence (and which folded in 1984). But Byers also found that the association could use the law to fend off demands that member institutions compensate and facilitate the academic success of male students of color and first-generation and working-class students in revenue sports. Duderstadt, the former University of Michigan president, blamed football for his and other athletic departments' struggles to achieve a gender balance in resource allocation without cutting men's programs. "It is this absurd practice of tolerating in football a men's athletics program several times as large as any other sport," he wrote, "that makes it so hard to achieve gender equity."[99] We can't assist Black and brown male athletes, the NCAA and college administrators could claim, because of the cost of women's sports, and we can't build women's sports because of the needs of Black and brown male athletes. The NCAA had discovered, or stumbled on, a tactic that Scott had warned against in *The Athletic Revolution*: It had isolated one revolt from another, leaving them "fighting among themselves" for what it said were maxed-out resources.[100] A crisis was never, for it, a crisis. It was how it gained and maintained control of the ever-bigger business of college sports.

Scandal has, as Watterson observed, always been a part of college sports. But the late 1980s set a new standard for bad news, and the reform talk got louder. In 1986, University of Maryland basketball star Len Bias died of a cocaine overdose in his dorm room, hours after returning from the NBA draft, where the Boston Celtics had selected him second overall. Critics rushed in, most blaming "at-risk" student-athletes for living above what they imagined as the meritocratic rules governing higher education.[101] "The offenses committed by athletes against people and property cast a shadow across American campuses," one longtime *Sports Illustrated* staff writer declared.[102] "One does not have the civil rights to take drugs," Jesse Jackson said in a news conference in Washington, DC, after Bias's death. The reverend called on universities and colleges to get serious about drug enforcement, to take "responsibility in this war against drugs." He thought it was time for athletic departments to institute randomized drug testing of athletes. Red Auerbach, the president and general manager of the Celtics, agreed. "Forget the civil rights and the invasion of privacy," he said. "Rules are made to be broken."[103]

The culture wars had begun, and the Right didn't hesitate to frame Bias's death as an inevitable outcome of the moral failings of liberal higher education. William Bennett, then the secretary of education and later the first Bush administration's director of the Office of National Drug Control Policy, urged college administrators to enact hardline anti-drug measures. "If our academic and cultural institutions have become so 'sophisticated' that they have forgotten their elementary duties and responsibilities," he said in a speech to the Heritage Foundation, "then it is time for us to call them back to first principles."[104] Nancy Reagan, then telling schoolchildren to "just say no," wrote in the *Washington Post* that she blamed "naive" college leaders who "deny that students could get any kind of drug they wanted on campus" for Bias's death. The first lady, maintaining the color-blind posture of her husband's administration, did not mention that Bias was Black, and the *Post* ran her column under the title "The Need for Intolerance."[105] A UMD task force recommended, as Jackson and Auerbach had, randomized drug testing of athletes, and universities and colleges across the United States took sometimes invasive actions to limit drug use among students. (Boston University announced that all residential students would need to sign a release giving officers the right to search their dorm rooms.) The reaction to Bias's death prompted lawmakers to introduce the Anti-Drug Abuse Act of 1986, which mandated new minimum sentences for low-level drug crimes, including infamous minimums for crack cocaine charges that were as much as a hundred times higher than minimums for the powder form most associated with white elites. (It mattered little, it seems, that Bias had not used crack on the night of his death.) Lawmakers and news media cast Black college athletes – the most visible Black students at predominantly white universities – as a "racialized threat of contamination," Theresa Runstedtler writes. Bias and his Black teammates did not belong in College Park and may even, some now thought, threaten the well-being of nonathletes – the real students who had earned and valued their seats in the classroom.[106]

Reagan and others were careful not to correlate Bias's overdose with his Blackness, but they didn't hesitate to conclude that it had something to do with his status as a student-athlete. In the *Post*, the first lady offered two examples of the costs of "our live-and-let-live society": Bias and Don Rogers, the twenty-three-year-old safety for the Cleveland Browns who had died of a cocaine overdose a week after the basketball star. Bias was, Reagan wrote, "full of talent and potential." Rogers was "another gifted athlete sacrificed to cocaine." The two young Black men had failed to cultivate the "personal, moral responsibility" that might have saved them.[107] Bias and Rogers had been blessed with a gift, a kind of masculine excess, that had, she suggested, made them stars on the court and the field but that had also left them vulnerable to the kind of risk-taking behavior that killed them. The Black athlete of 1986 lacked the masculine restraint of her husband, the former movie cowboy, Reagan seemed to say. Their athletic giftedness constituted an excess. It was too much, uncontrollable, dangerous. It had delivered them to two of the nation's finest public universities (UCLA for Rogers) and now threatened the character of American higher education. In 1979, the clinician Joanna Bunker Rohrbaugh had asked, in *Psychology Today*, "How can a woman be feminine and a 'jock'?"[108] She observed that female athletes faced greater gender stigma in basketball and track and field than in swimming and diving without acknowledging that the former tended to be mixed-race and mixed-class and the latter white and middle class. For the women of color on the basketball and track teams, race gendered their sports. For

Bias and Rogers, gender racialized theirs. Rohrbaugh's story, "Femininity on the Line," ran alongside an image of a young white woman on one knee in a grass-stained football uniform. She grits her teeth and wears, as if entering the Rose Bowl for Rogers's Bruins, a line of burnt cork across her cheeks – the slightest touch of athletic blackface.

If conservatives found in Bias's death a case for new draconian drug laws, liberals discovered in it a need for educational reform. Bias, it turned out, had failed three courses in his final semester and withdrawn from two more. Four of his teammates had failed more than one course after the end of the basketball season. The *New York Times* declared it "the scandal behind the tragedy." "The present corrupt standards," the editorial board wrote, "can ruin young lives as quickly as cocaine."[109] The *San Francisco Chronicle* described drugs as "the immediate cause of the tragedy" and a failure to educate as the broader context that had enabled the overdose death.[110] The *Washington Post* book critic Jonathan Yardley called it a "golden opportunity" for reform. Athletes must, he argued, meet the same standard for admission as nonathletes. Admitting students who could not get in on their own academic merit was, he believed, dooming them to failure and the athletic department to scandal.[111]

Conservatives and liberals agreed on the need for reform. Conservatives wanted to police athletes' bodies with randomized drug testing. Liberals wanted to regulate their access to higher education with stricter admission standards. Conservatives thought that athletes had received a gift from God, an excess that could, like drugs, endanger the athletes and their classmates. Liberals thought that they had received a gift from the institution, an undeserved seat that threatened the meritocratic ideal. All could agree, in the aftermath of his death, that Len Bias had wasted a gift and left behind a trail of unforgivable debt – to his school, the Celtics, the fans, his coach and teammates, God, himself.

Bias's death was, as Runstedtler and others argue, used to advance the war on drugs. It was also used to undermine affirmative action. The 1978 *Bakke* decision had transformed affirmative action from a form of modest redistribution into an elective but dominant institutional commitment to cultivating diverse learning environments – environments to which, as Justice Powell envisioned them, all could contribute, from a Black woman to "a farm boy from Idaho" to "potential stockbrokers."[112] The court had ruled that institutions could not set aside seats for students of color, as the UC Davis medical school had, but that they could award a "plus" to candidates who would contribute to what they deemed a diverse class.[113] (In the 2023 *Students for Fair Admissions* decision that ended race-based affirmative action, Powell's kitchen-sink definition was a favorite target of the conservative justices. Neil Gorsuch argued that it allowed universities and colleges to "simply assert an interest in diversity and discriminate as they please.")[114]

Most liberal lawmakers continued to affirm Powell's version of affirmative action until the emergence of the New Democrats in the late 1980s. The New Democrats embraced an aesthetic of multiculturalism, including an unrelenting celebration of historic "firsts," but orchestrated a liberal retreat from affirmative action in hiring and admissions. In 1990, their leader, the young Arkansas governor Bill Clinton, issued a statement on behalf of the centrists, declaring, "We endorse [Andrew] Jackson's credo of equal opportunity for all, and special privileges for none." In a frontal attack on President Johnson's 1965 vision of "equality as a result," Clinton and his allies declared that they believed "the promise of America is equal opportunity, not equal outcomes."[115] Johnson's endorsement of redistributive affirmative action was, to them, a harmful restraint on free market competition and, worse, a violation of the nation's abiding faith in fairness, and nothing embodied the values of competition and fairness like sports. The New Democrats declared 1990 a "turning point," and it was, and it came on the heels of ever-louder calls to regulate the gifts of the student-athlete.[116]

Bias's death and a flood of recruiting violations, including the cartoonish scandal at Southern Methodist – it involved a booster-furnished $400,000 slush fund and ended the career of the sitting governor of Texas – led to the formation of the headline-making Knight Commission on Intercollegiate Athletics. The Knight Foundation, the creation of brothers John and James, who together owned the *Akron Beacon Journal* and the *Miami Herald*, assembled what it (and an enamored press) never failed to describe as a "blue-ribbon" commission of current and former college leaders and CEOs. William Friday, the former president of the University of North Carolina, and Theodore Hesburgh, the former president of Notre Dame, served as cochairs. In 1991, after two years and $3 million, the commission delivered *Keeping Faith with the Student-Athlete*, in which it advocated for a "new structure of reform" that it called the "one-plus-three" model.[117] The "one" – "presidential control" – would be directed, it said, toward the "three" of "academic integrity, financial integrity, and independent certification." Though the commission directed a few words of criticism at the imbalanced economic structure of college sports – it recommended hard limits on coaches' salaries, season length, and practice hours – it didn't venture far from the usual reform talk. The commission defined what it, echoing John Underwood, called "the problem" as a growing gulf between big-time football and basketball and the academic life of the nation's universities and colleges. Football and basketball had to be brought into line, it suggested, commending the controversial 1983 reform of athlete admissions as having "served intercollegiate athletics well." "It is time to build on and extend its success," the commission concluded.[118] The Knight Commission earned glowing reviews from national news media, which almost never mentioned the incredible self-interest of presidents advocating for more presidential control or interrogated the distinction it made between commercial sports and noncommercial academics.

The Knight Foundation had done the NCAA a favor. Though the association's new executive director, Richard Schultz, served on the twenty-two-member commission, the foundation had taken some of the onus off the NCAA. It had created another organization with a mandate to reform and given casual observers a sense that, with all the college leaders involved and all the headlines the commission made, someone must be doing something to bring about change. The "confederated" structure of the NCAA has, as Hartmann observes, been among the association's greatest strengths, allowing it to delegate blame for structural failures while absorbing and rearticulating more radical forms of resistance at the level of the conference or individual institution.[119] The commission's recommendations, which the NCAA neither embraced nor rejected, criticized the association but also authorized it to clean house. The association got to be institution and activist.

The Knight Commission included fourteen current or former college administrators, four business executives, and one man from Washington: second-term congressman Tom McMillen. McMillen, a moderate Democrat serving Maryland's 4th District and a former NBA center, had retired from the league in 1986 to run for Congress. (At six-foot-eleven, he remains the tallest person to have ever served in either chamber.) The congressional rookie, then in his mid-thirties, joined four other men in Congress who had first made their names as athletes: Bill Bradley, Jim Bunning, Jack Kemp, and Mo Udall. Udall, the longtime Arizona congressman who had averaged five points a game in one season for the Denver Nuggets of the soon-defunct National Basketball League, called them the jock caucus. "I like having jocks on the hill, no matter their political persuasion," Udall, a Democrat, said. "We tend to be problem solvers, and we don't moan and groan about defeats."[120] The nickname caught on after *Sports Illustrated* used it as the title of a story about the ex-athletes in Congress. The jock caucus, five white men, three of them former college basketball standouts, did not resemble Len Bias's generation of student-athletes. But the old heads didn't hesitate to weigh in on what the kids were getting wrong.

McMillen, a Rhodes Scholar at the University of Maryland, where he had been one of the first star recruits of Len Bias's future coach Lefty Driesell, thought the issue could be a winner for him in a tough reelection bid. (His home in Crofton had been redrawn into the whiter, rural, more conservative 1st District.) In 1992, leveraging the attention he had received as a member of the Knight Commission to secure a book deal, he released his own recommendations as *Out of Bounds: How the American Sports Establishment Is Being Driven by Greed and Hypocrisy – and What Needs to Be Done about It*. The book was an odd blend of insistent calls for reform and wistful memories of his youth as a high-achieving

Congressman Tom McMillen and Senator Bill Bradley outside the Capitol Building in 1991. Photograph from CQ Roll Call via AP Images.

student who made a first career in basketball. The future of college sports should, he often seemed to suggest, look a lot more like his own past. "Unfortunately, not everyone is learning the same beneficial lessons [about teamwork, discipline, and desire] that I did," McMillen wrote. It will take a "concerted effort by all interested parties," he determined, "to rescue sports from their corrupting influences and return the games to their proper perspective."[121] The book, which did not get McMillen reelected, included an image of him seated on a bench at Oxford with a sweater over his shoulders and a hardbound volume in his hands. As a Rhodes Scholar, he wrote in the caption, "I relished the opportunity to study politics, economics, and philosophy, laying the groundwork for my later career in public service." His argument was hard to miss: He, the son of a dentist, had done college right; the basketball stars of 1992 were doing something wrong. He blamed Black athletes for harboring "dangerously delusional" dreams of NBA and NFL careers at higher rates than their white teammates and defenders of "marginal students" who, in fighting GPA and test-score minimums, acted as "apologists for failure" and surrendered to "the mediocrity of our present system."[122] Where, he and the Knight Foundation asked, had the Tom McMillens – who dreamed not of draft night but of tutorials at Oxford – gone?

The NCAA thought it might find them, the ideal amateurs, in women's sports. In 1992, it assembled a fifteen-member task force to define a "path toward measuring and realizing gender equity." The association had found that, twenty years since Title IX, men continued to constitute more than two-thirds of college athletes and receive far more resources, on and off the field, than their female counterparts. The task force defined the goal as a future in which "the participants in both men's and women's sports programs would accept as fair and equitable the overall program of the other gender." It recommended that member universities and colleges invest in what it called "emerging sports," which included badminton, bowling, crew, team handball, and other noncontact sports associated with the athletic clubs found in white, affluent communities.[123] The task force's findings contained a numbered list of criteria that it had used and that it now offered as a framework for other organizations. The seventh and shortest read, "Consider racial equity."[124] The task force's recommendations for growing women's sports suggest that it had considered and then decided against it. A blue-blooded amateurism was alive and well on the badminton courts and in the boat house.

But women's sports attracted little attention, good or bad, in the late 1980s and early 1990s, as national media investigated the scandals of men's football and basketball with a self-seriousness new to the business. "The whole tenor of sports journalism changed," one veteran broadcaster remembered of the time.[125] Young writers decided that they'd rather be Woodward and Bernstein than Grantland Rice, and they had a lot of muck to rake.

Rick Telander embodied the new combativeness. The Kansas City Chiefs had drafted him, an All–Big Ten cornerback out of Northwestern, in the eighth round of the 1971 NFL draft. He didn't make the roster, and two years later, at the height of the Watergate scandal, he joined the *Sports Illustrated* staff. Telander later described football writing as defined by either "heroes and champions" or "nastiness and pain."[126] He had written both, he said, but he had made his name with stories of the latter. Though he may be best known for his 1976 book about street basketball culture in New York, *Heaven Is a Playground*, Telander often returned to a culture he knew well: the abusive benevolence of the college football program. His investigation of the sport culminated in 1989 with *The Hundred Yard Lie*, a "diatribe," he admitted, against the game around which he had organized his young life.[127] Telander recognized that, while the individual faults of star athletes might make better headlines, it distracted from the class distinction inherent in what he called the "amateur attitude."[128] The amateur ideal was not available to most athletes of color and first-generation and working-class students. His solution was to establish what he named the Age Group Professional Football League, or AGPFL, modeled after the minor leagues in other sports but with universities as title sponsors. (Telander estimated that between fifty and eighty universities would opt in. The rest could continue to field amateur football teams but could not charge admission for games or seek other sources of revenue.) Athletes would be between eighteen and twenty-two years old and "need not be college students." If they wished to attend the affiliated school, they would receive a one-year scholarship to be used when they wished for every year of service to the AGPFL. But they would have to be admitted to the school on their own academic merit.[129]

Unlike most reformers of the time, Telander was calling for large-scale structural change. Universities needed to either forfeit football revenue or get out their checkbooks, he thought. Half-measures wouldn't do. But his recommendations shared something with those of the NCAA and the Knight Commission. The association and the commission argued that academic standards for athletes ought to be raised. Telander argued that academic standards ought to be abolished, that athletes, whatever their academic standing, should receive an income in exchange for their labor. The trouble with the NCAA and the Knight Commission's solution was that it involved excluding some of the most visible students of color from American higher education. The trouble with Telander's was that it also, though it created an alternative route for young people who wished to earn a living from their sport, involved removing some of the most visible students of color from the classroom. His was the more honest assessment of college sports, but it also assumed an antagonism between athletics and academics, with the former a drag on and distraction from the latter. The NCAA, the Knight Commission, and Telander believed that the athletic department could be reformed in isolation from the rest of the institution, but it couldn't, and it can't. It frames how we imagine who earns an education and who receives one with a bow on it.

Far from damaging the NCAA, the reform talk of the 1980s may have saved it from change by creating the sense that someone somewhere must be doing something. "The NCAA has traveled a long road on gender equity," the association could claim a few years later, "and a similar distance on minority issues."[130] What else could have come of all the studies, commissions, and investigations that we'd heard so much about? It couldn't be nothing, could it?

Ivory Christian arrived at Texas Christian University at a moment, he heard, of crisis. Len Bias had died. The NCAA had hit SMU football with a one-year ban for brazen recruiting violations. The Knight Foundation announced that it would form a commission on college sports. Telander published his diatribe. But if college football was in a state of crisis, then it was the kind that it could live with. I taught at TCU from 2015 to 2023 and often assigned Bissinger's *Friday Night Lights* in undergraduate literature classes. Students, most of whom knew the TV show – and some of whom decided to attend college in Texas *because* of the TV show – were fascinated to learn that Christian had gone to TCU. The school was not as white as it had been, but it was white and rich, and students of all backgrounds didn't have a hard time imagining why Christian had felt alienated by his surroundings. That's anti-Blackness, they could say. White privilege. I feel the same way, some Black students and students of color would confess. But most students, some of whom were taking on crushing amounts of debt, were more ambivalent about Christian's status as a student-athlete. "Christian was treated well at TCU," Bissinger wrote in the epilogue, "and lived in a nice dorm along with other athletes and had a nice room."[131] Members of the football team seemed, to the nonathletes in the room, like they'd been given a great gift – rolling around the sunbaked campus in golf carts, their tuition covered, celebrities at a football-obsessed university in a football-obsessed city in a football-obsessed state. Black students had it tough. Student-athletes had it good. Black students deserved to be there, no doubt. Athletes? Their classmates weren't so sure.

The Supreme Court wasn't either. In oral argument in *Students for Fair Admissions v. Harvard*, the conservative justices on the court grilled Harvard's legal team about the admission of athletes, legacies, donors' children, and the children of faculty and staff. Justice Neil Gorsuch wondered whether Harvard could achieve "whatever it deemed racial diversity" by eliminating ALDC admits, as the admissions office called them. If Harvard was invested in bringing a diverse class to Cambridge, then why, he wanted to know, did it favor "squash athletes" and "those who row crew"?[132] Harvard's legal team didn't have a good answer. In 2019, the FBI had charged celebrities and business leaders with bribing college coaches to designate their nonathlete children as recruited athletes to increase their chances of admission. The investigation, codenamed Varsity Blues, had altered the image of the college athlete. Now, for some, including Gorsuch, athlete admissions brought to mind not Reggie Bush but the influencer daughter of Lori Laughlin, Olivia Jade (who was not, in fact, as her USC application suggested, an elite coxswain).[133] But why would the justice, a formidable debater, go to the "A" rather than the "L," the more obvious violation of the meritocratic ideal?

In her dissent in the 2023 decision, Justice Sonia Sotomayor, the longest-serving liberal on the court, also dwelled on the first letter in ALDC. Harvard had not, following *Bakke*, used race to "unfairly disadvantage some racial groups" but as one of a "multitude of dimensions" in a "holistic review," she wrote. Race-conscious admissions allowed universities and colleges to "select students with various unique attributes, including talented athletes."[134] Considering an applicant's racial background was, she suggested, as Gorsuch had, kind of like considering an applicant's athletic status. But she seemed to have a different kind of college athlete in mind. The liberal justice was defending the student-athlete, and the conservative justice, in a perhaps calculated reversal, was attacking the amateur. The liberal and the conservative agreed that athletes bore a gift. One thought that they brought a gift – the gift of their "unique attributes" – to Harvard, the other that they received an unmerited gift from it.

The student-athlete had been a white northern in the South and then a Black student on a white campus. The amateur had been a Princeton man and then a nonrevenue athlete. It seemed, as the highest court ended affirmative action and the introduction of NIL (name, image, likeness) deals transformed at least some NCAA sports, that we were witnessing another turn, another racialization, of the student-athlete. At TCU, students of all backgrounds were cautious when talking about race and affirmative action. But they'd tell you what they thought about athlete admissions. Whom, I had to wonder, were we talking about now?

5

Color Commentary

At the 2001 NFL draft, Chris "Boomer" Berman, ESPN's first and biggest star, took a moment to mark the distance that he and the network had traveled since it first broadcast the event twenty-one years earlier. "People thought we were nuts. 'You're reading the phonebook on national television!'" he recalled of the first televised draft, in which ESPN treated cable subscribers to twelve hours of nontelegenic men in suits rifling through binders in a crowded hotel ballroom. "Well, think again. Everybody watching coast to coast, all over the world. We're on ESPN.com. There's ESPN Radio. There's ESPN Zone [the network's now-defunct theme restaurant chain] with NFL player chat. We've got expert panels in Bristol."[1] More than 52,000 NFL officials, writers, and fans had crowded into the Theater at Madison Square Garden to see whom the Atlanta Falcons would take with the first pick. Berman, in a dark suit and loud tie, sat at a desk overlooking the theater stage with fellow commentators Chris Mortensen and Joe Theismann and draft "guru" Mel Kiper. At the ESPN offices in Bristol, Connecticut, a second team stood by to offer their takes, and the network had stationed others outside teams' "war rooms" in Baltimore, St. Louis, and elsewhere to interview general managers and coaches about their picks. Millions tuned in. Millions more had studied Kiper's mock drafts on TV and online. Some had created their own. ESPN had built a market for the meat market.

When ESPN president Chet Simmons first reached out to NFL commissioner Pete Rozelle about televising the draft, Rozelle thought he had to be kidding. Televise *what*? he asked. ESPN was then known for broadcasting Australian rules football, Irish hurling, and darts, and Simmons recognized that an affiliation with the NFL could go a long way toward legitimizing the fledgling cable network. He was more right than he could have known. "The draft is probably second only to the Super Bowl," Rozelle would admit ten years later. "It has become a major publicity tool."[2] The NFL draft made ESPN, and it transformed the NFL from seasonal entertainment into a year-round obsession.[3]

After a rambling introduction from Berman, the Falcons selected Michael Vick out of Virginia Tech. Vick, the first Black quarterback to ever lead a draft class, took the stage in a red Falcons hat and shook hands with commissioner Paul Tagliabue. A ticking clock in the bottom lefthand corner of the broadcast indicated fifteen minutes until the next pick. Berman, Mortensen, Theismann, and Kiper had time to talk. Berman turned to his colleagues: What do you think? Kiper: "It's a roll-of-the-dice type pick." Theismann, naming two of the five Black starting quarterbacks then in the league: "I absolutely think he will be at the level of a Daunte Culpepper or a Donovan McNabb at least." Mortensen: "I agree with Joe." All four of them voiced concern about Vick's limited time as a starter in college. (Vick had redshirted his freshman year and then declared for the draft after two seasons under center at Tech, at the age of twenty.) But they were wowed, they said, one after the other, by his athleticism. "The things that he possesses, the gifts that he has physically," Theismann said, "are not just things that you go out and learn."

Berman kicked things over to Bristol, where Mike Tirico, the one Black member of the broadcast team, served as moderator. What are your thoughts? Tirico asked his fellow commentators. "Well, he's a tremendous athlete," one said. But "he's lightyears away from being a polished NFL quarterback." "He's a great athlete who's going to have to learn," another echoed. Though ESPN had made Black "firsts" one of the network's go-to sociological framings, no one, in a marathon nine-hour broadcast, acknowledged the significance of Vick's draft number. The commentators stuck, as they might have said, to the Xs and Os. Vick was gifted and raw, a roll of the dice.

When the San Diego Chargers selected Drew Brees thirty-second overall, making him the second quarterback drafted, the ESPN team struck a different note. "Drew Brees is ready to play. He's got a chip on his shoulder [and] he is competitive," Mortensen said. "This is a real heady quarterback, an intelligent quarterback, and understands the game," Ron "Jaws" Jaworski added from the Bristol studio. Mortensen, Jaworski, and their colleagues credited Brees, a three-year starter at Purdue

Michael Vick at the 2001 NFL draft. Photograph by Mark Lennihan. From AP Photo.

who stood a fraction of an inch taller than Vick, with overcoming his short stature and weak arm by throwing overhanded and from his toes. Hours of talk and numbers-crunching boiled down to this: Vick, a six-foot-tall, 210-pound quarterback, had gifts you couldn't teach and much to learn; Brees, a six-foot-tall, 210-pound quarterback, had grit and much to teach.[4]

Football commentators and fans look back on Vick's career as transformative. He made four Pro Bowls, finished second in the MVP vote twice, and, in 2007, at the height of his career, served twenty-one months in prison for his involvement in a dogfighting ring. He ran for more than 6,000 yards over thirteen seasons – including a 1,000-yard season in 2006 – demonstrating to NFL GMs, who had long favored tall, stand-and-throw signal callers, that a team could win with a dual-threat quarterback. A generation of Black quarterbacks, whose coaches might have once, without Vick as a model, converted them to cornerbacks or wide receivers, followed: Robert Griffin III, Jalen Hurts, Lamar Jackson, Colin Kaepernick, Patrick Mahomes, Kyler Murray, Cam Newton, Dak Prescott, Deshaun Watson, Russell Wilson. But they were asked to assume more risk than the white quarterbacks they succeeded, and some, like Griffin and Prescott, have suffered gruesome, career-altering torn ligaments and broken legs while scrambling for yards. At the 2001 NFL draft, no one described Brees, who had run for 546 yards and 5 touchdowns in his final college season (to Vick's 617 and 8), as a dual threat, and in a twenty-year NFL career, he never ran for more than 130 yards in a season – a number Vick often tallied in a single game. Vick retired at thirty-five, Brees at forty-two. Vick, often hurt (and sometimes incarcerated), started 115 NFL games, Brees 286.

You have, I would guess, heard this before. The Black quarterback is the most overused metric for measuring Black advancement in sports. "For decades, NFL quarterbacks were not always the most gifted athletes on the team," Jason Reid, a staff writer for *Andscape*, ESPN's race and culture website, writes in his 2022 book *The Rise of The Black Quarterback*. "There had been one requirement, never plainly stated, that the game's owners and coaches had insisted on, an attribute that had nothing to do with talent: whiteness."[5] Racism had, in Reid's account, gotten in the way of the market; self-defeating owners and coaches had, due to bias, made bad choices about whom to draft and whom to start. Now, at last, the most gifted athletes were running NFL offenses, and they were Black. This is worth celebrating, Reid thinks. But to describe someone as gifted is also to suggest that they owe an ontological debt, and neither the owner nor the coach nor the fan has ever hesitated to claim it. Vick, with his God-given talent, owes us. Brees, with his undersized grit, deserves whatever he gets.[6]

Reid's own network has also claimed the debt of the gifted athlete by measuring it and turning that act of measuring into bankable entertainment. The gender theorist Jennifer Doyle observes that men often treat her like an intruder when she joins them in a conversation about soccer. The reason, she realizes, is that they aren't talking about soccer at all but about "their relationships to each other." The game allows them to "talk with enormous intensity of feeling about other men" with other men in "a delicate balance of tenderness and disavowal."[7] The staged conversations among the ESPN commentators during the 2001 NFL draft were homosocial and could be homoerotic: Look at that man's hands, his legs, his size! This could all be done, Doyle suggests, in the comfortable absence of women. But what Berman, Mortensen, Theismann, and Kiper were talking about, in their refuge from women, was gender. The commentators were engaged in acts of gendered racialization – naming gender excesses (Vick's athleticism) and norms (Brees's stature) as gifts and grit. Race did not get in the way of the market; it made it, including the media market over which ESPN reigned.

Look at us now! Berman could crow in 2001. The network on which he had starred since 1979, the year it launched, now ruled a growing cable business. (Streaming was then a distant, unimagined nightmare for the double-digit channels on the dial.) More than 85 million American homes had ESPN, and it controlled nineteen international markets, reaching a combined 109 million subscribers outside the United States.[8] It had created the X Games and the ESPYs, a radio network and a magazine. *Forbes* would later name ESPN "the world's most valuable media property," observing that it dwarfed ABC, which had bought the network in 1984 and constituted close to half of the value of Disney, which had bought ABC in 1996.[9] ESPN had transformed the tagline "the worldwide leader in sports" – a title that it gave itself at first in jest – from laugh line to fact, and Berman, soaking in his James Cameron moment, was the king of that world.

Berman was not Howard Cosell or Jack Buck or Bob Costas. He did not broadcast games or secure exclusive interviews. He was something else and, at first, something new. His role was not to furnish information – a cable subscriber could watch the game on network TV or check the box scores in the morning paper – but to model what to do with that information, to model, every evening as he ran through highlights, how to be a fan. "We never look at ESPN as a television network," a marketing executive said of the image it cultivated in the mid-1990s. "ESPN is a *sports fan*."[10] If the network was a fan, it was a fan that did a lot more than root for a favorite team. It taught viewers that the ideal fan was a scout, a general manager, and an amateur sociologist all rolled into one. Fandom was not a mere diversion; it was a vocation. The network's broadcast of the 2001 NFL draft had Berman, Mortensen, Theismann, and Kiper stationed at a desk in the Garden that would have suited an evening-news anchor. Their colleagues in Bristol, wearing suits and ties, sat in armchairs around a coffee table as Tirico, their Black colleague, invited them to share their take on Michael Vick, going around the circle, leaning in to hear.

The network added ESPN2 in 1993, ESPNews in 1996, and ESPN Classic in 1997. ESPN Deportes and ESPNU would soon follow. (The 2004 film *Dodgeball* would feature a fictional ESPN8, nicknamed "the Ocho." It felt, at the time, like a joke that wouldn't be a joke for long.) The network had discovered long ago that talk-and-highlight shows were the most affordable ratings earners, but, with a growing suite of channels, it had a lot of time to fill. What to talk about? Executives had learned the lesson of the network's success with the NFL draft. Viewers wanted to hear about the gift, and they would watch for hours.

Giftedness freed ESPN from having to choose between the two dominant racial ideologies of the time, color blindness and multiculturalism. At the 2001 draft, Berman and his colleagues never mentioned Vick's Blackness or Brees's whiteness, but it didn't take a critical race theorist to notice the racial undertones. Part of the intrigue of the draft coverage was the commentators' elaborate dance around the racial significance of the event. The talking heads were engaged in an hours-long discussion of race without race. Rewatching it now, I almost admire the color-blind acrobatics of the conversation. In the late 1990s, the philosopher David Theo Goldberg listened to a buffet of sports talk radio shows on a solo drive from Philadelphia to Phoenix. For thirty-five hours, he heard, from hosts like Jim Rome and Chris "Mad Dog" Russo, "racist expression coded as race neutrality, racialized exclusions as color blindness, racist discrimination as market choices."[11] "Antagonistic sports fandom," the media scholar Thomas Oates calls it.[12] The gift allowed ESPN to serve as an outlet for color-blind racial resentment but with some of the edges of talk radio sanded down. To call Vick gifted but raw, as the ESPN draft team did, was to suggest that the Falcons and their fans had given him something – an unearned chance at the big time – for which he now owed them a return on investment. Years before his indictment on dogfighting charges, the network had furnished fans with the language with which to react: Vick had wasted his gift.

Liberals could watch and see something else in the gifted athlete. The media historian Victoria Johnson identifies melodrama as "sports TV's defining narrative and aesthetic mode," and Travis Vogan suggests that ESPN has often leaned into multicultural stories of racism overcome and barriers broken to inflect the network's "culture with culture," setting it a brow above neighboring channels.[13] A liberal fan might have watched the 2001 NFL draft and dwelled not on Kiper's and Theismann's takes but on the scene of Vick backstage hugging his mother, Brenda, who was living in a too-small apartment in Newport News, Virginia, with her second husband and Michael's siblings. Vick had said he would move his mother into a nice house when he received his signing bonus, and he did. The twenty-year-old had received more than he deserved for throwing a football, sure, the liberal fan might say, but it was good to see him get his shot, and he would be sharing his gifts with Atlanta. "This guy connects with a young generation of fans," Mortensen said of Vick at the draft. "Atlanta needed something inspirational, and [the Falcons front office] provided it."[14] The color-blind fan condemned athletes identified as gifted for either wasting their talent or not being grateful enough for what they'd received. The liberal fan celebrated them as testaments to a meritocratic athlete market and for contributing their gifts to team and nation. Neither doubted, as they talked around the clock of God-given talent, that the gifted athlete owed a debt to the fan watching at home.[15]

ESPN had given your dad something to talk about. But it had gotten the rest of us talking as well. "If someone surreptitiously took everything but ESPN from my cable television package," the conservative columnist George Will wrote in 1994, "it might be months before I noticed."[16] If Will had taken a moment to scan all the unwatched channels, he would have discovered more of the same: commentators talking and talking and talking about business, celebrities, music, and food, as well as, perhaps, himself, offering his take on the midterm elections. ESPN, as media historians have chronicled, built the cable business on consumers' unsatiable desire to see their favorite teams. This was the kind of content for which consumers, then accustomed to free, advertising-subsidized television, would shell out.[17] But live broadcasting rights for can't-miss games were more than the ESPN of 1980 could afford. (Darts and reruns of last week's games were, it discovered, can-miss television.) The network, with a limited budget and twenty-four hours to fill, struck on a solution: Roll the cameras, and let them talk. The format, which network founder Bill Rasmussen borrowed from radio, turned commentators like Berman, Keith Olbermann, and Dan Patrick into stars who sometimes overshadowed the athletes they covered. (Executives, who butted heads with Olbermann from the time he arrived at the network in 1992, often worried that they might also overshadow ESPN.)[18] Other cable networks noticed, and before long they were all talking about the stock market, real estate, Congress, and coconut macaroons like it was last night's Yankees game.

Media scholars argue that, as our encounters with teams and athletes become ever more mediated, we ought to be thinking in terms not of "sport and media" but "sport as media" or of sports as a "media genre."[19] But the rise to dominance of the TV commentator through ESPN and then on to Bloomberg, Bravo, CNBC, CNN, the Food Network, Fox News, MSNBC, MTV, and VH1 tells a different story, not of sports as media but of media as sports. (In the 2000s, reality TV would also borrow the low-cost, high-talk formula.) Now ESPN vies with Fox News (ESPN for conservative news consumers) and MSNBC (ESPN for liberals) to be the highest-rated basic cable channel. "It was the last hurrah for the press," Frank Deford remembered of covering the NBA before cable and the internet. "After that, it became the media."[20]

In 2003, after a stint at Fox Sports, Olbermann launched an hour-long news show with MSNBC, *Countdown with Keith Olbermann*. The

Washington Post announced that it would go "head-to-head" with Fox News's *The O'Reilly Factor*.[21] The media columnist Jack Schafer declared it "*SportsCenter* for News Junkies."[22] For the next ten years, Olbermann delivered "special comments" and debated, with a rotating cast of guests, the Bush administration's wars in the Middle East, government failure in New Orleans before and after Hurricane Katrina, and the election of the first Black president of the United States. It was, he acknowledged, as if he'd never left his desk in Bristol.

The Entertainment and Sports Programming Network launched on September 7, 1979, with a double-header of men's softball games. "Yea, verily, a sampler of wonders," host Lee Leonard said, doing his best to sell the thin offerings. "Now softball is one of those rare sports that everybody knows something about. Why? Because we all play it on Sunday when we drink a little beer."[23] Leonard sat in a folding chair. The beige wall behind him was decorated with line drawings of athletes. It looked like he was sitting inside a Pee-Chee. The Bristol studio, still under construction, lacked running water. For the first month, Leonard and the crew had to use the porta-potties in the mud lot outside. After signing the largest-ever cable advertising contract with Anheuser-Busch, the networked debuted that night with two games featuring a team named for one of the brewer's biggest competitors, the Milwaukee Schlitz. A live interview with the head football coach of the University of Colorado aired without audio. An estimated 30,000 households tuned in. "It was a technical nightmare," the vice president of programming remembered. "Everything was fucked." Leonard, a veteran of NBC Sports, admitted that the executives "didn't really know what they were doing" and that "there was no way they were ready to go on the air."[24] But they did. And they gathered at the Holiday Inn in Plainville, Connecticut, to light cigars and drink champagne. "Here's to you, sports junkies," Rasmussen declared. "Rejoice!"[25]

Rasmussen, a former local TV host, took his own star turn in the first hour of ESPN's maiden broadcast. Standing on a boom lift beside two giant satellite dishes, Rasmussen described how they and an RCA satellite over the Pacific allowed a half-baked network in central Connecticut to reach 1.4 million homes throughout the United States. "Years ago, tales of Jules Verne and Buck Rogers were made of dreams and wild bits of imagination," he said. "Today, modern technology has taken those dreams and that imagination and turned it into a reality that allows us to bring a television picture into your home via satellite."[26]

Rasmussen had the invention of cable and satellite television to thank for ESPN, but cable and satellite had football and boxing to thank for their markets. In 1947, an appliance store owner in northeastern Arkansas named James Yates Davidson learned that a Tennessee radio station had received a license to launch one of the first television stations in the South. Davidson, a tinkerer who had served in communications for the Navy during World War II, knew that the signal wouldn't reach his small town, a hundred miles away, and that he couldn't sell television sets without television stations in the area. But he had an idea. He built a one-hundred-foot antenna tower next to his store and then offered to run cable lines from his antenna to residents' homes for an installation fee of $150 and a recurring service charge of $3 a month. He struggled to attract customers until he decided to install a cable to the American Legion Hall for the broadcast of a 1948 football game between Ole Miss and Tennessee, which the Rebels won 16–13. After the game, Davidson couldn't run cable fast enough, and before long he was building antennas and installing cable across the state. The fee and charges were high, but who could afford to miss the Vols game?

Satellite TV borrowed Davidson's scheme. In 1975, the new Home Box Office announced that it would shift from microwave to satellite transmission, making the network, then limited to the Northeast, available across the nation. Providers balked at the cost. Downlink receiver dishes could run as much as $100,000, and no one knew if customers, not yet accustomed to a basic-cable bill, would be willing to fork over an extra $10 a month for a single channel. HBO bought the rights to Muhammad Ali and Joe Frazier's third and final bout, the "Thrilla in Manila," and installed three receivers itself in the Southeast. Demand for HBO increased after the fight, a fourteen-round technical knockout for Ali, and satellite transmission took off. The receivers would be there when a former radio and TV newsman from Connecticut had an idea for his own channel. Football games and fights didn't earn the ratings of *Dallas* or *M*A*S*H*, at least not at first, but they attracted obsessives, the kind of consumers who would give Davidson $150 to run a cable to their homes or call to demand HBO in their area.

Rasmussen discovered what Davidson and HBO executives had before him. He liked to tell interviewers that he and his son had formulated the idea for ESPN while stuck in a traffic jam in a Mazda sedan without air conditioning outside Waterbury, Connecticut, in the summer of 1978. But Rasmussen had been testing the ESPN model for years in local radio and TV. From the early 1960s to the mid-1970s, he had hosted free-ranging shows, first on AM radio in Amherst, Massachusetts, where he covered UMass football and basketball, then on an NBC affiliate in nearby Springfield. At the TV station, he did shows twice a night – one at dinnertime, the second after eleven. "I mixed [highlights from local] sports, hockey broadcasts, and a variety of miscellaneous broadcasting adventures into the brewing experience pot from which ESPN ultimately evolved," he later wrote.[27] Rasmussen had learned from his time in local broadcasting how to fill hours with affordable, entertaining content that attracted regulars: you talked, about whatever. He did news as well. "Sports hosts talk politics. Politics hosts talk sports," as one radio producer later said. "A hot take is a hot take is a hot take."[28] Leonard would leave ESPN for CNN, where he'd host a news talk show. The conservative shock jock Rush Limbaugh would later join ESPN as an NFL commentator. Unlike the rights to broadcast an event, talk cost nothing, and it allowed audiences to form a bond with hosts that they never could with straight broadcasters. The radio and TV veteran knew that he couldn't build a network on men's softball. He had to build it on the chatter around the game.

Bill Rasmussen on the cover of the September 1979 issue of *Connecticut* magazine. From Hearst Magazine Media.

Some of that chatter, Rasmussen realized, would have to be about race. In 1965, after moving to the Springfield TV station, he met Muhammad Ali, then training in the neighboring town of Chicopee. Rasmussen recognized in Ali a new kind of athlete – bold, magnetic, conscious of his racial significance to Black and white fans. Ali liked something Rasmussen said at a media luncheon and, at least according to Rasmussen, invited the young TV host on a half-hour walk, in which they talked about "boxing, the state of black America, and press conferences." Rasmussen asked the fighter if he ever got tired of mugging for the camera. "It's about having fun," Ali told him. The interaction left Rasmussen wondering why, as he later told the journalist Michael Freeman, he "had met few black athletes [and not] pontificated much on the radio or television about sports and race."[29] Rasmussen had a similar reaction to the arrival of Julius Erving at UMass in 1968, observing how Dr. J had made the game more "entertaining and saleable."[30] Fans bought tickets because the team won but also to see Erving soar through the air. Black athletes had made a bout or a game more fun and, amid civil rights and Black Power, more worth talking about, Rasmussen thought, and he wondered whether there might be something for him in that talk.

Rasmussen's account of how Ali and Erving motivated him to found ESPN seems odd when considering the audience that the network first courted. "Pitch the rich," a 1979 advertisement in the trade magazine *Broadcasting* declared. "Reach affluent 18–34 year old men 7 days a week on the new ESPN Total-Sports Network." The ad boasted that more than half of ESPN viewer households had incomes of more than $50,000, that a third owned stocks, bonds, and mutual funds, and that more than eight out of ten served wine more than once a week. "If you've got the spots, we've got the sports."[31] The *Wall Street Journal*, the tennis ball manufacturer Penn, and Hilton Hotels were among the network's first advertisers. The *Pittsburgh Courier* criticized ESPN in 1981 for all but ignoring Black colleges and universities in the network's fall football schedule. "ESPN Blacks Out Black Colleges," the headline stated.[32] Rasmussen envisioned his Entertainment and Sports Programming Network covering a certain kind of athlete and selling that coverage to a certain kind of consumer: someone with a little extra income and, well, kind of like himself. When the network broadcast a football game between Florida A&M and the University of Miami in 1979 – making A&M the one HBCU to receive airtime in the network's first two years – it sought to serve the alumni not of the former but of the latter.[33]

The ESPN founder was fond of Ali and Erving but intuited that it didn't matter whether the network's viewers liked them. "Hate or dislike," the media scholar and historian of fan cultures Jonathan Gray writes, "can be just as powerful as can a strong and admiring, affective relationship." ESPN catered to the fan as well as the "antifan," as Gray calls the hatewatcher.[34] It sought the viewer who loved Ali and the one who thought he was a menace and would, waving a hand at the screen, announce it to friends at the bar and in the living room. In time, the network would seat them, the fan and the antifan, on a set together and let them argue it out until the next live event.[35]

If ESPN commentators modeled how to be a fan, they also suggested who could be a fan. Greg Gumbel, whom the network hired in 1979, admitted to James Andrew Miller and Tom Shales, in their best-selling book about the network, *Those Guys Have All the Fun*, that ESPN needed him because it didn't then have a single broadcaster of color on staff. Executives knew, he said, that the contrast between the talent on the field and in the studio could damage the network's image with advertisers as well as cable subscribers, including white subscribers. ("Now I'm awfully quick to point out that that's not the reason why they keep you," he added, and Gumbel remained with the network for ten years before moving to CBS.)[36] A longtime organizational consultant for ESPN wrote that he had long held "doubts about pushing diversity" in Bristol. "Sometimes it seems a little too PC for my taste," he said.[37] In the late 1990s, NAACP president Kweisi Mfume accused the network of an "outright denial of opportunity" to Black people.[38] Mfume wasn't seeing things; ESPN, though seeking a much wider audience by then, had long sold racial comfort to a core audience of viewers who, as their advertisers imagined them, subscribed to the *Wall Street Journal* and bought Penn tennis balls.

The more I learned about ESPN, the more I came to believe that *Those Guys Have All the Fun* is among the best and most accurate titles I've ever encountered. Miller and Shales, who seem to admire the network and the people who built it, do little editorializing; transcripts of longform interviews constitute almost the entire book. But it reads like a horror show of sexual harassment and intimidation. ESPN general counsel Andy Brilliant recalled a time when he and other executives competed to hire the best-looking female assistant, adding, "I must say, mine was the best by far; she was absolutely drop-dead gorgeous."[39] And that's the network's general counsel! "I know it's quite sexist," one VP told Miller and Shales, "but when you have a pretty girl around the office, it's a little bit happier than having an ugly girl."[40] Karie Ross, who joined ESPN as an anchor in 1987, making her the third female on-air talent at the network, remembered her coworkers turning on the Playboy Channel next to her desk and then standing around to see her reaction. She later stood during an all-hands meeting in the Bristol cafeteria and condemned what she described as a culture of harassment. "After I finished, you could hear a pin drop," she said. When Miller and Shales asked Berman about the meeting, the network's lead anchor remarked, "Karie was right, I'm sure of that. I liked her. She was a great-looking woman; still is, the last time I saw her."[41] You'd think the media would have received some media training.

Rasmussen didn't last long at the network he founded – other execs forced him out in 1980 – but, for a twelve-month stretch in the late 1970s, he made one brilliant move after another. He secured use of the RCA satellite Satcom 1 right before the cable gold rush (Disney, Time Inc., and Warner Brothers all called RCA soon after, and CNN founder Ted Turner would sue RCA for use of the satellite), convinced Getty Oil to invest $10 million in a nonexistent cable channel, and signed a deal with the NCAA to broadcast football and basketball games for next to nothing. But ABC and NBC still had first dibs on the best college games, which left ESPN airing lesser contests or rebroadcasting games that ABC or NBC had carried live. It needed something to distinguish itself from the terrestrial networks, and Rasmussen, the radio man and twice-a-night TV host, knew what it would be.

"Now, here's another innovation on ESPN," Leonard said in the network's first minutes on the air, "and it's going to be a big part of our future: the SportsCenter with George Grande." The camera then turned to Grande, who, seated behind a giant slab of a desk, announced that this – he patted the desk – "the SportsCenter," would be the channel's hub: "If it takes an interview, we'll do it. If it takes play-by-play, we'll do it. If it takes commentary, we'll do that too."[42] Without the resources to bid for the rights to broadcast the Rose Bowl or the World Series, ESPN turned to highlights and observation and, in time, transformed Grande's desk into one of the biggest brands in television. "Bristol Hits the Big League in Sports TV," a *New York Times* headline read.[43] "Too much of a good thing can be wonderful," the *Boston Globe* wrote.[44] Another journalist mused that ESPN investors must have "extrasensory perception and supernatural insight."[45] Their admiration was not for the network's Australian rules football or NCAA reruns but for a new form of talk – and before long, Satcom 1, hovering 20,000 miles above the Pacific, would be beaming to Earth almost nothing else.

As it matured, ESPN cultivated an identifiable voice that a growing universe of media would imitate. With around-the-clock events and shows, it stitched together once-isolated seasonal rituals into a buffet of highlight reels and stats that Berman and others overlaid with knowledgeable, irreverent narration. The anchors, with a fleet of writers and researchers, discussed last night's game as casual fans wished they could but with an off-the-cuff demeanor that suggested to viewers that perhaps they could do what Berman did and that others would want to listen. The ESPN tone – smart but never too serious, journalistic but entertaining, invested but at a slight remove – facilitated what Rasmussen had imagined when he met Ali and watched Dr. J at UMass: TV that could entice viewers with the racial significance of athletes while deflecting it, that could be about race and not about race, that could go there and then insist that it hadn't. It's just a game, man. Relax.

Not every viewer idolized Berman, of course. A consumer can be critical of the thing consumed. ESPN's trick was that the network's signature ironic distance let us all believe that we were the critical consumer. We were in on the joke. We knew it was all for fun. But the commentator also taught us where and how to read race in an age of color blindness and multiculturalism. Who had gifts you couldn't teach? Who had grit you had to earn? Who owed the fan? And whom did the fan owe? We could learn to draw the line ourselves at the commentator's Super Bowl, the NFL draft.

On April 29, 1980, the new network took out an ad in the *New York Times*: "Watch the NFL Draft *Live* Only on ESPN." Some diehards with cable tuned in to hear from the "live on-the-scene announcers" stationed in the drab ballroom of the New York Sheraton Hotel.[46] Most fans did not. Nielsen didn't rate the broadcast. But 1.7 million watched in 1988. Then 2.5 million in 1993 and 31 million in 2004 – all to see the network's commentators talk and talk and talk about athletes' bodies and character and market value.[47]

The National Football League first added a draft in 1936. The Philadelphia Eagles had finished a league-worst 2–9 in the 1934 season, and team owner Bert Bell, unable to attract the talent of the better financed Chicago Bears, Green Bay Packers, and New York Giants, recommended a college draft in which teams would select in the inverse order of their finish the season before. "Gentlemen," he said at the 1935 spring meetings, "I've always had the theory that football is like a chain. The league is no stronger than its weakest link – and I've been a weak link for so long that I should know."[48] Bell, who would later serve as league commissioner from 1946 to 1959, wanted, he said, good, hard-fought games, not blowouts. He wanted to sell tickets, and he didn't want to see fans heading for the exits at halftime and never returning. The other owners wanted to check rising salaries, and a draft would force the best college seniors to negotiate with just one team – take it or leave it, kid. The owners met at the Ritz-Carlton Hotel in Philadelphia, where Bell, doing little to strengthen his weak link, traded the rights to the first pick to Bears owner George Halas, who selected Heisman Trophy winner Jay Berwanger of the University of Chicago. When the *Chicago Tribune* interviewed Berwanger, a halfback, the next week, the UChicago senior said, "I believe the decision at Philadelphia last Saturday means the Chicago club has an option on my services if I decide to play pro football."[49] He decided against it, taking a then more lucrative job as a foam rubber salesman while coaching on the side. Bell didn't manage to sign any of his draft picks, and the Eagles finished the 1936 season 1–11.[50] He would later, as commissioner, coin the phrase "on any given Sunday" ("on any given Sunday, any team in the NFL can win"), which was true, unless you were Bell's own Eagles.[51]

When Chet Simmons called Pete Rozelle in 1980 about televising the NFL draft on his no-name cable channel, little about the event itself had changed since Berwanger chose the rubber business over the Chicago Bears. "There's nobody there," the producer of the first draft told Simmons when he learned of his assignment. "It's just a bunch of people on the phone."[52] The owners didn't get it either, refusing to authorize ESPN's broadcast for fear that agents would dominate a televised draft. Rozelle advised Simmons to cover it as a news event, and Simmons obliged, announcing a month before the event, "We are happy to televise a news event of this magnitude to our more than 4,000,000 subscribers."[53] The network stationed twenty-five-year-old anchor Bob Ley at the Bristol studio and Grande, the original *SportsCenter* host, at the Sheraton. Grande welcomed the audience to "a history-making day, not only for television but for the National Football League as well."[54] A digital clock in the left-hand corner of the screen ticked down from 13:34, marking the time, like a bomb in a crime thriller, until the Detroit Lions would make the first pick (running back Billy Simms of the University of Oklahoma). Ley and Grande traded airtime for the next twelve hours, with three others, including Berman, who conducted interviews on the ballroom floor with team officials and New York Jets fans more than willing to share their takes.

Simmons might have framed the 1980 NFL draft as news, but it functioned as the ultimate cross-promotional event, introducing college football fans to the NFL, NFL fans to college football, and all fans to ESPN. The network was not there to hold the league accountable. It was there to sell it, while associating the NFL's brand with ESPN's. The idea that it wasn't – that ESPN was an autonomous news organization with a code of standards and ethics – made the arrangement all the more lucrative. "The draft put us in business with the NFL, and that was huge," Simmons later said. Ley called it the network's "first step into the big time."⁵⁵ The NFL moved the draft from Tuesday–Wednesday to Sunday–Monday in 1988 to cater to ESPN's growing audience, and ESPN added year-round scouting and mock drafting for a contingent of superfans known as draftniks.

ESPN created an audience for the NFL draft, and fascination with the draft led to increased interest in how teams evaluated talent. Scouting organizations held the first centralized combines in 1982 and merged them into one event, the NFL scouting combine, in 1985. Commentators and draft watchers could now assess for themselves athletes' 40-yard dash, 20-yard shuttle, hand size, arm length, height, weight, vertical, and, with the dubious results of the Wonderlic test, intelligence. "Imagine being told to strip to your shorts. You stand in a line of other men, also almost naked," linebacker Tim Green remembered of the 1986 combine. "The line advances slowly toward the front of the room where, one by one, the men are weighed and measured with the cold efficiency of a slaughterhouse."⁵⁶ A scout wrote "LB" (linebacker) and a number with a fat black marker on the back of his hand. No one called him by his name for the rest of the day. He was his number. Green is white, but most of the men being measured and weighed with him were Black, and it didn't take much imagination to recognize other, historical associations. "It's dehumanizing, but it's necessary," Giants GM George Young said at the 1989 combine. "If we're going to pay a kid a lot of money to play football, we have a right to find out as much as we can. If we're going to buy 'em, we ought to see what we're buying."⁵⁷ Unlike the draft, the NFL did not allow a TV crew at the combine until 2004. Was this for the good of the athletes? For the scouts? Or had it read Young's words and known better than to allow him in front of a camera with hundreds of shirtless Black men?

The NFL also limited writers' access to the combine, and the ones who got in tended to interview white athletes who could laugh about walking around in their underwear before a bunch of middle-aged men in khakis. "I felt like a prize bull at the county fair," one remarked after the 1989 draft. "I have a big ass and a big belly. I suck in my gut, but it never does any good. It just makes a big crease in my belly."[58] Black athletes also joked about the combine – what else are you going to do as a twenty-two-year-old without a contract? – but registered their discomfort about holding out their arms for white men to measure. Keyshawn Johnson, the first overall pick in the 1996 draft and a future ESPN commentator, described the combine as a "whacked process" that seemed to serve no function other than to degrade college athletes who, with nothing in the bank and no alternative league, had no recourse. "I felt more like I was being prepped for a transplant than for pro football," he wrote in his 1997 memoir.[59] Johnson's $6.5 million signing bonus didn't allow him to forget his status as a 6-foot-3, 220-pound, 23.9-year-old asset in the market of athletic bodies.

Johnson dwelled on his interactions with scouts and his contract negotiations with the New York Jets, but it wasn't lost on him that, by 1996, they were no longer the main audience for all the timing and testing. The draft was entertainment for the millions of cable subscribers who had been tracking and debating the wide receiver's value as if they'd be making the call for the Jets. Should the team have taken a running back? Or another receiver, the smaller but faster Marvin Harrison? Was he worth it? Johnson had starred at USC, earning MVP honors at the 1995 Cotton Bowl and the 1996 Rose Bowl. He was used to the limelight. But the draft was, he acknowledged, something else. He felt surveilled. The surveillance was racialized – it doesn't take more than one visit to an NFL stadium to notice a difference between the watchers and the watched – but also racializing. Surveillance, as the sociologist Simone Browne writes, reflects but also creates social norms. Benedict Anderson observed that the "simultaneous consumption" of the news and the novel was an essential ingredient in the formation of modern national communities, his "imagined communities."[60] Browne adds that one thing news readers consumed together were fugitive slave ads, which, she suggests, formed a sense of national belonging through the collective surveillance of the enslaved. The NFL scouting combine is not, as some critics suggest, a slave block, but it also relies on a form of surveillance to construct social boundaries, form communities, and assess, in cold numbers, human value. There were white athletes at the combine and Black fans who followed the draft. Johnson could see the color line, but it had, after civil rights, blurred. Front offices and fans were there to measure his gift and determine what he owed the game and them. Johnson retired from the NFL in 2007 and, setting aside whatever discomfort he had felt in 1996, joined ESPN's draft team as a commentator.

ESPN subscribers had known Johnson's value long before contract time because of Kiper, the network's fulltime, year-round draft analyst. Kiper, a Baltimore native with tall, combed-back hair, had assembled his first end-to-end draft guide as a high school senior in 1979 and mailed it to every team in the NFL, asking for their feedback. He received amused letters from a few assistant GMs. He did it again the next year and felt validated watching ESPN's inaugural broadcast of the NFL draft from a Baltimore Colts event in the Inner Harbor. "There's got to be a market for this," he thought.[61] One hundred and thirty fellow draft enthusiasts bought his guide in 1981, 860 in 1982. ESPN brought him on in 1984, and he and his "big board," a term borrowed from the New York Stock Exchange, never left. A 1992 account of his rise to football-nerd fame described his audience as men "just like him – fanatics, obsessives, Rotisserie League wheeler-dealers, couch potatoes who get cable and satellite dishes to watch coaches' shows," men who "clog the lines of call-in radio shows and never tire of talking, talking, talking about sports," know-it-alls for whom "Kiper is both their guru and their apotheosis."[62] Kiper – six-foot-one, 195 pounds, Essex Community College – never harbored a dream to wear the uniform of his hometown Colts. He was living his dream, and a lot of people discovered, watching him, that they shared it.

Chris Berman (*left*) and Mel Kiper (*center*) at the 1987 NFL draft. Photograph by Paul Spinelli. From AP Photo.

Kiper and his fellow commentators framed the draft as a managerial challenge, allowing viewers to forget that scouting served not to reward talent but to extract it at the lowest cost. In 2017, political scientists at Penn State wrote in the *Washington Post* that their research had revealed "substantial racial differences in the language used to describe quarterback prospects." The draft evaluation for a Black quarterback had a much greater chance, they found, of including words like "weight," "big," and "frame" than the evaluation for a white quarterback of identical size.[63] The researchers determined that racial biases in how scouts framed combine results led to a "market inefficiency" in which "minority quarterbacks provide more value than expected, while white quarterbacks provide less than expected."[64] In the *Post*, they wrote about Deshaun Watson, who would be drafted twelfth overall by the Houston Texans and had been billed as a "tremendous athlete" with "big, strong hands" who could be "baited into bad-decision interceptions."[65] The researchers wanted a fair evaluation and draft number (and associated signing bonus) for Watson. But "market inefficiency" is the language of management, and signing athletes who "provide more value than expected" is a general manager's job. Racism in scouting comes across, against the authors' intentions, as, above all, something that smart GMs can use to their advantage.

In televising the 1980 draft, ESPN launched the era, our era, of managerial fandom. Who would you take at number one? Could you detect market inefficiencies? Valuable assets in the later rounds? Gil Brandt, the head scout for the Dallas Cowboys from 1960 to 1988, noticed how ESPN changed NFL fandom at the end of his career. "I think people don't know and understand what a 3-technique is or understand play calling," he said, "but they do think they can be general managers, and they say, 'Hey, why didn't this guy get drafted?'"[66] Fans had dreamed of being Roger Staubach and then, after ESPN brought the draft into their homes, some decided they'd rather be Brandt. The historians David Roediger and Elizabeth Esch argue that race management structured the formation of management science in the United States by introducing two enduring strategies: "racial competition" and "race development," the setting of one class of workers against another and the assurance that all could, through labor and sacrifice, advance as a class.[67] Sports leagues and franchises have used the management strategies that Roediger and Esch describe but also, with an assist from ESPN and an army of commentators, turned management itself into entertainment. Brandt didn't think that the new ESPN-watching, management-minded fans knew what they were talking about, and most didn't, but the network let them dream of trading in football bodies.

Movie studios took note. Management, once the villain in films like *The Natural* and *Eight Men Out*, took heroic form in *Moneyball*, the 2011 adaptation of the Michael Lewis bestseller, and the 2014 front-office drama *Draft Day*, in which Kevin Costner stars as the beleaguered GM of the Cleveland Browns. *Draft Day* borrows the structure of ESPN's draft broadcasts, beginning with a ticking clock ("12:55:48 ... until the Draft begins") and a voice-over from Chris Berman ("A day where lives are changed, fates are decided, dynasties are born").[68] The film culminates with Costner's character taking over the team's war room and executing a series of ingenious trades, assembling a low-cost, high-talent roster while making the dreams of two young Black men come true. The owner shakes his hand. His girlfriend (Jennifer Garner) gives him admiring looks. His mother tells him that his late father would have been proud of him. *Draft Day* was not a blockbuster, but it made almost $30 million at the box office. Not bad for a football movie with no football.

In ESPN's draft coverage, race was subtext. Elsewhere, it was the text. In the late 1990s, around the time the network added ESPN Classic, a channel dedicated to archival games and documentaries, it began testing a new tone that was more Aaron Sorkin than David Letterman. "As we approach the 21st Century where else can you find *anything* that knows no economic boundaries?" Berman said at the time. "Athletes, and certainly sports fans, are men and women, old and young, white and black. A millionaire and someone on welfare could have an intelligent discussion about yesterday's ballgame. Try that with any other subject."[69] In 1997, the network borrowed *Nightline* anchor Ted Koppel from ABC to moderate a live "town meeting" on race. The forum, held at Howard University and marking fifty years since Jackie Robinson's MLB debut, wasted no time in establishing Koppel's race cred. It began with the infamous interview he had conducted with Los Angeles Dodgers general manager Al Campanis in 1987 in which Campanis had attributed the lack of Black managers in Major League Baseball to Black people lacking "some of the necessities" for management. "That sounds like the same kind of garbage we were hearing forty years ago about players," Koppel had responded. "That really sounds like garbage."[70] The Dodgers had fired Campanis thirty-six hours later, and Koppel received praise for his handling of the interview and, ten years on, a call from

Bristol. ESPN, known for manic highlights and frat-boy gags, needed him for a rebrand.

Onstage, below giant images of Robinson swinging, sliding, and celebrating with his Dodgers teammates, Koppel welcomed the panelists – all men, five Black, four white – to reflect on "how far we have come" since 1947. Most, like media-trained athletes, said that sports had come far but not far enough. Harry Edwards, a regular at forums of this kind, refused the framing. "We have to remember that sport is going to be exactly and precisely where society is," he said. "People get the kind of sports institution that they support and that they deserve." Koppel, reenacting his role from the Campanis interview, asked MLB legal consultant Clifford Alexander to account for the continued absence of Black general and field managers in the league. The owner of the Arizona Diamondbacks had canceled at the last minute, and MLB had sent Alexander, a Black former secretary of the army, to fill in. "It pains me to have a black lawyer to answer questions that should be addressed to white owners," Koppel said. Alexander, dodging, redirected the newsman to the other leagues' also terrible record on front-office hiring. When a Black woman in the audience, an athlete at George Washington University, stood and asked why the forum didn't include any women, Koppel's answer – limited time, the state of the industry "as it is," not as "it should be" – earned him boos from the audience.[71] The event was a mess. It ran long. It lacked focus. It made Koppel, the leagues, and most of the panelists look bad. (The D-backs owner, Jerry Colangelo, was wise to duck it.) The town meeting had one winner: the network televising it. "First, no-brainer kudos: give ESPN credit," *USA Today* said of the town meeting, calling it "substantive" and a "welcome detour" from the shallowness of the usual fare.[72] ESPN managed, with a distinguished news anchor as host and an HBCU as setting, to situate itself above the racial drama of the leagues it covered and with which it did business, an enlightened venue for substantive talk.

NBA star Chris Webber, the one nonretired athlete onstage, noticed. Sonny Vaccaro, the marketing executive most famous for signing Michael Jordan to his first sneaker deal with Nike, told Koppel that he thought it was "incumbent upon people like Chris and Michael" to take a stand for the hiring of more Black coaches. Us? Webber asked. What about the people who own the teams and hire the coaches? What about media organizations that had broadcasting deals with the leagues and treated their owners with kid gloves? When the conversation turned to Black athletes leaving college early for the NBA, as Webber had after two seasons at Michigan, he reminded the audience that criticism of him and others didn't come out of nowhere but from organizations like the one then mediating his words. "They aren't Black writers writing these stories. They aren't Black people commentating shows like this," Webber, then twenty-three, said. "We don't have the power yet."[73] Vaccaro wanted to remind Webber that his athletic talent carried a social debt, and Webber told him that he had it backward; the NBA and ESPN owed him. Koppel continued asking the panel about the lack of Black GMs and coaches, but no one wanted to address Webber's observation that perhaps the organization staging the event was neither neutral nor blameless. In the first minutes of the forum and twice more, Koppel acknowledged that "nothing was going to change because of anything that was said" on the program.[74] Then why have it? Because talk sells. It sells cable packages and ads and, at the first ESPN town meeting on race, an image of civic engagement.

The town meeting showed ESPN straining to reach a wider audience. Though it had once seen a subscriber base of affluent white men as an asset, the network now recognized it as a limitation. It didn't want to be cast as entertainment for the aging white male boomer. It didn't want to be your father's TV channel. Chasing younger fans, the network had launched ESPN2, "the Deuce," in 1993. Resident wiseass Olbermann, in leather jacket, led a show called *SportsNight*. "Good evening, and welcome to the end of our careers," he said on the first episode. Former MTV host "Downtown" Julie Brown interviewed fans at bars as well as young athletes about their lives off the field. The channel had a graffiti logo and more anchors of color and women anchors than the original ESPN. In the first hour of the channel's debut, Brown chatted with a bewildered MC Hammer about the "sports things he likes" and delivered trivia (which NFL team drafted Bo Jackson?) in sunglasses. When Berman made a cameo, a caption announced, "He's not one of us."[75] Hosts traded their ties for T-shirts and denim. Skateboarding and BMX received airtime. One reviewer described the new channel as "a bunch of middle-aged guys pretending to be young and a bunch of white guys pretending to be black."[76] "The problem about the birth of ESPN2," one host remembered, "was, you can't try to be hip; either you are or you aren't."[77]

Network executives had to agree, and ESPN2 would, over time, shed the Gen-X aesthetic and come to serve as a channel for ESPN's leftover content. But the network continued to court a younger, multiracial audience, including with, it thought, the 1997 town meeting. The meeting had caught the attention of the Clinton White House, which had, that

June, launched the One America Initiative, a fifteen-month program intended to foster "a constructive national dialogue" on race through a series of televised forums and the circulation of a conversation guidebook.[78] The administration reached out to ESPN about holding a second town meeting, this time with the president of the United States as moderator, and the network agreed. President Clinton introduced the event by thanking ESPN "for doing this for a second time." Bob Ley, who had cohosted the first NFL draft on ESPN and now anchored *Outside the Lines*, followed by asking Jim Brown and John Thompson about the "temperature of race in sports."[79] Clinton, then embroiled in the scandal over his affair with White House intern Monica Lewinsky, receded into the background. He had found the ideal venue for his talking solution. ESPN had done this before.

Keyshawn Johnson, then going into his third season with the Jets, took over Webber's role as the one nonretired athlete invited and the most insightful media critic. When Ley asked him about the internal segregation of football rosters, referencing Jason Sehorn, a rare white cornerback, Johnson threw it back at him. "It comes from the media," he said. "I think that's where it starts, because back a while ago, the media points and targets certain athletes at certain positions. Most running backs are African American; most quarterbacks are white; most cornerbacks are African American, except Jason." Two years after going number one in the NFL draft, Johnson reminded Ley of the meat market that ESPN had turned into mass entertainment. All year, fans could listen to draft analysts talk about who looked like an NFL cornerback. Ley then turned to the audience, from which a young man, introducing himself as the vice president of his high school class, asked whether the belief that Black athletes "are physically equipped better" than white athletes constituted a form of antiwhite discrimination. Jim Brown almost fell out of his chair. We are "really not getting to the point," he said.[80]

But not getting to the point was the point. ESPN had built the cable business by demonstrating that talk could be lucrative, cost-effective entertainment and enshrined the idea, shared by Terry Gross and Rush Limbaugh, Rachel Maddow and Bill O'Reilly, that it was good for us. Conclusions were anathema to the commentator. (Imagine all the content lost if we could say that Jordan was greater than LeBron and move on.) Had President Clinton brought his national dialogue on race to ESPN? Or had ESPN brought it to him?

ESPN's second town meeting was smoother than the first. But the network and Clinton's team might have regretted inviting Thompson, who didn't hold back. Thompson on inclusion: "A lot of people [were] able to participate in the cotton field." Thompson on the lack of Black coaches: We allow for "a hell of a lot of white failing." When an audience member, another high school student, asked why Black athletes should be admitted to selective universities and colleges over nonathlete white students with higher test scores, Thompson, after a long, cautious answer from the president, said, "I think I need to bring to his attention that the athlete is not the only one that gets special preference. If your folks have a lot of money, you get special preference in university. If you are a son or daughter of an alumnus, you get special preference." Why, Thompson asked, do we see the admission advantage that an athlete receives as an institutional gift and other forms of advantage, including wealth, as earned? "Our society," he added, "is about special preference."[81] Sports, including college sports, have often served to draw the line between the advantages we deem legitimate and the ones we consider unfair, unearned, given. Thompson coached at Georgetown, the president's alma mater and then the thirteenth most selective school in the nation, and he'd heard it all.

Ley, looking uncomfortable, announced that they were out of time, but not before Thompson had challenged the premise on which ESPN and the White House had staged the event. Was talk good? Did it, as the president announced in creating his program, "bridge racial divides"?[82] Thompson wasn't convinced. Where Clinton and Ley saw progress, he saw chairs in a circle taking us around and around again.

ESPN continued to host town meetings on race, including one with President Barack Obama in 2016, but it discovered the ideal talk formula in 2001, with the introduction of *Pardon the Interruption*, or *PTI*. The format was straightforward: *Washington Post* colleagues Michael Wilbon and Tony Kornheiser debate the news of the day as a sidebar counts down the seconds remaining for each item and announces what the hosts will discuss next. *PTI* combined the rhetorical dueling of a traditional debate show with lighthearted mischief that showcased the affection that friends Wilbon, who is Black, and Kornheiser, who is white, have for each other – however much they may disagree about a team or a trade. It achieved what the town meetings never could: a feeling of racial reconciliation through dialogue. It let viewers believe that talk could bridge differences not because Wilbon and Kornheiser discussed race but because they almost never did. (President George W. Bush had staffers record the show for him, and his successor, President Obama, was a well-known fan.)[83] "The magic of the show is eleven words," Kornheiser said: "Black guy, white guy, yell at each other, love each other."[84] The magic of the show is race talk without race, a town meeting without the town. White fans worried that Campanis's fate could befall them. Did they know the correct words to use? Would they fumble the interview? Don't worry, ESPN reassured them, we're getting somewhere.[85]

Producer Mark Shapiro, who hired Wilbon and Kornheiser, has said that the idea for *PTI* came to him while watching CNN's news debate show *Crossfire* on the treadmill. "Wait a second, nowhere is debate better than in sports," he thought. "Sports is argument. Why don't we have a show like this?"[86] But Shapiro had it backward. *Crossfire*, which CNN launched in 1982, had learned the value of debate from the channel that led the cable boom, ESPN. It was ESPN for news junkies. ESPN had transformed sports into argument, CNN politics into sports.

CNN founder Ted Turner had, by the time Shapiro declared eureka on the treadmill, been chasing ESPN for a while. In 1996, his Turner Broadcasting merged with Time Warner, and one of his first moves as head of the mammoth cable networks division was to create CNN/SI, a rival channel to ESPN that combined the established brands of his news network and the magazine of Robert Boyle, Frank Deford, and Jack McCallum. Steve Bornstein, the executive who had led the launch of ESPN2, identified CNN/SI as a threat to more than his network's ratings. Of *Sports Illustrated*, James Michener once wrote, "Only *The New Yorker*, among contemporary magazines, has been as effective in sponsoring good writing with a wry touch."[87] Bornstein, not wanting his network to come off as the lowbrow CNN/SI, introduced ESPNews and then bought the Classic Sports Network, renaming it ESPN Classic. He ordered slates of documentaries and hired talent with more traditional backgrounds in broadcast journalism. He hosted forums on race. He teamed with the president of the United States. Michael Eisner, the Disney CEO and Bornstein's boss, called Turner and told him that, whatever it took, ESPN would "bury" CNN/SI.[88]

In 1998, Bornstein and ESPN went on offense. "Next," the first issue of *ESPN The Magazine* announced above the names Kobe, Alex, Kordell, and Eric (Bryant, Rodriguez, Stewart, and Lindros). Eisner acknowledged that it wasn't the time to be founding a magazine. "Our strategic planning division didn't want to go into the magazine business," he said. But he didn't care. He wanted to get even. One VP described the sentiment inside the executive suites as "*we should be attacking them.*"[89]

ESPN wanted to eat *Sports Illustrated*'s lunch, but it didn't seek to convert *SI* readers. It sought to attract teenagers and young adults, the children of *SI* subscribers, with an oversized format and shorter, skimmable stories that mimicked the look and structure of, well, watching ESPN. The media historian Travis Vogan attributes Bornstein's decisions in the mid-1990s, some of which seemed disconnected from the network's immediate financial interests (documentaries? a magazine?), to ESPN's strategic cultivation of a middlebrow aesthetic. It sought to attract viewers who wanted something a cut above – or at least the feeling that they were consuming something a cut above – without alienating viewers who tuned in for the highlights.[90] The magazine served a branding function for the network, but it was also an effort to bring the commentator's take to another medium. The network hired some renowned writers, including a few from *SI*, but the magazine read like a furious tour through the land of TV talk.

The network's greatest success in middlebrow branding came not from the medium but the message: from a liberal, idealistic, semi-intellectual, often historical engagement with race and gender. In 2009, the magazine debuted the annual Body Issue with six alternative covers – three men, three women, three Black, three white – featuring elite athletes in the buff. ESPN's PR team announced it as a "celebration and exploration of the athletic form" that honored "athletes of diverse shapes, sizes, genders and races within the boundaries of taste and frontiers of creativity upon which *ESPN The Magazine* and ESPN have built their reputations."[91] No one could miss that it was a shot at *SI*'s Swimsuit Issue, which had, since 1964, sold soft-core fantasies of size-zero models in bikinis on beaches. The first Body Issue featured golfers, motocross riders, a mixed martial artist, a rock climber, a skier, a stock car racer, the US women's softball team, all naked, their genitals obscured by a hand, a leg, a ball, or a glove. It had a bit of a Noah's ark feel; no race or gender or size would be more naked than the next. It included athletes with disabilities, a pregnant athlete in her third trimester (softball outfielder Jessica Mendoza), as well as athletes whom magazine readers might not otherwise encounter (a sumo wrestler, an ultramarathon runner). Though media scholars would find that the Body Issue, which ran until 2019, when the magazine folded, minimized female athleticism, oversexualized Black women athletes, and cast athletes with disabilities within ableist and heteronormative frameworks, liberal media applauded the diverse and inclusive roster of athletes, and advertisers bought every inch of the issue they could.[92] (The *Times* described the first Body Issue as a rare "bright spot" for the magazine business, as the internet and the recession took their toll on print.)[93] If fans felt weird about ogling athletes' bodies, the magazine reassured them that they shouldn't. As long as the athletes weren't all thin, able-bodied women, then the ogling was good, a gesture of recognition. We had, the issue suggested, not a right but an obligation to look.

Editors knew the criticism they might face. Of assigning the first Body Issue, editor in chief Gary Belsky said, "There's a reality that has to have us thinking about how we represent men versus women, thinking about how we represent men and women of different ethnicities."[94] Belsky's caution shows. Scholars acknowledge that, while something about the whole endeavor might feel off, the issue does not exhibit obvious racial or gender biases. The magazine achieved what one team of researchers called "equality in nudity."[95] But Belsky also assigned Alyssa Roenigk, a staff writer at the magazine, to write a preemptive defense of the issue's handling of women athletes. The executive editor of *Golf World*, learning that three LPGA golfers had agreed to bare it all for the magazine, had written a column in which he worried that the image of the trio naked, leaning against a golf cart, could distract from their athletic achievements. Roenigk countered that the issue allowed the golfers to build their individual brands and "promote a healthy, athletic body ideal" in a media environment saturated with images of model-thin women. "Other magazines show anorexic women and celebrities like Paris Hilton," Sandra Gal, one of the golfers, said. "This is about showing off our athleticism and how fit we have to be to play at this level."[96] The golfers had, Roenigk argued, made a wise business decision that acknowledged that men remained the dominant audience for golf, that men wanted to see beautiful women, and that they were beautiful women. The market doesn't care about fairness, she wrote. "In the real world, ratings and ticket sales – demand for the product – drive all." Roenigk attributed the WNBA's low ratings at the time to the league's failure to cater to male fans watching from home: "The folks in charge look around the bleachers and market a wholesome image to the few thousand fans they see (women, children, families) instead of a more provocative message to the many thousands they don't (men)."[97] The W was, she suggested, too queer for the big time. The Body Issue advocated a brand of neoliberal feminism that comes through in the title of Roenigk's story: "For Sale by Owner." ESPN's announcement of the first Body Issue described athletes' bodies as "their most important asset."[98]

What did the magazine mean in announcing the Body Issue as "diverse"? The word could refer to race, gender, sex, size, age, faith, fame (or lack thereof), and, over eleven annual issues, the list continued to grow. (Did a thoroughbred racehorse, as a nonhuman, count as diverse? In the logic of the Body Issue, perhaps.) The media scholar Jennifer McClearen observes that the Ultimate Fighting Championship, no one's idea of an antiracist or antisexist organization, has leaned into similar stories of difference, defined as an obstacle to athletic success, overcome. UFC, which signed a lucrative media rights deal with ESPN in 2018, "depicts all fighters" – from a queer Black woman to a hetero white man who struggled in school – "as possessing some form of difference," she writes.[99] "Branded difference," as she calls it, structured the Body Issue, allowing it to seem, at once, liberal and conservative. The issue did more than, as ESPN had sought to do for years, balance multiculturalism with color blindness; it merged them. If we all had a thing called difference, if we could all be diverse, then difference dissolved into a kind of diversified color blindness. Difference was good, and difference was nothing.

But the Body Issue was also a take-generating machine. Of the six original covers, the best-selling, by far, was of Serena Williams. The tennis star, coming off a third Wimbledon title that summer, sits naked on a flat surface, smiling, one hand reaching for her hair and the other held over her chest. She curls one leg underneath her and crosses the other. Williams, like the other five cover athletes, is set against a white background. A small caption beneath the decontextualized naked woman – no court, no net, no self-designed tennis outfit – identifies her as Serena Williams. In the issue, Roenigk commended Williams for using "her body as an instrument of empowerment."[100] Nicole Fleetwood offers a more nuanced reading, suggesting that Williams's "powerful mode of embodied presence" forces us as onlookers to "witness our investments in the signs that we employ to make sense of her athleticism and embodiment."[101] Claudia Rankine, unconvinced, sees in Williams's image a discouraging indication that "no amount of visibility will alter the ways in which one is perceived."[102] What did Williams's cover do? Did it assert? Subvert? Did it trace the limits of cultural recognition? The one thing we can say for sure: It sold a lot of copies. The debate surrounding the Body Issue might have been good for athletes – it might have earned them more endorsement deals and followers – but there's no doubt that it was good for ESPN. It recast the whole business of looking at athletes' bodies, ESPN's core business, as urgent, meaningful, and, above all, worth talking about.

For a decade, the Body Issue created its own media weather. Every issue received credit, often from ESPN itself, for some kind of breakthrough. When one of the 2014 covers showed stout Texas Rangers first baseman Prince Fielder swinging a bat, his round, tattooed stomach visible, the *Washington Post* declared the issue "democratic" and "an illustration of the diverse body types among those who call themselves athletes."[103] The 2016 issue included trans triathlete Chris Mosier. One of the 2018 covers featured Sue Bird and Megan Rapinoe. "First Transgender Athlete in

ESPN's 'Body Issue,'" a *Times* headline read after the release of the 2016 issue.[104] "First Same-Sex Couple on Cover of ESPN's Body Issue," the *Post* announced in 2018.[105] The magazine managed to turn the release of every Body Issue into a media event with a combination of some images that could have run in the Swimsuit Issue (with the addition of a swimsuit) and others that broke new ground, at least in ESPN's own universe of curated difference and never-ending firsts. Who needed a game? The takes were entertainment enough.

In 2004, ESPN introduced a show called *Dream Job*. The dream job was working for ESPN. Twelve contestants ranging in age from twenty-one to forty vied for a Mazda3 and a one-year contract as an anchor with the network. Mike Hall, a white college senior, won the first season and made his ESPN debut soon after, hosting shows on ESPNews and ESPNU for the next three years. (He left Bristol for the Big Ten Network in 2007.) *Dream Job* was an ESPN show about wanting to be on an ESPN show. It took over a time slot during which the network had been airing live NHL games. An average of about 300,000 North American households had tuned in to the games. More than a million watched Hall chase his

Mike Hall, winner of the first season of *Dream Job*, in his dorm room in Columbia, Missouri. Photograph by Parker Eshelman. From AP Photo/*Columbia Missourian*.

dream of talking about NHL games on television. Talk had gone from cut-rate filler for a network that couldn't afford much else to the main event.

"I'm not just satisfied with being [at ESPN]," Hall, with confetti in his hair, said after winning the show. "I want to get there and be great. I know it will take a lot of dedication, but I will work extremely hard to maximize the opportunity."[106] The Atlanta Falcons had not drafted Hall first overall. The NFL wasn't his dream. ESPN had given Hall a Mazda and told him to drive to Bristol. It wanted his take on Michael Vick.

6

Draft Capital

Le'Veon Bell was sorry. The twenty-seven-year-old running back, who had sat out the entire 2018 NFL season after failing to reach a long-term deal with his team, the Pittsburgh Steelers, had a message for his owners. "This is loooong overdue!" Bell tweeted to his 1.8 million followers the next summer. "But I want to take a moment to apologize to all the fantasy owners who picked me last year, I'm sorry I couldn't pull through for y'all." Most fantasy football sites had ranked him first or second on their draft boards, and millions of fantasy managers had bet their seasons on Bell delivering the kind of stat line he had in 2017, when he finished third in the league in rushing and second in yards from scrimmage. His agent had negotiated a new four-year deal with the New York Jets worth $52.5 million, including $27 million guaranteed, and Bell wanted his former owners – at their computers, on their phones – to know that they could count on him. "Trust me, this year's about to be wayyyy different," he wrote from his iPhone, signing off with a flourish of smiling devil emojis.[1]

Fantasy Twitter had not gotten over it. "This man is dead to me, don't ever want to see or [choose] him again #bum," a user named MV with a bible verse in his bio wrote. "You abandoned your teammates and you ain't shit," a man from South Carolina wrote. A Chicago man gave him the middle finger.[2] More than a few users asked Bell to send them the money they had lost in their leagues. "Venmo the $500 you cost me and we'll call it even. I picked you 4th overall," one tweeted. "My money long overdue too. You got yours now lemme get mine," another added.[3] Some included their Venmo usernames, as if believing that Bell might cover the losses of a bunch of strangers on Twitter. Others used the thread to debate whether and when to draft him next season. Did he still have it? Would he retain his value? Was he worth the investment of, as they say, draft capital?

The Bell fiasco originated in March 2018, when the Steelers, after negotiations broke down, informed the running back that the organization would be designating him with a franchise tag for the second consecutive season. The franchise tag gives teams the right to retain one athlete scheduled to become a free agent for an additional season at a non-negotiated salary determined by league averages and the athlete's most recent contract. In 2017, Bell had made $12.1 million on the franchise tag. In 2018, he would have made $14.5 million. But he didn't want to risk his health on another one-year deal. Bell, then twenty-six, was at his best, and he knew that a torn ACL or even a slight decline in carries and yards could cost him millions of dollars, leaving him with nothing more than a meager rookie contract and two nonnegotiable one-year deals. He decided to hold out. He missed training. His teammates criticized him. He missed week one, then another week, and another, infuriating Steelers fans. "I'm playing for strictly my value to the team," Bell told ESPN.com. "That's what I'm asking. I don't think I should settle for anything less than what I'm valued at." Quarterback Ben Roethlisberger and wide receiver Antonio Brown, who with Bell constituted what Pittsburgh media had dubbed the "killer Bs," had each received lucrative long-term contracts, and Bell felt he was "next in line."[4]

Steelers management disagreed. The introduction of advanced metrics to football front offices in the 2000s had softened the market for running backs, revealing that the best backs in the league might be, above all, the beneficiaries of first-rate offensive lines and that they often lost some of their effectiveness in their mid- to late twenties, near the end of their first contracts. A team might be best served, general managers realized, by drafting another running back every three or four years, signing him to a low-cost rookie deal, and then discarding him for another twenty-two-year-old when the contract ended. The Steelers had, in fact, drafted another running back, James Conner out of the University of Pittsburgh, in the third round of the 2017 draft, and with Bell holding out, Conner scored twelve touchdowns (tied for third in the league) and made the Pro Bowl. Steelers fans might have been frustrated to not see Bell on the field, but they moved on.

Fantasy managers did not. After a strained hamstring forced New York Giants running back Brandon Jacobs to miss a game during the

2013 season, he received a tweet from a man who had Jacobs on his fantasy team. "On [my] life Brandon if you don't rush for 50 yards and 2 touchdowns tonight it's over for you and your family," a user named Andre Raynor, addressing Jacobs with an anti-Black slur, wrote. (The user was, like Jacobs, Black.) Two minutes later, Raynor added, "Fulfill my orders stated in the previous tweet or that's yo life bruh and I'm not playing." The running back shared a screenshot of the death threat with his Twitter followers. "Look at what we deal with," he wrote. The Giants referred the tweet to the NFL's security team, and the user deactivated his account after first announcing that he had been joking. "Bro relax it's never that serious," he tweeted at Jacobs. "It's just Twitter."[5] Jacobs later told ESPN that he had decided to speak out about fan harassment because he could no longer get through dinner at a restaurant without fantasy managers visiting his table to tell him that they had him on their teams and needed him to score on Sunday.[6] The veteran running back returned from his hamstring strain, hurt his knee, and, after surgery, retired from the league.

Others shared Jacobs's concerns. After seeing a rookie teammate carted off the field with a broken ankle in 2017, Seattle Seahawks cornerback Richard Sherman had words for the fantasy industry. "I think a lot of people, a lot of fans out there have looked at players less like people because of fantasy football," he told the *Seattle Times*. "You aren't thinking 'hey man, this guy got hurt, he's really physically hurt and he is going to take some time to recover and it's probably going to affect his mental state and now he has a long rigorous rehab.' You are thinking 'oh man, he's messing up my fantasy team.'"[7] Sherman was worried about how fantasy altered fans' perception of athletes, but he wasn't, it turned out, too worried to cash in. In 2018, he announced that he had cofounded his own fantasy site, for which he would serve as chief brand ambassador. Fantasy football "has better connected fans to players and I think it helps them know players better, [as well as] the ups and downs [we] go through on the field," Sherman told *Forbes*.[8]

Bell had to agree. Fans knew him. Some of them might hate him. Some might harass him on Twitter. But they knew him, and Bell, in a league in which the average career lasts little more than three years, needed to be known. The running back had been moonlighting as a recording artist. In 2017, he released, under the stage name Juice, an album titled *Post Interview*. Amid his holdout, he issued a four-track EP titled *My Side of Things*, which, as you might guess, defended his decision to turn down the franchise tag. "Got this platform, I'ma use it / Just 'cause I play ball don't mean I can't make music," he declares, through a muffling autotune, on the track "Target."[9] As his career wound down, Bell challenged Jake Paul, the YouTuber-turned-boxer, to a fight. Paul didn't bite, but Bell later went toe to toe with mixed martial artist Uriah Hall (loss), YouTuber JMX (win), and fellow retired NFL running back Adrian Peterson (win). In 2022, he finished tenth on the eighth season of *The Masked Singer*, for which he wore a milkshake costume and 3D glasses. (He lost on the Haddaway Eurodance song "What Is Love.") He has created and organized video game tournaments and hosts an OnlyFans account (no sex work, a lot of talk about his favorite video game, *Super Smash Bros.*). Bell wanted the best NFL contract he could get, but he also needed to secure his wider market value as a recording artist, a boxer, a gamer, a singing milkshake – for which he looked not to the Steelers front office but to the fantasy managers on Twitter. "I'm sorry I couldn't pull through for y'all."[10]

NFL football is a Black game. More than half of the league identifies as Black or mixed race. Fantasy football is about as white as the NFL is Black. In 2014, the Fantasy Sports Trade Association (now the Fantasy Sports and Gaming Association) found that four out of five fantasy customers were white and that nine out of ten were men.[11] (The association has not released racial or gender data since, and I think we can imagine why.) For media scholars and sociologists, the whiteness of fantasy is evidence of a desire for racial management in neoliberal times. Fantasy, they write, encourages users to cultivate a "neoliberal subjectivity" orientated toward individual risk management.[12] It habituates them to "racial neoliberalism."[13] It entices them with a kind of "vicarious management."[14] It accustoms the fantasy manager to the league's mode of labor extraction as what one scholar calls a "God-Fan."[15] Branden Buehler, the author of *Front Office Fantasies*, seems to be straining to find something new to say when he argues that football management video games give fans a "sense of empowerment" and may spur "critical reflection" on the conditions of their own labor.[16] (I don't know. Does shooting your friends with an airsoft gun spur critical reflection on mass shootings?) The emerging consensus is that, as Kellen Hoxworth writes, "predominantly white, male fantasy participants partake in the making and remaking of race by incorporating the calculative operations of neoliberalism into their daily lives."[17] But what Hoxworth and other scholars locate in the Blackness of the NFL and whiteness of fantasy is not the making of race but the retracing of the Black/white color line. Fantasy football makes race not through the categories of Blackness and whiteness but through the related categories of investor and debtor, the fan who gives and the athlete who, blessed with an assumed gift, receives and owes. Athletic racialization holds the color line by blurring it. It converts Blackness into giftedness and giftedness into Blackness. "On [my] life Brandon if you don't rush for 50 yards and 2 touchdowns."[18]

Does fantasy football indoctrinate us into neoliberalism? Do all fantasy managers harbor front-office dreams? Wendy Brown, among the leading scholars of the Swiss-Army-knife term, defines neoliberalism as the economizing of once-noneconomic domains and a subtle shift in our own market consciousness from external exchange to an internal investment in the self as a form of human capital. We all, under the sign of neoliberalism, seek to enhance our future value, she writes, through self-investment (college, exercise) intended to attract new external investors (social-media followers, dates).[19] We don't need Brown to tell us that this is a degrading way to inhabit the world. We can feel it; we're exhausted. But why would we choose, in what little free time we may have, to simulate neoliberalism? Scholars would seem to suggest that fantasy managers have been lulled into a false consciousness that works against their own interests. Fantasy may force Bell to act as what Brown calls a "little capital," forever looking out for the value of his brand, but it sells the fantasy manager on something else: not the refinement of neoliberal consciousness but a flight from it.[20] The fan, also enduring the humiliations of late capitalism, gets to bet on the direction of someone else's value, the sturdiness of someone else's ligaments and tendons. We get to, for a moment at least, take off our own milkshake costumes.[21]

Some fantasy users dream of being the general manager of the Pittsburgh Steelers. But most don't. Does the growth of fantasy football stem from a desire to manage human capital or to not be human capital ourselves? Is it about identification with management, as most assume, or disidentification with labor? The cultural theorist Annie McClanahan suggests that, in all our Gramscian talk of neoliberal hegemony and common sense, we have lost sight of the material conditions – the decline of domestic manufacturing; wage stagnation; attacks on organized labor; the rise of the service sector, debt, offshoring, finance – that allowed for neoliberalism's rise to dominance. (Neoliberal thought originated in the late 1940s. So why, she asks, did it take until after 1973 for it to enter the West's ideological bloodstream?) She wonders whether neoliberalism marks not the wholesale economizing of noneconomic domains but the introduction of economic vulnerabilities into the lives of people once shielded from them – people like McClanahan and me, white humanities professors, the people most committed to the term. College-educated professionals are, she writes, "finding their own lives more and more similar to the conditions in which the marginally employed, the working poor, immigrants, and people of color have long had to survive."[22] In the age of a long economic downturn, fantasy managers, most of them white and male, may not dream of managing Le'Veon Bell, but they, as their own conditions begin to resemble the historical conditions of Black and immigrant labor, may fear becoming him.[23]

Fantasy football disassociates users from one of the most visible forms of manual labor in the United States. Not all users dream of management, but no one wants to be managed – their body and movements tracked, measured, scrutinized. Racial capitalism names the extraction of labor, land, and resources through the construction and maintenance of categories of differential human value. We often forget, as Jodi Melamed writes, that it entails, and would crumble without, "the production of social separateness." Racial capitalism is what she calls "a technology of antirelationality."[24] It disconnects us from one another as social beings so that it may reconnect us as owners/workers, creditors/debtors, settlers/exiles. Critics of fantasy football have tended to describe it as relational: It encourages an identification with management. But perhaps it is more antirelational than relational; perhaps it encourages a disidentification with forms of labor – manual, high-risk, short-term – once associated with Black people, people of color, and immigrants but now carried out by more and more white people of a declining middle class.[25]

The bible of antirelational fandom may be Michael Lewis's 2003 bestseller *Moneyball*, which recounts the shrewd, data-driven dealings of Oakland Athletics general manager Billy Beane during the 2002 MLB season. Beane, a former first-round draft pick who had flamed out by his mid-twenties, managed to assemble one of the best teams in the league (tied for first in wins with the much wealthier New York Yankees) on one of the smallest budgets (less than a third of New York's). The book's subtitle, *The Art of Winning an Unfair Game*, references two forms of unfairness: the unfairness of wealth (the A's small-market budget) and the unfairness of talent (Beane's struggles as an overrated athlete). The former, Lewis determines, can be overcome. The latter cannot. The former is earned. The latter is given. He quotes the baseball statistician Bill James, who in 1977 wrote, "If we're going to pay these guys $150,000 a year to do this, we should at least know how good they are."[26] James wasn't cutting athletes' checks, but he and Lewis and a million fantasy leagues encouraged us to believe that we were, that athletes owed us something for their talent and for our attention. *Moneyball* let us into Beane's world, but it also led us out of the athlete's, which is, the book lets us forget, much closer to our own.

Lewis is not a baseball writer. He is a financial journalist. He used baseball to communicate something about finance: that it was also a game of legitimate and illegitimate advantages, gifts and debts, winners and losers. Reading it, you could almost believe that you understood high finance – even if all you understood was that a walk was as good as a hit.

Le'Veon Bell made $45 million over eight seasons in the NFL. He has, I think we can agree, done all right. But the fantasy of fantasy football is neither being nor owning Bell. It is the fantasy of not being him, of not hustling for the next gig, of not aging out, being devalued, getting cut. It is the fantasy of not, as more and more of us do under late capitalism, singing for our supper.

Henry Waugh was tired of singing for his. Henry, the hero of Robert Coover's 1968 novel *The Universal Baseball Association*, is a friendless accountant who moonlights as the commissioner of an invented baseball league, the Universal Baseball Association of the novel's title, that he governs with three six-sided dice and rules of his own making. The young star of Coover's league is Damon Rutherford, a rookie ace who, we learn, has "a bag of tricks, all right" but whose secret was "control" – "power and control."[27] Henry dreams of having some of Rutherford's control; he hates his job and resents his boss, a "militant clock-watcher."[28] After Rutherford, with a roll of three consecutive sets of ones, gets beaned in the batter's box and killed, Henry sinks further and further into his fantasy, for which he has constructed fifty-six seasons of games (we meet him in Year LVI) as well as elaborate backstories for the men of the Knickerbockers, Pioneers, and Pastime Club. "There are box scores to be audited, trial balances of averages along the way, seasonal inventories, rewards and punishments to be meted out, life histories to be overseen," he tells a woman he brings home from the bar who doesn't yet know that Henry's association is a dice game.[29] Henry wanders over to a coworker's home after Rutherford's death. He is seeking something that might restore a sense of "precision, discipline, control" to his environment.[30] He can't find it. The Universal Baseball Association has taken over his life. The novel, Coover's second, came and went, unnoticed in 1968. (Coover would become better known for his 1977 historical satire *The Public Burning*.) In 2011, Overlook Press reissued *The Universal*

Baseball Association, and one critic after another declared it a classic: "one of the best baseball novels," a "deeply metaphysical and existential" story of "free will and predestination," and "more relevant now than ever before."[31] The novel had found its time.

The Universal Baseball Association was Coover's ode to Strat-O-Matic, the real-life make-believe baseball simulation game. Strat-O-Matic is also a three-dice game. Strat cards for individual batters determine the likelihood (the dice combinations) that they will reach base, hit a home run, strike out, ground into a double. Hal Richman, who created Strat-O-Matic, selling the first set out of his basement in 1961, did not invent the baseball board game. Obsessives could gather around the hearth for a game of Parlor Base-Ball Field as far back as 1866 ("calculated to instruct ladies, youths and amateur ball-players in the theory of the 'national game'"), and a designer from Wisconsin brought the first card-and-dice version, National Pastime, to market in 1931.[32] Neither sold. Richman and his rival, Richard Seitz, the inventor of APBA (American Professional Baseball Association), added a new dimension to the board game genre: They issued a card for every big leaguer every year, with their actual stats guiding the action. Variables in an advanced game of Strat-O-Matic included differences in hitting against lefties or righties, a starter's inning-by-inning "fatigue rating," and the effects of different MLB fields. A Strat manager could, like Henry Waugh, orchestrate an entire season of baseball without once tuning in to an MLB game or checking the box scores. Richman, an unathletic kid from Long Island, had first turned to baseball simulation games as a refuge from his father, a quick-tempered insurance executive.[33] He and his future customers also wanted Damon Rutherford's control, to feel that they had some say in a world of bad bosses, uptight dads, and dramatic social change.

For Bill Gamson, a research associate at the Harvard School of Public Health, simulation board games still lacked the day-to-day excitement of the real thing. He thought he could do better. In 1960, he had two friends over to his apartment, and for the next five hours, they hashed out the rules of what would become Gamson's Baseball Seminar. (He gave it an affected, academic name out of a fear that the authorities might mistake him for a bookie.) The Seminar followed the current MLB season, with the box scores rather than Strat cards and last year's numbers determining the outcome. It was an innovation that made Gamson, in the estimation of Sam Walker, author of *Fantasyland*, "the Thomas Edison" of fantasy baseball.[34] Managers bid for the services of big leaguers in an auction before the season and then tracked their stats in the *Sporting*

News through the summer. Whoever amassed the highest totals in eight categories won the Seminar and a little cash. Gamson, a sociologist, later left Harvard for the University of Michigan, and he took his Seminar with him.

Gamson recruited twenty-five colleagues to his Seminar, and one of them taught the rules to a bright undergraduate student named Dan Okrent. After graduation, Okrent, a Detroit native, moved to New York, where, as an ambitious young book editor, he managed to rise to editor in chief of Harcourt and get fired, all before the age of thirty. He may have, he later acknowledged, devoted a bit too much time to baseball board games. When *Newsweek* ran a story about Strat-O-Matic and APBA addicts in 1976 titled "Dice Baseball Fever," it included an image of Okrent in a Cubs hat and bowtie, hunched over his Strat cards and smoking a cigarette. Strat-O-Matic, he told *Newsweek*, "makes life worth living."[35] "I remember just getting an enormous amount of ridicule about that," he later said.[36] In 1980, Okrent, undaunted, combined elements of the Baseball Seminar and Strat-O-Matic to create Rotisserie League Baseball, naming his game after La Rotisserie Française, a, by all accounts, mediocre (and soon defunct) French restaurant on the East Side, at which he and his friends gathered to talk baseball. "All of us had a firm belief that we could do what [Dodgers general manager] Al Campanis could do," Okrent wrote of that first season. "Hadn't we been appraising talent all our lives? I mean, being a GM was *easy*."[37]

Rotisserie League Baseball was not much different from Gamson's Seminar, but Okrent and his friends had something that Gamson, living among other academics in Ann Arbor, didn't: connections. Tom Guinzburg, who had cofounded the *Paris Review* and led Viking Press, succeeding his father, managed the Burghers. Lee Eisenberg, the editor in chief of *Esquire* who had coined the term *power lunch*, oversaw the Eisenberg Furriers. Valerie Salembier, an executive at *Ms.* magazine and the one woman among the eleven original members, ran the Flambés. Okrent, the owner of the Okrent Fenokees and no slouch himself, would later serve as the ombudsman of the *New York Times*.

News of the league traveled fast. The *Times* caught wind of it – through a friend of a friend – and sent a writer to interview the rotisserie leaguers. Eisenberg booked a conference room at his magazine's office for the occasion. The resulting story, "For Major-League Addicts, a Way to Win a Pennant," ran in the summer of 1980 and led to segments on *CBS Morning News* and the *Today Show*.[38] Okrent contributed his own reflection on the league's first season, "The Year George Foster Wasn't

Worth $36," to *Inside Sports*. (Okrent had bid the exorbitant sum of $36 on outfielder George Foster of the Cincinnati Reds, whose numbers then declined.) Okrent's story included the rules of the game ("copyrighted © 1980 by the Rotisserie League"), and before long, roto had turned into a minor sensation, with leagues, authorized and otherwise, forming across the country.[39] Using their contacts in the book business, Okrent and his friends released *Rotisserie League Baseball* with Bantam in 1984, declaring their fantasy, in bold letters on the front cover, "the greatest game for baseball fans since baseball."[40]

The men of the first Rotisserie League, knowing they'd be mocked, decided to get ahead of the inevitable digs. When the *Times* writer asked them about Salembier, they said they worried that if she won, it could mean "the end of the league as we know it."[41] "Valerie has a tendency to draft cute players," another wrote.[42] Salembier, who would have a long career in Manhattan C-suites, could more than hold her own. "I've never dealt with such a dishonest group of men," she deadpanned in an

Left to right: Rotisserie League Baseball founders Bruce McCall, Glen Waggoner, Rob Fleder, Dan Okrent, Lee Eisenberg, Cork Smith, and Bob Sklar in 1980. Photograph by Fred R. Conrad. From Redux Pictures.

interview with *People* magazine. "They're cheats, thieves, sexists ... But I can't help myself, I love the game."[43] The men could laugh at themselves. "The Rotisserie League is silly," one acknowledged, "and we know that."[44] The rotisserie leaguers were enacting a nascent form of what sociologists Rebecca Kissane and Sarah Winslow call "jock statsculinity" – a merging of traditional masculine signifiers with knowledge-work nerd culture into a new source of male confidence and comfort.[45] It arose at a time of shifting gender norms and socioeconomic conditions and amid growing concerns about the future of work, including, it seems, among the most advantaged. When a foundation director who formed a Massachusetts-based league with Okrent wrote about fantasy baseball for the alumni magazine of his alma mater, *Harvard Magazine*, he said that it was one overwhelming feeling that had led him to the league: "powerlessness."[46]

The Harvard man wasn't alone. "It wasn't enough to watch baseball, or to study it in the box scores and leaders lists," Okrent wrote in 1984. "We all wished, in some way, to possess it, to control it."[47] Why would a bunch of well-off, college-educated men watch baseball and feel a sense of loss? Why would they, with much fuller lives than Coover's Henry Waugh, share his alienation and longing for control? Some suggest that the end of the reserve clause and the arrival of free agency, after a 1975 arbitration decision against Major League Baseball, left fans wanting some of that freedom of movement for themselves. The fan, some scholars suggest, would be a free agent now.[48] But the early rotisserie leaguers acknowledged that they were motivated by a sense of loss, not a desire to see what their labor might fetch on the free market. They didn't look at the MLB free agent, with his fluctuating market value and inevitable decline, and say, I want to be like him more than ever. They looked at the free agent and said, No thanks. The fantasy wasn't to be in the market but to get out of it. Publishing and media had entered a volatile age of conglomeration. Okrent, Guinzburg, Eisenberg, Salembier, and the rest were already free agents; they didn't need to fantasize about it.

The baseball historian Jules Tygiel once described the founding of the Rotisserie League as the launch of the game's "postmodern era."[49] It had destabilized a game's meaning. Two fans could sit side by side in the stands and witness two different games, one cheering for the Phillies to win, the other for Mike Schmidt to raise his batting average without costing the other team's starter the win. *Postmodern* is one way to describe it, but the long downturn – a decline in the rate of return since 1973, from which followed a decline in real wages and the rise of consumer debt and the financial sector – also seems to have motivated the fantasy.[50] Tygiel's term fits when considering the self-reflexive, ironic tone with which Okrent and others addressed the imagined economic structure of their league. "There being no Marvin Miller [the longtime head of the MLB Players Association] present, we quickly agreed to a form of price-fixing," Okrent joked. "That was, we thought, very owner-like."[51] Another early roto leaguer acknowledged that they had restored a version of the reserve clause.[52] Eisenberg wondered if they might have ruined baseball.[53] Scholars of games insist that they are much more than diversions, that they act as a social "compass" and have "actively shaped Americans' thinking about race, progress, and inequality."[54] But roto baseball's absurdism insulated it from criticism. When Peter Gethers and Glen Waggoner, who co-owned the Getherswag Goners, won the first season, they arrived at the "awards banquet" in rented tuxedos, and their friends showered them with ceremonial bottles of Yoo-Hoo. The one thing sillier than grown men with chocolate milk in their hair was the critic who insisted that grown men with chocolate milk in their hair said something about how we live now. The critic didn't get the joke. It meant nothing. It was a game with artificial stakes based on a game with artificial stakes.

But Okrent and others did acknowledge that they had turned to fantasy out of frustration with the labor negotiations and strikes of 1980 and 1981. They wanted some say, some Cooverian control. The strike year of 1981 also stands as the high-water mark for Black participation in Major League Baseball (at least if you, as MLB does, exclude all Afro-Caribbeans, including Afro–Puerto Ricans, as "Latino"), and the first roto leaguers were all white.[55] For the non–Cincinnati Reds diehard who may not know, George Foster, for whom Okrent regretted bidding $36, was Black. The whiteness of Rotisserie League Baseball was among the few things that the members didn't turn into a self-mocking gag. Did fantasy baseball arise from a desire to be the general manager ("I mean, being a GM was *easy*")?[56] Or a fear of having your labor casualized, made insecure (the foundation director's "powerlessness") – circumstances under which Black workers had long labored?[57]

Baseball fans had sought to own some trace of their idols before. When the Virginia tobacco manufacturer Allen and Ginter introduced the first mass-market cigarette cards in the 1880s, early sets included army generals, world leaders, stage actresses, and game birds. But none sold like baseball cards. The emerging trade in memorabilia demonstrated that consumers wanted to own athletes, or at least illustrations of athletes, like nothing else.[58] Rotisserie League Baseball fed that desire but also transformed it. The memorabilia collector wanted to be close to the athlete, to touch a bat that Babe Ruth once held. The roto owner wanted to make a bet, and win a few bucks and bragging rights, off Reggie Jackson's real-time swing. The desire for closeness had turned into something more like an investment, an uneven and alienating form of relation. The collector wanted to close the distance between athlete and fan, the roto owner to define it.

The originators of Rotisserie League Baseball tried for years to turn their idea into a business. They sold books and T-shirts. They held conventions. (Okrent: "Seventy, eighty, ninety dorks from around America came to join the ten founding dorks.")[59] They sent out cease-and-desist letters when others used the Rotisserie name. Okrent later estimated that each of the original members had collected around ten thousand or fifteen thousand dollars from their various, unsuccessful business ventures.[60] "The single most impressive thing about all of this," Gethers said in the 2010 ESPN documentary *Silly Little Game*, "is that we've created a $2 billion industry and none of us actually made any money off of this."[61] His fantasy remained a fantasy. But others took theirs to the bank, some to a big-league front office. The nerds, trained on Strat-O-Matic and Rotisserie League Baseball, armed with math degrees and statistical models, had arrived.

Okrent, a man whose late-night Strat-O-Matic binges could run to six hours, found someone more obsessed than him in the back pages of the *Sporting News*. A one-inch classified advertisement announced the arrival of the 1978 edition of something called the *Baseball Abstract*, whose subtitle described it as "baseball's most informative and imaginative review." Okrent mailed $4.50 to a PO box in Lawrence, Kansas, and received in return a homemade booklet of statistical arguments for why Roger Maris's home run record would fall, why fielders had committed more errors against winning than losing teams in the 1977 season, why the Red Sox's vaunted offense wasn't as good as most thought (Fenway Park), and why the Orioles' defense wasn't either (Baltimore Memorial Stadium). The author, a twenty-nine-year-old 7-Eleven clerk named Bill James, decried the state of baseball statistics and announced his abstract as an "attempt to devise ways to assess player performance" that general managers and scouts had "previously not measured or measured poorly." If a reader did not like what he had to say, "your money will be cheerlessly refunded," James wrote.[62] In 1977, the amateur statistician had sold 70 of his abstracts through the mail, netting, after subtracting the cost of materials, $93.77. (No one, to James's relief, asked for a refund.) The 1978 edition – the one Okrent bought – sold 300. Okrent thought he deserved a larger audience. "A whole new world opened up for me," he remembered of reading James, and he wrote the author a letter: "Who the hell are you? Where did you come from?"[63]

James had come from a town of 200 in northeastern Kansas. His father ran a butter station, which, before the consolidation of agribusiness, served as a local broker in the butterfat trade. In 1967, James moved down the road to Lawrence to attend the University of Kansas, where he studied economics and English, and, after short, undistinguished stints in the army and graduate school, settled into a small house with his wife and dedicated himself to the baseball numbers game. Okrent connected James with Eisenberg, the *Esquire* editor in chief, who assigned James the magazine's 1979 "baseball forecast." The magazine introduced him as a "fanatic, who did he not really exist, could have been invented by Robert Coover."[64] In his forecast, James assailed the Mets for "doing everything possible to neutralize the inherent advantage of playing in New York" and described Angels outfielder Dan Ford as "like a blind man staying overnight at a friend's apartment," determining where to heave the ball according to some "private cryptography as yet undeciphered."[65] Eisenberg loved it.

Okrent thought James was fascinating, and he convinced an editor at *Sports Illustrated* to let him write a story about a moonlighting baseball statistician whom no one had ever heard of before with an audience of 300. Okrent flew to the Midwest and followed James around. He discovered that James had also cut his teeth on Strat-O-Matic and other baseball simulation games. A historian at KU had invented a game called Ball Park Baseball in the late 1950s. It was, befitting the inventor's academic training, more historical than Gamson's Baseball Seminar or even Strat-O-Matic. James recalled a year in which his league simulated every American League season of the 1930s. In 1971, when James was a senior, a local resident created a theme restaurant where customers could eat, drink, and play Ball Park. A desire "to win that damn little league," James confessed, had "focused my interest in the game onto analytical questions." He dedicated his final abstract, in 1988, to his first Ball Park league.[66]

SI killed Okrent's story. A fact-checker had, according to Okrent, declared some of James's claims unverifiable. But the story had stuck with one editor, who resurrected it more than a year later, and James had his day in the sun. "He Does It by the Numbers" ran in the second month of the 1981 MLB season, right before the strike, and featured an image of James sitting cross-legged in the Kansas City Royals outfield doing calculations longhand on the back of a suitcase. He wears a coat and tie, his hair matted to his forehead, and the scoreboard behind him shows his formula for runs created, or RC, a method for determining the number of runs an individual hitter contributes to the team. Okrent described James as a fount of "iconoclastic information" challenging baseball traditionalism.[67] "A baseball field is so covered with statistics that nothing can happen there without leaving its tracks in the records," the stats man told Okrent. "There may be no other facet of American life, the activities of laboratory rats excepted, which is so extensively categorized, counted and recorded."[68] James did not invent the method he called, in an inelegant repurposing of the acronym for the Society for American Baseball Research, sabermetrics. Dodgers general manager Branch Rickey had hired a fulltime statistician to consult on roster decisions in the mid-1940s, and Earnshaw Cook, a metallurgist who dabbled in baseball statistics, released his foundational *Percentage Baseball* in 1964.[69] But Okrent had, with the *SI* story, anointed James the face of a movement. He connected him with a friend at Ballantine Books, which turned the abstract into a book for the masses, and, against all odds, it landed on the *New York Times* Best Seller list.[70]

James succeeded where others had failed by giving statistics, the domain of losers and dweebs, a rebel flair. "This is *outside* baseball," he wrote in the introduction to the 1984 abstract, throwing a jab at every show and magazine that claimed to take fans "inside the game." "This is a book about what baseball looks like if you step back from it and study it intensely and minutely, but from a distance."[71] James did not long to be close to big leaguers. He did not idolize athletes. He introduced himself as an anti-jock, unembarrassed that he'd never worn a uniform. He didn't have the credentials to walk into a big-league clubhouse and interview George Brett or Ozzie Smith, and he didn't want them. He invited his readers to join him on the noble outside. "*Since* we are outsiders, since the players are going to put up walls to keep us out here, let us use our position as outsiders to what advantage we can," he wrote.[72] Alan Schwarz, author of *The Numbers Games: Baseball's Long Fascination with Statistics*, credits the abstracts with having created "an earthquake that shook all of baseball."[73] James and his readers did not want to be athletes. Why would they? Athletes were numbers, and the statisticians ran the numbers.

James did not believe in the natural. In his 1986 *Historical Baseball Abstract*, he observed that the success of Irish American athletes in the 1890s had led some to believe that they were naturals "in the same stupid way that people today believe that blacks are born athletes."[74] Theories about racial differences in athleticism were a form of anti-Blackness but also, for James, something worse: a source of bad scouting. He imagined sabermetrics as a color-blind corrective to racist ideas about talent. If you stuck to the numbers rather than allowing the biases of the game's culture to cloud your vision, you would, he argued, make more accurate assessments of an athlete's value (and, oh yeah, as a bonus, you wouldn't promote anti-Black thought).

But James did believe in talent and sought, in abstract after abstract, to measure it. "Where does talent come from?" he asked in 1984, introducing what he called his "Value Approximation method."[75] James's method led him to an almost radical form of color blindness. He thought the handwringing over the declining number of African American big leaguers was absurd. Writers and fans ought to recognize, he argued, that "it really doesn't make any difference whether the best players are black or white," adding that "Latin America continued to produce more than its fair share of the top stars in the game."[76] James's outside baseball abstracted labor. Labor was a resource. It had a determinable value that the sabermetrician, cutting through cultural noise, aimed to calculate. A batter wasn't Black or white, American or Venezuelan but the runs he created. He was $((H + W - CS) \times (TB + 0.7SB))/(AB + W + CS)$.

James later acknowledged that his method, sabermetrics, was "the view from the marketplace."[77] He established a genre that Michael Lewis would elevate to an art. He introduced readers to the logic of the market and allowed them to believe that they could beat it (I know better than a bunch of old scouts and financial managers!) through a stick-and-ball game. In 2018, James got himself into trouble when he took aim at Scott Boras, the agent behind some of the biggest MLB contracts ever, including both of Alex Rodriguez's megadeals in the 2000s. "If the players all retired tomorrow, we would replace them, the game would go on," he wrote on Twitter. "In three years, it would make no difference whatsoever. The players are NOT the game, any more than the beer vendors are." Twitter lit into him. The Red Sox, for whom James then served as a consultant, issued a statement condemning his comments, and James deleted the tweet and admitted to the *New York Times* that he might have "phrased [the remark] in an offensive way."[78] But the tweet distilled one of the core ideas of sabermetrics: that athletic labor was fungible.

It didn't matter, for James, who took the field. What mattered was that they created runs on offense, limited runs on defense, and didn't cost more than the value of their numbers.

James was not going to admit it to the *Times* but the goal of sabermetrics, as used by an MLB front office, was to hold salaries down. "Is there any such thing as a major league baseball player who is underpaid?" he asked on Twitter, as the backlash to his original tweet formed.[79] Sabermetrics served to ensure against bloated contracts of the kind Boras is famous for and to discover labor value that, due to bad scouting, could be bought below market rate. James's methods functioned to limit the overvaluation of talent, but he didn't see them as antilabor because talent was, as he framed it, a kind of natural resource, there for the claiming. Athletes hadn't earned their talent. They'd received a gift from the baseball gods, and James couldn't see why he should listen to their grumbling. They'd all received more than they deserved. The outsiders were tired of giving.

James's outside baseball wouldn't be on the outside for long. Sandy Alderson, the general manager of the Oakland Athletics from 1983 to 1997, had ordered James's abstract after seeing the same ad as Okrent and decided to hire a like-minded man named Eric Walker. Alderson had discovered Walker, a former engineer, on the local NPR station, to which Walker contributed five-minute commentaries on the illogic of baseball scouting and management. The A's GM would listen to Walker on his commute to the Oakland Coliseum. Alderson bought Walker's 1982 book *The Sinister First Baseman and Other Observations*, in which Walker declared, "There's one number everyone knows and agrees with: *three*. Three outs and you're gone. Period." That number, Walker insisted, must "dominate planning."[80] A successful team should be built not around "manufacturing runs," as baseball men liked to say, but avoiding outs. The batter must, above all else, get on base. A walk, a then ignored achievement, would suffice. It wasn't an out. Alderson gave Walker a call. He wanted, he said, "some Bill James–like stuff that was proprietary to us."[81]

Alderson guided the A's to a World Series title in 1989 and began grooming a successor. (He and Walker deserve credit for the title, but Jose Conseco and Mark McGwire's steroid-fueled home run derby didn't hurt.) In 1993, Alderson elevated Billy Beane, an advance scout who had finished his lackluster MLB career with Oakland, to assistant general manager. He asked Walker to write a memo on his (and now the organization's) method for the newest front-office executive. Walker handed in a novella-length document with the wandering title "Winning Baseball: An Objective, Numerical, Analytic Analysis of the Principles and Practices Involved in the Design of a Winning Baseball Team," and it set Beane's brain on fire. "It was the first thing I had ever read that tried to take an objective view of baseball," Beane told Lewis.[82] The assistant GM bought every one of James's abstracts, including the homemade editions from 1977 to 1981, which he obtained from a collector. He had all twelve of them behind him on his office bookshelf – a badge of baseball-nerd honor – when the best-selling financial journalist walked in with a book idea.

The magic trick of Lewis's *Moneyball* is that he manages to turn Billy Beane, a handsome millionaire executive (Brad Pitt is more than believable as Beane in the film adaptation), into an underdog. In 1995, A's owner Walter Haas died, and his estate sold the franchise to two area businessmen, who, seeking the kind of return that Haas, an heir to the Levi Strauss fortune, never had, slashed the budget. In 1991, Oakland invested $39 million in roster salaries, the most in Major League Baseball. In 1997, Beane's first season as general manager, it invested $13 million, the lowest of all twenty-eight teams. Alderson, a Dartmouth and Harvard Law grad who by the age of thirty-six had risen through the ranks of a white-shoe San Francisco law firm and become the A's general counsel and then general manager, is, in Lewis's telling, a "complete outsider to baseball." The A's are the "financial underdog" of the league. Beane had embraced James's and Walker's "new, outsider's view of baseball."[83] Assistant GM Paul DePodesta, a twenty-nine-year-old Harvard graduate and Beane's righthand man, is "an outsider who had found a way to enter a place designed to keep outsiders out." Lewis describes Beane as a "human bridge" between "the fiefdom of Playing Pro Ball and the Republic of Thinking about How to Play Pro Ball" – the insiders and the outsiders, who, with their fancy educations, would strike most as the ultimate insiders.[84] Beane wasn't democratizing baseball, but the book, which made an eighteen-week run on the *New York Times* Best Seller list, gave the executive class a slick makeover and a veneer of meritocratic deservedness. Lewis mentions the Ivy League credentials of DePodesta and other Beane hires not as a sign of their class status but as an indicator that they are outsiders, that they don't belong in the locker room. They are struggling to win an unfair game, Lewis's subtitle announces, a game that is unfair not to baseball's vast working class – the minor leagues, the stadium staff – but to the misunderstood Harvard man.

Billy Beane (*left*) and Michael Lewis (*right*) in the Oakland Athletics' dugout in 2011. Photograph by Patrick Fraser. From Getty Images.

If Lewis has a favorite word, it may be *gift*. It is all over *Moneyball*. One athlete has "a gift for stealing bases," another "a gift for tailoring the game to [his] talents," another "a gift for getting on base."[85] Lewis, as others had before him, draws a line between gifts received and gifts given, but with a difference. He is not distinguishing one athlete from another but the athlete, who embodies the resource of giftedness, from the manager, who identifies and extracts it. A team needed some amount of athletic giftedness, but it alone was not enough. "To anyone with the natural gifts to become a professional baseball player, hitting was less a physical than a mental skill," Lewis writes. The latter could be taught, and "if you made the process a routine – if you got every player doing his part on the production line – you could pay a lot less than the going rate for runs."[86] He attributes the success of the small-budget A's to a baseline level of athletic giftedness combined with Beane's "gift for making grotesquely good deals" and the "gifts" of the ideas that DePodesta had borrowed from Wall Street traders.[87] Beane's method entailed signing athletes for less than their value, for finding labor value that others had overlooked. He was a bargain hunter. But Lewis tells a story in which the athlete receives a gift out of nowhere – from God or the luck of the genetic draw – and the shrewd general manager gives them the second gift, through advanced metrics, of noticing it. The athlete owes the GM, and Lewis invites his reader, removed from the manual labor of the athlete – because who wants to see themselves as an extractable resource? – to claim some of the debt.

Lewis thought baseball had a lot to learn from finance. "What was happening to capitalism," he wrote, five years before the financial crisis, "should have happened to baseball: the technical man with his analytical magic should have risen to prominence in baseball management, just as he was rising to prominence on, say, Wall Street."[88] Lewis's technical man – James, Walker, Beane, DePodesta – could lower labor costs by introducing better methods for measuring value. Traditional baseball management was handing out inflated contracts because it was using the wrong metrics – batting average, fielding errors, steals. Management needed to anchor salaries to value on the field, Lewis thought. The Oakland A's sought something more: to discover undervalued athletes whom it could sign for far less than the value of their labor. Smart management awarded contracts based on the value an athlete would deliver to the franchise; smarter management, Lewis believed, awarded contracts based on the value an athlete would deliver above the cost of their contract, stealing a little extra labor here and a little extra labor there, often from the Caribbean. Lewis took an interest in Beane and the A's because they had learned the lessons of Wall Street. He, one of the best-selling nonfiction writers of the decade, identified Wall Street as the model for the Athletics and the A's as a model for understanding finance. His readers, most of whom knew little about Wall Street, could feel like they did and forget, for a moment, that they were the undervalued labor, not the executive with clever ideas about how to make it more efficient.

Sandy Alderson had been an outsider of a kind when he took over as the A's general manager in 1983. He had attended an Ivy League college, Dartmouth. No other GM had. When Lewis shadowed Beane in 2002, little had changed: Three out of a hundred MLB executives held Ivy League degrees. (Beane had attended the University of California, San Diego, in the baseball offseason. He had turned down an offer from Stanford to enter the MLB draft as an eighteen-year-old, a decision he came to regret and that, in Lewis's hands, motivated his search for better scouting methods.) After the 2002 season, the Red Sox named twenty-eight-year-old Theo Epstein, a Yale grad, as their GM, and Epstein hired Bill James as an adviser. The Red Sox won the World Series in 2004, their first in eighty-six years, and every team concluded that they needed their own Ivy League wunderkind. In 2020, an ESPN investigation revealed that by then Ivy League grads constituted almost half of MLB's executive class and that most of the rest had attended similar institutions.[89] "We're just trying to run [our organization] like a Fortune 500 company," a female scout told ESPN, "and it just causes a very toxic, almost Wall Street-type environment."[90] Ken Williams of the Chicago White Sox, a rare Black executive in the league, told *USA Today* that he thought owners felt comfortable hiring young men who would have been well suited for a career at Goldman Sachs because they shared a background. "The Ivy League–educated, analytically based, PowerPoint-savvy individuals are being hired because they speak the same language as ownership groups," he said.[91] The outsiders had stormed the gate, and they looked an awful lot like the insiders.

But critics of big data have often let baseball off the hook. Cathy O'Neil, the author of *Weapons of Math Destruction*, sees baseball statistics as "a useful contrast to the toxic models" she finds in finance, insurance, and social-media marketing because it benefits from an immense data set and doesn't hide it from the rest of us.[92] Nate Silver, the founder of *FiveThirtyEight*, agrees, calling baseball a "rich and revealing exception" to the otherwise flawed use of statistical modeling. Publishers, seeing the success of *Moneyball* and *Freakonomics*, had encouraged Silver to write his own book about "nerds conquering the world."[93] He was dubious about the idea but didn't doubt that baseball fit the bill. Matthew Berry, who for fifteen years served as – and this was his real title – "senior fantasy sports analyst" at ESPN, has written about how fantasy baseball functioned as a social oasis for him as a Jewish kid in evangelical College Station, Texas, and others have told similar stories of finding belonging through roto and sabermetrics.[94] The 2011 film adaptation of *Moneyball* made more than $100 million at the box office, and Jonah Hill received an Oscar nomination for his turn as the numbers-crunching DePodesta character, the unsung nerd-hero of a movement. Relative to some other uses of big data and algorithms, baseball statistics can seem harmless. In 2010, Bill James made a cameo on *The Simpsons*, declaring, from Professor Frink's laptop, "I made baseball as much fun as doing your taxes."[95]

James touted sabermetrics as a way to counteract bias in baseball. The numbers didn't care, he would say, if your team's catcher was Black or white. But his dream of a color-blind game obscured how the introduction of advanced metrics reinforced a division not between athletes of different backgrounds but between fans, wielding statistical models, and athletes, reduced to bundles of numbers to be evaluated, bought, sold, or, their value exhausted, cut. The divide between the managerial fan and the laboring athlete carries forward and renovates the older, more legible racial divisions that James had in mind when he framed his methods as race neutral. The cultural theorists Neda Atanasoski and Kalindi Vora argue that Western liberalism defined the human through what they call a racial "surrogate relation." Western man came to know his freedom through the unfreedom of racial and gender surrogates – a relation that, they suggest, now structures how we encounter forms of labor that technological innovation devalues and obscures. "The idea that some bodies are meant solely for work informs fantasies about automation," Atanasoski and Vora write.[96] In the transformation of individuals and communities into data, McClanahan writes of credit scoring, the "categories of class, gender, and race are reaffirmed at the very site of their disavowal."[97] Fantasy managers, the fan inheritors of the sabermetrics movement, draw a line between themselves and their surrogates, offloading fears about their own insecure futures onto Black men dressed, in helmets and cleats, like robots.

James retired his abstract in 1988, citing burnout, but his influence could be felt in the iconoclastic fan blogs that emerged in the mid-2000s. In 2005, three TV writers using the names Ken Tremendous, Junior, and Dak launched *Fire Joe Morgan*, a semiserious crusade to get the Hall of Fame second baseman, one of the few Black broadcasters in Major League Baseball, removed from the booth for criticizing sabermetrics. "Joe Morgan, because of his penchant for ignorantly slamming Michael Lewis's *Moneyball*, seemed like a good figurehead to use in the title of the site," Dak wrote.[98] Another successful fan blog founded in 2005, *FreeDarko*, originated on the message board of a fantasy basketball league and also made a demand in its title: The bloggers wanted the Detroit Pistons to give Serbian center Darko Miličić, an infamous draft bust, more time on the court. *FreeDarko* advocated a new form of fandom in which consumers would not follow their local teams but, as in a fantasy league, invest in individual athletes. "We chase product, rather than waiting till we can brag about ours to others," one of the site's founders wrote in 2006. "Maybe this is the ultimate articulation of FreeDarko Liberated Fandom."[99] The *FreeDarko* bloggers didn't cheer for teams or root for hometown heroes. Like rotisserie leaguers before them, they imagined their own universe of investments, and because they had read some Bill James, they figured they knew better. One blog called for the removal of a Black man from a white-dominated field, the other for the elevation of a white man in a Black-dominated league. But it was all, they would say, in the numbers.[100]

The bloggers had a self-mocking sense of humor that Okrent would have admired. The creators of *Fire Joe Morgan* acknowledged that they were "total dicks."[101] But social media was about to kick into high gear, and the next generation of stat heads would move to Vegas and make the bloggers of the 2000s look, by comparison, like perfect gentlemen.

For the first season of Rotisserie League Baseball, Dan Okrent collected $250 from each team. The winners, Peter Gethers and Glen Waggoner, made off with $2,500 and some bottles of Yoo-Hoo. Devoting hundreds of hours to a fantasy league was not a way to get ahead. Seasons took months, and most fantasy managers weren't wagering more than a few hundred dollars in their leagues. It was a long game. Not until the late 2000s did it get shorter and, for some, more lucrative.

In 2003, a goateed accountant in reflective sunglasses named Chris Moneymaker won the 2003 World Series of Poker and a check for $2.5 million. Moneymaker (his real name) wore sunglasses because he'd honed his skills online, where face-to-face bluffing was not a factor, and his win set off a boom in online poker. Millions created accounts on sites like PartyPoker and PokerStars and, with or without skill, chased the good life. Congress took note and, in 2006, seeing a need to augment federal restrictions on interstate gambling for the internet age, enacted the Unlawful Internet Gambling Enforcement Act. The law declared it illegal for businesses to receive or facilitate financial transactions related to online betting.[102] But it included a carve-out for fantasy sports that few lawmakers remember discussing. "It was considered one of these de minimis issues, that's all I recall," Iowa congressman James Leach, who backed the bill, said.[103]

Some online poker sites shut down or moved overseas. Others hung on until April 15, 2011, known in gambling circles as "Black Friday," when the federal government seized the domain names of the largest remaining sites and issued indictments against their founders. Poker sharks had to find a new gig. In the summer of 2007, one of them, a blogger from Costa Mesa, California, named Kevin Bonnet, announced a new business venture. "I bring to you a website that compresses the Fantasy Sports experience to just a few action-packed hours, offers you the ability to profit long-term from your sports knowledge, and eliminates all of the hassles of standard fantasy sports offerings like season-long commitments," he wrote under his blogger name, Blinders, before unveiling the URL FantasySportsLive.com. The idea had come to him, he said, while reading the UIGEA. He directed readers to the UIGEA's fantasy carve-out, assuring them that his business followed the letter of the law. Bonnet thanked Senator Bill Frist, the lead architect of the bill, for "making a website like this possible." He titled his announcement "The Shot Heard Round the World."[104] He meant it as a joke, but the journalist Daniel Barbarisi, author of the 2017 book *Dueling with Kings*, would look back on it as a transformative moment for the industry: "Voila. Daily Fantasy Sports was born."[105]

That fall, another blogger, Chris Fargis, an Amherst grad in his late twenties, launched an almost identical DFS site called Instant Fantasy Sports. "The basic idea behind the site is that we take the time frame of season-long fantasy sports leagues and shrink it," he wrote. "The site will look familiar to many of you who are reading this blog because it's set up a lot like an online poker site."[106] Fargis also credited the UIGEA for having encouraged him to turn fantasy into a legal version of Texas hold 'em. Bonnet sold Fantasy Sports Live to an investment firm in 2013. Fargis sold Instant Fantasy Sports in 2008 to NBC, which relaunched it as SnapDraft.

It didn't take long for the emerging market for short-term fantasy gambling to consolidate. On a ten-hour flight from London to Austin, Texas, to attend the 2009 South by Southwest festival's tech conference Interactive, Nigel Eccles, the CEO of a floundering news-betting market called HubDub (where you could bet on things like the outcome of elections), read over the UIGEA and discovered what Bonnet and Fargis had. With more resources than the bloggers, he thought that he could transition his Edinburgh-based team to fantasy and build something better. He returned to the UK after the conference and, with almost no knowledge of baseball, basketball, or American football, founded FanDuel. Eccles and his cofounders commandeered a classroom at the University of Edinburgh to use as a makeshift office and built FanDuel into a behemoth, valued at more than a billion dollars by 2015, when it controlled about half the market. The other half belonged to the frattier, Boston-based DraftKings, the brainchild of three young ecommerce marketing managers who rode round after round of venture funding to the big time.[107] They had launched DraftKings, according to their own founding lore, after work on beer-pong tables they had converted into desks.

The 2015 NFL season brought an onslaught of advertising from FanDuel and DraftKings. The DFS rivals aired a combined 25,000 TV ads in the first month of the season, most during live broadcasts, on ESPN, and – offering some indication of how they imagined their audience – during reruns of *Cops* and *South Park*.[108] The marketing blitz attracted new users but also the New York State attorney general Eric Schneiderman, who, later that fall, declared DFS an illegal form of gambling under state law and issued cease-and-desist letters to FanDuel and DraftKings, both of which had offices in Manhattan.[109] The UIGEA had allowed fantasy and other simulation games on the grounds that they were games of skill. Schneiderman, citing the terrible odds of winning and accusations that a DraftKings content manager had made $350,000 in a FanDuel contest using inside information (he was later cleared), deemed DFS an illegal game of chance. FanDuel and DraftKings disagreed, of course, and around and around they went: Game of chance! Game of skill! It's like the lotto! It's like the stock market! A 2018 Supreme Court decision, which lifted a federal ban on most forms of state-sanctioned betting, rendered the debate moot, but not before both sides had yelled themselves hoarse.

The legal fight distracted from what FanDuel and DraftKings were selling in all that advertising. The industry knew that it needed an image makeover. In 2012, the head of the Fantasy Sports Trade Association admitted in an interview with media scholars Andrew Billings and Brody Ruihley that fantasy had cultural associations he considered obstacles to growth. "Because the word 'fantasy' was in there, it got tied to the Renaissance festival in people's mind," he said. "Everyone thought fantasy football players were walking around with a 20-sided dice in their pocket."[110] Whereas Okrent and James had leaned into the nerdiness of their obsessions, FanDuel and DraftKings sold consumers on an image reminiscent of an episode of *Entourage*: Vegas, Miami, cabanas, bottle service, homosocial bonding among interchangeable women in bikinis. Berry, the ESPN fantasy writer, acknowledged that he and the network welcomed the bros for how they rebranded fantasy as "just one of the things guys do." "What do guys like?" he asked. "They like movies where stuff blows up. They like fast cars. They like attractive women. They like cigars. They like going to Vegas."[111] FanDuel and DraftKings were selling DFS with an image of the good life: Make money without ever leaving the cabana.

Stephen A. Smith, the divisive ESPN host, didn't think that fantasy had much to offer Black fans. "Leisure time for black folks historically consists of direct interaction, the kind of experience you get at a family barbeque or hanging out with friends," he wrote in *ESPN The Magazine*. "Sitting in front of a computer screen pretending to be Bill Parcells? Sounds like work to me."[112] When researchers decided to investigate Smith's conclusion by interviewing Black fans, they determined that he was correct: Fantasy football lacked the cultural "richness" that attracted Black communities to live games.[113] But didn't non-Black communities also dedicate most of their leisure time before the internet to interacting with others face-to-face? And didn't they also favor culturally rich to culturally dull experiences? Jay Caspian Kang agreed with Smith that fantasy football could be labor intensive. When the *New York Times Magazine* asked him to write about the booming industry in 2016, he thought he'd turn in a story about the "bro culture" that reminded him of "the sweaty, sardonic camaraderie you typically see at high stakes poker events." But he found that the game didn't have the same thrill, that it "felt kind of like homework."[114]

Smith and Kang are right that fantasy can be a lot of work. I created a fantasy baseball league for my family in 2022 – for serious academic research, I said – and it felt like I'd taken a part-time job. But you wouldn't know what Kang discovered from watching a FanDuel or DraftKings ad. The two giants of DFS were selling a dream of income without labor, which is also the dream of the stock market: that if you are smart, you can turn a little money into a lot of money without lifting a finger. Their ads often featured men in T-shirts and shorts holding checks for a million or more dollars over their heads. It was the dream of all good scams, money for nothing. The retail investing service Robinhood launched in 2013 with a game-like interface and an ad announcing that you could now "trade just like the big guys."[115] The fantasy manager had heard this before.

More than Strat-O-Matic obsessives or rotisserie leaguers or sabermetricians, DFS users talk about their game as a form of investment. "I'm a day trader, so you're just day trading athletes instead of individual stocks and companies," Tommy Gelati, a world-class conman who gave himself the nickname "the wolf of DFS" and later resurfaced as a QAnon celebrity, told *Real Sports with Bryant Gumbel* in 2014. "The charting's the same. It's the same premises, same concepts – lot of data, lot of analytics."[116] Some of that market language arose from the industry's efforts to distance itself from gambling before the 2018 Supreme Court decision. When *Frontline* asked a college student in 2016 if DFS constituted gambling, he said, "No, it's not gambling at all. I consider it more of investing. I have a portfolio. I'm trying to diversify the portfolio by picking players every day. I'm trying to maximize returns." He then acknowledged that FanDuel had reached out to him before the interview and asked him not to use the word *gambling* in talking with *Frontline*.[117] The student had made, he said, hundreds of thousands of dollars on FanDuel. He was a shark. Schneiderman's office had found that nine out of ten DFS users lost money and that only a tiny fraction got ahead, so the student was the rare winner.[118] The *Frontline* team set out, it seems, to unmask DFS as a form of gambling, but by interviewing Gelati, the college student, and others making what looked like easy money, it burnished the image that the industry had sought to construct. When the *Boston Globe* asked Okrent about DFS in late 2015, he admitted to feeling like J. Robert Oppenheimer after the atomic bombings of Hiroshima and Nagasaki. "I meant it for peaceful purposes," he said.[119]

Football is hard, dangerous work. You can't watch a game and miss the sweat and the crushing hits. DFS users may have their own bruising jobs, so it is no wonder that they aren't dreaming of being a lineman. But in listening to men like Gelati and the college student and watching, as we all do now, a barrage of FanDuel and DraftKings ads, I don't detect a desire to either manage human capital or to cultivate users' own human capital. Wendy Brown writes, of neoliberalism, that "when everything is capital, labor disappears as a category, as does its collective form, class."[120] But labor exists in the world of fantasy football. What matters

A DraftKings advertisement at a train station in Hoboken, New Jersey. From STRMX via AP Photo.

is that it isn't the user's. DFS doesn't sell the user on an image of the self as capital or the athlete as capital but on the self as not labor. Smith asked why few Black fans could be found in fantasy leagues. He should have asked why so many white fans – and white men, most of all – could. What were they, hunched over their screens, dreaming of?

William Rhoden, the longtime *Times* columnist and author of *Forty Million Dollar Slaves*, thought fantasy had drawn a new, more rigid line between athletes and fans. In 2015, he interviewed Carolina Panthers running back Jonathan Stewart, who told him about some of his interactions with fantasy managers on social media. "I think they don't look at us as human anymore," Stewart told Rhoden. "I think they look at us as an opportunity." Rhoden argued that the then-live debate about whether DFS constituted a game of chance had masked the "desensitizing effect" it had on users, "numbing them to the pain and injuries that are the stock and trade of a violent game."[121] Fantasy had, Rhoden thought, alienated fans from athletes, desensitizing them to their labor and to the beatings they took on the field. He didn't mention that Stewart was Black or that most DFS users were white men, but it is clear from his other writing that he recognized the numbing effect of fantasy football as a racial numbing. Since 1973, wages had fallen, debt had risen, and organized labor had suffered one setback after another. White men, who had benefited more than any other subset of Americans from the long economic boom that followed World War II, found themselves with less and wondering where the rest had gone. Labor no longer looked like a route to the good life. You needed some other way to make money to dig yourself out of the hole. Gifted athletes seemed to be living their lost American dream – some of the last manual laborers to be doing well in the United States, at least until old age came for them, around thirty. Fantasy is, for some, a fantasy of management. But, for others, and for most, it is a fantasy of not being labor at a time in which labor has been devalued, surveilled, reduced to data, racialized. It is antirelational. In desensitizing fans to athletes' labor, as Rhoden suggests it does, fantasy also desensitizes fans to their own labor.[122]

A team of business school researchers decided to test Rhoden's conclusion. They designed a study that, using a series of associative exercises intended to reveal unconscious bias, sought to determine whether fantasy football "dehumanized" athletes, as Stewart alleged. The researchers found, contrary to the running back's remarks, that having an athlete on one's fantasy roster humanized them, that it took fantasy managers less time to match an athlete's headshot with words like "citizen" and "warm" if they had him on their fantasy team. Fantasy football should, they concluded, be "leveraged by athlete representatives to cultivate stronger and more favorable brand images."[123] But their control was the same fantasy managers' associative behavior with defensive athletes ineligible for fantasy. The researchers acknowledged that it wasn't a great control. They might have been measuring not an effect of fantasy football but a difference in how fans related to, say, a wide receiver and a cornerback, or the difference not between humanization and dehumanization but between degrees of dehumanization stemming from the culture of fantasy. They also didn't consider DFS, in which users did not form season-long connections to athletes. But the greatest limitation of this and other similar studies is that they assume that fantasy can be isolated from the wider culture of fandom. They can't. There is no control. Fantasy fandom is fandom.[124]

Michael Lewis thought that baseball ought to be more like finance, and he got his wish. "*Moneyball* is a poetic and seminal book," Kirk Goldsberry, the basketball writer and former head of strategic research for the San Antonio Spurs, said in a 2021 interview with *Harvard Data Science Review*, reflecting on the influence of Lewis's book. It was "a call to arms for sports teams to start thinking more like hedge funds." Goldsberry seemed unconcerned by the change. "Kirk, do you feel that this is a good thing?" the interviewer asked him. No, he admitted. But he did not consider it a bad thing either. *Moneyball* belonged to a "larger cultural shift," he said. "We're all quantitative. We're all data scientists now."[125]

The datafication of baseball and basketball had been good to Goldsberry. But it isn't clear that it has had, as he suggested, a neutral effect on the rest of us. "We talk about performers in sports a lot like Goldman Sachs might talk about an asset performance," he said.[126] Professional athletes make a lot more money than someone working the floor of an Amazon warehouse, but their industry has undergone a similar transformation, with every movement tracked, every inefficiency corrected, every dollar of value rung out of their labor. If they can't hit their marks, they're out – cut, fired.

Finance may have gained as much from Billy Beane as Beane did from it. In 2015, a medical research facility hired DePodesta to "jumpstart the 'Moneyball' of medicine."[127] Nate Silver's *FiveThirtyEight* wrote of "the 'Moneyball' of campaign advertising," the *Wall Street Journal* of the "'Moneyball' of the meat industry."[128] A member of the board of an online clothing retailer touted it as "the 'Moneyball" of fashion."[129] Investment banks were taking cues from Lewis and Beane as well. "Building a [sports team] roster is a lot like building a portfolio," a Morgan Stanley newsletter observed in 2021. "Teams would like to sign players with a value higher than their price."[130] Baseball teams were thinking more like hedge funds, and other businesses were thinking more like baseball teams.

When we watch a game and see athletes' every move measured and assigned a value, most of us don't dream of being them. We are them, with lower salaries, and we don't like it. In the age of downturn, the fans needed to find a new way to dream, and they found the Universal Baseball Association, Strat-O-Matic, roto, sabermetrics, fantasy. It was never the dream of being the general manager. It was the dream of, at last, getting out of the game.

Epilogue
Sports Norming

Roger Goodell pleaded poverty. On the eve of the 2013 season, the National Football League reached a $765 million settlement agreement with former players who had sued the league for concealing evidence of the long-term consequences of concussions. Critics of the agreement pointed to the league's almost $10 billion in annual revenue and asked how the maximum individual payout of $5 million, reserved for retired players diagnosed with ALS before the age of forty-five, could be sufficient. The NFL commissioner, who had made $44.2 million the previous year, thought he'd set the record straight. "I've seen some of these comments, first off that we make $10 billion [a year]," Goodell said at a news conference at the Manhattan headquarters of Tiffany and Co., which manufactures the Lombardi Trophy. "That's $10 billion of revenue. And there's a difference between making [profit] and revenue. So this [settlement] is a significant amount of money."[1] The commissioner's comments did not placate his critics. He could have chosen a better venue than the global headquarters of a luxury jeweler, with men in white gloves handling the Super Bowl trophy, to make a case that the NFL didn't have the resources to compensate retired players suffering from Alzheimer's, ALS, CTE, Parkinson's, and other forms of dementia.

The NFL, knowing that the cost of the settlement could run past $1 billion, built in some cost savings. A section tucked into the back of the agreement – page 116, exhibit A-2, section 4 – established procedures for estimating plaintiffs' cognitive functioning prior to or absent their exposure to football. A plaintiff's eligibility for a payout would depend on the difference between that estimate and his present, post-NFL condition. The agreement described a forthcoming "user manual" for clinicians that would include diagnostic criteria, cutoff scores for determining levels of impairment, and "demographically adjusted normative data for Caucasians and African Americans."[2] No one, neither advocates nor reporters, asked what that meant for plaintiffs. No one asked how the normative data would be used. Most of us didn't get to page 116, exhibit A-2, section 4.

The section turned out to be the seed of a scandal. The diagnostic manual, which the legal services firm Epiq produced in early 2017, required that, for at least some of the tests administered, clinicians apply comprehensive norms, or "Heaton norms," which use racial demographic data to estimate preexposure cognitive functioning.[3] Heaton norms, as we would learn, assume lower baseline ability for Black patients, setting the bar for impairment higher for Black former players than for their white co-plaintiffs. The practice of "race norming" built into the agreement an assumption that a Black person has and deserves a lower quality of life than a white person. A forty-five-year-old Black retired player with diminished cognitive functioning arrived at midlife where medical science assumed he would. A forty-five-year-old white retired player with identical test results did not, and the NFL might award him a few million dollars in racial damages.

Kevin Henry got nothing. The Black former defensive lineman, who retired in 2000 after eight seasons with the Pittsburgh Steelers, had received a diagnosis of moderate to severe cognitive decline but then had his claim denied. The NFL contended that Henry's physician had failed to apply a "full demographic model." The league had him reevaluated, and a second clinician found no impairment, attributing the discrepancy between the first and second evaluations to "different normative comparison groups."[4] Henry and another former player, Najeh Davenport, sued the NFL in 2020, alleging that the use of race norming "explicitly and deliberately" discriminated against Black plaintiffs. "Simply stated," their suit claimed, "the League sought to reduce the total cost of benefits paid to the Settlement Class, by greatly reducing benefits to the Black retirees who today make up the majority of both the Settlement Class and the NFL's workforce."[5] Goodell, who made $64 million that year, despite announcing at the onset of the COVID-19 pandemic that he had cut his own salary to $0 (bonuses constitute most of his compensation package), did not turn out empty pockets or lecture reporters on the difference between revenue and profit this time. The NFL agreed to eliminate race norming from the settlement agreement.

The revelation that the NFL had used race norming to deny Black plaintiffs' claims stirred outrage on the left. Few remembered that the practice had originated there. In 1971, the Supreme Court ruled in *Griggs v. Duke Power* that the Civil Rights Act of 1964 prohibited employers from making hiring decisions using tests that disqualified applicants of color at a "substantially higher rate" than white applicants. Employers may not, Chief Justice Warren Burger wrote, "provide equality of opportunity merely in the fabled offer of milk to the stork and the fox."[6] It had to be substantial equality, an equality of outcome. Some HR departments dropped testing after the *Griggs* decision. Others adopted within-group norming, converting applicants' raw test results into scores that reflected where their performance ranked within their demographic group. Liberals championed the practice, attributing the lower test scores of Black and brown applicants to broader social inequalities for which race norming, a form of affirmative action, might compensate. The National Academy of Sciences defended within-group norming in two separate book-length studies, observing in 1982 that unnormed tests "validate the existing social structure rather than opening it up" and promoting race norming in 1989 as an "effective way to balance the dual goals of productivity and racial equity."[7]

Conservatives rebelled. The psychologist Linda Gottfredson argued that liberals refused to acknowledge "substantial racial differences" and that race norming entailed a "considerable sacrifice in workforce productivity."[8] George Will, the conservative columnist, described race norming as a euphemism for affirmative action and affirmative action as "today's euphemism for reverse discrimination."[9] Richard Herrnstein and Charles Murray condemned it in *The Bell Curve* as unscientific and a threat to the nation's economic future.[10] Race norming didn't survive the first Bush administration. The Civil Rights Act of 1991 banned the practice in hiring and promotion.

Robert Heaton, a neuropsychologist at the University of California, San Diego, developed his Heaton norms then, when race norming belonged to a beleaguered racial liberalism. He believed that within-group scoring in clinical psychology could safeguard against the overdiagnosis and pathologization of Black and brown communities. Most neuropsychologists, he wrote in the manual from which the NFL later borrowed, measured patients against the standard of a white middle-class man with one or two years of college education. He insisted that "no single normative standard can be effective with individuals who have widely differing demographic characteristics."[11] The liberal defenders of race norming in employment testing had not set out to degrade Black intelligence. Heaton and his collaborators had not intended to create a tool that the NFL could use to deny damages to Black plaintiffs.

But they did. How did race norming transform from affirmative action to affirmative discrimination? The historian Daryl Michael Scott observes that liberal "pity" has long been the "flip side" of conservative "contempt."[12] One tips over into the other with the slightest shift in socioeconomic conditions. Michael Staub, the author of *The Mismeasure of Minds*, writes that the 1954 *Brown v. Board* decision established Black psychic damage – the evidence that appears to have convinced the Warren Court of the harms of segregation – as the basis of an emerging anti-Black antiracism that continues to inform liberal and conservative racial thought. He sees an unacknowledged historical line stretching from *Brown* to *The Bell Curve*.[13] The Heaton norms had, Scott's and Staub's histories suggest, anti-Blackness baked into them. Journalists and editorialists offered another kind of historical explanation, casting the settlement's use of race norming as "evidence of slavery's afterlife" and the NFL as a "plantation" for the twenty-first century.[14] Professional football, they argued, reproduced the system of anti-Black labor extraction that had prevailed under King Cotton. But neither explanation – race norming as a result of the anti-Black condescension of liberal social science or the long shadow of slavery – accounts for the industrial environment in which Henry and Davenport labored: professional sports. The concussion settlement was about the flaws of social science and durable forms of unfreedom. But it was also about sports, which do more, as this book has shown, than receive and propagate a racial order manufactured elsewhere.

Sports make race through the concept of giftedness. It is a concept that we don't often refuse. Who would not want to be gifted, talented, born with it? But the gift carries a debt. For Marcel Mauss, the feeling of indebtedness was not a bad thing; it bound people and communities together in relations of reciprocation that could perhaps even transcend the logic of the market.[15] The French anthropologist based his argument on the gift-giving practices of Indigenous peoples of the Pacific Northwest and Pacific Islands. He was not writing about the prevailing ethic of industrial capitalist societies or about giftedness. Athletic giftedness does not bind but alienates. It burdens the athlete with an ontological debt. The gifted athlete owes the sport, the team, the owner, the coach, the fan, God, nation. The cultural theorist Mimi Nguyen describes a similar kind of free-floating gift – the "gift of freedom" to the refugee – that carries a "stubborn remainder," a "trace" that may be called "race or gender" or, she adds, "debt."[16] Giftedness is not a lack but an unearned excess.

One way to interpret the use of race norming in the NFL concussion settlement is that it equated Blackness with an absence of cognitive health. Another is that it associated Blackness with a surplus of athletic skill – an innate gift bearing a debt that, without an identifiable lender, can be claimed by all. The former player racialized as gifted owed the league. The former player racialized as gritty, as an ungifted grinder, owed nothing; he would get his check. In the NFL's rejection of their claims, Henry and Davenport confronted the anti-Black practice of race norming but also another form of sorting and compensation they knew all too well. Call it sports norming, the Goodell norms. The NFL had collected a debt owed.[17]

W. E. B. Du Bois had done his own accounting. A year before Mauss published *Essai sur le don*, in 1924, Du Bois had returned to a theme of his most famous title, *The Souls of Black Folk*, in which he had described Black spirituals as "the greatest gift of the Negro people" to the United States.[18] Who, he wondered, had given what to the nation? And what did it owe the giver? In *The Gift of Black Folk*, he enumerated the many contributions of Black people, including plundered labor, to the United States. Some of that gift could be quantified. Some of it could not. Black people had, through emancipation and Reconstruction, given the nation a model of the freedom it espoused but did not practice. "No element in American life," he wrote, "has so subtly and yet clearly woven itself into the warp and woof of our thinking and acting as the American Negro."[19] Black people had given, and the nation had taken. Du Bois did not call for formal reparations in *The Gift of Black Folk*, but the thrust of his argument could not be missed: The United States would not exist without Black people. It carried a racial debt.

Du Bois's gift would never be repaid, and after the reforms of the civil rights era, many would assume that Black people owed the United States a debt for their rights and for the enactment of moderate forms of affirmative action. The gift of Black folk had been deformed. It now appeared as a gift *to* Black folk, and the professional athlete emerged as the paradigmatic gift recipient, the possessor of God-given talent and government-furnished social support. The Black retired players whom the NFL had normed out of damages had received enough, the league decided.

The concussion settlement hadn't been Kevin Henry's first encounter with NFL race norms. At the 1993 NFL scouting combine, the defensive lineman ran the 40-yard dash and 20-yard shuttle run, leapt as high and as far as he could, and took, as all prospects did, the Wonderlic Personnel Test, a short-form IQ test. The Wonderlic had been one of the tests at issue in the 1971 *Griggs v. Duke Power* case, in which the Supreme Court had found that the defendant's use of the test in hiring and promotion had violated the Civil Rights Act of 1964. The *Griggs* decision did not stop the NFL from adopting the Wonderlic in the mid-1970s as a standard scouting tool. Two Cal State Fullerton economists later found that a white prospect who improved from the 25th to the 75th percentile on the test could expect to rise an average of 14.7 positions in the draft, a leap that could add hundreds of thousands and sometimes millions of dollars to a signing bonus. A Black prospect could expect to rise an average of 6.4 positions.[20] A separate study of quarterbacks discovered a slight *negative* correlation between Wonderlic scores and NFL success.[21] The test served no other function than to introduce statistical noise and to reduce Black players' first paychecks.

The tests didn't end there. Teams also administered their own psychological tests. "I know it may be bothersome to the players," New York Giants GM George Young acknowledged of the additional testing. "But we're not embarrassed to ask them to take the test, and they're not embarrassed to ask us for lots of money." He explained that he used psychological testing to spot "problem areas" and "maladjusteds." A consultant for the Steelers, which drafted Henry in the fourth round, praised the team's testing for how it interrogated "family makeup, how someone functions socially, morally and ethically; self-satisfaction, identity." Henry had his own thoughts about the tests. "I hate them," he told the *Pittsburgh Post-Gazette* in 1994. "I don't think they prove anything."[22] He couldn't know then that the NFL would still be testing him long after he'd made his last tackle.

Henry had grown up in the small town of Mound Bayou, Mississippi, which formerly enslaved people had founded after Reconstruction as an independent Black community and which remained, in Henry's youth, almost entirely Black. He had accepted a scholarship offer from Mississippi State, he later told a reporter as a college senior, to prove that "I could come to a predominantly white school and play and get my degree and make it here."[23] He did. He led the MSU defense. He graduated. He made the NFL. In his rookie season, Steelers legend Steve Furness, who played on the team's famed Steel Curtain defensive line, declared him "a natural pass rusher."[24] Henry had to wonder, as he faced one test after another, what Mississippi State, what the NFL combine, what the Steelers had been measuring all along. Perhaps they had been looking for deficiencies, for red flags, as Young said. Or perhaps they had been measuring his gift and the debt they could claim. He would pay a steep price either way.

Brian Flores thought he had passed the test. On January 24, 2022, the former head coach of the Miami Dolphins received a congratulatory text from Bill Belichick, under whom he'd coached for eleven seasons with the New England Patriots. "Sounds like you have landed – congrats!!" Belichick wrote to his former assistant, whom the Dolphins had fired after two consecutive winning seasons in Miami, renewing criticism that the league failed to support Black coaches. "Did you hear something I didn't hear?" a confused Flores asked. "Giants?!?!?!" Belichick wrote. Flores had an interview scheduled with the New York Giants later that week. Had the team decided to hire him? Without interviewing him? Then it dawned on Flores. "Coach," he texted back, "are you talking to Brian Flores or Brian Daboll. Just making sure." Football writers had reported that the Giants had interviewed Daboll, another former Belichick assistant, a white offensive-minded coach, the week before. "Sorry – I fucked this up," Belichick wrote. "I think they are naming Daboll."[25] Belichick signed off, and Flores sat through his interview with the Giants knowing that he didn't have a shot. The team named Daboll head coach. The Giants had, Flores believed, invited him to New York merely to comply with the Rooney Rule, which required NFL teams to interview at least one candidate of color for high-ranking coaching and front-office positions. The Giants had invited him to a sham interview.

Flores, risking his future in the league, sued the Dolphins, the Giants, and the NFL, and he connected his suit to the one that Henry and Davenport had filed over the use of race norming in the concussion settlement. (The suit also named the Denver Broncos. Flores alleged that the team had interviewed him for the head coaching position in bad faith and that executives had arrived to his interview an hour late and hung over.) "The NFL took the position that white people simply have better baseline cognitive function than Black people. This is the very definition of racism," his lawyers wrote. "It also perhaps explains why the NFL and its Teams are so loathe to hire Black Head Coaches."[26] The lawsuit included headshots of all active head coaches, general managers, and franchise owners – one Black head coach (Mike Tomlin of the Pittsburgh Steelers), six Black GMs, and zero Black owners. How could a league in which Black men constituted almost 70 percent of the players on the field not employ more Black coaches and executives? Flores's lawyers alleged, on the second page of the fifty-eight-page suit, that the NFL was "segregated" and "managed much like a plantation" – it was the new Jim Crow, the new slavery.[27] The league assumed, they argued, that Henry and Davenport had lower baseline cognitive functioning than their white co-plaintiffs and that Flores didn't have the hardware for the top job.

Flores's lawyers had to make a blunt historical argument. Law is built on precedent and comparison. For Flores's suit to succeed, they had to draw a line from the discrimination he and other Black coaches faced to the most legible forms of anti-Blackness. But anti-Blackness would not survive if it did not change to meet emerging socioeconomic conditions. Flores made his career in an age of civil rights and high finance. The NFL could point to the affirmative steps it had taken to promote more Black coaches (the Rooney Rule), and franchises could shield themselves with the market: We have to make the moves that will allow us to remain competitive, they argue. Black coaches should be thanking us, they imply, for diverging from that market imperative to interview them as something other than deracinated labor. Flores's lawsuit assumed that discrimination must account for the demographic differences between the players on the field and the coaches on the sideline, that discrimination – assumptions about Black intelligence, white owners' comfort with people like themselves – must be disrupting the pipeline from player to coach. It is, no doubt. But the pipeline has also never been a pipeline for some because the league, sports media, and fans have seen their playing careers not as laborious preparation for coaching careers but as gifts. The Black player-turned-coach doesn't enter his second career with stripes earned but with debt accrued. Flores's suit would succeed or fail on the analogies his legal team drew to the past and to other industries. (His lead attorney sold himself as "America's most prominent #MeToo lawyer.")[28] But most analogies – the analogies through which we encounter science, immigration, crime, education, media, finance – run the other way. Sports are not "like" other industries; other industries are like sports.

The NFL's use of race norming and Flores's lawsuit made headlines because they showed clear evidence of color-line discrimination. The NFL had denied Black players' claims because they were Black. The firing of Flores and David Culley of the Houston Texans at the end of the 2021 regular season had dropped the number of Black head coaches in the league from three to one. But athletic racialization does more than strengthen a rigid color line inherited from the plantation or the Jim Crow South. It moves it. It bends and blurs it. It crosses it with other lines. It wields old norms and invents new ones. It inhabits conservative and liberal thought.

Flores's lawsuit blasted Roger Goodell for pandering to Black and progressive fans – painting "end racism" in end zones and allowing players to make a league-approved set of political statements on their helmets – in the wake of George Floyd's murder. But no one would mistake Goodell for an antiracist. Some might apply that label to the leaders of the WNBA, a league that had embraced athlete protest and political engagement and offered refuge to leftist and liberal sports fans fleeing the NFL and other scandal-plagued men's leagues. Jonquel Jones, a power forward then with the Connecticut Sun, had her own take. "It's all a popularity contest and politics in wbb [women's basketball]," the reigning WNBA MVP tweeted on February 18, 2022. "In mbb you just gottah be the best. In wbb you gottah be the best player, best looking, most marketable, most IG followers, just to sit at the endorsement table."[29] Jones, a queer Black woman from the Bahamas who prefers what she describes as a more masculine look, hoped that the MVP award would deliver the kind of sponsorship deals that she'd seen other players of her caliber land. Then, as she told the journalist Katie Barnes, no one called. The three best-selling jerseys in 2021 all belonged to white athletes (Sue Bird, Sabrina Ionescu, Diana Taurasi), and the players of color who did move merchandise tended to be hetero and more feminine in their presentation. (Jones, that season's MVP, didn't make the top ten.)[30] A'ja Wilson, the 2020 and 2022 MVP, observed that the WNBA attributed the imbalance to "what is marketable."[31] She was not as marketable, the W told her, as Bird, Ionescu, Taurasi – and, later, Caitlin Clark. The market set Jones's value, the league wanted us to believe, not it. The consumer had spoken. The WNBA is no NFL, but it also regulates a labor market – holding drafts, setting salary caps – and then turns around and blames that market for inequalities in compensation that tend to fall heaviest on athletes at one, two, or three removes from the white male American athlete. Can we blame differential human value in sports on the invisible hand of the market? Or might sports, where bodies collide in competition before a mass public, sometimes guide that hand?[32]

Jones did not sue the WNBA. Her grievance wasn't as clear-cut as Henry's and Davenport's or Flores's. She hadn't had a settlement claim denied or lost her job. But she appeared to suffer the fate of many masculine women athletes: Her achievements had been devalued by the assumption that she possessed an advantage, a gift, tied to the perceived excesses of her Blackness and how she embodied her gender. She would get paid, but the league and their sponsors would take a little off the top to balance things out. They would norm her compensation.

Brittney Griner had fared better than Jones. Nike had signed her to a sponsorship deal out of college in 2013, and Griner had, with the company's marketing machine behind her, led the WNBA in jersey sales as a rookie. (The Nike deal netted her a reported $15,000 a year. That's how you end up playing winter ball in Russia.)[33] But Griner could relate. "I've heard, 'Oh, she's not a female, she's a male.' I've been told that, 'Oh, she's tucking stuff,'" she told *ESPN The Magazine* in 2015 for the magazine's Body Issue. "But hey, that's my body and I look the way I look."[34] Griner, queer, Black, and six foot nine, shrugged it off. Bullied as a child, she had gotten comfortable with how she looked. Others hadn't. Critics of the Biden administration's handling of her 2022 incarceration in Russia wondered what the White House might do for an equivalent white male athlete. What if, they asked, Tom Brady had been arrested and sentenced to nine years in a penal colony for trace amounts of hashish oil? Griner had played on two gold-medal-winning Olympic basketball squads. Didn't the nation owe her? None of this could have surprised Griner. She had made a career in professional sports, where differential human values are set and shared with a public as eager to discuss who is overrated and overpaid as what is happening on the field and the court. Griner knew, as Jones discovered, that her gift bore a debt. How much was her life worth? Ask a basketball fan. They can show you the numbers.

The campaign to bar trans girls from participation in high school sports has crossed the racializing gift with a gendering deficit. The tale of the Black athlete's supposed biological gifts – gifts that put the white athlete at an insurmountable disadvantage – reappear in accounts of the cisgender female athlete's supposed deficits, deficits that bestow the trans female athlete with an insurmountable advantage. White men can't jump transforms into cis women can't run or swim. Athletic competition seems to short-circuit leftist and liberal talk of race and gender as social constructs. We hear instead about racial genes and gender hormones.[35] "The buck often stops," the gender scholar C. J. Jones writes, "with sports."[36]

I have argued in the preceding pages that sports belong to the culture industry, that they require a sports cultural studies. Bertolt Brecht would have agreed. He thought that theater could learn a lot from sports. "We pin our hopes to the sporting public," the German playwright declared in 1926. The theater lacked the fun of the football stadium, and it showed in the dwindling enthusiasm of the theatergoing crowd. He proposed a "smokers' theater," where attendees could puff on cigars as if at a boxing match.[37] How, he asked, could the arts compete? They couldn't, it turned out. In 2023, the NFL accounted for 93 of the 100 most-watched television programs.[38] Neither scripted nor reality TV compared, and contemporary theater had, as Brecht feared, all but disappeared from the realm of popular culture. The numbers might surprise non–football fans who consume a lot of political news. Didn't the Right hate the NFL? Didn't the Left? Hadn't one scandal or another sunk it? You'd think. But we can't, it seems, look away.

Watched live en masse at home and in public, sports might be the nation's last remaining consensus culture. We cling to it. We talk about it like the weather, turn to it for common ground. How 'bout that game? we ask. It's a beautiful thing, but it also compels us to ask what ideas form in and circulate through that consensus.

Griner's incarceration in Russia necessitated that we argued, in the language of sports capitalism and the state, for her value. But to argue for one person's or group's value is to assume that some other devalued person or group – the guilty, the unathletic – lacks value. It adopts and reinforces the market relations that create classes of creditors and debtors, givers and recipients. Value is a relational concept. It implies normative criteria for human worth, criteria we might name race or gender or that might come wrapped as a gift, hidden in bouquets. Could we organize sports on a concept other than value? What would it look like?

It is no longer possible to pretend, in an age of renewed athlete protest and a redoubled opposition to it, that sports exist apart from politics. What that politics will be remains to be determined. We pin our hopes to the critical sporting public.

Acknowledgments

I'm the real debtor. Thank you to my colleagues and students at Michigan State University and Texas Christian University. Thank you to Michael Lynch, Anna Mae Duane, and the University of Connecticut Humanities Institute, where, as a visiting fellow, I completed a first draft of this book.

Entering a new field can be intimidating, and I was fortunate to find a welcoming environment in the American Studies Association's Sports Studies Caucus. Thank you to M. Aziz, Noah Cohan, Annie Coleman, Courtney Cox, Frank Andre Guridy, Victoria Jackson, Theresa Runstedtler, and, most of all, Amira Rose Davis – a model for how to do this work at the highest level. Doug Hartmann has been a generous friend and mentor throughout. It would take weeks at the library to gather what I learn from an hour-long conversation with him. Thank you to Wally Lamb and his circle of writer friends for their thoughtful feedback. I'm grateful to Paula Dragosh for her meticulous editing and for enduring my errors. Cecelia Cancellaro and the whole team at Cambridge University Press made the difficult work of making a book easy. Thank you.

I'm lucky to come from a family of athletes and intellectuals. It was, perhaps, inevitable that I would write this book. Thank you to my parents for introducing me to the world of sports (and, well, to the world). Thank you to my brothers, Zack and Sam, to whom this book is dedicated, for the many days of hopping the fence at the end of the road on our way to practice.

Thank you to Ken Griffey Jr. for this moment: "Here is Junior to third base. They're going to wave him in. The throw to the plate will be late. The Mariners are going to play for the American League Championship! I don't believe it! It just continues! My oh my!"

I wrote this book over three years amid seven moves between five states. It was all worth it because Sam Gailey was there for every mile.

Notes

INTRODUCTION: THE NATURAL'S BOUQUETS

1. Bernard Malamud, *The Natural* (New York: Harcourt, Brace, 1952), 41.
2. Malamud, 169.
3. Philip Davis, *Bernard Malamud: A Writer's Life* (New York: Oxford University Press, 2007), 103.
4. Harry Sylvester, "With Greatest of Ease," *New York Times*, August 24, 1952.
5. Leslie A. Fiedler, *Love and Death in the American Novel* (New York: Criterion, 1960), 470, 469.
6. Ahmad Rashad, *Ahmad: Vikes, Mikes, and Something on the Backside*, with Peter Bodo (New York: Viking, 1988), 83.
7. Harry Edwards, "The Sources of the Black Athlete's Superiority," *Black Scholar* 3, no. 3 (1971): 33.
8. The literary scholar Jodi Melamed argues that we now live with a "flexible privilege/stigma divide" that has renewed old color-line racial categories with new cultural, economic, and ideological criteria for determining social value. We get not Black and white or brown and white but liberal/unpatriotic, multicultural/monocultural, global citizen/illegal. The historian Natalia Molina describes the renewal of racial categories as the transference of a "racial script" from one time and people to another. The political scientists Daniel HoSang and Joseph Lowndes call it "racial transference" and see the producer, the parasite, and the patriot as some of the dominant racial categories of our time. This book is about the divide constituted, the script transferred, the transference enacted through the athletic racial categories of gift and grit. Melamed, *Represent and Destroy: Rationalizing Violence in the New Racial Capitalism* (Minneapolis: University of Minnesota Press, 2011), 2; Molina, *How Race Is Made in America: Immigration, Citizenship, and the Historical Power of Racial Scripts* (Berkeley: University of California Press, 2014), 6; HoSang and Lowndes, *Producers, Parasites, and Patriots: Race and the New Right-Wing Politics of Precarity* (Minneapolis: University of Minnesota Press, 2019), 12.

9. Amy Bass, *Not the Triumph but the Struggle: The 1968 Olympics and the Making of the Black Athlete* (Minneapolis: University of Minnesota Press, 2002), 10.
10. Jacques Derrida, *Given Time: I. Counterfeit Money*, trans. Peggy Kamuf (Chicago: University of Chicago Press, 1992), 147.
11. Dan Gilbert, "Open Letter to Fans from Cleveland Majority Owner Dan Gilbert," NBA.com, July 8, 2010, www.nba.com/cavaliers/news/gilbert_letter_100708.html.
12. Michael Omi and Howard Winant, *Racial Formation in the United States: From the 1960s to the 1980s* (New York: Routledge, 1986), 64, 69.
13. Ruth Wilson Gilmore and Craig Gilmore, "Restating the Obvious," in *Indefensible State: The Architecture of the National Insecurity State*, ed. Michael Sorkin (New York: Routledge, 2008), 145.
14. Nikhil Pal Singh, *Race and America's Long War* (Berkeley: University of California Press, 2017), 145.
15. See Lisa Lowe, *The Intimacies of Four Continents* (Durham, NC: Duke University Press, 2015), 6–7.
16. See Joseph Darda, *Empire of Defense: Race and the Cultural Politics of Permanent War* (Chicago: University of Chicago Press, 2019); Darda, *How White Men Won the Culture Wars: A History of Veteran America* (Berkeley: University of California Press, 2021); and Darda, *The Strange Career of Racial Liberalism* (Stanford, CA: Stanford University Press, 2022).
17. Ruth Wilson Gilmore, *Golden Gulag: Prisons, Surplus, Crisis, and Opposition in Globalizing California* (Berkeley: University of California Press, 2007), 27.
18. Ben Carrington, *Race, Sport and Politics: The Sporting Black Diaspora* (Los Angeles: Sage, 2010), 66.
19. Bass, *Not the Triumph but the Struggle*, 48.
20. Douglas Hartmann, "Rethinking the Relationships between Sport and Race in American Culture: Golden Ghettos and Contested Terrain," *Sociology of Sport Journal*, no. 17 (2000): 245. See also Hartmann, *Race, Culture, and the Revolt of the Black Athlete: The 1968 Olympic Protests and Their Aftermath* (Chicago: University of Chicago Press, 2003), xii–xiii.
21. Raymond Williams, *Marxism and Literature* (Oxford: Oxford University Press, 1977), 126, 132.
22. Malamud, *Natural*, 79.
23. Malamud, 79, 80.
24. Malamud, 111.
25. Malamud, 241.
26. Gilbert, "Open Letter to Fans."
27. See Matthew Frye Jacobson, *Whiteness of a Different Color: European Immigrants and the Alchemy of Race* (Cambridge, MA: Harvard University Press, 1998), 91–135; and David R. Roediger, *Working toward Whiteness: How America's Immigrants Became White; The Strange Journey from Ellis Island to the Suburbs* (New York: Basic Books, 2005), 18–34.
28. *US Olympic Track and Field Trials*, aired July 16, 1988, on ABC.

29. Quoted in Randy Harvey, "Unfounded Rumors," *Los Angeles Times*, September 29, 1988.
30. Pat Connolly, "An Athlete to Remember, for a Variety of Reasons," *New York Times*, September 27, 1998.
31. Judith Butler, "Athletic Genders: Hyperbolic Instance and/or the Overcoming of Sexual Binarism," in "The Athlete's Body," ed. Hans Ulrich Gumbrecht et al., special issue, *Stanford Humanities Review* 6, no. 4 (1998): 110, 111.
32. Quoted in Jeff Gottlieb, "Seizure Led to FloJo's Death," *Los Angeles Times*, October 23, 1998.
33. Ian Thomsen, "Flo-Jo Leaves Risk of Drugs Still in Question," *New York Times*, September 26, 1998.
34. Jack Halberstam, *Female Masculinity* (Durham, NC: Duke University Press, 1998), 2.
35. The cultural theorist Neda Atanasoski describes the Cold War as inaugurating a "racial reorientation" in which a "cultural/ideological" divide has supplemented the "racial/biological" divide of the eighteenth and nineteenth centuries. The sociologist Roderick Ferguson observes that racialization in the United States has long worked through gender, with workers of color (or workers who would become "of color") racialized as "deviant in terms of gender and sexuality." Atanasoski, *Humanitarian Violence: The U.S. Deployment of Diversity* (Minneapolis: University of Minnesota Press, 2013), 7; Ferguson, *Aberrations in Black: Toward a Queer of Color Critique* (Minneapolis: University of Minnesota Press, 2004), 15.
36. See Billy Hawkins, *The New Plantation: Black Athletes, College Sports, and Predominantly White NCAA Institutions* (New York: Palgrave Macmillan, 2010). Nathan Kalman-Lamb, Derek Silva, and Johanna Mellis, alluding to Hawkins's book, describe the introduction of NIL (name, image, and likeness) deals for college athletes as "plantation dynamics, rearranged." Kalman-Lamb, Silva, and Mellis, "Race, Money, and Exploitation: Why College Sport Is Still the 'New Plantation,'" *Guardian*, September 7, 2021, www.theguardian.com/sport/2021/sep/07/race-money-and-exploitation-why-college-sport-is-still-the-new-plantation.
37. Race, the boxing writer Carlo Rotella argues, "too often proves to be a graveyard of analytical thinking." It must be addressed not as the destination but as a "stepping stone" to understanding emerging socioeconomic conditions. Rotella interviewed Larry Holmes and Gerry Cooney about their 1982 heavyweight title fight, which their teams had promoted as "Rocky, Rocky, Rocky," with Cooney in the role of Balboa, another great white hope out to redeem the race. Looking back on the racial marketing of the bout, Holmes and Cooney cringed. It sold pay-per-view buys, they acknowledged, but flattened their lives and motivations. The retired fighters did not accuse their management and writers of fabricating racial significance where there was none. Their frustration arose, it seems, from writers' failure to recognize how race had changed in their lifetimes, from how they clung to race as they knew it rather than tracking race as it formed. The fight was not Johnson–Jeffries or Louis–Schmeling. It was 1982, and it was different. It had to be. The athletic gift is a stepping stone, and this book follows it into

science journalism, immigration reform, the war on crime, the struggle for and against affirmative action, and the businesses of cable news and online gambling. Rotella, "The Stepping Stone: Larry Holmes, Gerry Cooney, and *Rocky*," in *In the Game: Race, Identity, and Sports in the Twentieth Century*, ed. Amy Bass (New York: Palgrave Macmillan, 2005), 239.
38. Marcel Mauss, *The Gift: Forms and Functions of Exchange in Archaic Societies*, trans. Ian Cunnison (Glencoe, IL: Free Press, 1954), 66.
39. Mauss, 75.
40. Mauss, 10.
41. See W. E. B. Du Bois, *The Gift of Black Folk: The Negroes in the Making of America* (Boston: Stratford, 1924).
42. Derrida, *Given Time*, 24.
43. David Graeber, *Toward an Anthropological Theory of Value: The False Coin of Our Own Dreams* (New York: Palgrave, 2001), 161.
44. Mauss, *Gift*, 74.
45. Saidiya V. Hartman, *Scenes of Subjection: Terror, Slavery, and Self-Making in Nineteenth-Century America* (New York: Oxford University Press, 1997), 132.
46. Mimi Thi Nguyen, *The Gift of Freedom: War, Debt, and Other Refugee Passages* (Durham, NC: Duke University Press, 2012), 5.
47. Howard Bryant, *The Heritage: Black Athletes, a Divided America, and the Politics of Patriotism* (Boston: Beacon Press, 2018), x. Bryant describes Paul Robeson as the "charter member and first casualty" of the Heritage for how he used "his talents to amplify the causes" of "less athletically gifted black people" around the world and how it cost him his career (xiv, 58). Bryant and others have suggested that Flo Jo's generation of Black athletes, the generation that arrived after civil rights and Black Power, neglected the Heritage, that they failed to service another kind of social debt.
48. Kenny Moore, "The Spoils of Victory," *Sports Illustrated*, April 10, 1989, 50.
49. Anise C. Wallace, "Next Stop, Madison Avenue," *New York Times*, October 27, 1988.
50. The philosopher Grant Farred refers to the dissonance in the life of star Black athletes as the "burden of over-representation," in which athletes are understood as "representative" and "exceptional," standing in for and rising above the communities from which they come. The historian Amira Rose Davis identifies the labor that Black women athletes have carried out as ambassadors for the nation – a nation that advertises itself as modeling racial and gender freedoms – as uncompensated "symbolic labor." In her ethnographic account of the historic Gleason's Gym, the sociologist Lucia Trimbur describes white-collar clients' attraction to training there as a desire for what they consider and construct as the "authentic racial identities" of Black and brown fighters and their trainers – a "racialized form of consumption." Farred, *The Burden of Over-representation: Race, Sport, and Philosophy* (Philadelphia: Temple University Press, 2018), 46; Davis, "'Watch What We Do': The Politics and Possibilities of Black Women's Athletics, 1910–1970" (PhD diss., Johns Hopkins University, 2016), 14; Trimbur, *Come Out Swinging: The Changing World of Boxing in Gleason's Gym* (Princeton, NJ: Princeton University Press, 2013), 140.

51. See Roy Terrell, "The Biggest Golf Hustler of Them All," *Sports Illustrated*, November 12, 1962, 31.
52. See John Andrews, "The Paymasters," in "Not Just a Game," supplement, *Economist*, June 6, 1998, 16.
53. Quoted in Zachary Schiller, "Advantage, Mark McCormack?," *Business Week*, September 27, 1993, 72.
54. Quoted in David Davies, "McCormack, the Man Who Wanted More," *Guardian*, May 16, 2003.
55. E. M. Swift, "The Most Powerful Man in Sports," *Sports Illustrated*, May 21, 1990, 100.
56. "The Rising Price of Has-Beens," *Economist*, September 8, 1990, 72.
57. Mark H. McCormack, *What They Don't Teach You at Harvard Business School: Notes from a Street-Smart Executive* (New York: Bantam, 1984), xii.
58. Matthew Futterman, *Players: The Story of Sports and Money, and the Visionaries Who Fought to Create a Revolution* (New York: Simon and Schuster, 2016), 3.
59. McCormack, *What They Don't Teach You*, 163.
60. Quoted in Swift, "Most Powerful Man in Sports," 116.
61. The literary scholar Noah Cohan observes that being a sports fan is an "autobiographical practice": Fans learn to make sense of their lives through the stories they consume and tell about their favorite athletes and teams. McCormack taught them to make sense of their finances through them as well and to make sense of sports through finance. Cohan, *We Average Unbeautiful Watchers: Fan Narratives and the Reading of American Sports* (Lincoln: University of Nebraska Press, 2019), 4.
62. Theodor W. Adorno, "Education after Auschwitz," in *Critical Models: "Interventions" and "Catchwords,"* trans. Henry W. Pickford (New York: Columbia University Press, 1998), 196–97, 197.
63. Adorno, 197.
64. C. L. R. James, *Beyond a Boundary* (London: Hutchinson, 1963), 51.
65. Max Horkheimer and Theodor W. Adorno, *Dialectic of Enlightenment*, trans. John Cumming (New York: Herder and Herder, 1972), 132. American cultural studies, as Bass observes, has been slow to address sports as culture. It still, as Adorno and Horkheimer did in the 1940s, tends to consider culture as constituted of literature, film, music, and news media. Sports historians have turned toward culture, but cultural studies hasn't turned back. This has never been true of British cultural studies, which has, from the beginning, seen sports as constitutive of what Stuart Hall described as the foundation of cultural studies: "cultural power," where "symbolic forms and meaning" meet "the organization of power." See Bass, "State of the Field: Sports History and the 'Cultural Turn,'" *Journal of American History* 101, no. 1 (2014): 153–54; Hall, "Culture and Power," interview by Peter Osborne and Lynne Segal, *Radical Philosophy*, no. 86 (1997): 24.
66. Mark H. McCormack to Olle Nyman, June 11, 1973, Mark H. McCormack Papers, mums700-b0003-f010-i052, Special Collections and University Archives, University of Massachusetts Library.

67. McCormack, *What They Don't Teach You*, 102.
68. Mark H. McCormack to Robert D. Kain, July 5, 1990, Mark H. McCormack Papers, mums700-b0015-f028-i012, Special Collections and University Archives, University of Massachusetts Library.
69. Mark H. McCormack to Robert D. Kain, Peter Johnson, and Barry Frank, August 9, 1991, Mark H. McCormack Papers, mums700-b0017-f045-i016, Special Collections and University Archives, University of Massachusetts Library.
70. Quoted in "Payne: Tiger to Be Judged on Sincerity," ESPN.com, April 7, 2010, www.espn.com/golf/masters10/news/story?id=5063768.
71. For more on *Sports Illustrated* in the Laguerre era, see Michael MacCambridge, *The Franchise: A History of "Sports Illustrated" Magazine* (New York: Hyperion, 1997), 103–43.
72. Frank Deford, "Sometimes the Bear Eats You: Confessions of a Sportswriter," *Sports Illustrated*, March 29, 2010, 54.
73. Bharat Anand and Kate Attea, *International Management Group* (Boston: Harvard Business Publishing, 2001), 1.
74. Quoted in Nadine Brozan, "Three Olympians Take the President for a Run," *New York Times*, July 17, 1993.
75. "President Clinton Participates in ESPN Race Town Hall," Office of the Press Secretary, White House, April 14, 1998, https://clintonwhitehouse4.archives.gov/WH/New/html/19980415-8261.html.
76. Quoted in Peter Baker and Michael A. Fletcher, "Clinton's Town Hall Taking Discussion of Race into Sports Arena," *New York Times*, April 14, 1998.
77. Quoted in James Bennett, "President Leads TV Discussion on Role of Race in Sports," *New York Times*, April 15, 1998.
78. Victor Ray, "A Theory of Racialized Organizations," *American Sociological Review* 84, no. 1 (2019): 35, 36.
79. Pierre Bourdieu, "Sport and Social Class," trans. Richard Nice, *Social Science Transformation* 17, no. 6 (1978): 822.
80. "Only at the level of the field of positions," Bourdieu wrote in *Distinction*, "is it possible to grasp both the generic interests associated with the fact of taking part in the game and the specific interests attached to the different positions." There is, he added, "no way out of the game of culture." Bourdieu, *Distinction: A Social Critique of the Judgement of Taste*, trans. Richard Nice (Cambridge, MA: Harvard University Press, 1984), 12.
81. Others have written about the relation between the racial state and the sports organization. Hartmann identifies the midnight basketball programs of the 1980s and '90s as a convergence of state and local racial interests that coalesced into a "commercial" for cut-rate neoliberal social programs. Hartmann, *Midnight Basketball: Race, Sports, and Neoliberal Social Policy* (Chicago: University of Chicago Press, 2016), 76.
82. "President Clinton Participates in ESPN Race Town Hall."
83. "President Clinton Participates in ESPN Race Town Hall."
84. Dan Sheinin, "Mariners Trade Griffey to Reds," *Washington Post*, February 11, 2000.
85. James, *Beyond a Boundary*, 150.

1 THE MISMEASURE OF SPORT

1. Quoted in "Bannister Offers Speculation about 'Advantages' for Blacks," *New York Times*, September 14, 1995.
2. Quoted in Tim Radford, "Black Runners 'at an Advantage,'" *Guardian*, September 14, 1995.
3. Ben Carrington, "Of Races, Hurdles and Sporting Chances," letter to the editor, *Independent*, September 19, 1995.
4. See Roger Mills, "Bannister's 'Theory' an Unacceptable One," *Tampa Bay Times*, September 17, 1995.
5. Jack McCallum and Kostya Kennedy, "A Different Race for Sir Roger," *Sports Illustrated*, September 25, 1995, 15.
6. The editors of *Nature* also weighed in on Bannister's comments, arguing that research into Black athletic success must account for cultural factors and suggesting that, given the historical misuses of that research, it might be "better to invest what goodwill there is in some quite different field." But they affirmed the intellectual value of rigorous genetic studies of anatomical racial difference. "Much benefit could come from well-planned studies," the editors wrote. "Bias-Free Interracial Comparisons," *Nature* 377, no. 6546 (1995): 184, 183.
7. Roger Bannister, "Beyond the Boundary," *Sports Illustrated*, August 13, 1979, 132.
8. Bannister had convened a joint meeting of the British Association of Sport Medicine and the British Olympic Association in 1973 to investigate altitude training. He acknowledged that the "heartwarming success" of East African distance runners had motivated the meeting. He claimed that East Africans were "endowed genetically and through acclimatization with certain benefits from living in an atmosphere deficient in oxygen" and invited attendees to consider drafting a "workable code to restrict or ban altitude training." He wanted a level playing field, for the West. Bannister, "Opening Remarks to a Joint Meeting of the British Association of Sport Medicine with the British Olympic Association," *British Journal of Sports Medicine* 8, no. 1 (1974): 3, 4.
9. Roger Bannister, "My Olympic Defeat Hurt So Much I Went after the Four-Minute Mile," interview by Alice Thomson, *Times*, July 28, 2012.
10. "Sometimes I am asked what I would do differently if I was starting my career today," Bannister wrote in a 2014 memoir. "The world has moved on and only certain athletic events would be open to me." Altitude tents and other training technologies could not, he concluded, offset the "natural advantages the East African runners possess." If Bannister felt cowed by the criticism he had received for his 1995 remarks, as his defenders suggested he and others had, he didn't show it. Bannister, *Twin Tracks* (London: Robson Press, 2014), 353, 338.
11. See R. M. Malina, "Racial/Ethnic Variation in the Motor Development and Performance of American Children," *Canadian Journal of Sport Sciences* 13, no. 2 (1988): 136–43.
12. Brett St. Louis, "Sport and Common-Sense Racial Science," *Leisure Studies* 23, no. 1 (2004): 32.

13. Ben Carrington and Ian McDonald, introduction to *"Race," Sport and British Society*, ed. Ben Carrington and Ian McDonald (London: Routledge, 2001), 6. Carrington later argued that the reason that most scientific studies find nothing more than the suggestion of "racio-performative *correlation*" is that there is no "ontological black athletic body" outside the lab. The "scientific gaze" had constituted it. Carrington, *Race, Sport and Politics: The Sporting Black Diaspora* (Los Angeles: Sage, 2010), 81, 80.
14. See Amy Bass, *Not the Triumph but the Struggle: The 1968 Olympics and the Making of the Black Athlete* (Minneapolis: University of Minnesota Press, 2002), 50.
15. John J. MacAloon, *This Great Symbol: Pierre de Coubertin and the Origins of the Modern Olympic Games* (Chicago: University of Chicago Press, 1981), 268, 271.
16. The Human Genome Project launched in 1990, inaugurating what the anthropologist Jonathan Marks calls the age of "genohype." The project used the "as a scientist" defense to beat back critics. As Marks summarizes the argument: "Genetics is science, and thus to be against what a geneticist says is to be against science. That argument may be wrong and stupid, but it has a lot of rhetorical force." The HGP had built a scientific shield for Bannister before he ever took the stage at the British Association for the Advancement of Science. Marks, *Why I Am Not a Scientist: Anthropology and Modern Knowledge* (Berkeley: University of California Press, 2009), 238, 239.
17. Malcolm Gladwell, "The Sports Taboo," *New Yorker*, May 19, 1997, 53.
18. Selina Soule, "Testimony before the United States Senate Committee on the Judiciary in Opposition to the Equality Act," Alliance Defending Freedom, March 17, 2021, https://adfmedialegalfiles.blob.core.windows.net/files/EqualityActTestimonySJC.pdf.
19. The gender historian Valerie Moyer argues that the heightened surveillance of women athletes' bodies in the 2010s descends from the War on Terror, when the state shifted from mass screening to targeted surveillance and called on citizens to monitor the behavior of others (if you see something, say something). Moyer describes it as a "seeping" surveillance that moves from the state to elite sports and then to high school track meets in Connecticut. Moyer, "The Seeping Surveillance of Sex in Sports," in "The Body Issue: Sports and the Politics of Embodiment," ed. Joseph Darda and Amira Rose Davis, special issue, *American Quarterly* 75, no. 3 (2023): 502.
20. Cheryl Cooky and Shari L. Dworkin, "Policing the Boundaries of Sex: A Critical Examination of Gender Verification and the Caster Semenya Controversy," *Journal of Sex Research* 50, no. 2 (2013): 108.
21. The criminologist Kathryn Henne notes the contradiction at the heart of sex-verification testing: Though athletic governing bodies insist that they value "natural bodies," their rules "can actually require athletes deemed too naturally masculine for women's sport to artificially modify their bodies." The ontological debt attached to the idea of giftedness has often served to resolve that contradiction. Henne, *Testing for Athlete Citizenship: Regulating Doping and Sex in Sport* (New Brunswick, NJ: Rutgers University Press, 2015), 88.

22. Jon Entine, *Taboo: Why Black Athletes Dominate Sports and Why We're Afraid to Talk about It* (New York: PublicAffairs, 2000), 13, 12–13.
23. Entine, 11.
24. Dean B. Cromwell, *Championship Technique in Track and Field*, with Al Wesson (New York: Whittlesey House, 1941), 5, 6.
25. Cromwell, 230, 231.
26. Cromwell, 6, 9.
27. Cromwell, 10, 11.
28. "The New York Meeting of the American Anthropological Association," *Science* 89, no. 2298 (1939): 30.
29. Franz Boas, "What Is a Race?," *Nation*, January 28, 1925, 91.
30. Franz Boas, "Racial Purity," *Asia*, May 1940, 231.
31. For more on how Boas's "vigorous opposition to prejudice and discrimination coexisted with his ongoing efforts to practice a science of physical anthropology" that remained "fundamentally racialized" (66), see Tracy Teslow, *Constructing Race: The Science of Bodies and Cultures in American Anthropology* (New York: Cambridge University Press, 2014), 32–73.
32. Ruth Benedict, *Race: Science and Politics* (New York: Modern Age Books, 1940), vi.
33. Benedict, 7.
34. Ruth Benedict and Gene Weltfish, *The Races of Mankind* (New York: Public Affairs Committee, 1943), 11, 16.
35. Benedict and Weltfish, 7.
36. Benedict and Weltfish, 11.
37. For more on the origins and evolution of the concept of ethnicity, see Matthew Frye Jacobson, *Roots Too: White Ethnic Revival in Post–Civil Rights America* (Cambridge, MA: Harvard University Press, 2006), 31–35; and David R. Roediger, *Working toward Whiteness: How America's Immigrants Became White; The Strange Journey from Ellis Island to the Suburbs* (New York: Basic Books, 2005), 27–34.
38. Frantz Fanon, *Black Skin, White Masks*, trans. Charles Lam Markmann (New York: Grove Press, 1967), 161.
39. Fanon, 161n25.
40. Fanon, 161.
41. Quoted in Charles Maher, "Blacks' Arms OK – but They Run Better," *Los Angeles Times*, March 28, 1968.
42. Quoted in Maher.
43. Quoted in Charles Maher, "Blacks Physically Superior? Some Say They're 'Hungrier,'" *Los Angeles Times*, March 26, 1968.
44. Charles Maher, "Why No Black Quarterbacks in Professional Football?," *Los Angeles Times*, March 27, 1968.
45. Martin Kane, "An Assessment of 'Black Is Best,'" *Sports Illustrated*, January 18, 1971, 74. The British endocrinologist James Tanner, the one source Kane named in making his claims, had studied the bodies of 137 athletes at the 1960 Rome Olympics. From measurements he took of twelve white athletes and just three Black athletes, he discerned "large significant racial differences in leg length, arm length and hip length." Kane seems to have

built his broad claims about Black and white bodies on Tanner's 137-athlete study. Tanner, *The Physique of the Olympic Athlete* (London: George Allen and Unwin, 1964), 51.
46. Kane, "Assessment of 'Black Is Best,'" 79–80.
47. Kane, 81.
48. Quoted in Kane, 79.
49. Harry Edwards, "The Sources of the Black Athlete's Superiority," *Black Scholar* 3, no. 3 (1971): 39, 33.
50. Paul Gilroy described the revival of scientific theories of Black athleticism in the 1990s as a "reversion to mystical, pre-Boasian accounts of racial difference." But Boas and others in his orbit contributed to that resurgence by founding their study of culture on and sorting it into biological racial categories. Critics on the left have struggled ever since with how to counter racial biologism without summoning an also biologized racial culturalism. Gilroy, *Between Camps: Nations, Cultures and the Allure of Race* (London: Penguin, 2000), 257.
51. Tom Brokaw, host, *Black Athletes: Fact and Fiction*, NBC Nightly News, aired April 25, 1989, on NBC.
52. Amby Burfoot, "White Men Can't Run," *Runner's World*, August 1992, 90. *Los Angeles Times* columnist Scott Ostler had mocked Johnson's comments at the time, writing, "Dear Brooks: pack a lunch. And while you're out there searching, bring back a white Spud Webb, a white Dominique Wilkens, a white O. J. Simpson, a white Jerry Rice, a white Bo Jackson and a white Wilt Chamberlin." Ostler, "White Athletes – Fact and Fiction: Destroying Myths," *Los Angeles Times*, April 27, 1989.
53. Burfoot, "White Men Can't Run," 90.
54. Burfoot, 91.
55. Frank Deford, ed., *The Best American Sports Writing, 1993* (Boston: Houghton Mifflin, 1993), 58.
56. Burfoot, "White Men Can't Run," 90.
57. Linda Villarosa, "The Other Kenyans," *Runner's World*, August 1992, 98.
58. Dave Prokop, foreword to *The African Running Revolution*, ed. Dave Prokop (Mountain View, CA: World Publications, 1975), 4.
59. John Manners, "In Search of an Explanation," in *The African Running Revolution*, ed. Dave Prokop (Mountain View, CA: World Publications, 1975), 31.
60. Manners, 35.
61. See Entine, *Taboo*, 190.
62. Kenny Moore, "Sons of the Wind," *Sports Illustrated*, February 26, 1990, 79.
63. Malina, "Racial/Ethnic Variation," 137.
64. Marks, the anthropologist, identifies the failure to distinguish genetic from cultural difference as the fundamental flaw of racial athleticism. "The great bulk of human behavioral/mental variation occurs *between* groups and is the product of historical forces," he writes. "The great bulk of genetic variation occurs *within* groups, and may indeed comprise part of the causal nexus of someone's life trajectory." Malina's biocultural model throws out the difference. Marks, "The Growth of Scientific Standards from Anthropology Days

to Present Days," in *The 1904 Anthropology Days and Olympic Games*, ed. Susan Brownell (Lincoln: University of Nebraska Press, 2008), 391.
65. Aileen Moreton-Robinson, *The White Possessive: Property, Power, and Indigenous Sovereignty* (Minneapolis: University of Minnesota Press, 2015), 192.
66. Valerie Lynn Dorsey, "One Running Back Doesn't Mind Being Different," *USA Today*, December 19, 1991.
67. Quoted in Peter King, "White Guys Can't Run," *Sports Illustrated*, September 7, 1992, 29.
68. S. L. Price, "Whatever Happened to the White Athlete?," *Sports Illustrated*, December 8, 1997, 34.
69. Quoted in King, "White Guys Can't Run."
70. John Hoberman, *Darwin's Athletes: How Sport Has Damaged Black America and Preserved the Myth of Race* (Boston: Houghton Mifflin, 1997), xxv.
71. Gladwell, "Sports Taboo," 51.
72. Gladwell, 53.
73. Robert E. Park and Ernest W. Burgess, *Introduction to the Science of Sociology* (Chicago: University of Chicago Press, 1921), 136. See also Ralph Ellison, introduction to *Shadow and Act* (New York: Random House, 1964), xx.
74. Entine, *Taboo*, 8, 337.
75. Entine, 10, 74. Entine later attributed his struggle to find a publisher for *Taboo* and the negative reviews it received to a harmful "racial sensitivity" among "Establishment whites and blacks." Entine, "Breaking the Taboo," *Index on Censorship* 29, no. 4 (2000): 64.
76. Entine, *Taboo*, 10.
77. Quoted in Jim Myers, "Examining the Races: Experts Scoff at Myths," *USA Today*, December 16, 1991.
78. Quoted in Scott Shane, "Genetics Research Increasingly Finds 'Race' a Null Concept," *Baltimore Sun*, April 4, 1999.
79. Marks, *Why I Am Not a Scientist*, 238.
80. Marks, "Growth of Scientific Standards," 393.
81. "General Secretary of IAAF Pierre Weiss on Caster Semenya," LetsRun.com video, 3:01, August 19, 2009, www.youtube.com/watch?v=FK7tLvuwr4c.
82. Quoted in Christopher Clarey, "Gender Test after a Gold-Medal Finish," *New York Times*, August 19, 2009.
83. See Karyn Maughan, Gill Gifford, and Reuters, "Caster's Ultimate Humiliation," *Star* (South Africa), September 16, 2009.
84. Quoted in Clarey, "Gender Test after a Gold-Medal Finish."
85. International Association of Athletics Federations, "IAAF Policy on Gender Verification," 2006, https://web.archive.org/web/20070112013204/www.iaaf.org/newsfiles/36983.pdf. For more on the history of sex-verification testing, see Henne, *Testing for Athlete Citizenship*, 87–114.
86. Quoted in Ariel Levy, "Either/Or," *New Yorker*, November 30, 2009, 50.
87. Cooky and Dworkin, "Policing the Boundaries of Sex," 108.
88. Judith Butler, "Wise Distinctions: Thoughts on Caster Semenya," *Los Angeles Review of Books*, November 20, 2009, www.lrb.co.uk/blog/2009/november/wise-distinctions.

89. Henne, *Testing for Athlete Citizenship*, 20.
90. Semenya has never identified as intersex. "I'm an African, I'm a woman, I'm a different woman," she told the *Guardian* in 2023. "That's the only term I can use." The sociologist Zine Magubane argues that American feminists who wished to embrace Semenya as intersex failed to recognize that intersex had been raced white in the United States (motivating corrective medical intervention, then white activism) but Black in South Africa (as a sign of Black gender deviance). Western feminists' celebration of Semenya as an intersex icon sometimes landed in South Africa, Magubane observes, as a familiar form of anti-Blackness. Tshepo Mokoena, "Caster Semenya: 'How Would I Label Myself? I'm an African. I'm a Different Woman,'" *Guardian*, October 28, 2023, www.theguardian.com/sport/2023/oct/28/athlete-caster-semenya-interview-im-a-woman-im-a-different-woman; Magubane, "Spectacles and Scholarship: Caster Semenya, Intersex Studies, and the Problem of Race in Feminist Theory," *Signs* 39, no. 3 (2014): 761–85.
91. Douglas G. Logan, "An Open Letter to President Bush," USA Track and Field, July 22, 2008, https://web.archive.org/web/20080726193730/www.usatf.org/news/view.aspx?DUID=USATF_2008_07_22_06_15_21.
92. Rebecca M. Jordan-Young and Katrina Karkazis, *Testosterone: An Unauthorized Biography* (Cambridge, MA: Harvard University Press, 2019), 10.
93. Epstein, *Sports Gene*, 61.
94. Epstein, xii.
95. Malcolm Gladwell, *Outliers: The Story of Success* (New York: Little, Brown, 2008), 40.
96. After an article in the magazine of the Association for Psychological Science attributed the 10,000 hours rule, a Gladwell coinage, to Ericsson, the psychologist distanced himself from the idea, which he described as a "provocative generalization" that failed to distinguish "deliberate practice" from the sheer accumulation of hours. Gladwell fired back, suggesting that Ericsson did not account for talent and resituating himself somewhere between Ericsson and his friend Epstein on the sliding scale of the training-talent debate. Ericsson, "The Danger of Delegating Education to Journalists: Why the APS *Observer* Needs Peer Review when Summarizing New Scientific Developments," 2012, https://web.archive.org/web/20140717041100/http://psy.fsu.edu/faculty/ericsson/2012%20Ericssons%20reply%20to%20APS%20Observer%20article%20Oct%2028%20on%20web.doc; quoted in Ben Carter, "Can 10,000 Hours of Practice Make You an Expert?," *BBC News Online*, March 1, 2014, www.bbc.com/news/magazine-26384712.
97. Epstein, *Sports Gene*, 18.
98. Epstein, 155, 32.
99. Epstein, 267, 282.
100. Malcolm Gladwell, "Man and Superman," *New Yorker*, September 9, 2013, 79, 80.
101. Gladwell, 80.
102. *Men's Health*, July–August 2006.

103. Christopher McDougall, "The Men Who Live Forever," *Men's Health*, July–August 2006, 182.
104. McDougall, 186.
105. Christopher McDougall, *Born to Run: A Hidden Tribe, Superathletes, and the Greatest Race the World Has Never Seen* (New York: Knopf, 2009).
106. Dennis M. Bramble and Daniel E. Lieberman, "Endurance Running and the Evolution of *Homo*," *Nature*, no. 432 (2004): 351. See also Daniel E. Lieberman and Dennis M. Bramble, "The Evolution of Marathon Running: Capabilities in Humans," *Sports Medicine* 37, nos. 4–5: 288–90.
107. McDougall, *Born to Run*, 239.
108. McDougall, 41.
109. Christopher McDougall, "Built for the Long Run," *Men's Health*, June 2009, 104.
110. McDougall, *Born to Run*, 131.
111. Dale Groom, "Cardiovascular Observations on Tarahumara Indian Runners – the Modern Spartans," *American Heart Journal* 81, no. 1 (1971): 304.
112. William S. Willis Jr., "Skeletons in the Anthropological Closet," in *Reinventing Anthropology*, ed. Dell H. Hymes (New York: Pantheon, 1972), 137, 126. The anthropologist Nicholas De Genova later echoed Willis's criticism, wondering what an "anthropology *of* the United States, rather than an anthropology merely *in* its national space," might look like. De Genova, "The Stakes of an Anthropology of the United States," *New Centennial Review* 7, no. 2 (2007): 232–33.
113. Philip J. Deloria, *Playing Indian* (New Haven, CT: Yale University Press, 1998), 191.
114. Jack Halberstam, *Female Masculinity* (Durham, NC: Duke University Press, 1998), 275.
115. Adharanand Finn, *Running with the Kenyans: Passion, Adventure, and the Secrets of the Fastest People on Earth* (New York: Ballantine, 2012), 18.
116. Quoted in Finn, *Running with the Kenyans*, 184.
117. Court of Arbitration for Sport, "CAS Arbitration: Caster Semenya, Athletics South Africa, and International Association of Athletics Federations Decision," press release, May 1, 2019, www.tas-cas.org/fileadmin/user_upload/Media_Release_Semenya_ASA_IAAF_decision.pdf.
118. Amby Burfoot, "Let Semenya Run Free … in the 1500," LetsRun.com, May 2, 2019, www.letsrun.com/news/2019/05/guest-column-by-amby-burfoot-let-semenya-run-free-in-the-1500/.

2 ROBERTO CLEMENTE ON THE BLACK/BROWN COLOR LINE

1. "Monte Irvin Delivers Hall of Fame Induction Speech," August 6, 1973, MLB video, 3:48, November 10, 2015, www.youtube.com/watch?v=cKIBPetDKVk.
2. Joseph Durso, "Clemente Is in Hall of Fame," *New York Times*, March 21, 1973.
3. James D. Heath, Sports Note Pad, *Atlanta Daily World*, July 29, 1973.

4. Quoted in Les Biederman, "Clouter Clemente: Popular Buc," *Sporting News*, September 5, 1964, 3.
5. Quoted in David Maraniss, *Clemente: The Passion and Grace of Baseball's Last Hero* (New York: Simon and Schuster, 2006), 25.
6. C. L. R. James, *Beyond a Boundary* (London: Hutchinson, 1963), 55.
7. James, 59.
8. C. L. R. James, *The Life of Captain Cipriani: An Account of British Government in the West Indies* (Nelson, Lancashire, UK: Coulton, 1932), 15.
9. See Bill Nuun Jr., "Clemente May Bring 'Rookie of the Year' Laurels to Pirates," *Pittsburgh Courier*, June 18, 1955.
10. Adrian Burgos Jr., *Playing America's Game: Baseball, Latinos, and the Color Line* (Berkeley: University of California Press, 2007), 179–80.
11. See Lisa Brock and Bijan Bayne, "Not Just Black: African-Americans, Cubans, and Baseball," in *Between Race and Empire: African-Americans and Cubans before the Cuban Revolution*, ed. Lisa Brock and Bijan Digna Castañeda Fuertes (Philadelphia: Temple University Press, 1998), 175.
12. Peter C. Bjarkman, *Baseball with a Latin Beat: A History of the Latin American Game* (Jefferson, NC: McFarland, 1994), 59.
13. For more on Latinos in and out of the amateur draft, see Adrian Burgos Jr. and Frank Andre Guridy, "Becoming Suspect in Usual Places: Latinos, Baseball, and Belonging in el Barrio del Bronx," in *Beyond el Barrio: Everyday Life in Latina/o America*, ed. Gina M. Pérez, Frank Andre Guridy, and Adrian Burgos Jr. (New York: New York University Press, 2010), 90–92.
14. Orlando Cepeda, *Baby Bull: From Hardball to Hard Time and Back*, with Herb Fagen (Dallas: Taylor Publishing, 1998), 3.
15. Nate Penn, "Whack!-ipedia," *GQ*, June 2007, 227.
16. Earl Lewis, "To Turn on a Pivot: Writing African Americans into a History of Overlapping Diasporas," *American Historical Review* 100, no. 3 (1995): 767.
17. Laura E. Gómez, *Inventing Latinos: A New Story of American Racism* (New York: New Press, 2020), 15.
18. The historian Samuel Regalado, for example, writes in *Viva Baseball!* that "the expansion of baseball's Latin contingent mirrored the growing importance of Latin cultures in the United States." The sport functions, for him, and most scholars, as a microcosm of the wider culture. Regalado, *Viva Baseball! Latin Major Leaguers and Their Special Hunger* (Urbana: University of Illinois Press, 1998), 4.
19. G. Cristina Mora, *Making Hispanics: How Activists, Bureaucrats, and Media Constructed a New American* (Chicago: University of Chicago Press, 2014), 12.
20. John Leonard, "Out of Left Field," *New York Times*, October 17, 1976.
21. Yomaira C. Figuero-Vásquez, *Decolonizing Diasporas: Radical Mappings of Afro-Atlantic Literatures* (Evanston, IL: Northwestern University Press, 2020), 9.
22. Roberto Clemente, "A Conversation with Clemente," interview by Sam Nover, WIIC-TV, October 8, 1972.

23. Burgos observes that MLB's commemoration of Black and Latino greats – he cites the Latino Legends promotion of 2005 and Mudcat Grant's Black Aces club – often imposes a "double invisibility" on Afro-Latinos: "too black to be perceived as Latino, too ethnic to be perceived as black," they are honored as neither Latino legends nor Black aces. Burgos, "Left Out: Afro-Latinos, Black Baseball, and the Revision of Baseball's Racial History," *Social Text* 21, no. 7 (2009): 47.
24. See Claire Jean Kim, *Asian Americans in an Anti-Black World* (Cambridge: Cambridge University Press, 2023), 10. Jared Sexton describes the practice of ignoring how non-Black people of color may participate in and benefit from anti-Blackness as "people-of-color blindness." Sexton, "People-of-Color Blindness: Notes on the Afterlife of Slavery," *Social Text* 28, no. 2 (2010): 48.
25. Burgos, "Left Out," 41; Brock and Bayne, "Not Just Black," 175.
26. Frank Andre Guridy, *Forging Diaspora: Afro-Cubans and African Americans in a World of Empire and Jim Crow* (Chapel Hill: University of North Carolina Press, 2010), 6, 4.
27. "Racial classifications in the archive," Lisa Lowe writes, serve the "colonial need" to silence the "unspoken 'intimacies'" between the colonized, the enslaved, the Indigenous, and the indentured. Afro-Latinos underwent a reracialization that sorted them into another, isolated archive, at Cooperstown and elsewhere. Lowe, *The Intimacies of Four Continents* (Durham, NC: Duke University Press, 2015), 35.
28. Robert H. Boyle, "The Private World of the Negro Ballplayer," *Sports Illustrated*, March 21, 1960, 16, 18.
29. Boyle, 18.
30. Quoted in Boyle, 19.
31. Alvin Harlow, "Unrecognized Stars," *Esquire*, September 1938, 75.
32. Boyle, "Private World of the Negro Ballplayer," 18.
33. Burgos, offering a corrective to White's account, writes that the Cuban Giants "initiated a practice within the U.S. baseball circuit that associated Cuban with nonwhite racial identity," a tradition that Pompez and rival club owner Abel Linares, who also owned a team called the Cuban Stars, continued. Brock and Bayne suggest that African Americans adopted the name not to hide their Blackness but to announce it, that it signaled Black players' support of the Cuban independence movement as a Black struggle against white domination. Burgos, *Cuban Star: How One Negro-League Owner Changed the Face of Baseball* (New York: Hill and Wang, 2011), 259n1; see Brock and Bayne, "Not Just Black," 176.
34. Louis A. Pérez Jr., *On Becoming Cuban: Identity, Nationality, and Culture* (Chapel Hill: University of North Carolina Press, 1999), 78.
35. Mora, *Making Hispanics*, 118.
36. Gómez, *Inventing Latinos*, 144.
37. Regalado, *Viva Baseball!*, 5.
38. Raúl Yzaguirre, "The Decade for Hispanics," *Agenda*, January–February 1980, 2.
39. Tod G. Hamilton, *Immigration and the Remaking of Black America* (New York: Russell Sage, 2019), 11.

40. Christina M. Greer, *Black Ethnics: Race, Immigration, and the Pursuit of the American Dream* (New York: Oxford University Press, 2013), 27.
41. "Yanks Bring Up First Negro Players," *Washington Post*, October 14, 1953.
42. For more on the impact of integration on Black and Latino labor in Major League Baseball, see Rob Ruck, *Raceball: How the Major Leagues Colonized the Black and Latin Game* (Boston: Beacon Press, 2011); and Alan Klein, "Latinizing the 'National Pastime,'" *International Journal of the History of Sports* 24, no. 2 (2007): 296–310. Funneling the best Black and Latino prospects into the majors "did little for the communities they left behind," the historian Ruck writes. "It actively destroyed or weakened institutions in the black community and the Caribbean" (xiii). Klein describes the academies that MLB clubs would later build on the islands as one component of an extractive "commodity chain" (307).
43. *A Long Way from Home: The Untold Story of Baseball's Desegregation*, directed by Gaspar González (Hammer and Nail Productions, 2018).
44. Jim Bouton, *Ball Four: My Life and Hard Times Throwing the Knuckleball in the Big Leagues* (New York: World Publishing, 1970), 31, 102, 338.
45. Felipe Alou, "Latin-American Ballplayers Need a Bill of Rights," *Sport*, November 1963, 76.
46. Alou, 77.
47. Alou, 78, 77.
48. The racial construction of one group derives from and affects the racial construction of others, Natalia Molina writes. "Once attitudes, practices, customs, policies, and laws are directed at one group, they are more readily available and hence more easily applied to other groups." But what she calls racial scripts can also offer shared forms of resistance, or "counterscripts," some of which the Afro-Dominican Alou borrowed from non-Latino Black baseball in demanding a Latino bill of rights. Molina, *How Race Is Made in America: Immigration, Citizenship, and the Historical Power of Racial Scripts* (Berkeley: University of California Press, 2014), 7.
49. Dick Young, Young Ideas, *Daily News*, August 26, 1965.
50. Bob Broeg, "Loss of One Turn No Stiff Penalty," *St. Louis Post-Dispatch*, August 24, 1965.
51. Joe Black, "How about That Marichal Mess?," *New York Amsterdam News*, September 11, 1965.
52. Clemente, "Conversation with Clemente."
53. Jim Brosnan, "A Pitcher-Author Writes His Book on Pirate Lineup," *Life*, October 10, 1960, 168, 174.
54. Jim Brosnan, "Now Pitching for St. Louis ... the Rookie Psychiatrist," *Sports Illustrated*, July 21, 1958, 12.
55. Jim Brosnan, *The Long Season* (New York: Harper and Brothers, 1960), 179, 247, v.
56. Brosnan, 247, v.
57. Jim Brosnan, *Pennant Race* (New York: Harper and Brothers, 1962), 186.
58. Roderick A. Ferguson, *The Reorder of Things: The University and Its Pedagogies of Minority Difference* (Minneapolis: University of Minnesota Press, 2012), 196.

59. Harold Charnofsky, "The Major League Professional Baseball Player: Self-Conception versus the Popular Image," *International Review of Sport Sociology* 3, no. 1 (1968): 40.
60. Charnofsky, 42, 45.
61. Charnofsky, 52.
62. Harold Charnofsky, "The Major League Professional Baseball Player: A Sociological Study" (PhD diss., University of Southern California, 1969), 291, 295.
63. "Clemente Happy over Winning Hit," *Baltimore Sun*, July 12, 1961.
64. Quoted in Bruce Markusen, *Roberto Clemente: The Great One* (Champaign, IL: Sports Publishing, 1998), 47.
65. Quoted in Arnold Hano, "Roberto Clemente, Man of Paradox," *Sport*, May 1965, 71; quoted in Milton Richman, Sports Parade, *Times-News* (Hendersonville, NC), April 21, 1971.
66. Clemente, "Conversation with Clemente."
67. Howard Cohn, "Roberto Clemente's Problem," *Sport*, May 1962, 54, 56.
68. Cohn, 56.
69. Hano, "Roberto Clemente," 69.
70. See Laura E. Gómez, *Manifest Destinies: The Making of the Mexican American Race* (New York: New York University Press, 2007), 151–52.
71. "Latin Athletes' 'Plight' Criticized," *Los Angeles Times*, August 23, 1966.
72. "Latins in Baseball Check Dollar Drain," *New York Times*, May 19, 1970.
73. Quoted in Bruce Markusen, *The Team That Changed Baseball: Roberto Clemente and the 1971 Pittsburgh Pirates* (Yardley, PA: Westholme, 2006), 216.
74. Markusen, 189.
75. Claire Jean Kim, *Bitter Fruit: The Politics of Black-Korean Conflict in New York City* (New Haven, CT: Yale University Press, 2000), 16.
76. Clemente, "Conversation with Clemente."
77. Quoted in Kal Wagenheim, *Clemente!* (New York: Praeger, 1973), 61.
78. Quoted in Markusen, *Roberto Clemente*, 21.
79. Quoted in Maraniss, *Clemente*, 83.
80. Bill Nuun Jr., "Record Crop of 41 Negro Stars on Rosters of Teams in National League," *Pittsburgh Courier*, April 18, 1959.
81. See Nuun, "Clemente May Bring 'Rookie of the Year' Laurels to Pirates."
82. William Webster, "How Democratic Is Baseball?," *Pittsburgh Courier*, July 3, 1954.
83. Quoted in Bill Nuun Jr., "Baker, Clemente Deny Liking Fort Myers's Bias in Housing," *Pittsburgh Courier*, February 25, 1961.
84. "Long-smoldering, Fed-up, Bob Clemente Erupts!," *Pittsburgh Courier*, July 15, 1961. See also Bill Christine, *Roberto!* (New York: Stadia Sports, 1973), 49–50.
85. Roberto Clemente, "Highlights in Baseball's Week: Guest Column," *Pittsburgh Courier*, June 4, 1960.
86. Sheep Jackson, From the Sidelines, *Call and Post*, August 21, 1965.
87. Quoted in Stan Isaacs, "Louisiana in Dark Showing Through," *Newsday*, July 23, 1964.

88. Jackie Robinson, "Cobwebs in Dark's Mind," *New York Amsterdam News*, August 15, 1964.
89. Alvin Dark, chapter 10, in *Baseball Has Done It*, ed. Jackie Robinson and Charles Dexter (Philadelphia: J. B. Lippincott, 1964), 107.
90. "J. Robinson-Mays Age Dying: The Latins, Whites Take Over Baseball," *New Pittsburgh Courier*, March 16, 1968.
91. Nuun, "Record Crop of 41 Negro Stars."
92. "J. Robinson-Mays Age Dying."
93. Sheep Jackson, From the Sidelines, *Call and Post*, May 13, 1967.
94. Sheep Jackson, From the Sidelines, *Call and Post*, August 21, 1965; Jackson, From the Sidelines, *Call and Post*, May 13, 1967.
95. Hamilton Bims, "Roberto Clemente: Sad End for a Troubled Man," *Ebony*, March 1973, 53.
96. A. S. "Doc" Young, *Great Negro Baseball Stars and How They Made the Major Leagues* (New York: A. S. Barnes, 1953), 187.
97. A. S. "Doc" Young, *Negro Firsts in Sports* (Chicago: Johnson Publishing, 1963), 156, 157.
98. A. S. "Doc" Young, Good Morning Sports!, *Chicago Daily Defender*, September 23, 1965.
99. Robert Peterson, *Only the Ball Was White* (Englewood Cliffs, NJ: Prentice-Hall, 1970), 15, vii.
100. Gunnar Myrdal, *An American Dilemma: The Negro Problem and Modern Democracy* (New York: Harper and Brothers, 1944), 1021.
101. Jules Tygiel, *Baseball's Great Experiment: Jackie Robinson and His Legacy* (New York: Oxford University Press, 1983), 9.
102. Jerry Izenberg, *Great Latin Sports Figures: The Proud People* (Garden City, NY: Doubleday, 1976), 25.
103. Most fans, Burgos writes, remain devoted to a "narrative of a self-correcting society where well-intentioned white folks prevail to correct race matters," and Afro-Latinos and Black baseball in the Afro-Atlantic "cultural sphere" does not fit into that narrative. Better to stick with, as Tygiel did, the American creed. Burgos, "Left Out," 55.
104. Donn Rogosin, *Invisible Men: Life in Baseball's Negro Leagues* (New York: Atheneum, 1983), 175.
105. Burgos, *Playing America's Game*, xiv.
106. Quoted in John Holway, *Voices from the Great Black Baseball Leagues* (New York: Dodd, Mead, 1975), 91, 226, 343.
107. Peterson, *Only the Ball Was White*, 96.
108. Rogosin, *Invisible Men*, 175.
109. William Brashler, *The Story of Negro League Baseball* (New York: Ticknor and Fields, 1994), 67–68.
110. Rogosin, *Invisible Men*, 157, 160, 177.
111. Quoted in Holway, *Voices from the Great Black Baseball Leagues*, 245.
112. Peterson, *Only the Ball Was White*, 18.
113. Sol White, *Sol White's History of Colored Base Ball, with Other Documents on the Early Black Game, 1886–1936*, ed. Jerry Malloy (Lincoln: University of Nebraska Press, 1995), 89, 10.

114. Harlow, "Unrecognized Stars," 75. The baseball journalist and historian Jerry Malloy, who edited and republished White's history in 1995, doubts that the name Cuban Giants would have fooled many fans at the time. Most would have been "accustomed to euphemistic references in the sporting press to black players as 'Cuban,' 'Spanish,' or even 'Arabian.'" But the name might have, he suspects, facilitated some bookings against white teams, none of which would have fallen for gibberish Spanish after taking the field against the non-Cuban Cuban Giants. Malloy, "Sol White and the Origins of African American Baseball," introduction to *Sol White's History of Colored Base Ball, with Other Documents on the Early Black Game, 1886–1936*, ed. Jerry Malloy (Lincoln: University of Nebraska Press, 1995), lxi.
115. Holway, *Voices from the Great Black Baseball Leagues*, 2.
116. Tygiel, *Baseball's Great Experiment*, 16.
117. William Brashler, preface to *The Bingo Long Traveling All-Stars and Motor Kings* (Urbana: University of Illinois Press, 1993), xi.
118. William Brashler, *The Bingo Long Traveling All-Stars and Motor Kings* (New York: Harper and Row, 1973), 241.
119. *The Bingo Long Traveling All-Stars and Motor Kings*, directed by John Badham (Universal Pictures, 1976).
120. In a book-length investigation of fictional works about the Black leagues, the literary scholar Emily Ruth Rutter argues that, in the absence of traditional recordkeeping, literature has taken on a "crucial archival role." But there we also find a Black baseball that, setting aside what Guridy terms the "Afro-diasporic linkages" between Black America and the Black Caribbean, waited for the moral arc of the universe to bend toward integration. Rutter, *Invisible Ball of Dreams: Literary Representations of Baseball behind the Color Line* (Jackson: University Press of Mississippi, 2018), 5; Guridy, *Forging Diaspora*, 4.
121. Amiri Baraka, *The Autobiography of Leroi Jones* (New York: Freundlich Books, 1984), 35, 36.
122. Roger Kahn, *The Boys of Summer* (New York: Harper and Row, 1972), 426.
123. See Jay Caspian Kang, "The Unbearable Whiteness of Baseball," *New York Times Magazine*, April 6, 2016; Gene Seymour, "Fade to White," *Nation*, November 2–9, 2020, 18–21, 25; and David Waldstein, "The National Pastime's Challenge: Prove Its Time Hasn't Passed," *New York Times*, October 25, 2021.
124. Chris Rock, guest, *Real Sports with Bryant Gumbel*, season 21, episode 4, aired April 21, 2015, on HBO.
125. Burgos and Guridy, "Becoming Suspect in Usual Places," 83.

3 BLACK ON BLACK

1. Richard Wright, "Joe Louis Uncovers Dynamite," *New Masses*, October 8, 1935, 18, 19.
2. Wright, 19.
3. Wright, 19, 18.

4. Maya Angelou, *I Know Why the Caged Bird Sings* (New York: Random House, 1969), 113, 115.
5. Randy Roberts, *Joe Louis: Hard Times Man* (New Haven, CT: Yale University Press, 2010), xi.
6. Quoted in E. Franklin Frazier, *Negro Youth at the Crossroads: Their Personality Development in the Middle States* (Washington, DC: American Council on Education, 1940), 190.
7. Frazier, 190.
8. St. Clair Drake and Horace R. Cayton, *Black Metropolis: A Study of Negro Life in a Northern City* (New York: Harcourt, Brace, 1945), 391, 403, 609.
9. For more on Louis's financial motivation for holding the color line, see Louis Moore, "Jimmy Bivins and the Duration Championship," in *The Bittersweet Science: Fifteen Writers in the Gym, in the Corner, and at Ringside*, ed. Carlo Rotella and Michael Ezra (Chicago: University of Chicago Press, 2017), 221.
10. Carlo Rotella and Michael Ezra, "Introduction: Bittersweetness," in *The Bittersweet Science: Fifteen Writers in the Gym, in the Corner, and at Ringside*, ed. Carlo Rotella and Michael Ezra (Chicago: University of Chicago Press, 2017), 5.
11. Elliott J. Gorn, "The Manassa Mauler and the Fighting Marine: An Interpretation of the Dempsey–Tunney Fights," *Journal of American Studies* 19, no. 1 (1985): 43. See also Gorn, *The Manly Arts: Bare-Knuckle Prize Fighting in America* (Ithaca, NY: Cornell University Press, 1986), 250–51.
12. Andrew M. Kaye, *The Pussycat of Prizefighting: Tiger Flowers and the Politics of Black Celebrity* (Athens: University of Georgia Press, 2004), 8.
13. Nicole R. Fleetwood, *On Racial Icons: Blackness and the Public Imagination* (New Brunswick, NJ: Rutgers University Press, 2015), 84.
14. James Baldwin, "The Fight: Patterson vs. Liston," *Nugget*, November 1963, 69, 33–34.
15. See Norman Mailer, "Ten Thousand Words a Minute," *Esquire*, February 1963, 109–20.
16. Frank Deford, "Sometimes the Bear Eats You: Confessions of a Sportswriter," *Sports Illustrated*, March 29, 2010, 62.
17. Stephen Chapman, "The Best Magazine in America," *Chicago Tribune*, April 5, 1984.
18. Quoted in Pierre Guilmant, "Jesse, McNeil Hit 'Silence,'" *Chicago Daily Defender*, August 19, 1970.
19. Alvin F. Poussaint, "Why Blacks Kill Blacks," *Ebony*, October 1970, 145. See also Poussaint, *Why Blacks Kill Blacks* (New York: Emerson Hall, 1972).
20. John H. Johnson, "Publisher's Statement," in "Black on Black Crime: The Causes, the Consequences, the Cures" special issue, *Ebony*, August 1979, 33.
21. The geographer David Wilson observes that conservative and liberal racial ideologies brought different understandings of the origins of violence to the war on crime of the 1980s but that they shared a belief that local culture had contributed to crime within Black communities. Wilson, *Inventing Black-on-Black Crime: Discourse, Space, and Representation* (Syracuse, NY: Syracuse University Press, 2005), 6.

22. For more on the binding debt of the gift of freedom for enslaved people and their descendants and for refugees in the Global North, see Saidiya V. Hartman, *Scenes of Subjection: Terror, Slavery, and Self-Making in Nineteenth-Century America* (New York: Oxford University Press, 1997), 132; and Mimi Thi Nguyen, *The Gift of Freedom: War, Debt, and Other Refugee Passages* (Durham, NC: Duke University Press, 2012), 3.
23. Lindon Barrett, *Blackness and Value: Seeing Double* (Cambridge: Cambridge University Press, 1999), 17, 28.
24. Quoted in Jack Newfield, *Only in America: The Life and Times of Don King* (New York: William Morrow, 1995), 253.
25. Quoted in "McNabb Says Owens's Criticism Amounts to 'Black-on-Black Crime,'" ESPN.com, February 1, 2006, www.espn.com/nfl/story?id=2315675.
26. Quoted in Ben Fowlkes, "'Rampage' Jackson, Rashad Evans and the Politics of Race in MMA," MMA Fighting, May 25, 2010, www.mmafighting.com/2010/05/25/rampage-jackson-rashad-evans-and-the-politics-of-race-in-mma.
27. Nikhil Singh argues that "policing makes race when it removes normative barriers to police violence." It makes race in drawing the line between whom the state defends and whom it deems a threat to that defended class, and it may take the form of a "war" at home or a "police action" overseas. Boxing invited fans to imagine where they would draw the line, to distinguish between the legitimate and the illegitimate combatant, the law-abiding boxer and the criminal pugilist. In the 1960s, they drew it not down the color line but through Blackness. Singh, *Race and America's Long War* (Berkeley: University of California Press, 2017), 67–68.
28. Jeffrey T. Sammons, *Beyond the Ring: The Role of Boxing in American Society* (Urbana: University of Illinois Press, 1988), xv.
29. Jack London, "In the Modern Stadium," *Australian Star*, December 28, 1908.
30. Jack London, *The Abysmal Brute* (New York: Century, 1913), 5.
31. John Lardner, "That Was Pugilism: White Hopes – I," *New Yorker*, June 25, 1949, 59.
32. Quoted in Lardner, 63.
33. John Lardner, "That Was Pugilism: White Hopes – II," *New Yorker*, July 2, 1949, 44, 41.
34. Lardner, "White Hopes – I," 56; Lardner, "White Hopes – II," 36.
35. A. J. Liebling, "Boxing with the Naked Eye," *New Yorker*, June 30, 1951, 36.
36. A. J. Liebling, "A Blow for Austerity," *New Yorker*, July 9, 1960, 77, 79.
37. F. Scott Fitzgerald, "Ring," *New Republic*, October 11, 1933, 254.
38. Leslie A. Fiedler, *Love and Death in the American Novel* (New York: Criterion, 1960), 521.
39. Liebling, "Boxing with the Naked Eye," 31. Rotella agrees with Liebling. Television, he writes, "has dominated the fights since it rose to power in the 1950s. That's when boxing began to become an esoteric electronic spectacle rather than a regular feature of neighborhood life." It's also when the American magazine elevated writing about boxing to the status

of literature – gentrification by subscription. Rotella, "Introduction: At Ringside," in *Cut Time: An Education at the Fights* (Chicago: University of Chicago Press, 2003), 6.

40. If "the color line in heavyweight boxing had gone for good," the literary scholar and boxing historian Kasia Boddy observes in her account of the sport's cultural life, it held strong in "heavyweight writing." Boddy, *Boxing: A Cultural History* (London: Reaktion, 2008), 310.
41. Ben Carrington, *Race, Sport and Politics: The Sporting Black Diaspora* (Los Angeles: Sage, 2010), 79, 80.
42. Lardner, "White Hopes – II," 37.
43. The magazine writer sorted fighters into the racial categories of what the literary scholar Gerald Early calls, borrowing from Ralph Ellison, the "trickster" and the "yokel." Early traces the image of the white yokel back to Willard, but Willard did not become a joke, at least for most fans, until near the end of Joe Louis's reign. Early, "The Black Intellectual and the Sport of Prizefighting," *Kenyon Review* 10, no. 3 (1988): 107.
44. Lardner, "White Hopes – I," 59.
45. Liebling, "Boxing with the Naked Eye," 31, 38; Liebling, "Blow for Austerity," 71.
46. Rotella argues that we should understand boxing as a form of labor that has, like other forms of blue-collar work, been devalued amid deindustrialization and globalization. He calls it "body work." The assignment of giftedness obscures the labor of some fighters more than others. The gifted athlete is not engaged in craft, is not working at it. Rotella, *Good with Their Hands: Boxers, Bluesmen, and Other Characters from the Rust Belt* (Berkeley: University of California Press, 2002), 5.
47. Commonwealth v. Collberg, 119 Mass. 350, 353 (1876). For an account of the sport's early legal challenges, see Sammons, *Beyond the Ring*, 3–29.
48. See Khalil Gibran Muhammad, *The Condemnation of Blackness: Race, Crime, and the Making of Modern Urban America* (Cambridge, MA: Harvard University Press, 2010), 13.
49. Grant Farred, *What's My Name? Black Vernacular Intellectuals* (Minneapolis: University of Minnesota Press, 2003), 22.
50. Baldwin, "Fight," 34.
51. Jim Murray, "Come Out Talking!," *Los Angeles Times*, November 7, 1963.
52. Quoted in Tex Maule, "The Baddest of All Looks over the Universe," *Sports Illustrated*, February 15, 1965, 21.
53. See Jonathan Eig, *Ali: A Life* (New York: Houghton Mifflin Harcourt, 2017), 138.
54. Murray Kempton, "'I Whipped Him and I'm Still Pretty,'" *New Republic*, March 7, 1964, 9.
55. Red Smith, "Without Salt," *New York Herald Tribune*, February 26, 1964.
56. Quoted in John Cottrell, *Muhammad Ali, Who Once Was Cassius Clay* (New York: Funk and Wagnalls, 1967), 94, 192.
57. Malcolm X, *The Autobiography of Malcolm X*, with Alex Haley (New York: Grove Press, 1965), 311.
58. Floyd Patterson, "I Want to Destroy Clay," with Milton Gross, *Sports Illustrated*, October 19, 1964, 43, 44.

59. Muhammad Ali, "*Playboy* Interview: Cassius Clay," by Alex Haley, *Playboy*, October 1964, 192.
60. Floyd Patterson, "Cassius Clay Must Be Beaten," *Sports Illustrated*, October 11, 1965, 80, 83.
61. Quoted in Gilbert Rogin, "Champion as Long as He Wants," *Sports Illustrated*, November 29, 1965, 24.
62. Harry Edwards, *The Revolt of the Black Athlete* (New York: Free Press, 1969), 34, 89.
63. Eldridge Cleaver, *Soul on Ice* (New York: McGraw-Hill, 1968), 162, 92.
64. Remnick devotes the first chapter of his 1998 biography *The King of the World* to Patterson's life and career ("Patterson grew up in a series of cold water flats in Brooklyn's Bedford-Stuyvesant ..."), establishing a thematic contrast between him and Ali. Cottrell, Hauser, and Eig construct their biographies through a succession of contrasting character studies – Ali as the un-Liston and un-Frazier, the anti-Patterson and anti-Foreman. Remnick, *The King of the World: Muhammad Ali and the Rise of an American Hero* (New York: Random House, 1998), 9.
65. Ishmael Reed, "A Palooka He Ain't," review of *The Greatest: My Own Story*, by Muhammad Ali, *New York Times Book Review*, November 30, 1975.
66. Muhammad Ali, *The Greatest: My Own Story*, with Richard Durham (New York: Random House, 1975), 247.
67. The Ali biographer Michael Ezra argues that Ali's "moral authority" shifted throughout his life in relation to whom the public perceived to be profiting from his image – the Louisville Sponsoring Group, the Nation of Islam, corporate sponsors. It also tracked, month to month, with whom he was fighting and the contrast that writers drew between him and other Black fighters. Ezra, *Muhammad Ali: The Making of an Icon* (Philadelphia: Temple University Press, 2009), 86.
68. Mailer, "Ten Thousand Words," 117.
69. Norman Mailer, "The White Negro: Superficial Reflections on the Hipster," *Dissent*, Summer 1957, 279.
70. Norman Mailer, "Evaluations: Quick and Expensive Comments on the Talent in the Room," in *Advertisements for Myself* (New York: G. P. Putnam's Sons, 1959), 471.
71. James Baldwin, "The Black Boy Looks at the White Boy," *Esquire*, May 1961, 106, 105.
72. Mailer, "Ten Thousand Words," 114.
73. Mailer, 114, 115, 116.
74. Baldwin, "Fight," 32, 34.
75. Baldwin, 69, 34.
76. Naomi Murakawa, *The First Civil Right: How Liberals Built Prison America* (New York: Oxford University Press, 2014), 3.
77. Stuart Hall et al., *Policing the Crisis: Mugging, the State, and Law and Order* (London: Macmillan, 1978), 332.
78. Norman Mailer, "Ego," *Life*, March 19, 1971, 18.
79. Norman Mailer, *The Fight* (New York: Little, Brown, 1975), 35.
80. Placide Tempels, *Bantu Philosophy*, trans. Colin King (Paris: Présence Africaine, 1959), 52.

81. Mailer, *Fight*, 42, 43.
82. Mailer, 47, 14, 35, 47.
83. George Plimpton, introduction to the 1993 edition, in *Shadow Box: An Amateur in the Ring* (New York: Lyons and Buford, 1993), 9.
84. Mailer, *Fight*, 47.
85. Mailer, 122. With his writing about Ali, Mailer was engaged in an act, not his first, of what the cultural historian Eric Lott calls Black mirroring, in which a white creator extracts "symbolic surplus value" from Black cultural labor – an extraction often obscured, Lott observes, by a Black creator's fame and sometimes substantial renumeration. Lott, *Black Mirror: The Cultural Contradictions of American Racism* (Cambridge, MA: Harvard University Press, 2017), 22.
86. Ishmael Reed, "Ishmael Reed on Ali," *Village Voice*, October 16, 1978, 24, 23, 24, 25.
87. Roger Riger, "The Greatest Fights of the Century," *Esquire*, December 1963, 188–89, 188, 189, 190, 191.
88. Amiri Baraka, "In the Ring (2)," *Nation*, June 29, 1964, 662.
89. Riger, "Greatest Fights," 191.
90. Finis Farr, *Black Champion: The Life and Times of Jack Johnson* (New York: Charles Scribner's Sons, 1964), 32, 33.
91. Miles Davis, "Yesternow," *Jack Johnson* (Columbia, 1971).
92. See Theresa Runstedtler, *Jack Johnson, Rebel Sojourner: Boxing in the Shadow of the Global Color Line* (Berkeley: University of California Press, 2012), 3, 259–60.
93. Quoted in Ali, *Greatest*, 389, 395.
94. Quoted in Remnick, *King of the World*, 224.
95. Ali was right about white folks' attitude toward Johnson at the height of his predecessor's fame. The gender historian Gail Bederman shows how the discourse of civilization in the Progressive era bound racial and gender dominance to "millennial assumptions about human evolutionary progress," fueling an obsession among white men with defeating Johnson, whose long reign as world champion destabilized a belief in their entitlement to rule over nation and home. But Johnson's image in the time of Black Power had ceased to challenge and could even reinforce a belief in social progress. Bederman, *Manliness and Civilization: A Cultural History of Gender and Race in the United States, 1880–1917* (Chicago: University of Chicago Press, 1995), 25.
96. James Earl Jones, "Jack Johnson Is Alive and Well … on Broadway," *Ebony*, June 1969, 60.
97. Howard Sackler, *The Great White Hope* (New York: Dial, 1968), 138; quoted in Pete Hamill, "Muhammad Ali: 'This Is about Me,'" *Life*, October 25, 1968, 68.
98. Quoted in Hamill, 68.
99. Sackler, *Great White Hope*, 169.
100. Ali, *Greatest*, 390.
101. That phrase, unforgivable blackness, comes from W. E. B. Du Bois. Geoffrey Ward used it as the title of his 2004 Johnson biography and then collaborated with Ken Burns on a 2005 documentary of the same name.

102. For more on Johnson's contribution to Black moviegoing culture and the 1912 congressional ban on fight films, see Dan Streible, *Fighting Pictures: A History of Boxing and Early Cinema* (Berkeley: University of California Press, 2008), 195–265. Streible describes Johnson as "the first black movie star" (195).
103. The film historian Samantha Sheppard argues that, though most sports movies tell circumscribed, unchallenging stories about Black athletes, the "Black sporting body on screen" acts as a "rendering force," breaking from generic conventions to "make larger claims about the meanings, resonances, and intra- and intertextuality of the Black body in motion and contest in American cinema and society." The Jack Jefferson we meet in the adaptation of *The Great White Hope* can be the filmmakers' Jack Jefferson but also dissent from and transcend their intentions. Sheppard, *Sporting Blackness: Race, Embodiment, and Critical Muscle Memory on Screen* (Berkeley: University of California Press, 2020), 6.
104. Simeon Booker, Washington Notebook, in "Black on Black Crime: The Causes, the Consequences, the Cures," special issue, *Ebony*, August 1979, 27.
105. Thomas Moore, "The Black-on-Black Crime Plague," *U.S. News and World Report*, August 22, 1988, 50.
106. George Plimpton, *Shadow Box* (New York: Putnam, 1977), 5, 7, 29. Plimpton's exhibition with Moore anticipated the gym culture that Lucia Trimbur investigates in *Come Out Swinging*, in which white-collar clients hire Black and brown trainers to introduce them to the "authentic" world of the working-class pugilist. (The white-collar clients she observes do not, like Plimpton, laugh at themselves. Their trainers may, after they've cashed their checks.) See Trimbur, *Come Out Swinging: The Changing World of Boxing in Gleason's Gym* (Princeton, NJ: Princeton University Press, 2013), 117–41.
107. Plimpton, *Shadow Box*, 306, 312.
108. George Plimpton, *Paper Tiger* (New York: Harper and Row, 1966), 2.
109. William Oscar Johnson, "And in This Corner ... NCR 315," *Sports Illustrated*, September 16, 1968, 35.
110. Don Page, "Computer Punchy from Fight Tapes," *Los Angeles Times*, December 2, 1967.
111. "Loser Dempsey May Sue Computer Promoter," *Boston Globe*, December 24, 1967.
112. Ali, *Greatest*, 300.
113. The media historian Travis Vogan shows how Ali and "attitudes surrounding" him "shaped closed-circuit's history, transformation, and intersection with cinema culture," from Ali-Liston I to *Rocky*. Vogan, *The Boxing Film: A Cultural and Transmedia History* (New Brunswick, NJ: Rutgers University Press, 2021), 76.
114. Shirley Povich, This Morning, *Washington Post*, May 21, 1965.
115. Jim Murray, "Ee-yi, Ee-yi, Yo," *Los Angeles Times*, February 21, 1964.
116. Quoted in Johnson, "And in This Corner," 41, 36.
117. "Muhammad Ali vs. Jim Jeffries," *The Best of the All-Time Heavyweight Tournament* (Ben Scott Recording, 1967).
118. Quoted in Johnson, "And in This Corner," 41.

119. Quoted in Robert Lipsyte, "The Computer Fight," *New York Times*, January 22, 1970; quoted in "Marciano Training for Ali?," *Boston Globe*, September 5, 1966.
120. Quoted in Ali, *Greatest*, 297.
121. Ali, 297.
122. Bud Collins, "Rocky Beats Clay by 'KO,'" *Boston Globe*, January 21, 1970.
123. *The Super Fight*, directed by Murry Woroner (Woroner Productions, 1970).
124. Quoted in "How Ali's Antics Broke Up Rocky," *Detroit Free Press*, January 25, 1970.
125. Quoted in "Computer Crowns Rocky Marciano," *Chicago Daily Defender*, January 22, 1970.
126. A. S. "Doc" Young, "Unfair to Muhammad Ali," *Chicago Daily Defender*, January 29, 1970.
127. Quoted in Thomas Hauser, *Muhammad Ali: His Life and Times* (New York: Simon and Schuster, 1991), 300.
128. Andrew Sarris, "Takes," *Village Voice*, November 22, 1976, 61.
129. *Rocky*, directed by John G. Avildsen (United Artists, 1976).
130. *Rocky III*, directed by Sylvester Stallone (MGM/United Artists, 1982).
131. See Matthew Frye Jacobson, *Roots Too: White Ethnic Revival in Post–Civil Rights America* (Cambridge, MA: Harvard University Press, 2006), 107.
132. Remnick, *King of the World*; Eig, *Ali*, 522.
133. Quoted in Jeffrey Goldberg, "Sore Winners," *New York Times Magazine*, August 16, 1998, 32.

4 HOW THE STUDENT-ATHLETE SUBSIDIZES THE AMATEUR

1. H. G. Bissinger, *Friday Night Lights: A Town, a Team, and a Dream* (Reading, MA: Addison-Wesley, 1990), 349.
2. Bissinger, 10.
3. Bissinger, 114, 115.
4. Bissinger, 288.
5. Bissinger, 116.
6. The sociologists Allen Sack and Ellen Staurowsky observe that "need-based aid would have allowed athletes to place educational priorities over those of sports without fear of losing financial aid." Christian could have finished his degree at TCU after leaving the team. Sack and Staurowsky, *College Athletes for Hire: The Evolution and Legacy of the NCAA's Amateur Myth* (Westport, CT: Praeger, 1998), 84.
7. John Edgar Wideman, *Brothers and Keepers* (New York: Holt, Rinehart, and Winston, 1984), 226, 227.
8. Ronald A. Smith, *The Myth of the Amateur: A History of College Athletic Scholarships* (Austin: University of Texas Press, 2021), 147.
9. Taylor Branch, "The Shame of College Sports," *Atlantic*, October 2011, 88.
10. Victoria Jackson, "'We're All Complicit to an Extent': How Team USA Uses College Football and Basketball as Funding Sources," *Athletic*, July 22, 2021, https://theathletic.com/2696130/2021/07/22/were-all-complicit-to-an-extent-how-team-usa-uses-college-football-and-basketball-as-funding-sources/.

11. Gail Bederman, *Manliness and Civilization: A Cultural History of Gender and Race in the United States, 1880–1917* (Chicago: University of Chicago Press, 1995), 18.
12. Harry Edwards, "The Black 'Dumb Jock': An American Sports Tragedy," *College Board Review*, no. 131 (1984): 8.
13. US Supreme Court, "Regents of the University of California v. Bakke: Oral Argument," October 12, 1977, Oyez, transcript and audio, 1:59:13, www.oyez.org/cases/1979/76-811.
14. Regents of the University of California v. Bakke, 438 US 265, 316, 313 (1978).
15. Quoted in Malcolm Moran, "Former USC President Defends Policies," *New York Times*, October 17, 1980.
16. Quoted in Malcolm Moran, "At USC, Issue Is Responsibility," *New York Times*, October 26, 1980. The self-interest of administrators and football coaches who defended athlete admissions as a form of affirmative action was hard to miss. "Whereas the colleges portrayed their athletic policies as affirmative action for minorities," John Watterson writes, "those policies benefited the football programs more than their star athletes." Watterson, *College Football: History, Spectacle, Controversy* (Baltimore: Johns Hopkins University Press, 2000), 331.
17. James J. Duderstadt, *Intercollegiate Athletics and the American University: A University President's Perspective* (Ann Arbor: University of Michigan Press, 2000), 191, x.
18. Murray Sperber, *College Sports Inc.: The Athletic Department vs. the University* (New York: Henry Holt, 1990), 1.
19. Christopher Newfield, *Unmaking the Public University: The Forty-Year Assault on the Middle Class* (Cambridge, MA: Harvard University Press, 2008), 10.
20. The historian of higher education John Thelin was a rare voice arguing, in a coauthored 1989 pamphlet titled *The Old College Try*, that "intercollegiate sports are de facto central – not peripheral – to a university's purpose" and should be named in institutions' mission statements. Others have echoed Thelin's argument since. For Christopher Findeisen, college sports are "our academic values laid bare." For Daniel Gilbert, athletes are "indispensable contributors" to a movement to "transform the neoliberal university." As far back as 1971, Jack Scott was arguing that sports were not extracurricular but "a microcosm of the whole of American education." Thelin and Lawrence L. Wiseman, *The Old College Try: Balancing Academics and Athletics in Higher Education* (Washington, DC: School of Education and Human Development, George Washington University, 1989), v; Findeisen, "'The One Place Where Money Makes No Difference': The Campus Novel from *Stover at Yale* through *The Art of Fielding*," *American Literature* 88, no. 1 (2016): 81; Gilbert, "Not (Just) about the Money: Contextualizing the Labor Activism of College Football Players," in "Sport in the University," ed. Noah Cohan et al., special issue, *American Studies* 55, no. 3 (2016): 2; Scott, *The Athletic Revolution* (New York: Free Press, 1971), 204.
21. Bissinger, *Friday Night Lights*, 57.
22. *Friday Night Lights*, directed by Peter Berg (Universal Pictures, 2004).

23. H. G. Bissinger, *Friday Night Lights: A Town, a Team, and a Dream*, 25th anniversary ed. (New York: Hachette, 2015), 394.
24. H. G. Bissinger, email message to author, December 14, 2022.
25. Bissinger, *Friday Night Lights*, 25th anniversary ed., 405.
26. Intercollegiate Athletic Association of the United States, *Proceedings of the First Annual Meeting* (New York: Intercollegiate Athletic Association of the United States, 1906), 33, 12.
27. R. Tait McKenzie, "The Chronicle of the Amateur Spirit," in *Proceedings of the Fifth Annual Convention of the National Collegiate Athletic Association* (New York: National Collegiate Athletic Association, 1910), 50, 54.
28. Since the first Harvard–Yale boat race in 1852, college athletes have received "financial favors," Smith, the historian, writes. College sports have "never been truly amateur." Smith, *Myth of the Amateur*, 1.
29. Quoted in "Colleges Adopt the 'Sanity Code' to Govern Sports," *New York Times*, January 11, 1948.
30. Walter Byers, *Unsportsmanlike Conduct: Exploiting College Athletes*, with Charles Hammer (Ann Arbor: University of Michigan Press, 1995), 1.
31. Quoted in "Three Basketball Aces on Kentucky Team Admit '49 Fix Here," *New York Times*, October 21, 1951.
32. Quoted in Alfred E. Clark, "Judge in Fix Case Condemns Kentucky Teams and Coach," *New York Times*, April 30, 1952.
33. Byers, *Unsportsmanlike Conduct*, 69.
34. See Constitution of the National Collegiate Athletic Association, in *1955–1956 Yearbook of the National Collegiate Athletic Association* (Kansas City, MO: National Collegiate Athletic Association, 1956), 3–13.
35. For more on how the NCAA navigated the threats of taxation and workers' rights in the 1950s, see Smith, *Myth of the Amateur*, 147–59.
36. Scott, *Athletic Revolution*, 175.
37. See, Sack and Staurowsky, *College Athletes for Hire*, 45.
38. John R. Thelin, *Going to College in the Sixties* (Baltimore: Johns Hopkins University Press, 2018), 141.
39. See Ira Katznelson, *When Affirmative Action Was White: An Untold Story of Racial Inequality in Twentieth-Century America* (New York: Norton, 2005), 113–41.
40. Byers later acknowledged that "the South wanted to use the grant-in-aid to plunder the rich resources of white athletes in other parts of the country." He called it a "reverse rerun of the Civil War," meaning, I guess, that the South now sought to forestall a reliance on uncompensated Black labor. Byers, *Unsportsmanlike Conduct*, 68.
41. "Ivy Group Agreement," November 20, 1945, box 38, folder 340, Alfred Whitney Griswold Records, Manuscripts and Archives, Yale University Library.
42. Robert F. Goheen to Everett D. Barnes and the Council of the NCAA, memorandum, April 13, 1966, box 566, "National Collegiate Athletic Association, General File, 1966" folder, Records of the President's Office: William H. Elkins, Special Collections and University Archives, University of Maryland Libraries.

43. John R. Thelin, *A History of American Higher Education*, 3rd ed. (Baltimore: Johns Hopkins University Press, 2019), 381.
44. Harry Edwards, *The Revolt of the Black Athlete* (New York: Free Press, 1969), 16.
45. Byers, *Unsportsmanlike Conduct*, 149.
46. Roderick Ferguson argues that we should see the constant talk of crisis at American universities and colleges since the 1970s – as well as some of the real crises instigated by market-driven reforms – as "part of an institutional and social backlash against the inroads made by student movements." The NCAA, I'm suggesting, offered lawmakers and administrators a model for how to wield the idea of a crisis against students. Ferguson, *We Demand: The University and Student Protests* (Berkeley: University of California Press, 2017), 4.
47. Michael Oriard, *Bowled Over: Big-Time College Football from the Sixties to the BCS Era* (Chapel Hill: University of North Carolina Press, 2009), 141; Howard W. Chudacoff, *Changing the Playbook: How Power, Profit, and Politics Transformed College Sports* (Urbana: University of Illinois Press, 2015), 24.
48. Quoted in James A. Michener, *Sports in America* (New York: Random House, 1976), 203.
49. Thelin observes that we often forget how long it took for some of the reforms of the 1960s to alter the demographics of the college campus. Ninety-five percent of all college students were white in 1960, 94 in 1965, and 95 again in 1969. "Racial diversity? It remained negligible," he writes. Thelin, *Going to College in the Sixties*, 13.
50. National Collegiate Athletic Association, *Proceedings of the 61st Annual Convention* (Kansas City, MO: National Collegiate Athletic Association, 1967), 121, 122. Clausen, unconcerned with conforming to an amateur ideal, admitted that he had looked to MLB and NFL contracts as models.
51. Byers, *Unsportsmanlike Conduct*, 155.
52. Jack Olsen, "The Cruel Deception," *Sports Illustrated*, July 1, 1968, 15.
53. Quoted in Olsen, 15–16.
54. Jack Olsen, "Pride and Prejudice," *Sports Illustrated*, July 8, 1968, 27.
55. Olsen, 27.
56. Quoted in Olsen, 24.
57. National Collegiate Athletic Association, *Proceedings of the 63rd Annual Convention* (Kansas City, MO: National Collegiate Athletic Association, 1969), 99.
58. National Collegiate Athletic Association, 100, 101.
59. National Collegiate Athletic Association, 102.
60. Gordon S. White Jr., "College Athletes Who Protest to Face Loss of Financial Aid," *New York Times*, January 9, 1969.
61. See Douglas Hartmann, *Race, Culture, and the Revolt of the Black Athlete: The 1968 Olympic Protests and Their Aftermath* (Chicago: University of Chicago Press, 2003), 185, 205.
62. Frank Andre Guridy observes that the racial integration of college football in Texas constituted a "realignment, rather than a demolition, of social hierarchies" because it unfolded within the existing administrative and economic

structure of athletic departments. A first generation of Black athletes would find themselves cast as icons of progress within college sports, not the transformation of them. Guridy, *The Sports Revolution: How Texas Changed the Culture of American Athletics* (Austin: University of Texas Press, 2021), 95.
63. Stuart Hall, "Race, Articulation and Societies Structured in Dominance," in *Sociological Theories: Race and Colonialism* (Paris: UNESCO, 1980), 342.
64. Daniel Martinez HoSang and Joseph E. Lowndes, *Producers, Parasites, and Patriots: Race and the New Right-Wing Politics of Precarity* (Minneapolis: University of Minnesota Press, 2019), 12.
65. John Underwood, "The Desperate Coach," *Sports Illustrated*, August 25, 1969, 70.
66. Quoted in Underwood, 70.
67. Underwood, 66.
68. Underwood, 76.
69. John Underwood, "Concessions – and Lies," *Sports Illustrated*, September 8, 1969, 31.
70. The critical race studies scholar David Leonard observes that fans' nostalgia for the athletes of another, better time often associates hard work, discipline, and self-sacrifice with whiteness, with the all-white teams of leather helmets, canvas sneakers, and Jim Crow. Leonard, *Playing while White: Privilege and Power on and off the Field* (Seattle: University of Washington Press, 2017), 7.
71. See National Collegiate Athletic Association, *Proceedings of the 67th Annual Convention* (Shawnee Mission, KS: National Collegiate Athletic Association, 1973), 123.
72. Byers, *Unsportsmanlike Conduct*, 164.
73. Lyndon B. Johnson, "Commencement Address at Howard University: 'To Fulfill These Rights,'" June 4, 1965, Lyndon Baines Johnson Presidential Library and Museum, www.lbjlibrary.org/object/text/commencement-address-howard-university-fulfill-these-rights-06-04-1965.
74. Quoted in John David Skretney, *The Ironies of Affirmative Action: Politics, Culture, and Justice in America* (Chicago: University of Chicago Press, 1996), 217.
75. The athletic department is a textbook example of what Victor Ray calls racialized organizations. It consolidates resources along racial lines. But it also racializes, introducing new categories of difference – the student-athlete, the amateur – that detach race from the color line and resurface in other domains, including the fight over affirmative action. See Ray, "A Theory of Racialized Organizations," *American Sociological Review* 84, no. 1 (2019): 26–53.
76. Scott, *Athletic Revolution*, 213.
77. George H. Hanford, *An Inquiry into the Need for and Feasibility of a National Study of Intercollegiate Athletics* (Washington, DC: American Council on Education, 1974), 26. For an account of the conversations that led to the Hanford report, see George H. Hanford, "We Should Speak the 'Awful Truth' about College Sports," *Chronicle of Higher Education*, May 30, 2003, B10–12.
78. Hanford, 47.

79. Roger W. Heyns, cover letter to *An Inquiry into the Need for and Feasibility of a National Study of Intercollegiate Athletics*, by George H. Hanford (Washington, DC: American Council on Education, 1974).
80. Hanford, *Inquiry*, 48.
81. Bart Barnes and Nancy Scannell, "No Sporting Chance," *Washington Post*, May 12, 1974.
82. Quoted in Barnes and Scannell.
83. Quoted in Jay Searcy, "Big Money Is Pointing More Women toward Pro Sports," *New York Times*, April 14, 1974.
84. The number of women among administrators and coaches also fell after the NCAA, which at first left the governance of women's sports to the Association for Intercollegiate Athletics for Women, added women's championships. See Linda Jean Carpenter, "The Impact of Title IX on Women's Intercollegiate Sports," in *Government and Sport: The Public Policy Issues*, ed. Arthur T. Johnson and James H. Frey (Totowa, NJ: Rowman and Allanheld, 1985), 67.
85. Amira Rose Davis, "'Watch What We Do': The Politics and Possibilities of Black Women's Athletics, 1910–1970" (PhD diss., Johns Hopkins University, 2016), 214.
86. See Deborah L. Brake, *Getting in the Game: Title IX and the Women's Sports Revolution* (New York: New York University, 2010), 17; and Welch Suggs, *A Place on the Team: The Triumph and Tragedy of Title IX* (Princeton, NJ: Princeton University Press, 2005), 32–44.
87. Quoted in Bill Gilbert and Nancy Williamson, "Women in Sport: A Progress Report," *Sports Illustrated*, July 29, 1974, 29.
88. Duderstadt, *Intercollegiate Athletics and the American University*, 191.
89. Quoted in Gordon S. White Jr., "N.C.A.A.'s High Aims Turn into Rights Controversy," *New York Times*, January 16, 1983.
90. National Collegiate Athletic Association, *Proceedings of the 77th Annual Convention* (Shawnee Mission, KS: National Collegiate Athletic Association, 1983), 104.
91. National Collegiate Athletic Association, 108.
92. Derrick E. White, *Blood, Sweat, and Tears: Jake Gaither, Florida A&M, and the History of Black College Football* (Chapel Hill: University of North Carolina Press, 2019), 8.
93. Intercollegiate Athletic Association of the United States, *Proceedings of the Fourth Annual Meeting* (New York: Intercollegiate Athletic Association of the United States, 1909), 32.
94. Watterson, *College Football*, xi.
95. Christopher Newfield, *The Great Mistake: How We Wrecked Public Universities and How We Can Fix Them* (Baltimore: Johns Hopkins University Press, 2016), 4.
96. John Thompson, *I Came as a Shadow: An Autobiography*, with Jesse Washington (New York: Henry Holt, 2020), 222.
97. Quoted in Jack Falla, *NCAA: The Voice of College Sports* (Mission, KS: National Collegiate Athletic Association, 1981), 175.
98. Falla, 163.
99. Duderstadt, *Intercollegiate Athletics and the American University*, 212.

100. Scott, *Athletic Revolution*, 211.
101. See Theresa Runstedtler, "Racial Bias: The Black Athlete, Reagan's War on Drugs, and Big-Time Sports Reform," in "Sport in the University," ed. Noah Cohan et al., special issue, *American Studies* 55, no. 3 (2016): 87.
102. Jerry Kirshenbaum, "An American Disgrace," *Sports Illustrated*, February 27, 1989, 16.
103. Quoted in "Bias's Death Prompts Calls to Step Up Drug War," *Los Angeles Times*, June 26, 1986.
104. William J. Bennett, "No Drugs on Campus," *New York Times*, July 11, 1986.
105. Nancy Reagan, "The Need for Intolerance," *Washington Post*, July 7, 1986.
106. Runstedtler, "Racial Bias," 90.
107. Reagan, "Need for Intolerance."
108. Joanna Bunker Rohrbaugh, "Femininity on the Line," *Psychology Today*, August 1979, 30.
109. "The Scandal behind the Tragedy," *New York Times*, June 28, 1986.
110. "Failed Athletes," *San Francisco Chronicle*, July 3, 1986.
111. Jonathan Yardley, "For the University of Maryland, a Golden Opportunity for Genuine Reform," *Washington Post*, July 7, 1986.
112. *Bakke*, 438 U.S. at 323, 322.
113. *Bakke*, 438 U.S. at 317.
114. Students for Fair Admissions v. Harvard, 600 US 181, 307 (2023).
115. Democratic Leadership Council, *The New Orleans Declaration: A Democratic Agenda for the 1990s* (Washington, DC: Democratic Leadership Council, 1990), i.
116. Democratic Leadership Council, 1. Newfield observes that athlete admissions have been the second-most scrutinized form of admissions advantage behind race-based affirmative action – and ahead of the advantage given to the children of alumni. But commentators often blurred the two categories. Criticism of athlete admissions facilitated the formation of a conservative–liberal consensus against affirmative action. Newfield, *Unmaking the Public University*, 178.
117. Knight Foundation Commission on Intercollegiate Athletics, *Keeping Faith with the Student-Athlete: A New Model for Intercollegiate Athletics* (Charlotte, NC: Knight Foundation, 1991), 11.
118. Knight Foundation Commission on Intercollegiate Athletics, 4, 16, 17.
119. Hartmann, *Race, Culture, and the Revolt of the Black Athlete*, 225.
120. Steve Wulf and Jack McCullum, "The Jock Caucus," *Sports Illustrated*, February 23, 1987, 66.
121. Tom McMillen, *Out of Bounds: How the American Sports Establishment Is Being Driven by Greed and Hypocrisy – and What Needs to Be Done about It*, with Paul Coggins (New York: Simon and Schuster, 1992), 20.
122. McMillen, 23, 97.
123. NCAA Gender-Equity Task Force, *Final Report of the NCAA Gender-Equity Task Force* (Kansas City, MO: National Collegiate Athletic Association, 1993), attachment A.

124. NCAA Gender-Equity Task Force, attachment B.
125. *Pony Excess*, directed by Thaddeus Matula (ESPN, 2010).
126. Rick Telander, *Like a Rose: A Celebration of Football* (Champaign, IL: Sports Publishing, 2004), 3.
127. Rick Telander, *The Hundred Yard Lie: The Corruption of College Football and What We Can Do to Stop It* (New York: Simon and Schuster, 1989), 35.
128. Telander, 51.
129. Telander, 213.
130. Joseph N. Crowley, *In the Arena: The NCAA's First Century* (Indianapolis: National Collegiate Athletic Association, 2006), 203.
131. Bissinger, *Friday Night Lights*, 349.
132. US Supreme Court, "Students for Fair Admissions v. President and Fellows of Harvard College: Oral Argument," October 31, 2022, Oyez, transcript and audio, 1:55:15, www.oyez.org/cases/2022/20-1199.
133. The case against Harvard and the Varsity Blues scandal motivated a reconsideration of who benefited most from athlete admissions. It was not, as one journalist after another discovered, students of color or students from working-class or poor backgrounds. The *Atlantic* described it as "affirmative action for affluent white kids" and observed that sports had "come to play a subtle, yet ludicrously powerful, role in the reproduction of elite status in the United States." Saahil Desai, "College Sports Are Affirmative Action for Rich White Students," *Atlantic*, October 23, 2018, www.theatlantic.com/education/archive/2018/10/college-sports-benefits-white-students/573688/; Derek Thompson, "The Cult of Rich-Kid Sports," *Atlantic*, October 2, 2019, www.theatlantic.com/ideas/archive/2019/10/harvard-university-and-scandal-sports-recruitment/599248/.
134. *Students*, 600 U.S. at 359 (2023).

5 COLOR COMMENTARY

1. *NFL Draft 2001*, aired April 21–22, 2001, on ESPN.
2. Quoted in Richard Whittingham, *The Meat Market: The Inside Story of the NFL Draft* (New York: Macmillan, 1992), 1.
3. For more on ESPN's early NFL draft coverage, see Craig Ellenport, "A Bold New Network, a Preposterous Idea: How the NFL Draft Came to TV," *Sports Illustrated*, April 22, 2020, www.si.com/nfl/2020/04/22/how-espn-televised-nfl-draft-for-the-first-time; Thomas P. Oates, *Football and Manliness: An Unauthorized Feminist Account of the NFL* (Urbana: University of Illinois Press, 2017), 54–93; Pete Williams, *The Draft: A Year Inside the NFL's Search for Talent* (New York: St. Martin's Griffin, 2006), 40–56; and Barry Wilner and Ken Rappoport, *On the Clock: The Story of the NFL Draft* (Lanham, MD: Taylor Trade Publishing, 2015), 111–30.
4. *NFL Draft 2001*.
5. Jason Reid, *The Rise of the Black Quarterback: What It Means for America* (New York: Andscape, 2022), 3.

6. Our investment in the Black quarterback as an indicator of racial progress reminds me of something that Anoop Mirpuri once wrote about Kobe Bryant. Public discussion of Kobe's Blackness and class status, he observed in 2011, tended to legitimate the fairness of contractual market relations (Kobe was rich!) while constructing and maintaining the racial distinctions through which the market functions by extracting labor and resources from some for the benefit of others. The NBA, advertisers, and basketball media, Mirpuri wrote, "conflated practices of reading with practices of consumption." In the age of ESPN, reading (the commentator's job) and consuming (the fan's job but modeled by the commentator) had become indistinguishable. Mirpuri, "Why Can't Kobe Pass (the Ball)? Race and the NBA in the Age of Neoliberalism," in *Commodified and Criminalized: New Racism and African Americans in Contemporary Sports*, ed. David J. Leonard and C. Richard King (Lanham, MD: Rowman and Littlefield, 2011), 114.
7. Jennifer Doyle, "Art and Desire," *World Literature Today* 85, no. 3 (2011): 45.
8. Lauren Janis, "ESPN: Home Field for Sports Addicts," *Columbia Journalism Review* 40, no. 4 (2001): 97; Dave Nagle, "ESPN, Inc.: 2001 in Review," ESPN Press Room, January 2, 2002, https://espnpressroom.com/us/press-releases/2002/01/espn-inc-2001-in-review/.
9. Kurt Badenhausen, "Why ESPN Is Worth $40 Billion as the World's Most Valuable Media Property," *Forbes*, November 9, 2012, www.forbes.com/sites/kurtbadenhausen/2012/11/09/why-espn-is-the-worlds-most-valuable-media-property-and-worth-40-billion/.
10. Quoted in James Andrew Miller and Tom Shales, *Those Guys Have All the Fun: Inside the World of ESPN* (New York: Little, Brown, 2011), 304.
11. David Theo Goldberg, "Call and Response: Sports, Talk Radio, and the Death of Democracy," *Journal of Sports and Social Issues* 22, no. 2 (1998): 220. Goldberg suggests that ESPN had taken over AM radio's former function of broadcasting games, leaving radio to act as "an arena for voicing opinion." But ESPN also led the talk trend, including on the AM dial. In 1992, it launched ESPN Radio. In 1993, it hired Rome to host ESPN2's *Talk2*, which amounted to a televised radio show. It would become a common format on the network.
12. Thomas P. Oates, "Antagonistic Sports Fandom," in "The Body Issue: Sports and the Politics of Embodiment," ed. Joseph Darda and Amira Rose Davis, special issue, *American Quarterly* 75, no. 3 (2023): 520.
13. Victoria Johnson, *Sports TV* (New York: Routledge, 2021), 118; Travis Vogan, *ESPN: The Making of a Sports Media Empire* (Urbana: University of Illinois Press, 2015), 4. Vogan credits ABC with taking the melodramatic elements of studio-era films like *Knute Rockne, All American* and *Pride of the Yankees* and recasting them within reassuring stories of racial reconciliation. It launched *Monday Night Football* in 1970, at the height of Black Power, weaving in human-interest segments about interracial teamwork and orchestrating "programming flows" that led the *MNF* audience to the 1971 Movie of the Week *Brian's Song* and the 1977 miniseries *Roots*.

A generation of future ESPN executives and hosts watched and, it seems, learned a lesson or two about how to lean left without ever leaning too far. Vogan, *ABC Sports: The Rise and Fall of Network Television* (Berkeley: University of California Press, 2018), 125.
14. *NFL Draft 2001.*
15. "Race is at the center of American television," David Leonard and Stephanie Troutman Robbins write. Johnson, reversing the terms, argues that "sports, as seen on TV, is the central shared venue for working through questions of community ideals, struggles over national and regional mythologies, and questions of representative citizenship." Race made TV, and sports TV has made race. Leonard and Robbins, introduction to *Race in American Television: Voices and Visions That Shaped a Nation*, ed. David J. Leonard and Stephanie Troutman Robbins (Santa Barbara, CA: Greenwood, 2021), xx; Johnson, *Sports TV*, 3.
16. George F. Will, "A Stupendous Mystery," *Newsweek*, May 16, 1994, 70.
17. See Thomas F. Corrigan, "Digging the Moat: The Political Economy of ESPN's Cable Carriage Fees," in *ESPN and the Changing Sports Media Landscape*, ed. Greg C. Armfield, John McGuire, and Adam Earnheardt (New York: Peter Lang, 2019), 47–48; Michael Freeman, *ESPN: The Uncensored History* (Lanham, MD: Taylor Trade Publishing, 2000), 111–25; Matthew Futterman, *Players: The Story of Sports and Money, and the Visionaries Who Fought to Create a Revolution* (New York: Simon and Schuster, 2016), 257–84; Victoria E. Johnson, "Historicizing TV Networking: Broadcasting, Cable, and the Case of ESPN," in *Media Industries: History, Theory, and Method*, ed. Jennifer Holt and Alisa Perren (Malden, MA: Wiley-Blackwell), 2009, 61; and Travis Vogan, *ESPN*, 11–41. Sports fans, Futterman writes, showed that "this was the sort of entertainment they couldn't live without," and ESPN rode that need to record-high subscriber fees (271).
18. See Freeman, *ESPN*, 3.
19. Brett Hutchins and David Rowe, *Sport beyond Television: The Internet, Digital Media, and the Rise of Networked Media Sport* (New York: Routledge, 2012), 10; Jason Kido Lopez, *Redefining Sports Media* (New York: Routledge, 2023), 3, 5.
20. Frank Deford, "Sometimes the Bear Eats You: Confessions of a Sportswriter," *Sports Illustrated*, March 29, 2010, 62.
21. Lisa de Moraes, "Haven't We Seen You Somewhere Before?," *Washington Post*, March 29, 2003.
22. Jack Shafer, "*SportsCenter* for Political Junkies," *Slate*, April 29, 2003, https://slate.com/news-and-politics/2003/04/sportscenter-for-news-junkies.html.
23. *SportsCenter*, aired September 7, 1979, on ESPN.
24. Quoted in Miller and Shales, *Those Guys Have All the Fun*, 40, 45.
25. Bill Rasmussen, *Sports Junkies Rejoice! The Birth of ESPN* (Hartsdale, NY: QV Publishing, 1983), 241.
26. *SportsCenter.*
27. Rasmussen, *Sports Junkies Rejoice!*, 35.

28. "Pardon the Interruption ... but Did Sports Debate Shows Change the World?," in *Good Sport with Jody Avirgan*, February 15, 2023, podcast, 39:13, www.ted.com/podcasts/good-sport/pardon-the-interruption-transcript.
29. Freeman, *ESPN*, 45.
30. Rasmussen, *Sports Junkies Rejoice!*, 31.
31. "Pitch the Rich," advertisement, *Broadcasting*, December 10, 1979, 81.
32. "ESPN Blacks Out Black Colleges," *New Pittsburgh Courier*, November 7, 1981.
33. Media scholars Greg Armfield and John McGuire observe how the network's "branded content across multiple media platforms" guides "how sports fans think and feel about the people who play and control these games" – the "ESPN effect," they call it. But the ESPN effect first moved in the reverse direction: The thoughts and feelings of some fans – college-educated white men from the Northeast – guided the content. Armfield and McGuire, "You've Come a Long Way, Baby," preface to *The ESPN Effect: Exploring the Worldwide Leader in Sports*, ed. John McGuire, Greg C. Armfield, and Adam Earnheardt (New York: Peter Lang, 2015), xvi.
34. Jonathan Gray, "Antifandom and the Moral Text: Television without Pity and Textual Dislike," *American Behavioral Scientist* 48, no. 7 (2005): 841.
35. Daniel HoSang and Joseph Lowndes observe that Blackness in the United States gets framed either as "the negation of the polity" or as a "redemptive subjectivity." The former framing is, they note, recruited to authorize the latter. Talk of Black athletes since civil rights, including on ESPN, has often unfolded as a negotiation between Blackness as negation and Blackness as affirmation – between seeing an assumed athletic gift as contaminating an otherwise fair market and seeing it as evidence of a market liberated from the inefficiencies of racism. The fan and the antifan can both find what they need in the gift. HoSang and Lowndes, *Producers, Parasites, and Patriots: Race and the New Right-Wing Politics of Precarity* (Minneapolis: University of Minnesota Press, 2019), 15.
36. Quoted in Miller and Shales, *Those Guys Have All the Fun*, 71.
37. Anthony F. Smith, *ESPN The Company: The Story and Lessons behind the Most Fanatical Brand in Sports*, with Keith Hollihan (Hoboken, NJ: John Wiley and Sons, 2009), 156.
38. Joe Schlosser, "NAACP Sees Boycott Ahead," *Broadcasting and Cable*, August 23, 1999, 4.
39. Quoted in Miller and Shales, *Those Guys Have All the Fun*, 95.
40. Quoted in Miller and Shales, 180.
41. Quoted in Miller and Shales, 178, 180.
42. *SportsCenter*.
43. Parton Keese, "Bristol Hits the Big League in Sports TV," *New York Times*, December 9, 1979.
44. Jack Craig, "ESPN: 24 Hours Is Not Too Much," *Boston Globe*, August 2, 1981.
45. William Oscar Johnson, "Sports Junkies of the U.S., Rejoice!," *Sports Illustrated*, July 23, 1979, 43.

46. "Watch the NFL Draft *Live* Only on ESPN," advertisement, *New York Times*, April 29, 1980.
47. See Williams, *Draft*, 53.
48. Quoted in Robert S. Lyons, *On Any Given Sunday: A Life of Bert Bell* (Philadelphia: Temple University Press, 2010), 57.
49. "Jay Berwanger Denies Asking $1,000 a Game," *Chicago Tribune*, February 11, 1936.
50. See Whittingham, *Meat Market*, 35.
51. Quoted in Lyons, *On Any Given Sunday*, 287.
52. Quoted in Ellenport, "Bold New Network."
53. ESPN, "ESPN to Televise NFL Selections," press release, March 31, 1980.
54. *NFL Draft 1980*, aired April 29, 1980, on ESPN.
55. Quoted in Miller and Shales, *Those Guys Have All the Fun*, 65.
56. Tim Green, *The Dark Side of the Game: My Life in the NFL* (New York: Warner Books, 1996), 5.
57. Quoted in Jill Liebler, "Maximum Exposure," *Sports Illustrated*, May 1, 1989, 38.
58. Quoted in Liebler, 38.
59. Keyshawn Johnson, *Just Give Me the Damn Ball! The Fast Times and Hard Knocks of an NFL Rookie*, with Shelley Smith (New York: Warner Books, 1997), 20.
60. See Simone Browne, *Dark Matters: On the Surveillance of Blackness* (Durham, NC: Duke University Press, 2015), 71–72; Benedict Anderson, *Imagined Communities: Reflections on the Origin and Spread of Nationalism* (London: Verso, 1983), 39.
61. Quoted in Ellenport, "Bold New Network."
62. Tom Junod, "The Dish from Mel," *Sports Illustrated*, April 27, 1992, 48.
63. Christopher Boylan, Ryan McMahon, and Burt L. Monroe, "NFL Draft Profiles Are Full of Racial Stereotypes. And That Matters for When Quarterbacks Get Drafted," *Washington Post*, April 27, 2017.
64. Christopher Boylan, Ryan McMahon, and Burt L. Monroe, "Racially Differentiated Language in NFL Scouting Reports," in *Proceedings of the 22nd ACM SIGKDD International Conference on Knowledge Discovery and Data Mining* (New York: Association for Computing Machinery, 2016).
65. Boylan, McMahon, and Monroe, "NFL Draft Profiles Are Full of Racial Stereotypes."
66. Quoted in Wilner and Rappoport, *On the Clock*, 114.
67. See David R. Roediger and Elizabeth D. Esch, *The Production of Difference: Race and the Management of Labor in U.S. History* (New York: Oxford University Press, 2012), 15.
68. *Draft Day*, directed by Ivan Reitman (Lionsgate, 2014).
69. Chris Berman, foreword to *SportsCentury*, ed. Michael MacCambridge (New York: Hyperion, 1999), 17.
70. *Nightline*, "A Tribute to Jackie Robinson," hosted by Ted Koppel, aired April 6, 1987, on ABC.

71. Quoted in "ESPN Town Meeting: 'Sports in Black and White,'" *Sports Business Daily*, March 3, 1997.
72. Michael Hiestand, "ESPN Forum Leaves Lots of Room for Sequel," *USA Today*, March 3, 1997.
73. Quoted in "ESPN Town Meeting."
74. Wendy Carpenter, "Lively Howard Forum Examines Race and Sports," *Washington Times*, March 3, 1997.
75. *SportsNight*, aired October 1, 1993, on ESPN2.
76. Jack McCallum, "*ET*2, ESPN?," *Sports Illustrated*, October 11, 1993, 11.
77. Quoted in Miller and Shales, *Those Guys Have All the Fun*, 262.
78. Exec. Order No. 13,050, 3 C.F.R. 207 (1997).
79. "President Clinton Participates in ESPN Race Town Hall," Office of the Press Secretary, White House, April 14, 1998, https://clintonwhitehouse4.archives.gov/WH/New/html/19980415-8261.html.
80. "President Clinton Participates in ESPN Race Town Hall."
81. "President Clinton Participates in ESPN Race Town Hall."
82. Exec. Order No. 13,050.
83. See Stephanie Mansfield, "Revenge of the Words: The Yak Attacks of Tony Kornheiser and Michael Wilbon on ESPN's *Pardon the Interruption* Prove That Friends Make the Best Arguments," *Sports Illustrated*, August 5, 2002, 54.
84. Pablo Torre, "The Legacy of PTI," in *ESPN Daily*, October 22, 2021, podcast, 45:22, www.espn.com/radio/play/_/id/32450255.
85. For more on the emergence of the sports debate show, see Taylor M. Henry and Thomas P. Oates, "'Sport Is Argument': Polarization, Racial Tension, and the Televised Sport Debate Format," *Journal of Sport and Social Issues* 44, no. 2 (2020): 154–74. Henry and Oates observe that ESPN shifted from the color blindness of *PTI* during the Bush administration to the "coded racial conflict" of shows like *First Take*, starring the less collegial interracial team of Skip Bayless and Stephen A. Smith, during the Obama administration (163).
86. James Andrew Miller, "*Pardon the Interruption*: Flaunt All Rules," in *Origins with James Andrew Miller*, January 3, 2018, podcast, 1:40:46, www.originsthepodcast.com/chapter2.
87. James A. Michener, *Sports in America* (New York: Random House, 1976), 323.
88. Quoted in Miller and Shales, *Those Guys Have All the Fun*, 404.
89. Quoted in Miller and Shales, *Those Guys Have All the Fun*, 404, 401.
90. See Vogan, *ESPN*, 4.
91. ESPN, "*ESPN The Magazine* Announces 'Body Issue' Athletes," press release, October 1, 2009, https://espnpressroom.com/us/press-releases/2009/10/espn-the-magazine-announces-body-issue-athletes/.
92. See Gregory A. Cranmer, Maria Brann, and Nicholas D. Bowman, "Male Athletes, Female Aesthetics: The Continued Ambivalence toward Female Athletes in ESPN's *The Body Issue*," *International Journal of Sports Communication* 7, no. 2 (2014): 145–65; Gregory A. Cranmer, Alexander L. Lancaster, and Tina M. Harris, "Shot in Black and White: Visualized

Framing in ESPN's *The Body Issue*," *International Journal of Sports Communication* 9, no. 2 (2016): 209–28; and Charlene Weaving and Jessica Samson, "The Naked Truth: Disability, Sexual Objectification, and the *ESPN Body Issue*," *Journal of the Philosophy of Sport* 45, no. 1 (2018): 83–100.

93. Stephanie Clifford, "Special Issues Are Bright Spots for Magazines," *New York Times*, October 11, 2009.
94. Quoted in Miller and Shales, *Those Guys Have All the Fun*, 673.
95. Kevin Hull, Lauren R. Smith, and Annelie Schmittel, "Form or Function? An Examination of *ESPN Magazine*'s 'Body Issue,'" *Visual Communication Quarterly* 22, no. 2 (2015): 113.
96. Quoted in Alyssa Roenigk, "For Sale by Owner," *ESPN The Magazine*, October 19, 2009, 110.
97. Roenigk.
98. "*ESPN The Magazine* Announces 'Body Issue' Athletes."
99. Jennifer McClearen, *Fighting Visibility: Sports Media and Female Athletes in UFC* (Urbana: University of Illinois Press, 2021), 16.
100. Roenigk, "For Sale by Owner," 110.
101. Nicole R. Fleetwood, *On Racial Icons: Blackness and the Public Imagination* (New Brunswick, NJ: Rutgers University Press, 2015), 103, 101.
102. Claudia Rankine, *Citizen: An American Lyric* (Minneapolis: Graywolf Press, 2014), 24.
103. Soraya Nadia McDonald, "What Prince Fielder and *ESPN The Magazine*'s 'Body Issue' Say about Us," *Washington Post*, July 9, 2014.
104. Liam Stack, "Chris Mosier Is First Transgender Athlete in ESPN's 'Body Issue,'" *New York Times*, June 23, 2016.
105. Meagan Flynn, "Seattle Sports Stars Sue Bird and Megan Rapinoe Are First Same-Sex Couple on Cover of ESPN's Body Issue," *Washington Post*, June 26, 2018.
106. ESPN, "Mike Hall Wins ESPN's *Dream Job*," press release, March 29, 2004, www.espn.com/eoe/dreamjob_press_release.html.

6 DRAFT CAPITAL

1. Le'Veon Bell (@LeVeonBell), "This Is Loooong Overdue!!," Twitter, July 29, 2019, 2:47 p.m., https://twitter.com/LeVeonBell/status/1155927944692264960.
2. MV (@mike_v773), "This Man Is Dead to Me," July 29, 2019, comment on Bell, "This is loooong overdue!!," https://twitter.com/mike_v733/status/1155944644187840512?s=20&t=BBqQwu_fyunSwxVAFfU5eQ; Robin Castles (@RobinCastles), "You Abandoned Your Teammates and You Ain't Shit," July 29, 2019, comment on Bell, "This Is Loooong Overdue!!," https://twitter.com/RobinCastles/status/1155939507629248513?s=20&t=BBqQwu_fyunSwxVAFfU5eQ; Lawsi Lightfoot (@Sonoflow7997), "[middle finger]," July 29, 2019, comment on Bell, "This Is Loooong Overdue!!," https://twitter.com/Sonoflaw7997/status/115593410000118857 92?s=20&t=BBqQwu_fyunSwxVAFfU5eQ.

3. geckofdc (@Captain9NYR), "@LeVeon Bell Venmo the $500 You Cost Me and We'll Call It Even," July 29, 2019, comment on Bell, "This Is Loooong Overdue!!," https://twitter.com/captain9nyr/status/1155938058094563329?s=20&t=BBqQwu_fyunSwxVAFfU5eQ; Will (@willborgo_), "@LeVeon Bell $willborgo My Money Long Overdue Too," July 29, 2019, comment on Bell, "This Is Loooong Overdue!!," https://twitter.com/willborgo_/status/1155944046721785856?s=20&t=BBqQwu_fyunSwxVAFfU5eQ.
4. Quoted in Jeremy Fowler, "Le'Veon Bell: 'I Don't Think I Should Settle for Anything Less than What I'm Valued at,'" ESPN.com, March 5, 2018, www.espn.com/nfl/story/_/id/22657079/leveon-bell-pittsburgh-steelers-gets-franchise-tag-again.
5. Quoted in Ralph Vacchiano, "NY Giants RB Brandon Jacobs Receives Death Threat via Twitter," *New York Daily News*, October 22, 2013, www.nydailynews.com/sports/football/giants/giants-jacobs-receives-death-threat-twitter-article-1.1492670.
6. See Kieran Darcy, "Giants' Brandon Jacobs Sounds Off," ESPN.com, October 23, 2013, www.espn.com/new-york/nfl/story/_/id/9869573/brandon-jacobs-new-york-giants-sounds-fantasy-football-players.
7. Quoted in Bob Condotta, "Richard Sherman: Fantasy Football Makes Some Fans Look at Players as Less than People," *Seattle Times*, October 2, 2017, www.seattletimes.com/sports/seahawks/chris-carson-injury-ignites-richard-sherman-rant-against-fantasy-football/.
8. Andy Frye, "Richard Sherman Gets Involved in the Future of Fantasy Football," *Forbes*, August 23, 2018, www.forbes.com/sites/andyfrye/2018/08/23/richard-sherman-gets-involved-in-the-future-of-fantasy-football/?sh=6783b8d2d710.
9. Le'Veon Bell [Juice], "Target," *My Side of Things* (Melodie Music, 2018).
10. Bell, "This Is Loooong Overdue!!"
11. Fantasy Sports Trade Association, "Industry Demographics," 2014, www.fsta.org/?page=demographics.
12. Andrew Baerg, "Draft Day: Risk, Responsibility, and Fantasy Football," in *Fantasy Sports and the Changing Sports Media Industry: Media, Players, and Society*, ed. Nicholas David Bowman, John S. W. Spinda, and Jimmy Sanderson (Lanham, MD: Lexington Books, 2016), 102.
13. Kellen Hoxworth, "Football Fantasies: Neoliberal Habitus, Racial Governmentality, and National Spectacle," *American Quarterly* 72, no. 1 (2020): 159.
14. Thomas P. Oates, "New Media and the Repackaging of NFL Fandom," *Sociology of Sport Journal* 26, no. 1 (2009): 32.
15. Nicholas Ware, "God-Fans of the Gridiron: *Madden*, Fantasy, Football, and Simulation," in *Football, Culture and Power*, ed. David Leonard, Kimberly B. George, and Wade Davis (New York: Routledge, 2017), 87, 89.
16. Branden Buehler, *Front Office Fantasies: The Rise of Managerial Sports Media* (Urbana: University of Illinois Press, 2023), 164, 165.
17. Hoxworth, "Football Fantasies," 157.
18. Quoted in Vacchiano, "NY Giants RB Brandon Jacobs Receives Death Threat."

19. See Wendy Brown, *Undoing the Demos: Neoliberalism's Stealth Revolution* (New York: Zone Books, 2016), 17–45.
20. Brown, 36.
21. Media studies scholars Kit Hughes and Evan Elkins observe how Silicon Valley has embraced the Golden State Warriors, winners of four NBA titles between 2015 and 2022, as an advertisement for "dataficd managerialism." The organization's use of wearable tech and second-by-second tracking of athletic labor has allowed tech firms to cast invasive forms of data collection as, they write, "exciting, fun, and a precondition to success." It may be, as others suggest, that fantasy managers wish to be the data-minded manager seated in the suite above the floor. Or they harbor a more humble desire: a break from being surveilled themselves. Hughes and Elkins, "Silicon Valley's Team: The Golden State Warriors, Datafied Managerialism, and Basketball's Racialized Geography," in "The Body Issue: Sports and the Politics of Embodiment," ed. Joseph Darda and Amira Rose Davis, special issue, *American Quarterly* 75, no. 3 (2023): 473, 477.
22. Annie McClanahan, "Serious Crises: Rethinking the Neoliberal Subject," *boundary 2* 46, no. 1 (2019): 121.
23. The philosopher Michael Bray argues that the twenty-first-century Left has often undermined itself by reinforcing a division between mental and manual labor and valuing the former over the latter. The result has been a class of young knowledge workers disconnected from and often loathed by a working class of manual and service workers. The division, he writes, remixes identifiable racial categories as "a category like 'Black' (or 'migrant') becomes redrawn along lines more or less coincident with those that separate manual from mental labor." Fantasy football allows users to forget their own embodied labor as well as, Bray's argument would suggest, the interests they share with other workers. Bray, *Powers of the Mind: Mental and Manual Labor in the Contemporary Political Crisis* (Bielefeld, Germany: Transcript, 2019), 131.
24. Jodi Melamed, "Racial Capitalism," *Critical Ethnic Studies* 1, no. 1 (2015): 78.
25. None of this is to suggest that it wouldn't make sense to want to own the Pittsburgh Steelers. The late twentieth and early twenty-first centuries have been good to the owner class. Owners have, as the historian Sean Dinces writes, accrued enormous fortunes since the 1980s as the broader "upward redistribution of resources" enhanced their "old monopoly powers." But most recognize that they aren't destined for the owner's box. They are fantasizing their way out of, not into, the economic conditions of the twenty-first century. Dinces, *Bulls Market: Chicago's Basketball Business and the New Inequality* (Chicago: University of Chicago Press, 2018), 6, 5.
26. Quoted in Michael Lewis, *Moneyball: The Art of Winning an Unfair Game* (New York: Norton, 2003), 72.
27. Robert Coover, *The Universal Baseball Association, Inc., J. Henry Waugh, Prop.* (New York: Random House, 1968), 33.
28. Coover, 35.
29. Coover, 27–28.
30. Coover, 87.

31. Matt Weiland, "A Veteran Baseball Novel Comes Off the Bench," *New York Times*, August 26, 2011; John Sexton, *Baseball as a Road to God: Seeing beyond the Game*, with Thomas Oliphant and Peter J. Schwartz (New York: Gotham, 2013), 66; Daniel Roberts, "Robert Coover's Dark Fantasy-Baseball Novel," *Paris Review*, September 18, 2017, www.theparisreview.org/blog/2017/09/18/robert-coovers-dark-fantasy-baseball-novel/.
32. "The Parlor Game of Base-Ball," advertisement, *Frank Leslie's Illustrated Newspaper*, December 8, 1866, 180. See also Edward J. Rielly, *Baseball: An Encyclopedia of Popular Culture* (Santa Barbara, CA: ABC-CLIO, 2000), 112. Inventor Francis Sebring advertised the game in an 1866 issue of *Frank Leslie's Illustrated Newspaper* ("the new and beautiful divertissement of base-ball"), but no sets survived, leading the cultural historian Edward Rielly to wonder whether Parlor Base-Ball Field ever existed outside of the magazine and Sebring's imagination.
33. Joe Lemire, "Strat-O-Matic More than a Game for Its Founders and Devotees," *Sports Illustrated*, February 10, 2011, www.si.com/more-sports/2011/02/10/strat-omatic.
34. Sam Walker, *Fantasyland: A Season on Baseball's Lunatic Fringe* (New York: Viking, 2006), 59.
35. Mary Alice Kellogg, "Dice Baseball Fever," *Newsweek*, August 23, 1976, 60.
36. Quoted in Lemire, "Strat-O-Matic More Than a Game."
37. Daniel Okrent, "The Year George Foster Wasn't Worth $36," *Inside Sports*, March 31, 1981, 89.
38. See Fred Ferretti, "For Major-League Addicts, a Way to Win a Pennant," *New York Times*, July 8, 1980.
39. Okrent, "Year George Foster Wasn't Worth $36," 90.
40. Glen Waggoner, ed., *Rotisserie League Baseball* (New York: Bantam, 1984). Andrew Billings, Nicholas Buzzelli, and Minghui Fan observe that fantasy has grown "in tandem" with media, media innovation being, they argue, "the key component to fantasy sports expansion," from the box score to the internet to the iPhone to a bunch of media insiders telling friends about something called Rotisserie League Baseball. Billings, Buzzelli, and Fan, "Growing in Tandem with Media: Fantasy Sport, Media Use, and the Formation of an Industry Giant," *International Journal of the History of Sport* 38, no. 1 (2021): 29.
41. Quoted in Ferretti, "For Major-League Addicts."
42. Steve Wulf, "For the Champion in the Rotisserie League, Joy Is a Yoo-Hoo Shampoo," *Sports Illustrated*, May 14, 1984, 15.
43. Quoted in Jack Friedman, "The Most Peppery Game since the Hot Stove League? It's Rotisserie Baseball," *People*, April 23, 1984, 42.
44. Wulf, "For the Champion in the Rotisserie League," 8.
45. Rebecca Joyce Kissane and Sarah Winslow, *Whose Game? Gender and Power in Fantasy Sports* (Philadelphia: Temple University Press, 2020), 53.
46. Conn Nugent, "How to Own a Baseball Team," *Harvard Magazine*, April 1981, 70.
47. Daniel Okrent, "The Year George Foster Wasn't Worth $36," introduction to *Rotisserie League Baseball*, ed. Glen Waggoner (New York: Bantam, 1984), 4.

48. See Andrew J. Ploeg, "A New Form of Fandom: How Free Agency Brought about Rotisserie League Baseball," *International Journal of the History of Sport* 38, no. 1 (2021): 7–27.
49. Jules Tygiel, *Past Time: Baseball as History* (New York: Oxford University Press, 2000), 198.
50. On the long downturn, see Robert Brenner, *The Economics of Global Turbulence: The Advanced Capitalist Economies from the Long Boom to the Long Downturn, 1945–2005* (London: Verso, 2006).
51. Okrent, "Year George Foster Wasn't Worth $36," *Inside Sports*, 89.
52. Wulf, "For the Champion in the Rotisserie League," 8.
53. Lee Eisenberg, "The Awful Truth about Rotisserie League Baseball," *New York Times*, April 8, 1990.
54. David J. Leonard, "Not a Hater, Just Keepin' It Real: Race- and Gender-Based Game Studies," *Games and Culture* 1, no. 1 (2006): 85; Tara Fickle, *The Race Card: From Gaming Technologies to Model Minorities* (New York: New York University Press, 2019), 2.
55. See Mark Armour and Daniel R. Levitt, "Baseball Demographics, 1947–2016," Society for American Baseball Research, https://sabr.org/bioproj/topic/baseball-demographics-1947-2016/.
56. Okrent, "Year George Foster Wasn't Worth $36," *Inside Sports*, 89.
57. Nugent, "How to Own a Baseball Team," 70.
58. See Dave Jamieson, *Mint Condition: How Baseball Cards Became an American Obsession* (New York: Atlantic Monthly Press, 2010), 11–29; and Nan Enstad, *Cigarettes, Inc.* (Chicago: University of Chicago Press, 2018), 28–30.
59. *Silly Little Game*, directed by Adam Kurland and Lucas Jansen (ESPN Films, 2010).
60. See Ben McGrath, "Dream Teams," *New Yorker*, April 13, 2015, 27.
61. *Silly Little Game*.
62. Bill James, *1978 Baseball Abstract: The 2nd Annual Edition of Baseball's Most Informative and Imaginative Review* (Lawrence, KS: self-pub., 1978), 1.
63. Quoted in Alan Schwarz, *The Numbers Game: Baseball's Lifelong Fascination with Statistics* (New York: Thomas Dunne Books, 2004), 122.
64. "Our Crystal Baseball," *Esquire*, April 24, 1979, 6.
65. Bill James, "1979 Baseball Forecast," *Esquire*, April 24, 1979, 65, 67.
66. Bill James, *The Bill James Baseball Abstract, 1988* (New York: Ballantine, 1988), i.
67. Daniel Okrent, "He Does It by the Numbers," *Sports Illustrated*, May 25, 1981, 42.
68. Quoted in Okrent, 45.
69. For detailed accounts of James's forerunners, including Rickey's statistician, Allan Roth, and Cook, see Schwarz, *Numbers Game*, 67–91.
70. For more on James's life and influence on the game, see Scott Gray, *The Mind of Bill James: How a Complete Outsider Changed Baseball* (New York: Doubleday, 2006).
71. Bill James, *The Bill James Baseball Abstract, 1984* (New York: Ballantine, 1984), 6.

72. James, 8.
73. Schwarz, *Numbers Game*, 112.
74. Bill James, *The Bill James Historical Baseball Abstract* (New York: Villard, 1986), 41.
75. James, *Bill James Baseball Abstract, 1984*, 31.
76. James, *Bill James Historical Baseball Abstract*, 252.
77. Quoted in Tyler Kepner, "Bill James, No Stranger to Controversy, Believes His Current One Is 'Unfortunate,'" *New York Times*, November 8, 2018.
78. Quoted in Kepner.
79. Bill James (@billjamesonline), "Is There Any Such Thing as a Major League Baseball Player Who Is Underpaid?," Twitter, November 8, 2018, https://web.archive.org/web/20181110102306/https://twitter.com/billjamesonline.
80. Eric Walker, *The Sinister First Baseman and Other Observations* (Millbrae, CA: Celestial Arts, 1982), 113.
81. Quoted in Lewis, *Moneyball*, 63.
82. Lewis, 62.
83. Lewis, 56, 123, 62.
84. Lewis, 140.
85. Lewis, 129, 178, 100.
86. Lewis, 59.
87. Lewis, 105, 135.
88. Lewis, 88.
89. Joon Lee, "Inside the Rise of MLB's Ivy League Culture: Stunning Numbers and a Question of What's Next," ESPN.com, June 30, 2020, www.espn.com/mlb/story/_/id/29369890/inside-rise-mlb-ivy-league-culture-stunning-numbers-question-next.
90. Quoted in Lee.
91. Quoted in Bob Nightengale, "'It's Just Getting Worse': MLB's 'Disgusting' Minority Hiring Woes Continue as Job Candidates Shut Out Again," *USA Today*, December 4, 2019, www.usatoday.com/story/sports/mlb/columnist/bob-nightengale/2019/12/04/mlb-general-managers-executives-winter-meetings/2604488001/.
92. Cathy O'Neil, *Weapons of Math Destruction: How Big Data Increases Inequality and Threatens Democracy* (New York: Crown, 2016), 17.
93. Nate Silver, *The Signal and the Noise: Why So Many Predictions Fail – but Some Don't* (New York: Penguin Press, 2012), 10, 9.
94. See Matthew Berry, *Fantasy Life: The Outrageous, Uplifting, and Heartbreaking World of Fantasy Sports from the Guy Who's Lived It* (New York: Riverhead Books, 2013), 7.
95. *The Simpsons*, season 22, episode 3, "MoneyBart," aired October 10, 2010, on Fox.
96. Neda Atanasoski and Kalindi Vora, *Surrogate Humanity: Race, Robots, and the Politics of Technological Futures* (Durham, NC: Duke University Press, 2019), 5, 33.
97. Annie McClanahan, *Dead Pledges: Debt, Crisis, and Twenty-First-Century Culture* (Stanford, CA: Stanford University Press, 2017), 66.

98. Dak [Dave King], "Some Questions and Some Answers," *Fire Joe Morgan*, April 20, 2005, www.firejoemorgan.com/2005/04/some-questions-and-some-answers.html.
99. Bethlehem Shoals [Nathanial Friedman], "Save Your Claws, Chew Angles," *FreeDarko*, November 7, 2006, https://freedarko.blogspot.com/2006/11/save-your-claws-chew-angles.html.
100. For more on *Fire Joe Morgan* and *FreeDarko*, see Noah Cohan, *We Average Unbeautiful Watchers: Fan Narratives and the Reading of American Sports* (Lincoln: University of Nebraska Press, 2019), 155–63. Cohan sees *FJM*, *FreeDarko*, and Jessica Luther's feminist blog *Power Forward* as evidence of how the blog-era internet offered fans the means of articulating alternative narratives and forming chosen communities that they couldn't find in traditional media. A lot of the takes offered on *FJM* and *FreeDarko* are now dominant ones – and may make you miss the time when they were alternative.
101. Dak [Dave King], "Some Questions and Some Answers."
102. See Unlawful Internet Gambling Enforcement Act of 2006, 31 U.S.C. § 5363 (2006).
103. Quoted in David McCabe, "How the Daily Fantasy Sports Industry Was Born," *The Hill*, September 24, 2015, https://thehill.com/policy/technology/254744-how-the-daily-fantasy-sports-industry-was-born/.
104. Blinders [Kevin Bonnet], "The Shot Heard Round the World," *Blinders*, June 21, 2007, http://blinderspoker.blogspot.com/2007/06/shot-heard-round-world.html.
105. Daniel Barbarisi, *Dueling with Kings: High Stakes, Killer Sharks, and the Get-Rich Promise of Daily Fantasy Sports* (New York: Touchstone, 2017), 12.
106. Chris Fargis, "My New Business Venture: Instant Fantasy Sports," *Twenty-One Outs Twice*, September 14, 2007, http://twentyoneoutstwice.blogspot.com/2007/09/my-new-business-venture-instant-fantasy.html.
107. For more on the formation of DFS and the struggle between FanDuel and DraftKings for market share, see Albert Chen, *Billion Dollar Fantasy: The High-Stakes Game between FanDuel and DraftKings That Upended Sports in America* (New York: Houghton Mifflin Harcourt, 2019).
108. See Anthony Crupi, "Fantasy Sports Sites DraftKings, FanDuel September Spend Tops $100 Million," *Ad Age*, September 30, 2015, https://adage.com/article/media/draftkings-fanduel-spe/300658.
109. For a detailed account of the legal battle over DFS, see Chen, *Billion Dollar Fantasy*, 99–186.
110. Quoted in Andrew C. Billings and Brody J. Ruihley, *The Fantasy Sports Industry: Games within Games* (London: Routledge, 2014), 68.
111. Quoted in Billings and Ruihley, 75.
112. Stephen A. Smith, "Why Don't Black People Play Fantasy? Allow Me to Explain," *ESPN The Magazine*, September 8, 2008, 18.
113. Joris Drayer and Brendan Dwyer, "Perception of Fantasy Is Not Always the Reality: An Exploratory Examination into Blacks' Lack of Participation in Fantasy Sports," *International Journal of Sports Management* 14 (2013): 98.

114. Jay Caspian Kang, "How the Daily Fantasy Sports Industry Turns Fans into Suckers," *New York Times Magazine*, January 6, 2016, www.nytimes.com/2016/01/06/magazine/how-the-daily-fantasy-sports-industry-turns-fans-into-suckers.html.
115. "Robinhood," Robinhood video, February 20, 2014, 1:51, https://vimeo.com/87163777.
116. *Real Sports with Bryant Gumbel*, season 20, episode 9, "Risky Business," aired September 23, 2014, on HBO.
117. *Frontline*, season 34, episode 3, "The Fantasy Sports Gamble," aired February 9, 2016, on PBS.
118. Eric T. Schneiderman, memorandum of law in support of motion for a preliminary injunction against DraftKings, Inc., New York State Office of the Attorney General, November 17, 2015, 10.
119. Quoted in Dan Shaughnessy, "The Accidental Godfather of Fantasy Sports," *Boston Globe*, October 13, 2015.
120. Brown, *Undoing the Demos*, 38.
121. William C. Rhoden, "Fantasy Sports' Real Crime: Dehumanizing the Athletes," *New York Times*, November 25, 2015.
122. "In the game of capitalism," the media scholar Todd Boyd wrote of Black NBA stars at the turn of the century, "a game that was built on the backs of the free labor of slaves, it seems appropriate that someone other than White people should someday reap some of the benefits." He declared their success "the redefinition of the American Dream." The trouble came from white fans who agreed with him and who felt that Kevin Garnett and Allen Iverson's American dream had come at the cost of their own. Boyd "The Game Is to Be Sold, Not to Be Told," in *Basketball Jones: America above the Rim*, ed. Todd Boyd and Kenneth L. Shropshire (New York: New York University Press, 2000), xii; Boyd, *Young, Black, Rich, and Famous: The Rise of the NBA, the Hip Hop Invasion, and the Transformation of American Culture* (New York: Doubleday, 2003), 6.
123. See Ben Larkin, Brendan Dwyer, and Chad Goebert, "Man or Machine: Fantasy Football and Dehumanization of Athletes," *Journal of Sport Management* 34, no. 5 (2020): 412.
124. In her study of (non-American) football in Chile, Brenda Elsey urges historians to address the game not as "a byproduct of something else" but as "what really happens." In the United States, fantasy, advanced metrics, and the chatter around them have muddied the waters, making it more difficult than ever to watch a game and agree on what occurred, on how to demarcate the event. Elsey, *Citizens and Sportsmen: Fútbol and Politics in Twentieth-Century Chile* (Austin: University of Texas Press, 2011), 1.
125. "Tracking the (Money) Balls: How Data Science Is Becoming a Game Changer," in *Harvard Data Science Review Podcast*, March 19, 2021, podcast, 28:27, https://hdsr.mitpress.mit.edu/podcast.
126. "Tracking the (Money) Balls."
127. "'Moneyball' Comes to Medicine," Scripps Health, December 20, 2015, www.scripps.org/news_items/5588-moneyball-comes-to-medicine.

128. John Sides, "The Moneyball of Campaign Advertising," *FiveThirtyEight* (blog), *New York Times*, October 5, 2011, https://archive.nytimes.com/fivethirtyeight.blogs.nytimes.com/2011/10/05/the-moneyball-of-campaign-advertising-part-1/; Patrick Thomas, "Chicken Producers Have Own 'Moneyball,'" *Wall Street Journal*, December 14, 2023.
129. Quoted in Michael J. de la Merced and Katie Benner, "As Department Stores Close, Stitch Fix Expands Online," *New York Times*, May 10, 2017.
130. Michael J. Mauboussin and Dan Callahan, "Turn and Face the Strange: Overcoming Barriers to Change in Sports and Investing," *Consilient Observer*, September 8, 2021, www.morganstanley.com/im/en-us/individual-investor/insights/articles/turn-and-face-the-strange.html.

EPILOGUE: SPORTS NORMING

1. Quoted in Neil Best, "Roger Goodell Says NFL Concussion Lawsuit Settlement in Best Interest of Players, Too," *Newsday*, September 4, 2013.
2. Class Action Settlement Agreement (as Amended), Turner et al. v. National Football League (*In re* National Football League Players' Concussion Injury Litigation), No. 2:12-md-02323-AB (ED Pa. 2015), at 116.
3. Will Hobson, "How 'Race-Norming' Was Built into the NFL Concussion Settlement," *Washington Post*, August 2, 2021.
4. Class Action Complaint, Henry et al. v. National Football League, No. 2:20-cv-04165 (ED Pa. 2020), at 4.
5. Class Action Complaint, *Henry*, at 1, 3.
6. Griggs et al. v. Duke Power Co., 401 US 424, 426, 424 (1971).
7. Alexandra K. Wigdor and Wendell R. Garner, eds., *Ability Testing: Uses, Consequences, and Controversies* (Washington, DC: National Academy Press, 1982), 24; John A. Hartigan and Alexandra K. Wigdor, eds., *Fairness in Employment Testing: Validity Generalization, Minority Issues, and the General Aptitude Test Battery* (Washington, DC: National Academy Press, 1989), 280.
8. Linda S. Gottfredson, "The Science and Politics of Race-Norming," *American Psychologist* 49, no. 11 (1994): 955.
9. George F. Will, "Seeing Nothing Normal in 'Race-Norming,'" *Baltimore Sun*, May 23, 1991.
10. Richard J. Herrnstein and Charles Murray, *The Bell Curve: Intelligence and Class Structure in American Life* (New York: Free Press, 1994), 503–5.
11. Richard K. Heaton et al., *Revised Comprehensive Norms for an Expanded Halstead-Reitan Battery: Demographically Adjusted Neuropsychological Norms for African Americans and Caucasian Adults* (Lutz, FL: Psychological Assessment Resources, 2004), 6.
12. Daryl Michael Scott, *Contempt and Pity: Social Policy and the Image of the Damaged Black Psyche, 1880–1996* (Chapel Hill: University of North Carolina Press, 1997), xviii.
13. Michael E. Staub, *The Mismeasure of Minds: Debating Race and Intelligence between "Brown" and "The Bell Curve"* (Chapel Hill: University of North

Carolina Press, 2018), 3. Staub writes that the *Brown* decision moved racial liberalism from "a discussion of economic and social injustice to a debate over racial intelligence" and the psychological costs of segregation, a move that aligned it with racial conservatism in imagining Black environments as harmful to children's cognitive development. Race norming emerged from that unacknowledged political consensus as a practice at once conservative, liberal, and anti-Black.

14. Chelsey R. Carter and Tracie Canada, "The NFL's Racist 'Race Norming' Is an Afterlife of Slavery," *Scientific American*, July 8, 2021, www.scientificamerican.com/article/the-nfls-racist-race-norming-is-an-afterlife-of-slavery/; Steve Almond, "The NFL Is a Billion Dollar 'Plantation,'" WBUR.org, February 9, 2022, www.wbur.org/cognoscenti/2022/02/09/nfl-superbowl-race-norming-brian-flores-steve-almond.

15. Gift-giving offered evidence, Mauss wrote in 1925, that "all is not yet couched in terms of purchase and sale" and that "our morality is not solely commercial." Mauss, *The Gift: Forms and Functions of Exchange in Archaic Societies*, trans. Ian Cunnison (Glencoe, IL: Free Press, 1954), 63.

16. Mimi Thi Nguyen, *The Gift of Freedom: War, Debt, and Other Refugee Passages* (Durham, NC: Duke University Press, 2012), 18–19.

17. Of Henry and Davenport's lawsuit, Dave Zirin, the longtime sports editor for the *Nation*, observed that the NFL's "comfort with 'race norming' feels more like a part of a bigger picture than an outdated manual or a clinician's snafu." The league has also made other forms of norming, on and off the field, comfortable for fans. Zirin, "So What the Hell Is Race Norming?," *Nation*, March 12, 2021, www.thenation.com/article/society/race-norming-nfl-concussions/.

18. W. E. B. Du Bois, *The Souls of Black Folk: Essays and Sketches* (Chicago: A. C. McClurg, 1903), 251.

19. W. E. B. Du Bois, *The Gift of Black Folk: The Negroes in the Making of America* (Boston: Stratford, 1924), iii.

20. Andrew Gill and Vitor Brajer, "Wonderlic, Race, and the NFL Draft," *Journal of Sports Economics* 13, no. 6 (2012): 649.

21. David J. Berri and Rob Simmons, "Catching a Draft: On the Process of Selecting Quarterbacks in the National Football League Amateur Draft," *Journal of Productivity Analysis* 35, no. 1 (2009): 47n22.

22. Quoted in Ed Bouchette, "Final Exam: Steelers Throw New Mental Test at Would-Be Draftees," *Pittsburgh Post-Gazette*, April 24, 1994.

23. Mike Knobler, "Against the Tide: Henry Has No Regrets about Playing for State," *Clarion-Ledger*, December 20, 1992.

24. Quoted in Ed Bouchette, "Rookie in a Rush to Make Name for Self: Henry Tries to Impress Steelers," *Pittsburgh Post-Gazette*, August 12, 1993.

25. Class Action Complaint, Flores v. National Football League et al., No. 1:22-cv-00871 (SDNY 2022), at 7.

26. Class Action Complaint, *Flores*, at 4.

27. Class Action Complaint, *Flores*, at 2.

28. "Douglas H. Wigdor," Wigdor LLP, 2023, www.wigdorlaw.com/our-team/douglas-h-wigdor/.

29. Jonquel Jones (@jus242), "It's all a popularity contest and politics in wbb," Twitter, February 18, 2022, 2:16 a.m., https://twitter.com/jus242/status/1494571538720436229.
30. "WNBA's Most Popular Merchandise," WNBA.com, September 23, 2021, www.wnba.com/news/wnbas-most-popular-merchandise/.
31. Quoted in Katie Barnes, "Jonquel Jones and the Untold Story of the WNBA's Reigning MVP," ESPN.com, June 22, 2022, www.espn.com/wnba/story/_/id/34109460/jonquel-jones-untold-story-wnba-reigning-mvp.
32. Lucia Trimbur writes that dwelling on "the uniqueness of American football's rules of play and patterns of violence" has short-circuited connections between it and other organized sports, including low- and noncontact sports. We need, she argues, to hold leagues to an industry-wide "duty of care" that would connect the NFL to the WNBA and provide "protections for an international group of current and future workers." Trimbur, "Lights Out: Concussion Research, the National Football League, and Employer Duty of Care," in *The Palgrave Handbook of Sport, Politics, and Harm*, ed. Stephen Wagg and Allyson M. Pollock (London: Palgrave Macmillan, 2021), 159, 169.
33. Kate Fagan, "Owning the Middle," *ESPN The Magazine*, June 10, 2013, 88.
34. Quoted in "Brittney Griner," *ESPN The Magazine*, July 20, 2015, 110.
35. For an account of the gendered racialization of testosterone, see Rebecca M. Jordan-Young and Katrina Karkazis, *Testosterone: An Unauthorized Biography* (Cambridge, MA: Harvard University Press, 2019), 159–201.
36. C. J. Jones, "Unfair Advantage Discourse in USA Powerlifting: Toward a Transfeminist Sport Studies," *TSQ* 8, no. 1 (2021): 59. The queer theorist Jennifer Doyle observes that sports governing bodies cannot abide a female athlete who might "measure human capacity." The sociologist Travers, who goes by a mononym, argues that the gender segregation of sports functions to "justify extensive opportunity structures and disproportionate patterns of remuneration for male athletes" and normalize gender inequality in the non-sporting world. The enormous scale of the campaign against trans athletes, who denaturalize gender segregation, testifies to a broad, enduring commitment to gender inequality in national political life. Doyle, "Dirt Off Her Shoulders," introduction to "The Athlete Issue," ed. Jennifer Doyle, special issue of *GLQ* 19, no. 4 (2013): 421; Travers, *The Trans Generation: How Trans Kids (and Their Parents) Are Creating a Gender Revolution* (New York: New York University Press, 2018), 96.
37. Bertolt Brecht, "Emphasis on Sport," in *Brecht on Theatre: The Development of an Aesthetic*, trans. John Willett (New York: Hill and Wang, 1964), 6, 8.
38. See Anthony Crupi, "NFL Swallows TV Whole, Notching 93 of the Year's Top 100 Broadcasts," *Sportico*, January 5, 2024, www.sportico.com/business/media/2024/nfl-posts-93-of-top-100-tv-broadcasts-2023-1234761753/. Including college football and the Super Bowl lead-out show (*Next Level Chef*), the sport accounted for 98 of the 100 most watched programs.

Bibliography

Adorno, Theodor W. "Education after Auschwitz." In *Critical Models: "Interventions" and "Catchwords,"* translated by Henry W. Pickford, 191–204. New York: Columbia University Press, 1998.
Ali, Muhammad. *The Greatest: My Own Story.* With Richard Durham. New York: Random House, 1975.
Ali, Muhammad. "*Playboy* Interview: Cassius Clay." By Alex Haley. *Playboy,* October 1964, 67–82, 190–92.
Almond, Steve. "The NFL Is a Billion Dollar 'Plantation.'" WBUR.org, February 9, 2022. www.wbur.org/cognoscenti/2022/02/09/nfl-superbowl-race-norming-brian-flores-steve-almond.
Alou, Felipe. "Latin-American Ballplayers Need a Bill of Rights." *Sport,* November 1963.
Anand, Bharat, and Kate Attea. *International Management Group.* Boston: Harvard Business Publishing, 2001.
Anderson, Benedict. *Imagined Communities: Reflections on the Origin and Spread of Nationalism.* London: Verso, 1983.
Andrews, John. "The Paymasters." In "Not Just a Game." Supplement, *Economist,* June 6, 1998, 14–17.
Angelou, Maya. *I Know Why the Caged Bird Sings.* New York: Random House, 1969.
Armfield, Greg C., and John McGuire. "You've Come a Long Way, Baby." Preface to *The ESPN Effect: Exploring the Worldwide Leader in Sports,* edited by John McGuire, Greg C. Armfield, and Adam Earnheardt, xiii–xvii. New York: Peter Lang, 2015.
Armour, Mark, and Daniel R. Levitt. "Baseball Demographics, 1947–2016." Society for American Baseball Research. https://sabr.org/bioproj/topic/baseball-demographics-1947-2016/.
Atanasoski, Neda. *Humanitarian Violence: The U.S. Deployment of Diversity.* Minneapolis: University of Minnesota Press, 2013.
Atanasoski, Neda, and Kalindi Vora. *Surrogate Humanity: Race, Robots, and the Politics of Technological Futures.* Durham, NC: Duke University Press, 2019.

Badenhausen, Kurt. "Why ESPN Is Worth $40 Billion as the World's Most Valuable Media Property." *Forbes*, November 9, 2012. www.forbes.com/sites/kurtbadenhausen/2012/11/09/why-espn-is-the-worlds-most-valuable-media-property-and-worth-40-billion/.
Baerg, Andrew. "Draft Day: Risk, Responsibility, and Fantasy Football." In *Fantasy Sports and the Changing Sports Media Industry: Media, Players, and Society*, edited by Nicholas David Bowman, John S. W. Spinda, and Jimmy Sanderson, 99–119. Lanham, MD: Lexington Books, 2016.
Baker, Peter, and Michael A. Fletcher. "Clinton's Town Hall Taking Discussion of Race into Sports Arena." *New York Times*, April 14, 1998.
Baldwin, James. "The Black Boy Looks at the White Boy." *Esquire*, May 1961, 102–6.
Baldwin, James. "The Fight: Patterson vs. Liston." *Nugget*, November 1963, 32–34, 67–70.
Bannister, Roger. "Beyond the Boundary." *Sports Illustrated*, August 13, 1979, 130–38.
Bannister, Roger. "My Olympic Defeat Hurt So Much I Went after the Four-Minute Mile." Interview by Alice Thomson. *Times*, July 28, 2012.
Bannister, Roger. "Opening Remarks to a Joint Meeting of the British Association of Sport Medicine with the British Olympic Association." *British Journal of Sports Medicine* 8, no. 1 (1974): 3–4.
Bannister, Roger. *Twin Tracks*. London: Robson Press, 2014.
"Bannister Offers Speculation about 'Advantages' for Blacks." *New York Times*, September 14, 1995.
Baraka, Amiri. *The Autobiography of Leroi Jones*. New York: Freundlich Books, 1984.
Baraka, Amiri. "In the Ring (2)." *Nation*, June 29, 1964, 661–62.
Barbarisi, Daniel. *Dueling with Kings: High Stakes, Killer Sharks, and the Get-Rich Promise of Daily Fantasy Sports*. New York: Touchstone, 2017.
Barnes, Bart, and Nancy Scannell. "No Sporting Chance." *Washington Post*, May 12, 1974.
Barnes, Katie. "Jonquel Jones and the Untold Story of the WNBA's Reigning MVP." ESPN.com, June 22, 2022. www.espn.com/wnba/story/_/id/34109460/jonquel-jones-untold-story-wnba-reigning-mvp.
Barrett, Lindon. *Blackness and Value: Seeing Double*. Cambridge: Cambridge University Press, 1999.
Bass, Amy. *Not the Triumph but the Struggle: The 1968 Olympics and the Making of the Black Athlete*. Minneapolis: University of Minnesota Press, 2002.
Bass, Amy. "State of the Field: Sports History and the 'Cultural Turn.'" *Journal of American History* 101, no. 1 (2014): 148–72.
Bederman, Gail. *Manliness and Civilization: A Cultural History of Gender and Race in the United States, 1880–1917*. Chicago: University of Chicago Press, 1995.
Bell, Le'Veon [Juice]. "Target." *My Side of Things*. Melodie Music, 2018.
Bell, Le'Veon (@LeVeonBell). "This is looooong overdue!!" Twitter, July 29, 2019, 2:47 p.m. https://twitter.com/LeVeonBell/status/1155927944692264960.
Benedict, Ruth. *Race: Science and Politics*. New York: Modern Age Books, 1940.
Benedict, Ruth, and Gene Weltfish. *The Races of Mankind*. New York: Public Affairs Committee, 1943.

Bennett, James. "President Leads TV Discussion on Role of Race in Sports." *New York Times*, April 15, 1998.
Bennett, William J. "No Drugs on Campus." *New York Times*, July 11, 1986.
Berman, Chris. Foreword to *SportsCentury*, edited by Michael MacCambridge, 17. New York: Hyperion, 1999.
Berri, David J., and Rob Simmons. "Catching a Draft: On the Process of Selecting Quarterbacks in the National Football League Amateur Draft." *Journal of Productivity Analysis* 35, no. 1 (2009): 37–49.
Berry, Matthew. *Fantasy Life: The Outrageous, Uplifting, and Heartbreaking World of Fantasy Sports from the Guy Who's Lived It.* New York: Riverhead Books, 2013.
Best, Neil. "Roger Goodell Says NFL Concussion Lawsuit Settlement in Best Interest of Players, Too." *Newsday*, September 4, 2013.
"Bias-Free Interracial Comparisons." *Nature* 377, no. 6546 (1995): 183–84.
"Bias's Death Prompts Calls to Step Up Drug War." *Los Angeles Times*, June 26, 1986.
Biederman, Les. "Clouter Clemente: Popular Buc." *Sporting News*, September 5, 1964, 3–4.
Billings, Andrew C., Nicholas R. Buzzelli, and Minghui Fan. "Growing in Tandem with Media: Fantasy Sport, Media Use, and the Formation of an Industry Giant." *International Journal of the History of Sport* 38, no. 1 (2021): 28–40.
Billings, Andrew C., and Brody J. Ruihley. *The Fantasy Sports Industry: Games within Games.* London: Routledge, 2014.
Bims, Hamilton. "Roberto Clemente: Sad End for a Troubled Man." *Ebony*, March 1973, 52–60.
The Bingo Long Traveling All-Stars and Motor Kings. Directed by John Badham. Universal Pictures, 1976.
Bissinger, H. G. Email message to author. December 14, 2022.
Bissinger, H. G. *Friday Night Lights: A Town, a Team, and a Dream.* Reading, MA: Addison-Wesley, 1990.
Bissinger, H. G. *Friday Night Lights: A Town, a Team, and a Dream.* 25th anniversary ed. New York: Hachette, 2015.
Bjarkman, Peter C. *Baseball with a Latin Beat: A History of the Latin American Game.* Jefferson, NC: McFarland, 1994.
Black, Joe. "How about That Marichal Mess?" *New York Amsterdam News*, September 11, 1965.
Blinders [Kevin Bonnet]. "The Shot Heard Round the World." *Blinders*, June 21, 2007. http://blinderspoker.blogspot.com/2007/06/shot-heard-round-world.html.
Boas, Franz. "Racial Purity." *Asia*, May 1940, 231–34.
Boas, Franz. "What Is a Race?" *Nation*, January 28, 1925, 89–91.
Boddy, Kasia. *Boxing: A Cultural History.* London: Reaktion, 2008.
Booker, Simeon. Washington Notebook. In "Black on Black Crime: The Causes, the Consequences, the Cures." Special issue, *Ebony*, August 1979, 27.
Bouchette, Ed. "Final Exam: Steelers Throw New Mental Test at Would-Be Draftees." *Pittsburgh Post-Gazette*, April 24, 1994.
Bouchette, Ed. "Rookie in a Rush to Make Name for Self: Henry Tries to Impress Steelers." *Pittsburgh Post-Gazette*, August 12, 1993.

Bourdieu, Pierre. *Distinction: A Social Critique of the Judgement of Taste*. Translated by Richard Nice. Cambridge, MA: Harvard University Press, 1984.
Bourdieu, Pierre. "Sport and Social Class." Translated by Richard Nice. *Social Science Transformation* 17, no. 6 (1978): 819–40.
Bouton, Jim. *Ball Four: My Life and Hard Times Throwing the Knuckleball in the Big Leagues*. New York: World Publishing, 1970.
Boyd, Todd. "The Game Is to Be Sold, Not to Be Told." In *Basketball Jones: America above the Rim*, edited by Todd Boyd and Kenneth L. Shropshire, ix–xii. New York: New York University Press, 2000.
Boyd, Todd. *Young, Black, Rich, and Famous: The Rise of the NBA, the Hip Hop Invasion, and the Transformation of American Culture*. New York: Doubleday, 2003.
Boylan, Christopher, Ryan McMahon, and Burt L. Monroe. "NFL Draft Profiles Are Full of Racial Stereotypes. And That Matters for When Quarterbacks Get Drafted." *Washington Post*, April 27, 2017.
Boylan, Christopher, Ryan McMahon, and Burt L. Monroe. "Racially Differentiated Language in NFL Scouting Reports." In *Proceedings of the 22nd ACM SIGKDD International Conference on Knowledge Discovery and Data Mining*. New York: Association for Computing Machinery, 2016.
Boyle, Robert H. "The Private World of the Negro Ballplayer." *Sports Illustrated*, March 21, 1960, 16–19, 74–84.
Brake, Deborah L. *Getting in the Game: Title IX and the Women's Sports Revolution*. New York: New York University, 2010.
Bramble, Dennis M., and Daniel E. Lieberman. "Endurance Running and the Evolution of *Homo*." *Nature*, no. 432 (2004): 345–52.
Branch, Taylor. "The Shame of College Sports." *Atlantic*, October 2011, 80–110.
Brashler, William. *The Bingo Long Traveling All-Stars and Motor Kings*. New York: Harper and Row, 1973.
Brashler, William. Preface to *The Bingo Long Traveling All-Stars and Motor Kings*, vii–xv. Urbana: University of Illinois Press, 1993.
Brashler, William. *The Story of Negro League Baseball*. New York: Ticknor and Fields, 1994.
Bray, Michael. *Powers of the Mind: Mental and Manual Labor in the Contemporary Political Crisis*. Bielefeld, Germany: Transcript, 2019.
Brecht, Bertolt. "Emphasis on Sport." In *Brecht on Theatre: The Development of an Aesthetic*, trans. John Willett, 6–9. New York: Hill and Wang, 1964.
Brenner, Robert. *The Economics of Global Turbulence: The Advanced Capitalist Economies from the Long Boom to the Long Downturn, 1945–2005*. London: Verso, 2006.
"Brittney Griner." *ESPN The Magazine*, July 20, 2015, 108–11.
Brock, Lisa, and Bijan Bayne. "Not Just Black: African-Americans, Cubans, and Baseball." In *Between Race and Empire: African-Americans and Cubans before the Cuban Revolution*, edited by Lisa Brock and Digna Castañeda Fuertes, 168–204. Philadelphia: Temple University Press, 1998.
Broeg, Bob. "Loss of One Turn No Stiff Penalty." *St. Louis Post-Dispatch*, August 24, 1965.

Brokaw, Tom, host. *Black Athletes: Fact and Fiction.* NBC Nightly News. Aired April 25, 1989, on NBC.
Brosnan, Jim. *The Long Season.* New York: Harper and Brothers, 1960.
Brosnan, Jim. "Now Pitching for St. Louis ... the Rookie Psychiatrist." *Sports Illustrated*, July 21, 1958, 12–15, 57.
Brosnan, Jim. *Pennant Race.* New York: Harper and Brothers, 1962.
Brosnan, Jim. "A Pitcher-Author Writes His Book on Pirate Lineup." *Life*, October 10, 1960, 168, 173–80.
Brown, Wendy. *Undoing the Demos: Neoliberalism's Stealth Revolution.* New York: Zone Books, 2016.
Browne, Simone. *Dark Matters: On the Surveillance of Blackness.* Durham, NC: Duke University Press, 2015.
Brozan, Nadine. "Three Olympians Take the President for a Run." *New York Times*, July 17, 1993.
Bryant, Howard. *The Heritage: Black Athletes, a Divided America, and the Politics of Patriotism.* Boston: Beacon Press, 2018.
Buehler, Branden. *Front Office Fantasies: The Rise of Managerial Sports Media.* Urbana: University of Illinois Press, 2023.
Burfoot, Amby. "Let Semenya Run Free ... in the 1500." LetsRun.com, May 2, 2019. www.letsrun.com/news/2019/05/guest-column-by-amby-burfoot-let-semenya-run-free-in-the-1500/.
Burfoot, Amby. "White Men Can't Run." *Runner's World*, August 1992, 89–95.
Burgos, Adrian, Jr. *Cuban Star: How One Negro-League Owner Changed the Face of Baseball.* New York: Hill and Wang, 2011.
Burgos, Adrian, Jr. "Left Out: Afro-Latinos, Black Baseball, and the Revision of Baseball's Racial History." *Social Text* 21, no. 7 (2009): 37–58.
Burgos, Adrian, Jr. *Playing America's Game: Baseball, Latinos, and the Color Line.* Berkeley: University of California Press, 2007.
Burgos, Adrian, Jr., and Frank Andre Guridy. "Becoming Suspect in Usual Places: Latinos, Baseball, and Belonging in el Barrio del Bronx." In *Beyond el Barrio: Everyday Life in Latina/o America*, edited by Gina M. Pérez, Frank Andre Guridy, and Adrian Burgos Jr., 81–99. New York: New York University Press, 2010.
Butler, Judith. "Athletic Genders: Hyperbolic Instance and/or the Overcoming of Sexual Binarism." In "The Athlete's Body," edited by Hans Ulrich Gumbrecht, Ted Leland, Rick Schavone, and Jeffrey T. Schnapp, 103–11. Special issue, *Stanford Humanities Review* 6, no. 4 (1998).
Butler, Judith. "Wise Distinctions: Thoughts on Caster Semenya." *Los Angeles Review of Books*, November 20, 2009. www.lrb.co.uk/blog/2009/november/wise-distinctions.
Byers, Walter. *Unsportsmanlike Conduct: Exploiting College Athletes.* With Charles Hammer. Ann Arbor: University of Michigan Press, 1995.
Carpenter, Linda Jean. "The Impact of Title IX on Women's Intercollegiate Sports." In *Government and Sport: The Public Policy Issues*, edited by Arthur T. Johnson and James H. Frey, 62–78. Totowa, NJ: Rowman and Allanheld, 1985.
Carpenter, Wendy. "Lively Howard Forum Examines Race and Sports." *Washington Times*, March 3, 1997.

Carrington, Ben. "Of Races, Hurdles and Sporting Chances." Letter to the editor. *Independent*, September 19, 1995.
Carrington, Ben. *Race, Sport and Politics: The Sporting Black Diaspora*. Los Angeles: Sage, 2010.
Carrington, Ben, and Ian McDonald. Introduction to *"Race," Sport and British Society*, edited by Ben Carrington and Ian McDonald, 1–26. London: Routledge, 2001.
Carter, Ben. "Can 10,000 Hours of Practice Make You an Expert?" *BBC News Online*, March 1, 2014. www.bbc.com/news/magazine-26384712.
Carter, Chelsey R., and Tracie Canada. "The NFL's Racist 'Race Norming' Is an Afterlife of Slavery." *Scientific American*, July 8, 2021. www.scientificamerican.com/article/the-nfls-racist-race-norming-is-an-afterlife-of-slavery/.
Castles, Robin (@RobinCastles). "You abandoned your teammates and you ain't shit." July 29, 2019, comment on Bell, "This is loooong overdue!!" https://twitter.com/RobinCastles/status/1155939507629248513?s=20&t=BBqQwu_fyunSwxVAFfU5eQ.
Cepeda, Orlando. *Baby Bull: From Hardball to Hard Time and Back*. With Herb Fagen. Dallas: Taylor Publishing, 1998.
Chapman, Stephen. "The Best Magazine in America." *Chicago Tribune*, April 5, 1984.
Charnofsky, Harold. "The Major League Professional Baseball Player: Self-Conception versus the Popular Image." *International Review of Sport Sociology* 3, no. 1 (1968): 39–55.
Charnofsky, Harold. "The Major League Professional Baseball Player: A Sociological Study." PhD diss., University of Southern California, 1969.
Chen, Albert. *Billion Dollar Fantasy: The High-Stakes Game between FanDuel and DraftKings That Upended Sports in America*. New York: Houghton Mifflin Harcourt, 2019.
Christine, Bill. *Roberto!* New York: Stadia Sports, 1973.
Chudacoff, Howard W. *Changing the Playbook: How Power, Profit, and Politics Transformed College Sports*. Urbana: University of Illinois Press, 2015.
Clarey, Christopher. "Gender Test after a Gold-Medal Finish." *New York Times*, August 19, 2009.
Clark, Alfred E. "Judge in Fix Case Condemns Kentucky Teams and Coach." *New York Times*, April 30, 1952.
Class Action Complaint, Flores v. National Football League et al. No. 1:22-cv-00871 (SDNY 2022).
Class Action Complaint, Henry et al. v. National Football League. No. 2:20-cv-04165 (ED Pa. 2020).
Class Action Settlement Agreement (as Amended), Turner et al. v. National Football League (*In re* National Football League Players' Concussion Injury Litigation). No. 2:12-md-02323-AB (ED Pa. 2015).
Cleaver, Eldridge. *Soul on Ice*. New York: McGraw-Hill, 1968.
Clemente, Roberto. "A Conversation with Clemente." Interview by Sam Nover. WIIC-TV, October 8, 1972.

Clemente, Roberto. "Highlights in Baseball's Week: Guest Column." *Pittsburgh Courier*, June 4, 1960.
"Clemente Happy over Winning Hit." *Baltimore Sun*, July 12, 1961.
Clifford, Stephanie. "Special Issues Are Bright Spots for Magazines." *New York Times*, October 11, 2009.
Cohan, Noah. *We Average Unbeautiful Watchers: Fan Narratives and the Reading of American Sports*. Lincoln: University of Nebraska Press, 2019.
Cohn, Howard. "Roberto Clemente's Problem." *Sport*, May 1962, 54–56, 100–3.
"Colleges Adopt the 'Sanity Code' to Govern Sports." *New York Times*, January 11, 1948.
Collins, Bud. "Rocky Beats Clay by 'KO.'" *Boston Globe*, January 21, 1970.
Commonwealth v. Collberg. 119 Mass. 350 (1876).
"Computer Crowns Rocky Marciano." *Chicago Daily Defender*, January 22, 1970.
Condotta, Bob. "Richard Sherman: Fantasy Football Makes Some Fans Look at Players as Less than People." *Seattle Times*, October 2, 2017. www.seattletimes.com/sports/seahawks/chris-carson-injury-ignites-richard-sherman-rant-against-fantasy-football/.
Connolly, Pat. "An Athlete to Remember, for a Variety of Reasons." *New York Times*, September 27, 1998.
Constitution of the National Collegiate Athletic Association. In *1955–1956 Yearbook of the National Collegiate Athletic Association*, 3–13. Kansas City, MO: National Collegiate Athletic Association, 1956.
Cooky, Cheryl, and Shari L. Dworkin. "Policing the Boundaries of Sex: A Critical Examination of Gender Verification and the Caster Semenya Controversy." *Journal of Sex Research* 50, no. 2 (2013): 103–11.
Coover, Robert. *The Universal Baseball Association, Inc., J. Henry Waugh, Prop*. New York: Random House, 1968.
Corrigan, Thomas F. "Digging the Moat: The Political Economy of ESPN's Cable Carriage Fees." In *ESPN and the Changing Sports Media Landscape*, edited by Greg G. Armfield, John McGuire, and Adam Earnheardt, 37–51. New York: Peter Lang, 2019.
Cottrell, John. *Muhammad Ali, Who Once Was Cassius Clay*. New York: Funk and Wagnalls, 1967.
Court of Arbitration for Sport. "CAS Arbitration: Caster Semenya, Athletics South Africa, and International Association of Athletics Federations Decision." Press release. May 1, 2019. www.tas-cas.org/fileadmin/user_upload/Media_Release_Semenya_ASA_IAAF_decision.pdf.
Craig, Jack. "ESPN: 24 Hours Is Not Too Much." *Boston Globe*, August 2, 1981.
Cranmer, Gregory A., Maria Brann, and Nicholas D. Bowman. "Male Athletes, Female Aesthetics: The Continued Ambivalence toward Female Athletes in ESPN's *The Body Issue*." *International Journal of Sports Communication* 7, no. 2 (2014): 145–65.
Cranmer, Gregory A., Alexander L. Lancaster, and Tina M. Harris. "Shot in Black and White: Visualized Framing in ESPN's *The Body Issue*." *International Journal of Sports Communication* 9, no. 2 (2016): 209–28.
Cromwell, Dean B. *Championship Technique in Track and Field*. With Al Wesson. New York: Whittlesey House, 1941.

Crowley, Joseph N. *In the Arena: The NCAA's First Century.* Indianapolis: National Collegiate Athletic Association, 2006.
Crupi, Anthony. "Fantasy Sports Sites DraftKings, FanDuel September Spend Tops $100 Million." *Ad Age*, September 30, 2015. https://adage.com/article/media/draftkings-fanduel-spe/300658.
Crupi, Anthony. "NFL Swallows TV Whole, Notching 93 of the Year's Top 100 Broadcasts." *Sportico*, January 5, 2024. www.sportico.com/business/media/2024/nfl-posts-93-of-top-100-tv-broadcasts-2023-1234761753/.
Dak [Dave King]. "Some Questions and Some Answers." *Fire Joe Morgan*, April 20, 2005. www.firejoemorgan.com/2005/04/some-questions-and-some-answers.html.
Darcy, Kieran. "Giants' Brandon Jacobs Sounds Off." ESPN.com, October 23, 2013. www.espn.com/new-york/nfl/story/_/id/9869573/brandon-jacobs-new-york-giants-sounds-fantasy-football-players.
Darda, Joseph. *Empire of Defense: Race and the Cultural Politics of Permanent War.* Chicago: University of Chicago Press, 2019.
Darda, Joseph. *How White Men Won the Culture Wars: A History of Veteran America.* Berkeley: University of California Press, 2021.
Darda, Joseph. *The Strange Career of Racial Liberalism.* Stanford, CA: Stanford University Press, 2022.
Dark, Alvin. Chapter 10. In *Baseball Has Done It*, edited by Jackie Robinson and Charles Dexter, 106–9. Philadelphia: J. B. Lippincott, 1964.
Davies, David. "McCormack, the Man Who Wanted More." *Guardian*, May 16, 2003.
Davis, Amira Rose. "'Watch What We Do': The Politics and Possibilities of Black Women's Athletics, 1910–1970." PhD diss., Johns Hopkins University, 2016.
Davis, Miles. "Yesternow." *Jack Johnson*. Columbia, 1971.
Davis, Philip. *Bernard Malamud: A Writer's Life.* New York: Oxford University Press, 2007.
De Genova, Nicholas. "The Stakes of an Anthropology of the United States." *New Centennial Review* 7, no. 2 (2007): 231–77.
de la Merced, Michael J., and Katie Benner. "As Department Stores Close, Stitch Fix Expands Online." *New York Times*, May 10, 2017.
de Moraes, Lisa. "Haven't We Seen You Somewhere Before?" *Washington Post*, March 29, 2003.
Deford, Frank. "Sometimes the Bear Eats You: Confessions of a Sportswriter." *Sports Illustrated*, March 29, 2010, 52–62.
Deford, Frank, ed. *The Best American Sports Writing, 1993.* Boston: Houghton Mifflin, 1993.
Deloria, Philip J. *Playing Indian.* New Haven, CT: Yale University Press, 1998.
Democratic Leadership Council. *The New Orleans Declaration: A Democratic Agenda for the 1990s.* Washington, DC: Democratic Leadership Council, 1990.
Derrida, Jacques. *Given Time: I. Counterfeit Money.* Translated by Peggy Kamuf. Chicago: University of Chicago Press, 1992.

Desai, Saahil. "College Sports Are Affirmative Action for Rich White Students." *Atlantic*, October 23, 2018. www.theatlantic.com/education/archive/2018/10/college-sports-benefits-white-students/573688/.
Dinces, Sean. *Bulls Market: Chicago's Basketball Business and the New Inequality*. Chicago: University of Chicago Press, 2018.
Dorsey, Valerie Lynn. "One Running Back Doesn't Mind Being Different." *USA Today*, December 19, 1991.
"Douglas H. Wigdor." Wigdor LLP, 2023. www.wigdorlaw.com/our-team/douglas-h-wigdor/.
Doyle, Jennifer. "Art and Desire." *World Literature Today* 85, no. 3 (2011): 44–45.
Doyle, Jennifer. "Dirt Off Her Shoulders." Introduction to "The Athlete Issue," edited by Jennifer Doyle, 419–33. Special issue, *GLQ* 19, no. 4 (2013).
Draft Day. Directed by Ivan Reitman. Lionsgate, 2014.
Drayer, Joris, and Brendan Dwyer. "Perception of Fantasy Is Not Always the Reality: An Exploratory Examination into Blacks' Lack of Participation in Fantasy Sports." *International Journal of Sports Management* 14 (2013): 81–102.
Du Bois, W. E. B. *The Gift of Black Folk: The Negroes in the Making of America*. Boston: Stratford, 1924.
Du Bois, W. E. B. *The Souls of Black Folk: Essays and Sketches*. Chicago: A. C. McClurg, 1903.
Duderstadt, James J. *Intercollegiate Athletics and the American University: A University President's Perspective*. Ann Arbor: University of Michigan Press, 2000.
Durso, Joseph. "Clemente Is in Hall of Fame." *New York Times*, March 21, 1973.
Early, Gerald. "The Black Intellectual and the Sport of Prizefighting." *Kenyon Review* 10, no. 3 (1988): 44–65.
Edwards, Harry. "The Black 'Dumb Jock': An American Sports Tragedy." *College Board Review*, no. 131 (1984): 8–13.
Edwards, Harry. *The Revolt of the Black Athlete*. New York: Free Press, 1969.
Edwards, Harry. "The Sources of the Black Athlete's Superiority." *Black Scholar* 3, no. 3 (1971): 32–41.
Eig, Jonathan. *Ali: A Life*. New York: Houghton Mifflin Harcourt, 2017.
Eisenberg, Lee. "The Awful Truth about Rotisserie League Baseball." *New York Times*, April 8, 1990.
Ellenport, Craig. "A Bold New Network, a Preposterous Idea: How the NFL Draft Came to TV." *Sports Illustrated*, April 22, 2020. www.si.com/nfl/2020/04/22/how-espn-televised-nfl-draft-for-the-first-time.
Ellison, Ralph. Introduction to *Shadow and Act*, xi–xxiii. New York: Random House, 1964.
Elsey, Brenda. *Citizens and Sportsmen: Fútbol and Politics in Twentieth-Century Chile*. Austin: University of Texas Press, 2011.
Enstad, Nan. *Cigarettes, Inc.* Chicago: University of Chicago Press, 2018.
Entine, Jon. "Breaking the Taboo." *Index on Censorship* 29, no. 4 (2000): 62–64.
Entine, Jon. *Taboo: Why Black Athletes Dominate Sports and Why We're Afraid to Talk about It*. New York: PublicAffairs, 2000.
Epstein, David. *The Sports Gene: Inside the Science of Extraordinary Athletic Performance*. New York: Current, 2013.

Ericsson, K. Anders. "The Danger of Delegating Education to Journalists: Why the APS *Observer* Needs Peer Review When Summarizing New Scientific Developments." 2012. https://web.archive.org/web/20140717041100/http://psy.fsu.edu/faculty/ericsson/2012%20Ericssons%20reply%20to%20APS%20Observer%20article%20Oct%2028%20on%20web.doc.
ESPN. "*ESPN The Magazine* Announces 'Body Issue' Athletes." Press release. October 1, 2009. https://espnpressroom.com/us/press-releases/2009/10/espn-the-magazine-announces-body-issue-athletes/.
ESPN. "ESPN to Televise NFL Selections." Press release. March 31, 1980.
ESPN. "Mike Hall Wins ESPN's *Dream Job*." Press release. March 29, 2004. www.espn.com/eoe/dreamjob_press_release.html.
"ESPN Blacks Out Black Colleges." *New Pittsburgh Courier*, November 7, 1981.
"ESPN Town Meeting: 'Sports in Black and White.'" *Sports Business Daily*, March 3, 1997.
Exec. Order No. 13,050. 3 C.F.R. 207–8 (1997).
Ezra, Michael. *Muhammad Ali: The Making of an Icon*. Philadelphia: Temple University Press, 2009.
Fagan, Kate. "Owning the Middle." *ESPN The Magazine*, June 10, 2013, 76–89.
"Failed Athletes." *San Francisco Chronicle*, July 3, 1986.
Falla, Jack. *NCAA: The Voice of College Sports*. Mission, KS: National Collegiate Athletic Association, 1981.
Fanon, Frantz. *Black Skin, White Masks*. Translated by Charles Lam Markmann. New York: Grove Press, 1967.
Fantasy Sports Trade Association. "Industry Demographics." 2014. www.fsta.org/?page=demographics.
Fargis, Chris. "My New Business Venture: Instant Fantasy Sports." *Twenty-One Outs Twice*, September 14, 2007. http://twentyoneoutstwice.blogspot.com/2007/09/my-new-business-venture-instant-fantasy.html.
Farr, Finis. *Black Champion: The Life and Times of Jack Johnson*. New York: Charles Scribner's Sons, 1964.
Farred, Grant. *The Burden of Over-Representation: Race, Sport, and Philosophy*. Philadelphia: Temple University Press, 2018.
Farred, Grant. *What's My Name? Black Vernacular Intellectuals*. Minneapolis: University of Minnesota Press, 2003.
Ferguson, Roderick A. *Aberrations in Black: Toward a Queer of Color Critique*. Minneapolis: University of Minnesota Press, 2004.
Ferguson, Roderick A. *The Reorder of Things: The University and Its Pedagogies of Minority Difference*. Minneapolis: University of Minnesota Press, 2012.
Ferguson, Roderick A. *We Demand: The University and Student Protests*. Berkeley: University of California Press, 2017.
Ferretti, Fred. "For Major-League Addicts, a Way to Win a Pennant." *New York Times*, July 8, 1980.
Fickle, Tara. *The Race Card: From Gaming Technologies to Model Minorities*. New York: New York University Press, 2019.
Fiedler, Leslie A. *Love and Death in the American Novel*. New York: Criterion, 1960.

Figuero-Vásquez, Yomaira C. *Decolonizing Diasporas: Radical Mappings of Afro-Atlantic Literatures*. Evanston, IL: Northwestern University Press, 2020.
Findeisen, Christopher. "'The One Place Where Money Makes No Difference': The Campus Novel from *Stover at Yale* through *The Art of Fielding*." *American Literature* 88, no. 1 (2016): 67–91.
Finn, Adharanand. *Running with the Kenyans: Passion, Adventure, and the Secrets of the Fastest People on Earth*. New York: Ballantine, 2012.
Fitzgerald, F. Scott. "Ring." *New Republic*, October 11, 1933, 254–55.
Fleetwood, Nicole R. *On Racial Icons: Blackness and the Public Imagination*. New Brunswick, NJ: Rutgers University Press, 2015.
Flynn, Meagan. "Seattle Sports Stars Sue Bird and Megan Rapinoe Are First Same-Sex Couple on Cover of ESPN's Body Issue." *Washington Post*, June 26, 2018.
Fowler, Jeremy. "Le'Veon Bell: 'I Don't Think I Should Settle for Anything Less than What I'm Valued at.'" ESPN.com, March 5, 2018. www.espn.com/nfl/story/_/id/22657079/leveon-bell-pittsburgh-steelers-gets-franchise-tag-again.
Fowlkes, Ben. "'Rampage' Jackson, Rashad Evans and the Politics of Race in MMA." MMA Fighting, May 25, 2010. www.mmafighting.com/2010/05/25/rampage-jackson-rashad-evans-and-the-politics-of-race-in-mma.
Frazier, E. Franklin. *Negro Youth at the Crossroads: Their Personality Development in the Middle States*. Washington, DC: American Council on Education, 1940.
Freeman, Michael. *ESPN: The Uncensored History*. Lanham, MD: Taylor Trade Publishing, 2000.
Friday Night Lights. Directed by Peter Berg. Universal Pictures, 2004.
Friedman, Jack. "The Most Peppery Game since the Hot Stove League? It's Rotisserie Baseball." *People*, April 23, 1984, 40–42.
Frontline. Season 34, episode 3, "The Fantasy Sports Gamble." Aired February 9, 2016, on PBS.
Frye, Andy. "Richard Sherman Gets Involved in the Future of Fantasy Football." *Forbes*, August 23, 2018. www.forbes.com/sites/andyfrye/2018/08/23/richard-sherman-gets-involved-in-the-future-of-fantasy-football/?sh=6783b8d2d710.
Futterman, Matthew. *Players: The Story of Sports and Money, and the Visionaries Who Fought to Create a Revolution*. New York: Simon and Schuster, 2016.
geckofdc (@Captain9NYR). "@LeVeon Bell Venmo the $500 you cost me and we'll call it even." July 29, 2019, comment on Bell, "This is loooong overdue!!" https://twitter.com/captain9nyr/status/1155938058094563329?s=20&t=BBqQwu_fyunSwxVAFfU5eQ.
"General Secretary of IAAF Pierre Weiss on Caster Semenya." LetsRun.com video, 3:01, August 19, 2009. www.youtube.com/watch?v=FK7tLvuwr4c.
Gilbert, Bill, and Nancy Williamson. "Women in Sport: A Progress Report." *Sports Illustrated*, July 29, 1974, 26–31.
Gilbert, Dan. "Open Letter to Fans from Cleveland Majority Owner Dan Gilbert." NBA.com, July 8, 2010. www.nba.com/cavaliers/news/gilbert_letter_100708.html.

Gilbert, Daniel A. "Not (Just) about the Money: Contextualizing the Labor Activism of College Football Players." In "Sport in the University," edited by Noah Cohan, Daniel A. Gilbert, Theresa Runstedtler, Tyran Kai Steward, and Lucia Trimbur, 19–34. Special issue, *American Studies* 55, no. 3 (2016).

Gill, Andrew, and Vitor Brajer. "Wonderlic, Race, and the NFL Draft." *Journal of Sports Economics* 13, no. 6 (2012): 642–53.

Gilmore, Ruth Wilson. *Golden Gulag: Prisons, Surplus, Crisis, and Opposition in Globalizing California*. Berkeley: University of California Press, 2007.

Gilmore, Ruth Wilson, and Craig Gilmore. "Restating the Obvious." In *Indefensible State: The Architecture of the National Insecurity State*, edited by Michael Sorkin, 141–62. New York: Routledge, 2008.

Gilroy, Paul. *Between Camps: Nations, Cultures and the Allure of Race*. London: Penguin, 2000.

Gladwell, Malcolm. "Man and Superman." *New Yorker*, September 9, 2013, 76–80.

Gladwell, Malcolm. *Outliers: The Story of Success*. New York: Little, Brown, 2008.

Gladwell, Malcolm. "The Sports Taboo." *New Yorker*, May 19, 1997, 50–55.

Goheen, Robert F. Memorandum to Everett D. Barnes and the Council of the NCAA. April 13, 1966. Box 566, "National Collegiate Athletic Association, General File, 1966" folder. Records of the President's Office: William H. Elkins. Special Collections and University Archives, University of Maryland Libraries.

Goldberg, David Theo. "Call and Response: Sports, Talk Radio, and the Death of Democracy." *Journal of Sports and Social Issues* 22, no. 2 (1998): 212–23.

Goldberg, Jeffrey. "Sore Winners." *New York Times Magazine*, August 16, 1998, 30–33.

Gómez, Laura E. *Inventing Latinos: A New Story of American Racism*. New York: New Press, 2020.

Gómez, Laura E. *Manifest Destinies: The Making of the Mexican American Race*. New York: New York University Press, 2007.

Gorn, Elliott J. "The Manassa Mauler and the Fighting Marine: An Interpretation of the Dempsey–Tunney Fights." *Journal of American Studies* 19, no. 1 (1985): 27–47.

Gorn, Elliott J. *The Manly Arts: Bare-Knuckle Prize Fighting in America*. Ithaca, NY: Cornell University Press, 1986.

Gottfredson, Linda S. "The Science and Politics of Race-Norming." *American Psychologist* 49, no. 11 (1994): 955–63.

Gottlieb, Jeff. "Seizure Led to FloJo's Death." *Los Angeles Times*, October 23, 1998.

Graeber, David. *Toward an Anthropological Theory of Value: The False Coin of Our Own Dreams*. New York: Palgrave, 2001.

Gray, Jonathan. "Antifandom and the Moral Text: Television without Pity and Textual Dislike." *American Behavioral Scientist* 48, no. 7 (2005): 840–58.

Gray, Scott. *The Mind of Bill James: How a Complete Outsider Changed Baseball*. New York: Doubleday, 2006.

Green, Tim. *The Dark Side of the Game: My Life in the NFL*. New York: Warner Books, 1996.
Greer, Christina M. *Black Ethnics: Race, Immigration, and the Pursuit of the American Dream*. New York: Oxford University Press, 2013.
Griggs et al. v. Duke Power Co. 401 US 424 (1971).
Groom, Dale. "Cardiovascular Observations on Tarahumara Indian Runners – the Modern Spartans." *American Heart Journal* 81, no. 1 (1971): 304–14.
Guilmant, Pierre. "Jesse, McNeil Hit 'Silence.'" *Chicago Daily Defender*, August 19, 1970.
Guridy, Frank Andre. *Forging Diaspora: Afro-Cubans and African Americans in a World of Empire and Jim Crow*. Chapel Hill: University of North Carolina Press, 2010.
Guridy, Frank Andre. *The Sports Revolution: How Texas Changed the Culture of American Athletics*. Austin: University of Texas Press, 2021.
Halberstam, Jack. *Female Masculinity*. Durham, NC: Duke University Press, 1998.
Hall, Stuart. "Culture and Power." Interview by Peter Osborne and Lynne Segal. *Radical Philosophy*, no. 86 (1997): 24–41.
Hall, Stuart. "Race, Articulation and Societies Structured in Dominance." In *Sociological Theories: Race and Colonialism*, 305–45. Paris: UNESCO, 1980.
Hall, Stuart, Chas Critcher, Tony Jefferson, John Clarke, and Brian Roberts. *Policing the Crisis: Mugging, the State, and Law and Order*. London: Macmillan, 1978.
Hamill, Pete. "Muhammad Ali: 'This Is about Me.'" *Life*, October 25, 1968, 67–68.
Hamilton, Tod G. *Immigration and the Remaking of Black America*. New York: Russell Sage, 2019.
Hanford, George H. *An Inquiry into the Need for and Feasibility of a National Study of Intercollegiate Athletics*. Washington, DC: American Council on Education, 1974.
Hanford, George H. "We Should Speak the 'Awful Truth' about College Sports." *Chronicle of Higher Education*, May 30, 2003, B10–12.
Hano, Arnold. "Roberto Clemente, Man of Paradox." *Sport*, May 1965, 68–74.
Harlow, Alvin. "Unrecognized Stars." *Esquire*, September 1938, 75, 119–20.
Hartigan, John A., and Alexandra K. Wigdor, eds. *Fairness in Employment Testing: Validity Generalization, Minority Issues, and the General Aptitude Test Battery*. Washington, DC: National Academy Press, 1989.
Hartman, Saidiya V. *Scenes of Subjection: Terror, Slavery, and Self-Making in Nineteenth-Century America*. New York: Oxford University Press, 1997.
Hartmann, Douglas. *Midnight Basketball: Race, Sports, and Neoliberal Social Policy*. Chicago: University of Chicago Press, 2016.
Hartmann, Douglas. *Race, Culture, and the Revolt of the Black Athlete: The 1968 Olympic Protests and Their Aftermath*. Chicago: University of Chicago Press, 2003.
Hartmann, Douglas. "Rethinking the Relationships between Sport and Race in American Culture: Golden Ghettos and Contested Terrain." *Sociology of Sport Journal*, no. 17 (2000): 229–53.
Harvey, Randy. "Unfounded Rumors." *Los Angeles Times*, September 29, 1988.

Hauser, Thomas. *Muhammad Ali: His Life and Times*. New York: Simon and Schuster, 1991.
Hawkins, Billy. *The New Plantation: Black Athletes, College Sports, and Predominantly White NCAA Institutions*. New York: Palgrave Macmillan, 2010.
Heath, James D. Sports Note Pad. *Atlanta Daily World*, July 29, 1973.
Heaton, Richard K., S. Walden Miller, Michael J. Taylor, and Michael Grant. *Revised Comprehensive Norms for an Expanded Halstead-Reitan Battery: Demographically Adjusted Neuropsychological Norms for African Americans and Caucasian Adults*. Lutz, FL: Psychological Assessment Resources, 2004.
Henne, Kathryn E. *Testing for Athlete Citizenship: Regulating Doping and Sex in Sport*. New Brunswick, NJ: Rutgers University Press, 2015.
Henry, Taylor M., and Thomas P. Oates. "'Sport Is Argument': Polarization, Racial Tension, and the Televised Sport Debate Format." *Journal of Sport and Social Issues* 44, no. 2 (2020): 154–74.
Herrnstein, Richard J., and Charles Murray. *The Bell Curve: Intelligence and Class Structure in American Life*. New York: Free Press, 1994.
Heyns, Roger W. Cover letter to *An Inquiry into the Need for and Feasibility of a National Study of Intercollegiate Athletics*, by George H. Hanford. Washington, DC: American Council on Education, 1974.
Hiestand, Michael. "ESPN Forum Leaves Lots of Room for Sequel." *USA Today*, March 3, 1997.
Hoberman, John. *Darwin's Athletes: How Sport Has Damaged Black America and Preserved the Myth of Race*. Boston: Houghton Mifflin, 1997.
Hobson, Will. "How 'Race-Norming' Was Built into the NFL Concussion Settlement." *Washington Post*, August 2, 2021.
Holway, John. *Voices from the Great Black Baseball Leagues*. New York: Dodd, Mead, 1975.
Horkheimer, Max, and Theodor W. Adorno. *Dialectic of Enlightenment*. Translated by John Cumming. New York: Herder and Herder, 1972.
HoSang, Daniel Martinez, and Joseph E. Lowndes. *Producers, Parasites, and Patriots: Race and the New Right-Wing Politics of Precarity*. Minneapolis: University of Minnesota Press, 2019.
"How Ali's Antics Broke Up Rocky." *Detroit Free Press*, January 25, 1970.
Hoxworth, Kellen. "Football Fantasies: Neoliberal Habitus, Racial Governmentality, and National Spectacle." *American Quarterly* 72, no. 1 (2020): 155–79.
Hughes, Kit, and Evan Elkins. "Silicon Valley's Team: The Golden State Warriors, Datafied Managerialism, and Basketball's Racialized Geography." In "The Body Issue: Sports and the Politics of Embodiment," edited by Joseph Darda and Amira Rose Davis, 471–99. Special issue, *American Quarterly* 75, no. 3 (2023).
Hull, Kevin, Lauren R. Smith, and Annelie Schmittel. "Form or Function? An Examination of *ESPN Magazine*'s 'Body Issue.'" *Visual Communication Quarterly* 22, no. 2 (2015): 106–17.
Hutchins, Brett, and David Rowe. *Sport beyond Television: The Internet, Digital Media, and the Rise of Networked Media Sport*. New York: Routledge, 2012.

Intercollegiate Athletic Association of the United States. *Proceedings of the First Annual Meeting*. New York: Intercollegiate Athletic Association of the United States, 1906.
Intercollegiate Athletic Association of the United States. *Proceedings of the Fourth Annual Meeting*. New York: Intercollegiate Athletic Association of the United States, 1909.
International Association of Athletics Federations. "IAAF Policy on Gender Verification." 2006. https://web.archive.org/web/20070112013204/www.iaaf.org/newsfiles/36983.pdf.
Isaacs, Stan. "Louisiana in Dark Showing Through." *Newsday*, July 23, 1964.
"Ivy Group Agreement." November 20, 1945. Box 38, folder 340. Alfred Whitney Griswold Records. Manuscripts and Archives, Yale University Library.
Izenberg, Jerry. *Great Latin Sports Figures: The Proud People*. Garden City, NY: Doubleday, 1976.
"J. Robinson-Mays Age Dying: The Latins, Whites Take Over Baseball." *New Pittsburgh Courier*, March 16, 1968.
Jackson, Sheep. From the Sidelines. *Call and Post*, August 21, 1965.
Jackson, Sheep. From the Sidelines. *Call and Post*, May 13, 1967.
Jackson, Victoria. "'We're All Complicit to an Extent': How Team USA Uses College Football and Basketball as Funding Sources." *Athletic*, July 22, 2021. https://theathletic.com/2696130/2021/07/22/were-all-complicit-to-an-extent-how-team-usa-uses-college-football-and-basketball-as-funding-sources/.
Jacobson, Matthew Frye. *Roots Too: White Ethnic Revival in Post–Civil Rights America*. Cambridge, MA: Harvard University Press, 2006.
Jacobson, Matthew Frye. *Whiteness of a Different Color: European Immigrants and the Alchemy of Race*. Cambridge, MA: Harvard University Press, 1998.
James, Bill. *1978 Baseball Abstract: The 2nd Annual Edition of Baseball's Most Informative and Imaginative Review*. Lawrence, KS: self-published, 1978.
James, Bill. "1979 Baseball Forecast." *Esquire*, April 24, 1979, 64–67.
James, Bill. *The Bill James Baseball Abstract, 1984*. New York: Ballantine, 1984.
James, Bill. *The Bill James Baseball Abstract, 1988*. New York: Ballantine, 1988.
James, Bill. *The Bill James Historical Baseball Abstract*. New York: Villard, 1986.
James, Bill (@billjamesonline). "Is there any such thing as a major league baseball player who is underpaid?" Twitter, November 8, 2018. https://web.archive.org/web/20181110102306/https://twitter.com/billjamesonline.
James, C. L. R. *Beyond a Boundary*. London: Hutchinson, 1963.
James, C. L. R. *The Life of Captain Cipriani: An Account of British Government in the West Indies*. Nelson, Lancashire, UK: Coulton, 1932.
Jamieson, Dave. *Mint Condition: How Baseball Cards Became an American Obsession*. New York: Atlantic Monthly Press, 2010.
Janis, Lauren. "ESPN: Home Field for Sports Addicts." *Columbia Journalism Review* 40, no. 4 (2001): 96–97.
"Jay Berwanger Denies Asking $1,000 a Game." *Chicago Tribune*, February 11, 1936.
Johnson, John H. "Publisher's Statement." In "Black on Black Crime: The Causes, the Consequences, the Cures." Special issue, *Ebony*, August 1979, 32–33.

Johnson, Keyshawn. *Just Give Me the Damn Ball! The Fast Times and Hard Knocks of an NFL Rookie*. With Shelley Smith. New York: Warner Books, 1997.
Johnson, Lyndon B. "Commencement Address at Howard University: 'To Fulfill These Rights.'" June 4, 1965. Lyndon Baines Johnson Presidential Library and Museum. www.lbjlibrary.org/object/text/commencement-address-howard-university-fulfill-these-rights-06-04-1965.
Johnson, Victoria E. "Historicizing TV Networking: Broadcasting, Cable, and the Case of ESPN." In *Media Industries: History, Theory, and Method*, edited by Jennifer Holt and Alisa Perren, 57–68. Malden, MA: Wiley-Blackwell, 2009.
Johnson, Victoria E. *Sports TV*. New York: Routledge, 2021.
Johnson, William Oscar. "And in This Corner ... NCR 315." *Sports Illustrated*, September 16, 1968, 34–49.
Johnson, William Oscar. "Sports Junkies of the U.S., Rejoice!" *Sports Illustrated*, July 23, 1979, 43.
Jones, C. J. "Unfair Advantage Discourse in USA Powerlifting: Toward a Transfeminist Sport Studies." *TSQ* 8, no. 1 (2021): 58–74.
Jones, James Earl. "Jack Johnson Is Alive and Well ... on Broadway." *Ebony*, June 1969, 54–61.
Jones, Jonquel (@jus242). "It's all a popularity contest and politics in wbb." Twitter, February 18, 2022, 2:16 a.m. https://twitter.com/jus242/status/1494571538720436229.
Jordan-Young, Rebecca M., and Katrina Karkazis. *Testosterone: An Unauthorized Biography*. Cambridge, MA: Harvard University Press, 2019.
Junod, Tom. "The Dish from Mel." *Sports Illustrated*, April 27, 1992, 46–52.
Kahn, Roger. *The Boys of Summer*. New York: Harper and Row, 1972.
Kalman-Lamb, Nathan, Derek Silva, and Johanna Mellis. "Race, Money, and Exploitation: Why College Sport Is Still the 'New Plantation.'" *Guardian*, September 7, 2021. www.theguardian.com/sport/2021/sep/07/race-money-and-exploitation-why-college-sport-is-still-the-new-plantation.
Kane, Martin. "An Assessment of 'Black Is Best.'" *Sports Illustrated*, January 18, 1971, 72–83.
Kang, Jay Caspian. "How the Daily Fantasy Sports Industry Turns Fans into Suckers." *New York Times Magazine*, January 6, 2016. www.nytimes.com/2016/01/06/magazine/how-the-daily-fantasy-sports-industry-turns-fans-into-suckers.html.
Kang, Jay Caspian. "The Unbearable Whiteness of Baseball." *New York Times Magazine*, April 6, 2016.
Katznelson, Ira. *When Affirmative Action Was White: An Untold Story of Racial Inequality in Twentieth-Century America*. New York: Norton, 2005.
Kaye, Andrew M. *The Pussycat of Prizefighting: Tiger Flowers and the Politics of Black Celebrity*. Athens: University of Georgia Press, 2004.
Keese, Parton. "Bristol Hits the Big League in Sports TV." *New York Times*, December 9, 1979.
Kellogg, Mary Alice. "Dice Baseball Fever." *Newsweek*, August 23, 1976, 60–61.

Kempton, Murray. "'I Whipped Him and I'm Still Pretty.'" *New Republic*, March 7, 1964, 9–10.

Kepner, Tyler. "Bill James, No Stranger to Controversy, Believes His Current One Is 'Unfortunate.'" *New York Times*, November 8, 2018.

Kim, Claire Jean. *Asian Americans in an Anti-Black World*. Cambridge: Cambridge University Press, 2023.

Kim, Claire Jean. *Bitter Fruit: The Politics of Black-Korean Conflict in New York City*. New Haven, CT: Yale University Press, 2000.

King, Peter. "White Guys Can't Run." *Sports Illustrated*, September 7, 1992, 28–29.

Kirshenbaum, Jerry. "An American Disgrace." *Sports Illustrated*, February 27, 1989, 16–19.

Kissane, Rebecca Joyce, and Sarah Winslow. *Whose Game? Gender and Power in Fantasy Sports*. Philadelphia: Temple University Press, 2020.

Klein, Alan. "Latinizing the 'National Pastime.'" *International Journal of the History of Sports* 24, no. 2 (2007): 296–310.

Knight Foundation Commission on Intercollegiate Athletics. *Keeping Faith with the Student-Athlete: A New Model for Intercollegiate Athletics*. Charlotte, NC: Knight Foundation, 1991.

Knobler, Mike. "Against the Tide: Henry Has No Regrets about Playing for State." *Clarion-Ledger*, December 20, 1992.

Lardner, John. "That Was Pugilism: White Hopes – I." *New Yorker*, June 25, 1949, 56–67.

Lardner, John. "That Was Pugilism: White Hopes – II." *New Yorker*, July 2, 1949, 36–46.

Larkin, Ben, Brendan Dwyer, and Chad Goebert. "Man or Machine: Fantasy Football and Dehumanization of Athletes." *Journal of Sport Management* 34, no. 5 (2020): 403–16.

"Latin Athletes' 'Plight' Criticized." *Los Angeles Times*, August 23, 1966.

"Latins in Baseball Check Dollar Drain." *New York Times*, May 19, 1970.

Lee, Joon. "Inside the Rise of MLB's Ivy League Culture: Stunning Numbers and a Question of What's Next." ESPN.com, June 30, 2020. www.espn.com/mlb/story/_/id/29369890/inside-rise-mlb-ivy-league-culture-stunning-numbers-question-next.

Lemire, Joe. "Strat-O-Matic More than a Game for Its Founders and Devotees." *Sports Illustrated*, February 10, 2011. www.si.com/more-sports/2011/02/10/strat-omatic.

Leonard, David J. "Not a Hater, Just Keepin' It Real: Race- and Gender-Based Game Studies." *Games and Culture* 1, no. 1 (2006): 83–88.

Leonard, David J. *Playing while White: Privilege and Power on and off the Field*. Seattle: University of Washington Press, 2017.

Leonard, David J., and Stephanie Troutman Robbins. Introduction to *Race in American Television: Voices and Visions That Shaped a Nation*, edited by David J. Leonard and Stephanie Troutman Robbins, xvii–xxvi. Santa Barbara, CA: Greenwood, 2021.

Leonard, John. "Out of Left Field." *New York Times*, October 17, 1976.

Levy, Ariel. "Either/Or." *New Yorker*, November 30, 2009, 46–59.

Lewis, Earl. "To Turn on a Pivot: Writing African Americans into a History of Overlapping Diasporas." *American Historical Review* 100, no. 3 (1995): 765–87.
Lewis, Michael. *Moneyball: The Art of Winning an Unfair Game*. New York: Norton, 2003.
Lieberman, Daniel E., and Dennis M. Bramble. "The Evolution of Marathon Running: Capabilities in Humans." *Sports Medicine* 37, nos. 4–5: 288–90.
Liebler, Jill. "Maximum Exposure." *Sports Illustrated*, May 1, 1989, 38–46.
Liebling, A. J. "A Blow for Austerity." *New Yorker*, July 9, 1960, 66–80.
Liebling, A. J. "Boxing with the Naked Eye." *New Yorker*, June 30, 1951, 31–38.
Lightfoot, Lawsi (@Sonoflow7997). "[middle finger]." July 29, 2019, comment on Bell, "This is loooong overdue!!" https://twitter.com/Sonoflaw7997/status/1155934100001185792?s=20&t=BBqQwu_fyunSwxVAFfU5eQ.
Lipsyte, Robert. "The Computer Fight." *New York Times*, January 22, 1970.
Logan, Douglas G. "An Open Letter to President Bush." USA Track and Field, July 22, 2008. https://web.archive.org/web/20080726193730/www.usatf.org/news/view.aspx?DUID=USATF_2008_07_22_06_15_21.
London, Jack. *The Abysmal Brute*. New York: Century, 1913.
London, Jack. "In the Modern Stadium." *Australian Star*, December 28, 1908.
A Long Way from Home: The Untold Story of Baseball's Desegregation. Directed by Gaspar González. Hammer and Nail Productions, 2018.
"Long-smoldering, Fed-up, Bob Clemente Erupts!" *Pittsburgh Courier*, July 15, 1961.
Lopez, Jason Kido. *Redefining Sports Media*. New York: Routledge, 2023.
"Loser Dempsey May Sue Computer Promoter." *Boston Globe*, December 24, 1967.
Lott, Eric. *Black Mirror: The Cultural Contradictions of American Racism*. Cambridge, MA: Harvard University Press, 2017.
Lowe, Lisa. *The Intimacies of Four Continents*. Durham, NC: Duke University Press, 2015.
Lyons, Robert S. *On Any Given Sunday: A Life of Bert Bell*. Philadelphia: Temple University Press, 2010.
MacAloon, John J. *This Great Symbol: Pierre de Coubertin and the Origins of the Modern Olympic Games*. Chicago: University of Chicago Press, 1981.
MacCambridge, Michael. *The Franchise: A History of "Sports Illustrated" Magazine*. New York: Hyperion, 1997.
Magubane, Zine. "Spectacles and Scholarship: Caster Semenya, Intersex Studies, and the Problem of Race in Feminist Theory." *Signs* 39, no. 3 (2014): 761–85.
Maher, Charles. "Blacks' Arms OK – but They Run Better." *Los Angeles Times*, March 28, 1968.
Maher, Charles. "Blacks Physically Superior? Some Say They're 'Hungrier.'" *Los Angeles Times*, March 26, 1968.
Maher, Charles. "Why No Black Quarterbacks in Professional Football?" *Los Angeles Times*, March 27, 1968.
Mailer, Norman. "Ego." *Life*, March 19, 1971, 18–36.
Mailer, Norman. "Evaluations: Quick and Expensive Comments on the Talent in the Room." In *Advertisements for Myself*, 463–73. New York: G. P. Putnam's Sons, 1959.

Mailer, Norman. *The Fight*. New York: Little, Brown, 1975.
Mailer, Norman. "Ten Thousand Words a Minute." *Esquire*, February 1963, 109–20.
Mailer, Norman. "The White Negro: Superficial Reflections on the Hipster." *Dissent*, Summer 1957, 276–93.
Malamud, Bernard. *The Natural*. New York: Harcourt, Brace, 1952.
Malina, R. M. "Racial/Ethnic Variation in the Motor Development and Performance of American Children." *Canadian Journal of Sport Sciences* 13, no. 2 (1988): 136–43.
Malloy, Jerry. "Sol White and the Origins of African American Baseball." Introduction to *Sol White's History of Colored Base Ball, with Other Documents on the Early Black Game, 1886–1936*, edited by Jerry Malloy, xiii–lxiv. Lincoln: University of Nebraska Press, 1995.
Manners, John. "In Search of an Explanation." In *The African Running Revolution*, edited by Dave Prokop, 26–39. Mountain View, CA: World Publications, 1975.
Mansfield, Stephanie. "Revenge of the Words: The Yak Attacks of Tony Kornheiser and Michael Wilbon on ESPN's *Pardon the Interruption* Prove That Friends Make the Best Arguments." *Sports Illustrated*, August 5, 2002, 52–56.
Maraniss, David. *Clemente: The Passion and Grace of Baseball's Last Hero*. New York: Simon and Schuster, 2006.
"Marciano Training for Ali?" *Boston Globe*, September 5, 1966.
Marks, Jonathan. "The Growth of Scientific Standards from Anthropology Days to Present Days." In *The 1904 Anthropology Days and Olympic Games*, edited by Susan Brownell, 383–96. Lincoln: University of Nebraska Press, 2008.
Marks, Jonathan. *Why I Am Not a Scientist: Anthropology and Modern Knowledge*. Berkeley: University of California Press, 2009.
Markusen, Bruce. *Roberto Clemente: The Great One*. Champaign, IL: Sports Publishing, 1998.
Markusen, Bruce. *The Team That Changed Baseball: Roberto Clemente and the 1971 Pittsburgh Pirates*. Yardley, PA: Westholme, 2006.
Mauboussin, Michael J., and Dan Callahan. "Turn and Face the Strange: Overcoming Barriers to Change in Sports and Investing." *Consilient Observer*, September 8, 2021. www.morganstanley.com/im/en-us/individual-investor/insights/articles/turn-and-face-the-strange.html.
Maughan, Karyn, Gill Gifford, and Reuters. "Caster's Ultimate Humiliation." *Star* (South Africa), September 16, 2009.
Maule, Tex. "The Baddest of All Looks over the Universe." *Sports Illustrated*, February 15, 1965, 20.
Mauss, Marcel. *The Gift: Forms and Functions of Exchange in Archaic Societies*. Translated by Ian Cunnison. Glencoe, IL: Free Press, 1954.
McCabe, David. "How the Daily Fantasy Sports Industry Was Born." *The Hill*, September 24, 2015. https://thehill.com/policy/technology/254744-how-the-daily-fantasy-sports-industry-was-born/.
McCallum, Jack. "*ET2*, ESPN?" *Sports Illustrated*, October 11, 1993, 11.

McCallum, Jack, and Kostya Kennedy. "A Different Race for Sir Roger." *Sports Illustrated*, September 25, 1995, 15.
McClanahan, Annie. *Dead Pledges: Debt, Crisis, and Twenty-First-Century Culture*. Stanford, CA: Stanford University Press, 2017.
McClanahan, Annie. "Serious Crises: Rethinking the Neoliberal Subject." *boundary 2* 46, no. 1 (2019): 103–32.
McClearen, Jennifer. *Fighting Visibility: Sports Media and Female Athletes in UFC*. Urbana: University of Illinois Press, 2021.
McCormack, Mark H. To Olle Nyman, June 11, 1973. Mark H. McCormack Papers, mums700-b0003-f010-i052. Special Collections and University Archives, University of Massachusetts Library.
McCormack, Mark H. To Robert D. Kain, July 5, 1990. Mark H. McCormack Papers, mums700-b0015-f028-i012. Special Collections and University Archives, University of Massachusetts Library.
McCormack, Mark H. To Robert D. Kain, Peter Johnson, and Barry Frank, August 9, 1991. Mark H. McCormack Papers, mums700-b0017-f045-i016, Special Collections and University Archives, University of Massachusetts Library.
McCormack, Mark H. *What They Don't Teach You at Harvard Business School: Notes from a Street-Smart Executive*. New York: Bantam, 1984.
McDonald, Soraya Nadia. "What Prince Fielder and *ESPN The Magazine*'s 'Body Issue' Say about Us." *Washington Post*, July 9, 2014.
McDougall, Christopher. *Born to Run: A Hidden Tribe, Superathletes, and the Greatest Race the World Has Never Seen*. New York: Knopf, 2009.
McDougall, Christopher. "Built for the Long Run." *Men's Health*, June 2009, 102–6.
McDougall, Christopher. "The Men Who Live Forever." *Men's Health*, July–August 2006, 180–91.
McGrath, Ben. "Dream Teams." *New Yorker*, April 13, 2015, 26–32.
McKenzie, R. Tait. "The Chronicle of the Amateur Spirit." In *Proceedings of the Fifth Annual Convention of the National Collegiate Athletic Association*, 40–55. New York: National Collegiate Athletic Association, 1910.
McMillen, Tom. *Out of Bounds: How the American Sports Establishment Is Being Driven by Greed and Hypocrisy – and What Needs to Be Done about It*. With Paul Coggins. New York: Simon and Schuster, 1992.
"McNabb Says Owens's Criticism Amounts to 'Black-on-Black Crime.'" ESPN.com, February 1, 2006. www.espn.com/nfl/story?id=2315675.
Melamed, Jodi. "Racial Capitalism." *Critical Ethnic Studies* 1, no. 1 (2015): 76–85.
Melamed, Jodi. *Represent and Destroy: Rationalizing Violence in the New Racial Capitalism*. Minneapolis: University of Minnesota Press, 2011.
Michener, James A. *Sports in America*. New York: Random House, 1976.
Miller, James Andrew. "*Pardon the Interruption*: Flaunt All Rules." In *Origins with James Andrew Miller*, January 3, 2018. Podcast, 1:40:46. www.originsthepodcast.com/chapter2.
Miller, James Andrew, and Tom Shales. *Those Guys Have All the Fun: Inside the World of ESPN*. New York: Little, Brown, 2011.

Mills, Roger. "Bannister's 'Theory' an Unacceptable One." *Tampa Bay Times*, September 17, 1995.
Mirpuri, Anoop. "Why Can't Kobe Pass (the Ball)? Race and the NBA in the Age of Neoliberalism." In *Commodified and Criminalized: New Racism and African Americans in Contemporary Sports*, edited by David J. Leonard and C. Richard King, 95–120. Lanham, MD: Rowman and Littlefield, 2011.
Mokoena, Tshepo. "Caster Semenya: 'How Would I Label Myself? I'm an African. I'm a Different Woman.'" *Guardian*, October 28, 2023. www.theguardian.com/sport/2023/oct/28/athlete-caster-semenya-interview-im-a-woman-im-a-different-woman.
Molina, Natalia. *How Race Is Made in America: Immigration, Citizenship, and the Historical Power of Racial Scripts*. Berkeley: University of California Press, 2014.
"'Moneyball' Comes to Medicine." Scripps Health, December 20, 2015. www.scripps.org/news_items/5588-moneyball-comes-to-medicine.
"Monte Irvin Delivers Hall of Fame Induction Speech." August 6, 1973. MLB video, 3:48, November 10, 2015. www.youtube.com/watch?v=cKIBPetDKVk.
Moore, Kenny. "Sons of the Wind." *Sports Illustrated*, February 26, 1990, 72–84.
Moore, Kenny. "The Spoils of Victory." *Sports Illustrated*, April 10, 1989, 50–55.
Moore, Louis. "Jimmy Bivins and the Duration Championship." In *The Bittersweet Science: Fifteen Writers in the Gym, in the Corner, and at Ringside*, edited by Carlo Rotella and Michael Ezra, 211–24. Chicago: University of Chicago Press, 2017.
Moore, Thomas. "The Black-on-Black Crime Plague." *U.S. News and World Report*, August 22, 1988, 48–53.
Mora, G. Cristina. *Making Hispanics: How Activists, Bureaucrats, and Media Constructed a New American*. Chicago: University of Chicago Press, 2014.
Moran, Malcolm. "At USC, Issue Is Responsibility." *New York Times*, October 26, 1980.
Moran, Malcolm. "Former USC President Defends Policies." *New York Times*, October 17, 1980.
Moreton-Robinson, Aileen. *The White Possessive: Property, Power, and Indigenous Sovereignty*. Minneapolis: University of Minnesota Press, 2015.
Moyer, Valerie. "The Seeping Surveillance of Sex in Sports." In "The Body Issue: Sports and the Politics of Embodiment," edited by Joseph Darda and Amira Rose Davis, 501–18. Special issue, *American Quarterly* 75, no. 3 (2023).
"Muhammad Ali vs. Jim Jeffries." *The Best of the All-Time Heavyweight Tournament*. Ben Scott Recording, 1967.
Muhammad, Khalil Gibran. *The Condemnation of Blackness: Race, Crime, and the Making of Modern Urban America*. Cambridge, MA: Harvard University Press, 2010.
Murakawa, Naomi. *The First Civil Right: How Liberals Built Prison America*. New York: Oxford University Press, 2014.
Murray, Jim. "Come Out Talking!" *Los Angeles Times*, November 7, 1963.
Murray, Jim. "Ee-yi, Ee-yi, Yo." *Los Angeles Times*, February 21, 1964.
MV (@mike_v773). "This man is dead to me." July 29, 2019, comment on Bell, "This is loooong overdue!!" https://twitter.com/mike_v733/status/1155944644187840512?s=20&t=BBqQwu_fyunSwxVAFfU5eQ.

Myers, Jim. "Examining the Races: Experts Scoff at Myths." *USA Today*, December 16, 1991.
Myrdal, Gunnar. *An American Dilemma: The Negro Problem and Modern Democracy*. New York: Harper and Brothers, 1944.
Nagle, Dave. "ESPN, Inc.: 2001 in Review." ESPN Press Room, January 2, 2002. https://espnpressroom.com/us/press-releases/2002/01/espn-inc-2001-in-review/.
National Collegiate Athletic Association. *Proceedings of the 61st Annual Convention*. Kansas City, MO: National Collegiate Athletic Association, 1967.
National Collegiate Athletic Association. *Proceedings of the 63rd Annual Convention*. Kansas City, MO: National Collegiate Athletic Association, 1969.
National Collegiate Athletic Association. *Proceedings of the 67th Annual Convention*. Shawnee Mission, KS: National Collegiate Athletic Association, 1973.
National Collegiate Athletic Association. *Proceedings of the 77th Annual Convention*. Shawnee Mission, KS: National Collegiate Athletic Association, 1983.
NCAA Gender-Equity Task Force. *Final Report of the NCAA Gender-Equity Task Force*. Kansas City, MO: National Collegiate Athletic Association, 1993.
"The New York Meeting of the American Anthropological Association." *Science* 89, no. 2298 (1939): 29–30.
Newfield, Christopher. *The Great Mistake: How We Wrecked Public Universities and How We Can Fix Them*. Baltimore: Johns Hopkins University Press, 2016.
Newfield, Christopher. *Unmaking the Public University: The Forty-Year Assault on the Middle Class*. Cambridge, MA: Harvard University Press, 2008.
Newfield, Jack. *Only in America: The Life and Times of Don King*. New York: William Morrow, 1995.
NFL Draft 1980. Aired April 29, 1980, on ESPN.
NFL Draft 2001. Aired April 21–22, 2001, on ESPN.
Nguyen, Mimi Thi. *The Gift of Freedom: War, Debt, and Other Refugee Passages*. Durham, NC: Duke University Press, 2012.
Nightengale, Bob. "'It's Just Getting Worse': MLB's 'Disgusting' Minority Hiring Woes Continue as Job Candidates Shut Out Again." *USA Today*, December 4, 2019. www.usatoday.com/story/sports/mlb/columnist/bob-nightengale/2019/12/04/mlb-general-managers-executives-winter-meetings/2604488001/.
Nightline. "A Tribute to Jackie Robinson." Hosted by Ted Koppel. Aired April 6, 1987, on ABC.
Nugent, Conn. "How to Own a Baseball Team." *Harvard Magazine*, April 1981, 54–56, 70.
Nuun, Bill, Jr. "Baker, Clemente Deny Liking Fort Myers's Bias in Housing." *Pittsburgh Courier*, February 25, 1961.
Nuun, Bill, Jr. "Clemente May Bring 'Rookie of the Year' Laurels to Pirates." *Pittsburgh Courier*, June 18, 1955.
Nuun, Bill, Jr. "Record Crop of 41 Negro Stars on Rosters of Teams in National League." *Pittsburgh Courier*, April 18, 1959.
O'Neil, Cathy. *Weapons of Math Destruction: How Big Data Increases Inequality and Threatens Democracy*. New York: Crown, 2016.

Oates, Thomas P. "Antagonistic Sports Fandom." In "The Body Issue: Sports and the Politics of Embodiment," edited by Joseph Darda and Amira Rose Davis. Special issue, *American Quarterly* 75, no. 3 (2023): 519–41.
Oates, Thomas P. *Football and Manliness: An Unauthorized Feminist Account of the NFL*. Urbana: University of Illinois Press, 2017.
Oates, Thomas P. "New Media and the Repackaging of NFL Fandom." *Sociology of Sport Journal* 26, no. 1 (2009): 31–49.
Okrent, Daniel. "He Does It by the Numbers." *Sports Illustrated*, May 25, 1981, 40–51.
Okrent, Daniel. "The Year George Foster Wasn't Worth $36." *Inside Sports*, March 31, 1981, 88–90.
Okrent, Daniel. "The Year George Foster Wasn't Worth $36." Introduction to *Rotisserie League Baseball*, edited by Glen Waggoner, 3–7. New York: Bantam, 1984.
Olsen, Jack. "The Cruel Deception." *Sports Illustrated*, July 1, 1968, 12–27.
Olsen, Jack. "Pride and Prejudice." *Sports Illustrated*, July 8, 1968, 18–31.
Omi, Michael, and Howard Winant. *Racial Formation in the United States: From the 1960s to the 1980s*. New York: Routledge, 1986.
Oriard, Michael. *Bowled Over: Big-Time College Football from the Sixties to the BCS Era*. Chapel Hill: University of North Carolina Press, 2009.
Ostler, Scott. "White Athletes – Fact and Fiction: Destroying Myths." *Los Angeles Times*, April 27, 1989.
"Our Crystal Baseball." *Esquire*, April 24, 1979, 6.
Page, Don. "Computer Punchy from Fight Tapes." *Los Angeles Times*, December 2, 1967.
"Pardon the Interruption ... but Did Sports Debate Shows Change the World?" In *Good Sport with Jody Avirgan*, February 15, 2023. Podcast, 39:13. www.ted.com/podcasts/good-sport/pardon-the-interruption-transcript.
Park, Robert E., and Ernest W. Burgess. *Introduction to the Science of Sociology*. Chicago: University of Chicago Press, 1921.
"The Parlor Game of Base-Ball." Advertisement. *Frank Leslie's Illustrated Newspaper*, December 8, 1866, 180.
Patterson, Floyd. "Cassius Clay Must Be Beaten." *Sports Illustrated*, October 11, 1965, 78–98.
Patterson, Floyd. "I Want to Destroy Clay." With Milton Gross. *Sports Illustrated*, October 19, 1964, 42–61.
"Payne: Tiger to Be Judged on Sincerity." ESPN.com, April 7, 2010. www.espn.com/golf/masters10/news/story?id=5063768.
Penn, Nate. "Whack!-ipedia." *GQ*, June 2007, 224–27, 244–45.
Pérez, Louis A., Jr. *On Becoming Cuban: Identity, Nationality, and Culture*. Chapel Hill: University of North Carolina Press, 1999.
Peterson, Robert. *Only the Ball Was White*. Englewood Cliffs, NJ: Prentice-Hall, 1970.
"Pitch the Rich." Advertisement. *Broadcasting*, December 10, 1979, 81.
Plimpton, George. Introduction to the 1993 edition. In *Shadow Box: An Amateur in the Ring*, 9–10. New York: Lyons and Buford, 1993.
Plimpton, George. *Paper Tiger*. New York: Harper and Row, 1966.

Plimpton, George. *Shadow Box*. New York: Putnam, 1977.
Ploeg, Andrew J. "A New Form of Fandom: How Free Agency Brought about Rotisserie League Baseball." *International Journal of the History of Sport* 38, no. 1 (2021): 7–27.
Pony Excess. Directed by Thaddeus Matula. ESPN, 2010.
Poussaint, Alvin F. "Why Blacks Kill Blacks." *Ebony*, October 1970, 143–50.
Poussaint, Alvin F. *Why Blacks Kill Blacks*. New York: Emerson Hall, 1972.
Povich, Shirley. This Morning. *Washington Post*, May 21, 1965.
"President Clinton Participates in ESPN Race Town Hall." Office of the Press Secretary, White House, April 14, 1998. https://clintonwhitehouse4.archives.gov/WH/New/html/19980415-8261.html.
Price, S. L. "Whatever Happened to the White Athlete?" *Sports Illustrated*, December 8, 1997, 30–42.
Prokop, Dave. Foreword to *The African Running Revolution*. Edited by Dave Prokop, 4. Mountain View, CA: World Publications, 1975.
Radford, Tim. "Black Runners 'at an Advantage.'" *Guardian*, September 14, 1995.
Rankine, Claudia. *Citizen: An American Lyric*. Minneapolis: Graywolf Press, 2014.
Rashad, Ahmad. *Ahmad: Vikes, Mikes, and Something on the Backside*. With Peter Bodo. New York: Viking, 1988.
Rasmussen, Bill. *Sports Junkies Rejoice! The Birth of ESPN*. Hartsdale, NY: QV Publishing, 1983.
Ray, Victor. "A Theory of Racialized Organizations." *American Sociological Review* 84, no. 1 (2019): 26–53.
Reagan, Nancy. "The Need for Intolerance." *Washington Post*, July 7, 1986.
Real Sports with Bryant Gumbel. Season 20, episode 9, "Risky Business." Aired September 23, 2014, on HBO.
Reed, Ishmael. "Ishmael Reed on Ali." *Village Voice*, October 16, 1978, 1, 23–30.
Reed, Ishmael. "A Palooka He Ain't." Review of *The Greatest: My Own Story*, by Muhammad Ali. *New York Times Book Review*, November 30, 1975.
Regalado, Samuel O. *Viva Baseball! Latin Major Leaguers and Their Special Hunger*. Urbana: University of Illinois Press, 1998.
Regents of the University of California v. Bakke. 438 US 265 (1978).
Reid, Jason. *The Rise of the Black Quarterback: What It Means for America*. New York: Andscape, 2022.
Remnick, David. *The King of the World: Muhammad Ali and the Rise of an American Hero*. New York: Random House, 1998.
Rhoden, William C. "Fantasy Sports' Real Crime: Dehumanizing the Athletes." *New York Times*, November 25, 2015.
Richman, Milton. Sports Parade. *Times-News* (Hendersonville, NC), April 21, 1971.
Rielly, Edward J. *Baseball: An Encyclopedia of Popular Culture*. Santa Barbara, CA: ABC-CLIO, 2000.
Riger, Roger. "The Greatest Fights of the Century." *Esquire*, December 1963, 188–91.
"The Rising Price of Has-Beens." *Economist*, September 8, 1990, 72.
Roberts, Daniel. "Robert Coover's Dark Fantasy-Baseball Novel." *Paris Review*, September 18, 2017. www.theparisreview.org/blog/2017/09/18/robert-coovers-dark-fantasy-baseball-novel/.

Roberts, Randy. *Joe Louis: Hard Times Man*. New Haven, CT: Yale University Press, 2010.
"Robinhood." Robinhood video, February 20, 2014, 1:51. https://vimeo.com/87163777.
Robinson, Jackie. "Cobwebs in Dark's Mind." *New York Amsterdam News*, August 15, 1964.
Rock, Chris, guest. *Real Sports with Bryant Gumbel*. Season 21, episode 4. Aired April 21, 2015, on HBO.
Rocky. Directed by John G. Avildsen. United Artists, 1976.
Rocky III. Directed by Sylvester Stallone. MGM/United Artists, 1982.
Roediger, David R. *Working toward Whiteness: How America's Immigrants Became White; The Strange Journey from Ellis Island to the Suburbs*. New York: Basic Books, 2005.
Roediger, David R., and Elizabeth D. Esch. *The Production of Difference: Race and the Management of Labor in U.S. History*. New York: Oxford University Press, 2012.
Roenigk, Alyssa. "For Sale by Owner." *ESPN The Magazine*, October 19, 2009, 108–13.
Rogin, Gilbert. "Champion as Long as He Wants." *Sports Illustrated*, November 29, 1965, 20–24.
Rogosin, Donn. *Invisible Men: Life in Baseball's Negro Leagues*. New York: Atheneum, 1983.
Rohrbaugh, Joanna Bunker. "Femininity on the Line." *Psychology Today*, August 1979, 30–42.
Rotella, Carlo. *Good with Their Hands: Boxers, Bluesmen, and Other Characters from the Rust Belt*. Berkeley: University of California Press, 2002.
Rotella, Carlo. "Introduction: At Ringside." In *Cut Time: An Education at the Fights*. Chicago: University of Chicago Press, 2003.
Rotella, Carlo. "The Stepping Stone: Larry Holmes, Gerry Cooney, and *Rocky*." In *In the Game: Race, Identity, and Sports in the Twentieth Century*, edited by Amy Bass, 237–63. New York: Palgrave Macmillan, 2005.
Rotella, Carlo, and Michael Ezra. "Introduction: Bittersweetness." In *The Bittersweet Science: Fifteen Writers in the Gym, in the Corner, and at Ringside*, edited by Carlo Rotella and Michael Ezra, 1–7. Chicago: University of Chicago Press, 2017.
Ruck, Rob. *Raceball: How the Major Leagues Colonized the Black and Latin Games*. Boston: Beacon Press, 2011.
Runstedtler, Theresa. *Jack Johnson, Rebel Sojourner: Boxing in the Shadow of the Global Color Line*. Berkeley: University of California Press, 2012.
Runstedtler, Theresa. "Racial Bias: The Black Athlete, Reagan's War on Drugs, and Big-Time Sports Reform." In "Sport in the University," edited by Noah Cohan, Daniel A. Gilbert, Theresa Runstedtler, Tyran Kai Steward, and Lucia Trimbur, 85–116. Special issue, *American Studies* 55, no. 3 (2016).
Rutter, Emily Ruth. *Invisible Ball of Dreams: Literary Representations of Baseball behind the Color Line*. Jackson: University Press of Mississippi, 2018.
Sack, Allen L., and Ellen J. Staurowsky. *College Athletes for Hire: The Evolution and Legacy of the NCAA's Amateur Myth*. Westport, CT: Praeger, 1998.
Sackler, Howard. *The Great White Hope*. New York: Dial, 1968.

Sammons, Jeffrey T. *Beyond the Ring: The Role of Boxing in American Society*. Urbana: University of Illinois Press, 1988.
Sandomir, Richard. "*Dream Job*, the Nightmare, Showing Now on ESPN." *New York Times*, March 6, 2004.
Sarris, Andrew. "Takes." *Village Voice*, November 22, 1976, 61.
"The Scandal behind the Tragedy." *New York Times*, June 28, 1986.
Schiller, Zachary. "Advantage, Mark McCormack?" *Business Week*, September 27, 1993, 64–73.
Schlosser, Joe. "NAACP Sees Boycott Ahead." *Broadcasting and Cable*, August 23, 1999, 4.
Schneiderman, Eric T. Memorandum of law in support of motion for a preliminary injunction against DraftKings, Inc. New York State Office of the Attorney General, November 17, 2015.
Schwarz, Alan. *The Numbers Game: Baseball's Lifelong Fascination with Statistics*. New York: Thomas Dunne Books, 2004.
Scott, Daryl Michael. *Contempt and Pity: Social Policy and the Image of the Damaged Black Psyche, 1880–1996*. Chapel Hill: University of North Carolina Press, 1997.
Scott, Jack. *The Athletic Revolution*. New York: Free Press, 1971.
Searcy, Jay. "Big Money Is Pointing More Women toward Pro Sports." *New York Times*, April 14, 1974.
Sexton, Jared. "People-of-Color Blindness: Notes on the Afterlife of Slavery." *Social Text* 28, no. 2 (2010): 31–56.
Sexton, John. *Baseball as a Road to God: Seeing beyond the Game*. With Thomas Oliphant and Peter J. Schwartz. New York: Gotham, 2013.
Seymour, Gene. "Fade to White." *Nation*, November 2–9, 2020, 18–21, 25.
Shafer, Jack. "*SportsCenter* for Political Junkies." *Slate*, April 29, 2003. https://slate.com/news-and-politics/2003/04/sportscenter-for-news-junkies.html.
Shane, Scott. "Genetics Research Increasingly Finds 'Race' a Null Concept." *Baltimore Sun*, April 4, 1999.
Shaughnessy, Dan. "The Accidental Godfather of Fantasy Sports." *Boston Globe*, October 13, 2015.
Sheinin, Dan. "Mariners Trade Griffey to Reds." *Washington Post*, February 11, 2000.
Sheppard, Samantha N. *Sporting Blackness: Race, Embodiment, and Critical Muscle Memory on Screen*. Berkeley: University of California Press, 2020.
Shoals, Bethlehem [Nathanial Friedman]. "Save Your Claws, Chew Angles." *FreeDarko*, November 7, 2006. https://freedarko.blogspot.com/2006/11/save-your-claws-chew-angles.html.
Sides, John. "The Moneyball of Campaign Advertising." *FiveThirtyEight* (blog). *New York Times*, October 5, 2011. https://archive.nytimes.com/fivethirtyeight.blogs.nytimes.com/2011/10/05/the-moneyball-of-campaign-advertising-part-1/.
Silly Little Game. Directed by Adam Kurland and Lucas Jansen. ESPN Films, 2010.
Silver, Nate. *The Signal and the Noise: Why So Many Predictions Fail – but Some Don't*. New York: Penguin Press, 2012.
The Simpsons. Season 22, episode 3, "MoneyBart." Aired October 10, 2010, on Fox.
Singh, Nikhil Pal. *Race and America's Long War*. Berkeley: University of California Press, 2017.

Skretney, John David. *The Ironies of Affirmative Action: Politics, Culture, and Justice in America*. Chicago: University of Chicago Press, 1996.
Smith, Anthony F. *ESPN The Company: The Story and Lessons behind the Most Fanatical Brand in Sports*. With Keith Hollihan. Hoboken, NJ: John Wiley and Sons, 2009.
Smith, Red. "Without Salt." *New York Herald Tribune*, February 26, 1964.
Smith, Ronald A. *The Myth of the Amateur: A History of College Athletic Scholarships*. Austin: University of Texas Press, 2021.
Smith, Stephen A. "Why Don't Black People Play Fantasy? Allow Me to Explain." *ESPN The Magazine*, September 8, 2008, 18.
Soule, Selina. "Testimony before the United States Senate Committee on the Judiciary in Opposition to the Equality Act." Alliance Defending Freedom, March 17, 2021. https://adfmedialegalfiles.blob.core.windows.net/files/Equality ActTestimonySJC.pdf.
Sperber, Murray. *College Sports Inc.: The Athletic Department vs. the University*. New York: Henry Holt, 1990.
SportsCenter. Aired September 7, 1979, on ESPN.
SportsNight. Aired October 1, 1993, on ESPN2.
St. Clair, Drake, and Horace R. Cayton. *Black Metropolis: A Study of Negro Life in a Northern City*. New York: Harcourt, Brace, 1945.
St. Louis, Brett. "Sport and Common-Sense Racial Science." *Leisure Studies* 23, no. 1 (2004): 31–46.
Stack, Liam. "Chris Mosier Is First Transgender Athlete in ESPN's 'Body Issue.'" *New York Times*, June 23, 2016.
Staub, Michael E. *The Mismeasure of Minds: Debating Race and Intelligence between "Brown" and "The Bell Curve."* Chapel Hill: University of North Carolina Press, 2018.
Streible, Dan. *Fighting Pictures: A History of Boxing and Early Cinema*. Berkeley: University of California Press, 2008.
Students for Fair Admissions v. Harvard. 600 US 181 (2023).
Suggs, Welch. *A Place on the Team: The Triumph and Tragedy of Title IX*. Princeton, NJ: Princeton University Press, 2005.
The Super Fight. Directed by Murry Woroner. Woroner Productions, 1970.
Swift, E. M. "The Most Powerful Man in Sports." *Sports Illustrated*, May 21, 1990, 98–120.
Sylvester, Harry. "With Greatest of Ease." *New York Times*, August 24, 1952.
Tanner, J. M. *The Physique of the Olympic Athlete*. London: George Allen and Unwin, 1964.
Telander, Rick. *Like a Rose: A Celebration of Football*. Champaign, IL: Sports Publishing, 2004.
Telander, Rick. *The Hundred Yard Lie: The Corruption of College Football and What We Can Do to Stop It*. New York: Simon and Schuster, 1989.
Tempels, Placide. *Bantu Philosophy*. Translated by Colin King. Paris: Présence Africaine, 1959.
Terrell, Roy. "The Biggest Golf Hustler of Them All." *Sports Illustrated*, November 12, 1962, 28–34.
Teslow, Tracy. *Constructing Race: The Science of Bodies and Cultures in American Anthropology*. New York: Cambridge University Press, 2014.

Thelin, John R. *Going to College in the Sixties.* Baltimore: Johns Hopkins University Press, 2018.
Thelin, John R. *A History of American Higher Education.* 3rd ed. Baltimore: Johns Hopkins University Press, 2019.
Thelin, John R., and Lawrence L. Wiseman. *The Old College Try: Balancing Academics and Athletics in Higher Education.* Washington, DC: School of Education and Human Development, George Washington University, 1989.
Thomas, Patrick. "Chicken Producers Have Own 'Moneyball.'" *Wall Street Journal*, December 14, 2023.
Thompson, Derek. "The Cult of Rich-Kid Sports." *Atlantic*, October 2, 2019. www.theatlantic.com/ideas/archive/2019/10/harvard-university-and-scandal-sports-recruitment/599248/.
Thompson, John. *I Came as a Shadow: An Autobiography.* With Jesse Washington. New York: Henry Holt, 2020.
Thomsen, Ian. "Flo-Jo Leaves Risk of Drugs Still in Question." *New York Times*, September 26, 1998.
"Three Basketball Aces on Kentucky Team Admit '49 Fix Here." *New York Times*, October 21, 1951.
Torre, Pablo. "The Legacy of PTI." In *ESPN Daily*, October 22, 2021. Podcast, 45:22. www.espn.com/radio/play/_/id/32450255.
"Tracking the (Money) Balls: How Data Science Is Becoming a Game Changer." In *Harvard Data Science Review Podcast*, March 19, 2021. Podcast, 28:27. https://hdsr.mitpress.mit.edu/podcast.
Travers. *The Trans Generation: How Trans Kids (and Their Parents) Are Creating a Gender Revolution.* New York: New York University Press, 2018.
Trimbur, Lucia. *Come Out Swinging: The Changing World of Boxing in Gleason's Gym.* Princeton, NJ: Princeton University Press, 2013.
Trimbur, Lucia. "Lights Out: Concussion Research, the National Football League, and Employer Duty of Care." In *The Palgrave Handbook of Sport, Politics, and Harm*, edited by Stephen Wagg and Allyson M. Pollock, 156–71. London: Palgrave Macmillan, 2021.
Tygiel, Jules. *Baseball's Great Experiment: Jackie Robinson and His Legacy.* New York: Oxford University Press, 1983.
Tygiel, Jules. *Past Time: Baseball as History.* New York: Oxford University Press, 2000.
Underwood, John. "Concessions – and Lies." *Sports Illustrated*, September 8, 1969, 29–40.
Underwood, John. "The Desperate Coach." *Sports Illustrated*, August 25, 1969, 66–76.
Unlawful Internet Gambling Enforcement Act of 2006. 31 USC § 5361–67 (2006).
US Olympic Track and Field Trials. Aired July 16, 1988, on ABC.
US Supreme Court. "Regents of the University of California v. Bakke: Oral Argument." October 12, 1977. Oyez. Transcript and audio, 1:59:13. www.oyez.org/cases/1979/76-811.

US Supreme Court. "Students for Fair Admissions v. President and Fellows of Harvard College: Oral Argument." October 31, 2022. Oyez. Transcript and audio, 1:55:15. www.oyez.org/cases/2022/20-1199.
Vacchiano, Ralph. "NY Giants RB Brandon Jacobs Receives Death Threat via Twitter." *New York Daily News*, October 22, 2013. www.nydailynews.com/sports/football/giants/giants-jacobs-receives-death-threat-twitter-article-1.1492670.
Villarosa, Linda. "The Other Kenyans." *Runner's World*, August 1992, 96–103.
Vogan, Travis. *ABC Sports: The Rise and Fall of Network Television*. Berkeley: University of California Press, 2018.
Vogan, Travis. *The Boxing Film: A Cultural and Transmedia History*. New Brunswick, NJ: Rutgers University Press, 2021.
Vogan, Travis. *ESPN: The Making of a Sports Media Empire*. Urbana: University of Illinois Press, 2015.
Wagenheim, Kal. *Clemente!* New York: Praeger, 1973.
Waggoner, Glen, ed. *Rotisserie League Baseball*. New York: Bantam, 1984.
Waldstein, David. "The National Pastime's Challenge: Prove Its Time Hasn't Passed." *New York Times*, October 25, 2021.
Walker, Eric. *The Sinister First Baseman and Other Observations*. Millbrae, CA: Celestial Arts, 1982.
Walker, Sam. *Fantasyland: A Season on Baseball's Lunatic Fringe*. New York: Viking, 2006.
Wallace, Anise C. "Next Stop, Madison Avenue." *New York Times*, October 27, 1988.
Ware, Nicholas. "God-Fans of the Gridiron: Madden, Fantasy, Football, and Simulation." In *Football, Culture and Power*, edited by David Leonard, Kimberly B. George, and Wade Davis, 86–99. New York: Routledge, 2017.
"Watch the NFL Draft Live Only on ESPN." Advertisement. *New York Times*, April 29, 1980.
Watterson, John Sayle. *College Football: History, Spectacle, Controversy*. Baltimore: Johns Hopkins University Press, 2000.
Weaving, Charlene, and Jessica Samson. "The Naked Truth: Disability, Sexual Objectification, and the ESPN Body Issue." *Journal of the Philosophy of Sport* 45, no. 1 (2018): 83–100.
Webster, William. "How Democratic Is Baseball?" *Pittsburgh Courier*, July 3, 1954.
Weiland, Matt. "A Veteran Baseball Novel Comes Off the Bench." *New York Times*, August 26, 2011.
White, Derrick E. *Blood, Sweat, and Tears: Jake Gaither, Florida A&M, and the History of Black College Football*. Chapel Hill: University of North Carolina Press, 2019.
White, Gordon S., Jr. "College Athletes Who Protest to Face Loss of Financial Aid." *New York Times*, January 9, 1969.
White, Gordon S., Jr. "N.C.A.A.'s High Aims Turn into Rights Controversy." *New York Times*, January 16, 1983.
White, Sol. *Sol White's History of Colored Base Ball, with Other Documents on the Early Black Game, 1886–1936*. Edited by Jerry Malloy. Lincoln: University of Nebraska Press, 1995.

Whittingham, Richard. *The Meat Market: The Inside Story of the NFL Draft.* New York: Macmillan, 1992.
Wideman, John Edgar. *Brothers and Keepers.* New York: Holt, Rinehart, and Winston, 1984.
Wigdor, Alexandra K., and Wendell R. Garner, eds. *Ability Testing: Uses, Consequences, and Controversies.* Washington, DC: National Academy Press, 1982.
Will (@willborgo_). "@LeVeon Bell $willborgo my money long overdue too." July 29, 2019, comment on Bell, "This is loooong overdue!!" https://twitter.com/willborgo_/status/1155944046721785856?s=20&t=BBqQwu_fyunSwxVAFfU5eQ.
Will, George F. "Seeing Nothing Normal in 'Race-Norming.'" *Baltimore Sun*, May 23, 1991.
Will, George F. "A Stupendous Mystery." *Newsweek*, May 16, 1994, 70.
Williams, Pete. *The Draft: A Year Inside the NFL's Search for Talent.* New York: St. Martin's Griffin, 2006.
Williams, Raymond. *Marxism and Literature.* Oxford: Oxford University Press, 1977.
Willis, William S., Jr. "Skeletons in the Anthropological Closet." In *Reinventing Anthropology*, edited by Dell H. Hymes, 121–52. New York: Pantheon, 1972.
Wilner, Barry, and Ken Rappoport. *On the Clock: The Story of the NFL Draft.* Lanham, MD: Taylor Trade Publishing, 2015.
Wilson, David. *Inventing Black-on-Black Crime: Discourse, Space, and Representation.* Syracuse, NY: Syracuse University Press, 2005.
"WNBA's Most Popular Merchandise." WNBA.com, September 23, 2021. www.wnba.com/news/wnbas-most-popular-merchandise/.
Wright, Richard. "Joe Louis Uncovers Dynamite." *New Masses*, October 8, 1935, 18–19.
Wright, Richard. "A Rejoinder." *New Leader*, February 3, 1964, 15–22.
Wulf, Steve. "For the Champion in the Rotisserie League, Joy Is a Yoo-Hoo Shampoo." *Sports Illustrated*, May 14, 1984, 8–18.
Wulf, Steve, and Jack McCullum. "The Jock Caucus." *Sports Illustrated*, February 23, 1987, 62–74.
X, Malcolm. *The Autobiography of Malcolm X.* With Alex Haley. New York: Grove Press, 1965.
"Yanks Bring Up First Negro Players." *Washington Post*, October 14, 1953.
Yardley, Jonathan. "For the University of Maryland, a Golden Opportunity for Genuine Reform." *Washington Post*, July 7, 1986.
Young, A. S. "Doc." Good Morning Sports! *Chicago Daily Defender*, September 23, 1965.
Young, A. S. "Doc." *Great Negro Baseball Stars and How They Made the Major Leagues.* New York: A. S. Barnes, 1953.
Young, A. S. "Doc." *Negro Firsts in Sports.* Chicago: Johnson Publishing, 1963.
Young, A. S. "Doc." "Unfair to Muhammad Ali." *Chicago Daily Defender*, January 29, 1970.
Young, Dick. Young Ideas. *Daily News*, August 26, 1965.
Yzaguirre, Raúl. "The Decade for Hispanics." *Agenda*, January–February 1980, 2.
Zirin, Dave. "So What the Hell Is Race Norming?" *Nation*, March 12, 2021. www.thenation.com/article/society/race-norming-nfl-concussions/.

Index

Aaron, Hank, 56, 77
Abysmal Brute, The (London), 91
Adorno, Theodor, 15–16, 229n65
Advertisements for Myself (Mailer), 99
affirmative action, 5, 119–20, 143–44, 228n37
    athlete admissions in relation to, 150–51, 175, 251n16, 256n116, 257n133
    introduction of, 134
    movement against, 134–35, 216
    New Democrats on, 144
    race norming as, 214–15
    for white men, 127
    See also *Regents of the University of California v. Bakke*; *Students for Fair Admissions v. Harvard*
African Running Revolution, The, 36–37
Alderson, Sandy, 198–99, 201
Alexander, Clifford, 172
Alexander, Jane, 107
Ali, Muhammad, *103*, 129
    in *All-Time Heavyweight Tournament* (radio program), 109–10
    antifans, 162–63
    Black heavyweight champions, 87
    against Black opponents, 94–98, 247n64, 247n67
    Black-on-Black crime, 89
    in closed-circuit broadcasts, 109–10, 249n113
    colorism of, 98
    Johnson, Jack, compared to, 106–7, 248n95
    Mailer on, 102–4, 248n85
    McCormack on, 16
    middlebrow magazine, 17
    national acceptance of, 114–15
    NYPD argument about, 115
    at Olympic Games, 1960 (Rome), 87
    Rasmussen on, 162, 165
    in Rumble in the Jungle (Ali–Foreman), 102–3, 108
    in *Super Fight, The*, 110–12, 112
    in Thrilla in Manila (Ali–Frazier III), 160
    See also Black-on-Black boxing matches
Allen, Maury, 108
Allen, Newt, 80
Allen and Ginter (tobacco manufacturer), 193
Alliance Defending Freedom (ADF), 27
All-Time Heavyweight Tournament (radio program), 109–10
Almonte, Danny, 84
Alou, Felipe, 65–66, 73, 79, 240n48
altitude training, 24–25, 38, 48, 231n8
amateur
    affirmative action, 150
    as class status, 118, 123, 127, 136, 148
    Ivy League, 127
    as NCAA founding ideal, 118, 122–23
    student-athlete contrasted with, 121, 126, 133–34, 139
    as subsidized by student-athlete, 118–19, 135
    as white, 119, 135, 257n133

305

amateur (cont.)
  women's sports, 147
  See also NCAA (National Collegiate Athletic Association); student-athlete
American Anthropological Association, 29
American Council on Education, 136, 138
American Sociological Association, 70
analytics. See sports analytics
Anderson, Benedict, 168
Angelou, Maya, 86
anthropology, 29–32, 37, 51, 233n31
Anti-Drug Abuse Act of 1986, 142
antiwar movement, 131, 135
APBA (American Professional Baseball Association) (tabletop game), 189–90
Armfield, Greg, 260n33
Armies of the Night, The (Mailer), 103
Armstrong, Lance, 47
Ashford, Evelyn, 7
Asiago, Delilah, 36
Association for Intercollegiate Athletics for Women, 140, 255n84
Atanasoski, Neda, 203, 227n35
athletes with disabilities, 131, 135, 177
Athletic Revolution, The (J. Scott), 126, 141
Auerbach, Red, 141
Autobiography of Malcolm X, The (X with Haley), 96

Baer, Max, 85, 86
Balboa, Rocky, 108, 112–14, 227n37
Baldwin, James, 88–89, 98–101
Ball Park Baseball (tabletop game), 195
Bannister, Roger, 23–28, 47, 231n8, 231n10
Bantu Philosophy (Tempels), 102
Baraka, Amiri, 82–84, 104–5
Barbary Shore (Mailer), 99
Barnes, Katie, 220
Baseball Abstract (B. James), 195–97
baseball cards, 56, 193–94
Baseball Hall of Fame, 73, 79, 84
  Clemente, Roberto, in, 54–55, 58, 60, 239n27
Baseball Has Done It (J. Robinson and Dexter), 77
Baseball Seminar, 189–90, 195. See also fantasy sports
Baseball's Great Experiment (Tygiel), 79
Bass, Amy, 3, 5, 26, 229n65
Bayi, Filbert, 24–25
Bayless, Skip, 262n85
Bayne, Bijan, 56, 239n33

Beane, Billy, 187–88, 198–201, 200, 210
Beat generation, 99, 103
Bederman, Gail, 119, 248n95
Belichick, Bill, 218
Bell, Bert, 165–66
Bell, James "Cool Papa," 82
Bell, Le'Veon, 182–88
Bell Curve, The (Herrnstein and C. Murray), 41, 214–15
Belsky, Gary, 178
Benedict, Ruth, 29–31
Bennett, William, 141
Berg, Peter, 121
Berman, Chris, 158, 165, 171
  in *Draft Day*, 171
  on ESPN2, 173
  as model fan, 156
  at NFL draft, 152–53, 155–57, 166, 169
  on sexual harassment at ESPN, 164
  See also ESPN
Bernstein, Carl, 148
Berry, Matthew, 202, 206
Berwanger, Jay, 166
Best American Sports Writing, 1993 (Deford), 34, 36
Bias, Len, 141–44, 149
Biden, Joe, 221
Biederman, Les, 71
Big K.R.I.T., 121
Bigger Thomas (Wright character), 96
Bikila, Abebe, 36
Billings, Andrew, 206, 266n40
Bingo Long Traveling All-Stars and Motor Kings, The (Brashler), 82
Bingo Long Traveling All-Stars and Motor Kings, The (film), 61, 82
Bird, Sue, 179, 220
Bissinger, Buzz, 116, 149
Bjarkman, Peter, 56
Black, Joe, 68, 74
"Black Athlete, The" (Olsen), 17, 129, 132
Black Athletes: Fact and Fiction (NBC Nightly News), 25, 34
Black baseball diaspora
  competing diasporas within, 57
  historical erasure of, 60, 82, 243n120
  memory of, 56, 77–78, 82–84
  See also Latin American baseball leagues
Black baseball leagues
  dissolution of, 64
  historical recovery of, 79–82

Irvin in, 54–55
  memory of, 68, 76–77, 82–83
"Black Boy Looks at the White Boy, The"
  (Baldwin), 99
Black Champion (Farr), 105–6
"Black on Black Crime" (*Ebony*), 107
Black Power movement, 162, 258n13
  Ali as icon of, 97
  backlash to, 113
  Johnson, Jack, as icon of, 106, 248n95
  legacy of, 228n47
Black quarterbacks, 154–55, 170, 258n6
Black/brown color line, 55–57, 59–60, 64.
  See also racialization
Blackmun, Harry, 119–20
Black/nonwhite binary, 60. *See also*
  racialization
Black-on-Black boxing matches
  Ali in, 94–98
  criminal associations with, 94, 101
  embodiments of Blackness contrasted,
    88, 98, 245n27
  giftedness, 90
  in *Rocky III*, 113–14
  white identification with, 104
Black-on-Black crime, 89–90, 101, 107–8,
    114, 244n21
  in sports, 90–91
Blass, Steve, 73
Boas, Franz, 29–33, 41, 233n31, 234n50
Boddy, Kasia, 246n40
Body Issue (*ESPN The Magazine*),
    177–80, 221
Bolt, Usain, 25
Bonnet, Kevin, 204–5
Boras, Scott, 197–98
Borg, Björn, 14–15
Boricua movement, 62
Born to Run (McDougall), 48–52
Bornstein, Steve, 176–77
Boston Marathon, 33, 52–53
Bouchard, Claude, 34
Bourdieu, Pierre, 19, 230n80
Bouton, Jim, 64–65
Boyd, Todd, 270n122
Boyle, Robert, 60–61, 176
Braddock, Jim, 109, 137
Bradley, Bill, 145, 146
Brady, Tom, 221
Bramble, Dennis, 49–50
Branch, Taylor, 118
Brandt, Gil, 170

Brashler, William, 79–82
Bratton, William, 115
Bray, Michael, 265n23
Brecht, Bertolt, 221–22
Brees, Drew, 153–55, 157
Brett, George, 196
Brian's Song, 258n13
Brilliant, Andy, 163
British Association for the Advancement
  of Science (BAAS), 23–25, 232n16
Brock, Lisa, 56, 239n33
Broeg, Bob, 67–68
Brokaw, Tom, 34
Brooklyn Dodgers, 68, 74, 196
  integration of, 1, 56, 64, 83
Brosnan, Jim, 68–70, 73
Brown, Antonio, 183
Brown, Bundini, 106
Brown, "Downtown" Julie, 173
Brown, Jim, 18, 19, 20, 174
Brown, Roscoe, 136
Brown, Wendy, 186, 208
Brown v. Board of Education, 68, 79, 215,
    272n13
Browne, Simone, 168
Bryant, Bear, 128
Bryant, Howard, 12, 228n47
Bryant, Kobe, 176, 258n6
Buchanan, Pat, 134–35
Buck, Jack, 156
Buehler, Branden, 185
Bunning, Jim, 145
Burfoot, Amby, 33–35, 52–53
Burger, Warren, 214
Burgos, Adrian, Jr.
  on Afro-Latino baseball players,
    239n23, 242n103
  on Almonte, 84
  on Cuban Giants, 239n33
  on Latino baseball history, 56, 80
  on MLB draft, 238n13
Burns, Ken, 248n101
Bush, George H. W., 214
Bush, George W., 45, 175
business advice literature, 14, 188, 197
Butler, Judith, 41
  on athletic genders, 8–10
  on Semenya, 44
Buzzelli, Nicholas, 266n40
Byers, Walter, 125, 252n40
  early challenges at NCAA, 123–24
  invention of student-athlete, 124–25

Byers, Walter (cont.)
    resistance to Title IX, 136, 140
    response to revolt of Black athletes,
        128–29, 134
    See also amateur; NCAA (National
    Collegiate Athletic Association);
    student-athlete

Cabinet Committee on Opportunities for
    Spanish-Speaking People, 62
Cameron, James, 156
Campanella, Roy, 74
Campanis, Al, 171–72, 176, 190
Camus, Albert, 17
Cardoso, Bill, 108
Carlos, John, 97
Carnegie Corporation, 136
Carrington, Ben, 5, 24, 26, 93, 232n13
Cayton, Bill, 105
Cayton, Horace, Jr., 87
census, US, 57, 62–63, 72
Census Bureau, 62–63
Cepeda, Orlando, 57, 65, 77–79
*Championship Technique in Track and
    Field* (Cromwell), 28–29, 32
Charles, Ezzard, 94
Charnofsky, Harold, 70–71, 73
Chataway, Chris, 36
Chemweno, Mary, 36
Chicago Police Department, 85–86, 89,
    98, 115
Chicano movement, 62
Christian, Ivory, 122, 124
    in *Friday Night Lights* (Bissinger), 121–22
    at TCU, 116–17, 119, 127, 133, 149
    See also student-athlete
"Chronicle of the Amateur Spirit, The"
    (McKenzie), 123
Chudacoff, Howard, 128
Churro, Victoriano, 49
Chuvalo, George, 97
Civil Rights Act of 1964, 12, 137, 214
Civil Rights Act of 1991, 214
Clark, Caitlin, 220
Clausen, Dick, 129, 253n50
Cleaver, Eldridge, 97
Clemente, Roberto, 59, 75, 83
    as advocate for Latino baseball players,
        72–73
    in Black Pittsburgh, 73–74, 84
    on Black/brown color line, 68
    Brosnan on, 68–69
    diasporic consciousness of, 81
    as gifted, 58–59
    Hall of Fame induction of, 54–55
    Irvin, 55, 60, 83
    Nuun, 74–76
    reracialization of, 56, 59–60, 73
    sportswriters, 71–72
Clemente, Vera Zabala, 54
Clendenon, Donn, 59
Cleveland Cavaliers, 3–4
Clinton, Bill, 21
    at ESPN town meeting, 17–20, 19, 173–75
    at Olympic Games, 1996 (Atlanta), 115
    closed-circuit broadcasting, 109–10,
        249n113
CNN, 158, 161, 164, 176
CNN/SI, 176
Cobb, Ty, 2
Cohan, Noah, 229n61, 269n100
Cohn, Howard, 71–72
Colangelo, Jerry, 172
Cold War, 9, 227n35
College Sports Inc. (Sperber), 121
Collins, Bud, 111
Coltrane, John, 74
Come Out Swinging (Trimbur), 249n106
Conner, James, 183
Connolly, Pat, 7–8
Conseco, Jose, 198
Cook, Earnshaw, 196
Cooky, Cheryl, 43
Cooney, Gerry, 227n37
Coover, Robert, 188–89, 192–93, 195
Cops, 205
Cornelius, William "Sug," 81
Cosell, Howard, 156
Costas, Bob, 156
Costner, Kevin, 171
Cottrell, John, 97, 247n64
Countdown with Keith Olbermann, 158
Court of Arbitration for Sport, 52
Cromwell, Dean, 28–29, 29, 52
Crossfire, 176
Cruz, Joaquim, 7
CTE (chronic traumatic
    encephalopathy), 212
Cuban Giants, 61, 81–82, 239n33,
    243n114
Culley, David, 219
Culpepper, Daunte, 153
cultural studies, 221, 229n65
culture industry, 15, 221
culture wars, 24, 141
Cusma, Elisa, 42

Index

Daboll, Brian, 218
Dallas, 160
Daniel Barbarisi, 205
Daniels, Jack, 36
Dark, Alvin, 66, 77
Darwin's Athletes (Hoberman), 39–40
Dassler, Adolf, 13
Davenport, Najeh
   in Flores lawsuit, 218–19
   in NFL, 215
   NFL concussion settlement, 213, 216, 220, 272n17
Davidson, James Yates, 160
Davies, Nick, 43
Davis, Amira Rose, 137, 228n50
Davis, Miles, 74, 106
Deer Park, The (Mailer), 99
Deford, Frank, 17, 34, 88–89, 158, 176
Dempsey, Jack, 104–5, 109
Dent, Jim, 16
DePodesta, Paul, 199–202
Derrida, Jacques, 3, 11
"Desperate Coach, The" (Underwood), 132
Dillard, Harrison, 29
DiMaggio, Joe, 86
Dinces, Sean, 265n25
Distinction (Bourdieu), 230n80
Dodgeball, 156
Dole, Bob, 21
Donner le temps. See *Given Time* (Derrida)
Dorsey, Phil, 74, 75
Doyle, Jennifer, 155, 273n36
Draft Day, 171
DraftKings, 205–6, 208. See also fantasy sports
Dream Job, 180–81, 180
Driesell, Lefty, 146
Drug Enforcement Administration, 68
Du Bois, W. E. B., 11, 216, 248n101
Duderstadt, James, 120–21, 138, 140
Dueling with Kings (Barbarisi), 205
dumb jock, 119, 127
Dundee, Angelo, 106
Dworkin, Shari, 43

Early, Gerald, 246n43
Eccles, Nigel, 205
Edwards, Harry
   on Ali, 97
   on *Black Athletes: Fact and Fiction* (NBC Nightly News), 34
   on education of Black athletes, 119
   at Koppel ESPN town meeting, 172

   on natural athleticism, 2
   rebuttal to Kane, 33
   revolt of Black athletes, 128
Eig, Jonathan, 98, 247n64
Eight Men Out, 171
Eisenberg, Lee, 190, 191, 192, 195
Eisner, Michael, 176
El Guerrouj, Hicham, 39
Elkins, Evan, 265n21
Ellis, Jimmy, 87
Ellison, Ralph, 40
Elsey, Brenda, 270n124
Entine, Jon, 28, 40–41, 46, 52, 235n75
Entourage, 206
Epstein, David, 37, 45–47, 52, 236n96
Epstein, Theo, 201
Ericsson, Anders, 46, 236n96
Erving, Julius, 162, 165
Esch, Elizabeth, 170
ESPN, 4, 17
   Clinton town meeting, 17–20, 19, 173–75
   culture of, 163–64
   ESPN Classic, 156, 171, 176
   ESPN2, 156, 173, 176, 258n11
   humor, 164–65, 172
   Koppel town meeting, 171–73
   launch of, 159–62, 164, 260n33
   market dominance of, 155–56, 259n17
   middlebrow culture, 171, 176–77
   as modeling commentary, 158–59, 174, 176, 258n11
   as modeling fandom, 156, 163–65, 170–71, 258n6
   NFL draft on, 152–55, 165–71, 257n3
   race talk on, 156–58, 260n35, 262n85
   as racializing organization, 19
   reconciliation of color blindness and multiculturalism, 156–58, 165, 179
   See also Berman, Chris; *Dream Job*; *First Take*; Kiper, Mel; *Pardon the Interruption (PTI)*
ESPN The Magazine, 176–80
Essai sur le don. See *Gift, The* (Mauss)
ethnicity, 233n37
   Latinos as, 57
   white people as, 2, 6–7, 31–32
   See also racialization
Evans, Lee, 128
Evans, Rashad, 90
Ewell, Barney, 29
Ezra, Michael, 247n67

Falla, Jack, 140
Fan, Minghui, 266n40
FanDuel, 205–8. *See also* fantasy sports
Fanon, Frantz, 38
fans, 14–17
　Adorno on, 15
　antifans, 163, 260n35
　disassociation from labor, 187–88, 208–9
　ESPN as model for, 156, 164–65, 170–71
　harassment of athletes, 183–84, 209
　as investors, 14–17, 21, 203, 229n61
　James, C. L. R., on, 15, 22
　as managers, 170–71, 202–3
fantasy sports
　Bell, Le'Veon, 182–83
　daily fantasy sports (DFS), 205–10
　disassociation from labor, 186–87, 208–9, 265n23
　harassment of athletes, 183–84, 209
　humor, 193
　media innovation, 266n40
　neoliberalism, 185–86
　See also Baseball Seminar; DraftKings; FanDuel; Okrent, Dan; Rotisserie League Baseball
Fantasy Sports and Gaming Association, 185, 206
Fantasyland (S. Walker), 189
Fargis, Chris, 205
Farr, Finis, 105–6
Farred, Grant, 95, 228n50
Favre, Brett, 90
Female Masculinity (Halberstam), 51
"Femininity on the Line" (Rohrbaugh), 143
Ferguson, Roderick, 70, 227n35, 253n46
Fiedler, Leslie, 2, 92
Fielder, Prince, 179
Fight, The (Mailer), 102–4
Figueroa-Vásquez, Yomaira, 58
Findeisen, Christopher, 251n20
Finn, Adharanand, 51–52
Fire Joe Morgan, 203–4, 269n100
First Four Minutes (Bannister), 28
First Take, 262n85
Fitzgerald, F. Scott, 92
FiveThirtyEight, 202, 210
Fleder, Rob, 191
Fleetwood, Nicole, 88, 179
Fleisher, Nat, 110
Flores, Brian, 218–20
Ford, Dan, 195
Foreman, George, 87, 102–3, 108

Foster, George, 191, 193
Frankfurt school, 15
Frazier, E. Franklin, 87
Frazier, Joe, 87, 160
FreeDarko, 203, 269n100
Freeman, Michael, 162
Fresh Prince of Bel-Air, The, 20
Frick, Ford, 65–66
Friday, William, 144
Friday Night Lights (Bissinger), 116–17, 149
Friday Night Lights (film), 121
Friday Night Lights (TV show), 149
Friend, Bob, 74
Front Office Fantasies (Buehler), 185
Furness, Steve, 217
Futterman, Matthew, 14, 259n17

Gal, Sandra, 178
Gamson, Bill, 189–90, 195
García, Silvio, 83
Garner, Jennifer, 171
Garnett, Kevin, 270n122
Gehrig, Lou, 86
Gelati, Tommy, 207–8
genetics, 27, 34, 37, 40
　biocultural approach, 25, 38, 234n64
　Entine on, 40–41
　Epstein, David, on, 45–47
　Human Genome Project, 232n16
　"slave genes" theory, 25, 33
　See also Gladwell, Malcolm: on genetics; Marks, Jonathan; Kidd, Kenneth; *Sports Gene, The* (Epstein); *Taboo* (Entine)
Gethers, Peter, 193, 204
GI Bill, 127
gift
　of Black people, 11, 216
　Derrida on, 3, 11
　education of athletes as, 119, 122, 128–29, 175
　of freedom, 12, 90, 215, 245n22
　Graeber on, 11
　labor as, 10–11, 22
　Mauss on, 10–11, 215, 272n15
Gift, The (Mauss), 10–11, 216
Gift of Black Folk, The (Du Bois), 11, 216
giftedness
　affirmative action, 120, 134, 150, 175
　of Ali, 115
　of Black boxers, 89–90
　of Black quarterbacks, 155

as capital excess, 10, 15, 94
after civil rights, 5–6, 12, 216
of Clemente, Roberto, 58–59
Clinton on, 20
debt of, 3–4, 11–12, 215–16
  Bias, 143
  as communal burden, 6, 12–13
  conversion between racial and gender,
    27–28, 221
  to fans, 158
  to general manager, 200–1
  Jones, Marion, 45
  Latino athletes, 59, 65
  Edwards on, 33
as gender excess, 10, 27–28, 142, 220–21
  Black women athletes, 45
  Griffith Joyner, 8
  Semenya, 43–44
  Vick, 155
of Indigenous in relation to Black
  athletes, 38, 49
labor, 246n46
of Latino in relation to Black athletes, 65
as mechanism of racialization, 3, 5, 7,
  185–86, 225n8
in *Moneyball* (M. Lewis), 187–88, 200–1
in NFL concussion settlement, 216
reconciliation of color blindness and
  multiculturalism, 156–58
regulation of, 45, 47, 84, 144, 232n21
science of, 25
sports analytics as measuring, 198
sports commentary, 155–58, 165, 168,
  260n35
of student-athletes, 126–28, 131–32, 150
transformation into grit, 9–10, 114
of Vick, 153–54
of white athletes, 6–7
See also grit; racialization
Gilbert, Dan (Cleveland Cavaliers owner),
  3–4, 6
Gilbert, Daniel (historian), 251n20
Gilmore, Ruth Wilson, 4
Gilroy, Paul, 234n50
Giuliani, Rudy, 115
Given Time (Derrida), 11
Gladwell, Malcolm, 14, 52
  10,000 hours rule, 46, 236n96
  on genetics, 26–27, 39–40
  on performance-enhancing drugs, 47–48
  on racial in relation to gender binary, 40
Goldberg, David Theo, 157, 258n11
Goldfinger, 110

Goldsberry, Kirk, 210
Gómez, Laura, 57, 62
Goodell, Roger, 10, 212–13, 216, 220
Gorn, Elliott, 87
Gorsuch, Neil, 144, 150
Gottfredson, Linda, 214
Gould, Stephen Jay, 41
Graeber, David, 11
Graf, Steffi, 9
Gramsci, Antonio, 95, 186
Grande, George, 164, 166
Grant, Mudcat, 239n23
Gray, Jonathan, 162–63
Great Latin Sports Figures
  (Izenberg), 80
Great Migration, 6
Great Negro Stars and How
  They Made the Majors Leagues
  (Doc Young), 78–79
great white hope
  Ali as, 98
  Balboa as, 113–14
  Black boxers as, 101
  Cooney as, 227n37
  cultural return of, 105–7, 109,
    111–12
  disappearance of, 87–89, 115
  as dope, 91–92
  invention of, 93
  as kitsch, 114
  Louis against, 87
  Marciano as, 111
Great White Hope, The (film), 107,
  249n103
Great White Hope, The (Sackler), 105–7,
  113
Greatest, The (Ali), 98
"Greatest Fights of the Century, The"
  (*Esquire*), 104–5
Green, Tim, 167
Greenlee, Gus, 74
Greer, Christina, 63
Griffey, Ken, Jr., 20–22, 46
Griffey, Ken, Sr., 21, 46
Griffin, Robert, III, 154–55
Griffith Joyner, Florence, 17, 228n47
  after civil rights, 12
  commercial success of, 12–13
  Navratilova compared to, 9–10
  at Olympic Games, 1988 (Seoul), 8, 12
  at US Olympic Track and Field Trials,
    1988, 7–8
Griggs v. Duke Power, 214, 217

Griner, Brittney, 221–22
grit
  of Bannister, 25
  of Brees, 154–55
  as class status, 51
  as earned advantage, 28
  as gender norm, 155
  giftedness in relation to, 3, 9–10, 114, 216
  sports commentary, 165
  of white athletes, 65, 130
  See also giftedness; racialization
Groom, Dale, 50
Gross, Terry, 174
Guinzburg, Tom, 190, 192
Gumbel, Greg, 163
Guridy, Frank Andre, 60, 84, 238n13, 243n120, 253n62

Haas, Walter, 199
Haddaway, 185
Halberstam, Jack, 10, 51
Haley, Alex, 96
Hall, Mike, 180–81, *180*
Hall, Stuart, 131–32, 229n65
Hall, Uriah, 185
Hamilton, Tod, 63
Hamilton, Tyler, 47
Hanford, George, 136, 138, 254n77
Hano, Arnold, 72
Harris, Charles "Teenie," 59
Harrison, Marvin, 168
Hartman, Saidiya, 12, 245n22
Hartmann, Douglas, 5, 131, 145, 230n81
Harvard Business School, 17
Hauser, Thomas, 98, 247n64
HBCUs (historically Black colleges and universities)
  football games on ESPN, 162
  Koppel ESPN town meeting, 172
  response to NCAA academic reforms, 138–39
  Title IX at, 137
HBO, 160
"He Does It by the Numbers" (Okrent), 196
Heaton, Robert, 214–15
Heaton norms. *See* race norming
Heaven Is a Playground (Telander), 148
Heinz, W. C., 88
Hemingway, Ernest, 92
Henne, Kathryn, 44, 232n21
Henry, Charles, 130–31

Henry, Kevin
  in Flores lawsuit, 218–19
  in NFL, 215–18
  NFL concussion settlement, 213, 216, 220, 272n17
Henry, Taylor, 262n85
Herrnstein, Richard, 214
Herskovits, Melville, 29
Hesburgh, Theodore, 144
Higher Education Act of 1965, 128
Hill, Jonah, 202
Historical Baseball Abstract, The (B. James), 197
History of Colored Base Ball (S. White), 81
Hobbs, Roy (Malamud character), 1–3, 6–7, 65
Hoberman, John, 39–40
Holm, Stefan, 46–47
Holmes, Larry, 87, 227n37
Holway, John, 79, 81
"Hometown Hero" (Big K.R.I.T.), 121
Horkheimer, Max, 15–16, 229n65
HoSang, Daniel Martinez, 132, 225n8, 260n35
House Un-American Activities Committee, 88
Hoxworth, Kellen, 185
Hughes, Kit, 265n21
Human Genome Project, 34, 232n16
Hundred Yard Lie, The (Telander), 148
Hunter, David, 41
Hurston, Zora Neale, 29
Hurts, Jalen, 154

IAAF (International Association of Athletics Federations), 52
  as racializing organization, 19
  sex-verification testing of, 27, 41–44, 48, 52
IMG (International Management Group), 13, 16–17
Immigration Act of 1924, 6
Immigration and Nationality Act of 1965
  Black immigrants, 63
  Black/brown color line, 82
  as gift, 59
  Latinos as ethnicity, 57
  racialization of language, 72
  reracialization of Afro-Latinos, 83

Index

In and Out of the Ring (Jack Johnson), 105
"In Search of an Explanation" (Manners), 37
Indigenous athletes, 2
   Black athletes in relation to, 38, 48–49
   See also Kalenjin people (East Africa); Tarahumara people (northern Mexico)
International Olympic Committee (IOC), 24, 43–44, 52
Invisible Men (Rogosin), 80
Ionescu, Sabrina, 220
Irvin, Monte, 83
   Clemente, Roberto, 55, 60
   diasporic consciousness of, 84
   Hall of Fame induction of, 54–55
   integration of MLB, 56
Iverson, Allen, 270n122
Ivy League, 127
Izenberg, Jerry, 79

Jack Johnson (M. Davis), 106
Jackson, Bo, 173
Jackson, Jesse, 89, 141
Jackson, Lamar, 154
Jackson, Quinton "Rampage," 90
Jackson, Reggie, 194
Jackson, Sheep, 76–78
Jackson, "Shoeless" Joe, 2, 6
Jackson, Victoria, 119
Jacobs, Brandon, 183–84, 186
Jacobs, Jim, 105–6
Jacobson, Matthew Frye, 114, 233n37
Jade, Olivia, 150
James, Bill, 201, 206, 267n70
   Baseball Abstract, 194–96
   with Boston Red Sox, 197, 201
   color blindness of, 196–97, 202–3
   influence on fan blogs, 203
   influence on Oakland Athletics, 198–99
   on labor, 187, 197–98
   See also sports analytics
James, C. L. R.
   on American fans, 15, 22
   on Black/brown color line, 55–56
   diasporic consciousness of, 81, 84
James, LeBron, 3–4, 6, 174
Jaworski, Ron, 153
Jeffries, Jim, 101
   in *All-Time Heavyweight Tournament* (radio program), 109–10
   as great white hope, 91, 227n37
   in *Great White Hope, The* (Sackler), 107
   as white dope, 92–93

Jepkosgei, Janeth, 41
JMX, 185
jock caucus, 145–46
Johansson, Ingemar, 87, 92, 94
Johnson, Brooks, 34, 234n52
Johnson, Jack, 91, 108
   cultural renaissance of, 105–7, 248n95
   in fight films, 107, 249n102
   great white hope, 91, 227n37
   Louis contrasted with, 87–88, 91
Johnson, John H., 89
Johnson, Keyshawn, 19, 168–69, 174
Johnson, Lyndon, 134
Johnson, Randy, 21
Johnson, Victoria, 157, 259n15
Jones, C. J., 221
Jones, James Earl, 82, 105–7, 113
Jones, Jonquel, 220–21
Jones, Marion, 44–45
Jordan, Michael, 13, 15, 172, 174
Jordan-Young, Rebecca, 45
Joyner, Al, 17
Joyner-Kersee, Jackie, 18
Jurek, Scott, 50–51

Kaepernick, Colin, 154
Kahn, Roger, 83
Kalenjin people (East Africa), 2, 36–37
Kane, Martin, 32–33, 233n45
Kang, Jay Caspian, 207
Karkazis, Katrina, 45
Kaye, Andrew, 87
Kearns, Doc, 105
Keeping Faith with the Student-Athlete (Knight Commission on Intercollegiate Athletics), 144
Keino, Kipchoge "Kip," 36
Kelly, George, 54
Kemp, Jack, 145
Kempton, Murray, 95
Ken Griffey Jr. Presents Major League Baseball (Super Nintendo game), 21
Ken Griffey Jr.'s Winning Run (Super Nintendo game), 21
Kennedy, Kostya, 24
Kerouac, Jack, 99
Kidd, Kenneth, 26, 40
Kim, Claire Jean, 60, 73
King, Billie Jean, 137
King, Don, 16, 90, 114
King, Martin Luther, Jr., 97, 118
King, Peter, 38
King of the World, The (Remnick), 247n64

Kiper, Mel
  career of, 168–69
  at NFL draft, 153, 155–57, 169
  See also ESPN
Kissane, Rebecca, 192
Klein, Alan, 240n42
Knight, James, 144
Knight, John, 144
Knight Commission on Intercollegiate
  Athletics, 144–45, 148–49
Knight Foundation, 144, 147, 149
Knute Rockne, All American, 258n13
Koppel, Ted, 171–73
Kornheiser, Tony, 175–76
Koufax, Sandy, 67

labor
  of Black women athletes, 228n50
  Black/brown color line, 63–64
  boxing as, 246n46
  concussions, 273n32
  fans as managers of, 170–71, 202–3
  fantasy sports as disassociation from,
    186–87, 192–93, 207–9, 265n23
  as gift, 10–11, 22
  integration of MLB, 64, 75, 240n42
  James, Bill, on, 197–98
  of Latin American baseball players, 72
  in Moneyball (M. Lewis), 200–1
  sports as model for valuation of, 220
  of student-athletes, 118–19, 130, 135, 137
  under neoliberalism, 185–87
Laguerre, André, 17, 88–89, 129, 132
Lardner, John, 91–94, 103
Lardner, Ring, 2, 69, 91–92
Latin American baseball leagues
  in Black baseball circuit, 60, 68, 76
  in Black baseball history, 80–81
  Irvin in, 54–55
  recruitment from, 56, 64, 72
  See also Black baseball diaspora
Laughlin, Lori, 150
Lawrence, Brooks, 69
Leach, James, 204
LeBow, Guy, 110
Leonard, David, 254n70, 259n15
Leonard, Lee, 159, 161, 164
Letterman, David, 171
level playing field, 3, 27–28, 47–48,
    144, 231n8
Lewinsky, Monica, 18, 174
Lewis, Carl, 34, 35

Lewis, Michael, 200
  antirelational fandom, 187–88
  business advice literature, 14, 188, 197
  influence on fan blogs, 203
  influence on sports industry, 210
  influence outside sports, 210–11
  Moneyball, 171, 199–201
  See also sports analytics
Ley, Bob, 17–18, 166–67, 174–75
Lieberman, Daniel, 49–50
Liebling, A. J., 88, 91–94, 103, 245n39
Life of Captain Cipriani, The (C. L. R.
  James), 55
Limbaugh, Rush, 161, 174
Lindros, Eric, 176
Liston, Sonny, 115
  against Ali, 95–96, 104, 109–10
  in All-Time Heavyweight Tournament
    (radio program), 110
  Black heavyweight champions, 87
  in "Greatest Fights of the Century, The"
    (Esquire), 104–5
  in Patterson–Liston I, 88, 98–102, 100, 104
  See also Black-on-Black
  boxing matches
Little, Kevin, 39
Little Big League, 20
Little League World Series, 84
Logan, Doug, 45
Lombardi, Vince, 32
London, Jack, 91–92
long downturn, 187, 192–93, 209, 211,
    267n50
Long Season, The (Brosnan),
    69–70
Lott, Eric, 248n85
Louis, Joe, 86, 98, 137, 246n43
  in All-Time Heavyweight Tournament
    (radio program), 109
  Baldwin on, 88
  as Black hero, 85–87
  in "Greatest Fights of the Century, The"
    (Esquire), 104
  patriotism of, 95
  waning racial significance of, 94
  against white dopes, 91–92
  against white opponents, 87, 94,
    227n37, 244n9
Lowe, Lisa, 4, 239n27
Lowndes, Joseph, 132, 225n8, 260n35
LPGA (Ladies Professional Golf
  Association) Tour, 178

Luce, Henry, 17
Luther, Jessica, 269n100

MacAloon, John, 26
Maddow, Rachel, 174
Magubane, Zine, 236n90
Maher, Charles, 32
Mahomes, Patrick, 154
Mailer, Norman, 103, 105
  as Ali fan, 102–4, 108–9, 248n85
  at Patterson-Liston I, 88–89, 98–101
Maiyoro, Nyandika, 36
Major League Baseball Featuring Ken Griffey Jr. (Nintendo 64 game), 21
Making Hispanics (Mora), 58
Malamud, Bernard, 1–2, 6–7
Malina, Robert, 25, 34, 38
Malloy, Jerry, 243n114
Mann, Thomas, 15
Mann Act, 91
Manners, John, 36–37
Manners, Robert, 37
Mäntyranta, Eero, 47
Maple, Jack, 115
Marciano, Rocky, 87, 94
  in *All-Time Heavyweight Tournament* (radio program), 109
  in "Greatest Fights of the Century, The" (*Esquire*), 104–5
  in *Super Fight, The*, 110–12, 112
Marichal, Juan
  fight with Roseboro, 57, 66–68, 67, 76, 79
  integration of MLB, 56
Maris, Roger, 194
Marks, Jonathan, 41, 232n16, 234n64. *See also* genetics
Martínez, Conchita, 9
Martinez, Edgar, 21
Martínez-Patiño, Maria, 43, 46
M*A*S*H, 160
Masked Singer, The, 185
Mauss, Marcel, 10–11, 215–16, 272n15
Mays, Willie, 56, 67, 71, 77–78
Mazeroski, Bill, 73
MC Hammer, 173
McCall, Bruce, 191
McCallum, Jack, 24, 176
McClanahan, Annie, 186–87, 203
McClearen, Jennifer, 178
McCormack, Mark, 13–17, 21, 229n61.
  See also sports management
McDonald, Ian, 26

McDougall, Christopher, 48–52
McGuire, John, 260n33
McGwire, Mark, 198
McKenzie, R. Tait, 123
McMillen, Tom, 145–47, 146
McNabb, Donovan, 90, 153
Mead, Margaret, 29
Meadows, Jenny, 41
Melamed, Jodi, 187, 225n8
Melville, Herman, 92
Mendoza, Jessica, 177
Meredith, Burgess, 113
Meyer, Dutch, 133
Mfume, Kweisi, 163
Michener, James, 128, 176
middlebrow magazine, 245n39
  Ali, 98
  boxing in, 104
  ESPN The Magazine as, 177
  prestige of sportswriting, 92, 101
  Sports Illustrated as, 17, 88
  See also sportswriting
Miles, Boobie, 121, 139
Miličić, Darko, 203
Miller, James Andrew, 163–64
Miller, Marvin, 193
Mingus, Charles, 74
Miñoso, Minnie, 56, 78–79
Mirpuri, Anoop, 258n6
Mismeasure of Minds, The (Staub), 215
MLB (Major League Baseball), 21
  Black/brown color line, 68, 75
  Black/nonwhite binary, 60
  free agency, 192
  integration of, 54, 56–57
  as racializing organization, 19, 58, 64, 82, 84
  as white democracy, 75
MLB draft, 238n13
Molina, Natalia, 225n8, 240n48
Monday Night Football, 258n13
Moneyball (film), 171, 199, 202
Moneyball (M. Lewis), 171, 199–201
  antirelational fandom, 187–88
  as business advice literature, 188
  commercial success of, 202
  influence on fan blogs, 203
  influence on sports industry, 210
  influence outside sports, 210–11
  See also sports analytics
Moneymaker, Chris, 204
Moon, Wally, 56

Moore, Archie, 108, 249n106
Moore, Kenny, 37–38
Moore, Louis, 244n9
Mora, G. Cristina, 58, 62
Morceli, Noureddine, 23
Moreton-Robinson, Aileen, 38
Morgan, Joe, 203
Morrison, Toni, 98
Mortensen, Chris, 152–53, 155–57
Mosier, Chris, 179
Moyer, Valerie, 232n19
Mr. T, 113
Muhammad, Khalil Gibran, 94
Murakawa, Naomi, 101
Murray, Charles, 41, 214
Murray, Jim, 95, 110
Murray, Kyler, 154
My Side of Things (L. Bell), 184
Myrdal, Gunnar, 79
Myth of the Amateur, The (Ronald Smith), 118

NAACP (National Association for the Advancement of Colored People), 96, 163
Naked and the Dead, The (Mailer), 99
Nation of Islam (NOI), 95, 97, 247n67
National Academy of Sciences, 214
National Pastime (tabletop game), 189
Native Son (Wright), 85
Natural, The (film), 2, 171
Natural, The (Malamud), 1–2, 6–7
natural athleticism. *See* giftedness
Navratilova, Martina, 8–10
NBA (National Basketball Association), 3–4, 172–73, 258n6
NBA draft, 141
NCAA (Falla), 140
NCAA (National Collegiate Athletic Association), 119
academic reforms of, 138–40, 148–49
under Byers, 123–25, 125
formation of, 122–23
home rule, 123
invention of student-athlete, 117–18, 124–27, 252n35
Knight Commission on Intercollegiate Athletics, 145
NIL (name, image, likeness), 151
resistance to Title IX, 136, 140
response to revolt of Black athletes, 128–31, 133–34

sanity code, 123
use of crisis, 138–39, 141, 253n46
women's sports, 140–41, 147, 255n84
See also amateur; Byers, Walter; student-athlete
NCR 315 computer, 109–11
Negro Firsts in Sports (Doc Young), 78–79
Nelson, Bert, 32
neoliberalism, 14, 178, 185–87, 208, 230n81
New Democrats, 144
New York Police Department (NYPD), 115
New York Yankees, 20, 64, 68–69, 187
Newark Eagles, 54, 82–84. *See also* Black baseball leagues
Newfield, Christopher, 121, 139, 256n116
Newfield, Jack, 90
Newton, Cam, 154
NFL (National Football League), 10
concussion settlement, 212–14, 216
Flores lawsuit, 218–20
Henry, Kevin, in, 217–18
market dominance of, 222
as racializing organization, 19
scouting combine, 167–68, 216–17
NFL draft, 169
Draft Day, 171
on ESPN, 152–55, 165–71, 257n3
introduction of, 165–66
Vick at, 154, 157
Nguyen, Mimi Thi, 12, 215, 245n22
Nicklaus, Jack, 13–14
Nike, 172, 221
NIL (name, image, likeness), 151
Nixon, Richard, 68, 134
Norton, Ken, 87
Nover, Sam, 68
Numbers Game, The (Schwarz), 196
Nuun, Bill, Jr., 74–76

Oakland Athletics, 187, 198–201, 200
Oates, Thomas, 157, 262n85
Obama, Barack, 175, 262n85
O'Brien, Davey, 122
Okrent, Dan, 198, 204, 206
on daily fantasy sports, 208
on James, Bill, 194–96
Rotisserie League Baseball, 190–94, *191*, 204
See also fantasy sports
Olbermann, Keith, 158–59, 173
Old College Try, The (Thelin and Wiseman), 251n20

Index

Olsen, Jack, 17, 129–30, 132, 135
Olympic Games, 1936 (Berlin), 13, 26, 28
Olympic Games, 1960 (Rome), 36, 87, 233n45
Olympic Games, 1964 (Innsbruck, Austria), 47
Olympic Games, 1968 (Mexico City), 5, 36–37, 43, 97
Olympic Games, 1988 (Seoul), 8, 12
Olympic Games, 1996 (Atlana), 115
Olympic Games, 2000 (Sydney), 43
Olympic Games, 2012 (London), 25, 42
Olympic Project for Human Rights, 97, 128
O'Malley, Walter, 83
Omi, Michael, 4
One America Initiative (Clinton), 174
O'Neil, Cathy, 202
Only the Ball Was White (R. Peterson), 79, 81
Operation Breadbasket (Southern Christian Leadership Conference), 89
O'Reilly, Bill, 174
O'Reilly Factor, The, 159
Oriard, Michael, 128
Ostler, Scott, 234n52
"Other Kenyans, The" (Villarosa), 35–36
Out of Bounds (McMillen), 146
Outside the Lines, 174
Owens, Jesse, 13, 28
Owens, Terrell, 90

Pagán, José, 66
Page, Don, 109
Palmer, Arnold, 13–14
Paper Lion (Plimpton), 108
Pardon the Interruption (PTI), 175–76, 262n85
Park, Robert E., 40
Parlor Base-Ball Field (tabletop game), 189, 266n32
Pasquel, Jorge, 80
passing
 as Cuban, 61, 81–82, 243n114
 as Indigenous, 82
Patrick, Dan, 158
Patterson, Floyd, 100
 against Ali, 96–97, 247n64
 Black heavyweight champions, 87
 Liebling on, 92, 94
 in Patterson–Liston I, 88, 98–102, 104
 Patterson–Liston I, 88, 95, 99–101, *100*. *See also* Black-on-Black boxing matches
Patton, Mel, 29

Paul, Jake, 185
Paul, Rich, 14
Pele, 13
Pennant Race (Brosnan), 70
Percentage Baseball (Cook), 196
Pérez, Louis, 62
performance-enhancing drugs, 8, 39, 44–45, 47, 84
Perkins, Maxwell, 92
Permian High School football team, 116–17, 121, 122, 139
Peters, Brock, 105
Peterson, Adrian, 185
Peterson, Robert, 79–81
PGA (Professional Golf Association) Tour, 13, 16
Philip Deloria, 51
Pitt, Brad, 199
Pittsburgh Courier, 74–78
Pittsburgh Crawfords, 74
Pittsburgh Pirates, 56, 59, 68, 73
Pittsburgh Steelers, 74, 218, 265n25
 Bell, Le'Veon, contract dispute, 182–83, 185–86
 Henry, Kevin, 213, 217
Player, Gary, 14
Plimpton, George, 103, 108–9, 249n106
Pompez, Alex, 61, 64, 239n33
Poussaint, Alvin, 89
Povich, Shirley, 110
Powell, Lewis, 120, 143–44
Power, Vic, 64, 79
Power Forward, 269n100
Prescott, Dak, 154–55
President's Council on Physical Fitness, 17
Price, S. L., 39
Pride of the Yankees, 258n13
Proehl, Ricky, 38
Pryor, Richard, 82
Public Burning, The (Coover), 188

Quarry, Jerry, 106
Quimare Gutiérrez, Arnulfo, 50, 51

"Race and Sports" (*USA Today*), 25, 38
race norming, 213–16, 218, 272n13, 272n17
Race: Science and Politics (Benedict), 30
Races of Mankind, The (Benedict and Weltfish), 30–31
Racial Formation in the United States (Omi and Winant), 4

racial state, 4, 18–19, 230n81
racialization, 58
  of Afro-Latinos, 59–60, 69, 82–84, 239n27
  athletic, 3–5, 10, 84
  census as mechanism of, 62–63
  crime, 101
  of fantasy sports, 185–86
  gendered, 9–10, 40, 132, 227n35
    as excess of athleticism, 26–28, 45, 142–43, 155, 220–21
    racial in relation to gender binary, 35
    testosterone, 45, 273n35
  ideological, 9–10, 227n35
  of language, 58–59, 65, 72
  in NFL concussion settlement, 216, 219–20
  of student-athletes, 119, 129, 131–32, 135, 151
  surveillance as, 168
  See also Black/brown color line; Black/nonwhite binary; ethnicity; giftedness; grit
racializing organizations, 4–5, 18–19, 58, 64, 254n75
Rankine, Claudia, 179
Rapinoe, Megan, 179
Rashad, Ahmad, 2
Rasmussen, Bill, 158–62, 161, 164–65
Ray, Victor, 18–19, 254n75
Reagan, Nancy, 141
Reagan, Ronald, 114
Redford, Robert, 2
Reed, Ishmael, 98, 104
Regalado, Samuel, 238n18
Regents of the University of California v. Bakke, 119–20, 143–44. *See also* affirmative action
Reid, Jason, 155
Remnick, David, 98, 106, 247n64
Renfroe, Othello, 80
revolt of Black athletes, 128, 130, 133–34
  inspiration for wider rebellion, 131–32, 135–36
Revolt of the Black Athlete, The (Edwards), 128
Rhoden, William, 209
Rice, Grantland, 148
Richardson, Spec, 65
Richman, Hal, 189
Rickey, Branch, 64, 78, 83, 196
Rielly, Edward, 266n32

Riger, Roger, 105
Riggs, Bobby, 137
Rise of The Black Quarterback, The (Reid), 155
Roberts, Randy, 86
Robeson, Paul, 88, 228n47
Robinhood, 207
Robinson, Frank, 56
Robinson, Jackie, 68, 74
  as gifted, 65
  as inspiration for *The Natural* (Malamud), 1–2
  integration of Major League Baseball, 56, 61, 64, 77–78
  Koppel ESPN town meeting, 171–72
  as legend, 78–79
  Robeson contrasted with, 88
Rock, Chris, 83
Rocky, 112–13
Rocky II, 113
Rocky III, 113–14
Rocky Balboa, 113
Rocky Super Action Boxing (ColecoVision game), 114
Rodriguez, Alex, 21, 176, 197
Roediger, David, 170, 233n37
Roenigk, Alyssa, 178–79
Roethlisberger, Ben, 183
Rogers, Don, 142–43
Rogosin, Donn, 79–80
Rohrbaugh, Joanna Bunker, 142–43
Rome, Jim, 157, 258n11
Rooney Rule (NFL), 218–19
Roots, 258n13
Roseboro, John, 57, 66–68, 67, 76, 79
Ross, Karie, 163–64
Rotella, Carlo, 227n37, 245n39, 246n46
Rotisserie League Baseball, 190–94, 191, 204, 266n40. *See also* fantasy sports
Rozelle, Pete, 152–53, 166
Ruck, Rob, 240n42
Ruihley, Brody, 206
Rumble in the Jungle (Ali–Foreman), 102–4, 108. *See also* Black-on-Black boxing matches
Running with the Kenyans (Finn), 52
Runstedtler, Theresa, 106, 142–43
Rupp, Adolph, 124
Russo, Chris "Mad Dog," 157
Ruth, Babe, 86, 194
Rutter, Emily Ruth, 243n120
Ryun, Jim, 36

Index

sabermetrics. *See* sports analytics
Sack, Allen, 250n6
Sackler, Howard, 105
Safir, Howard, 115
Salembier, Valerie, 190–92
Sammons, Jeffrey, 91
Sanders, Miles, 121
Sarris, Andrew, 113
Satcom 1 (RCA satellite), 159, 164
Savinova, Mariya, 42
Savold, Lee, 92–94
Schmeling, Max, 109, 227n37
Schmidt, Mike, 192
Schneiderman, Eric, 206, 208
Schultz, Joe, 65
Schultz, Richard, 145
Schwarz, Alan, 196
Scott, Daryl Michael, 215
Scott, Jack, 126, 135, 141, 251n20
Seattle Mariners, 20–21
Sebring, Francis, 266n32
Sehorn, Jason, 174
Seitz, Richard, 189
Selassie, Haile, 87
Semenya, Caster, 41–43, 42, 52–53, 236n90
Sexton, Jared, 239n24
sex-verification testing, 42–44, 232n19, 232n21
Shadow Box (Plimpton), 108
Shales, Tom, 163–64
Shanklin, Donnie, 130
Shapiro, Mark, 176
Sheffield, Gary, 57, 84
Sheppard, Samantha, 249n103
Sherman, Richard, 184
Silly Little Game, 194
Silver, Nate, 202, 210
Simmons, Chet, 152–53, 166–67
Simms, Billy, 166
Simpson, O. J., 13
Simpsons, The, 20, 202
Singh, Nikhil Pal, 4, 245n27
Sinister First Baseman and Other Observations, The (E. Walker), 198
Sirma, Susan, 36
Sklar, Bob, *191*
Smith, Cork, *191*
Smith, Ozzie, 196
Smith, Red, 88, 96
Smith, Ronald, 118, 252n28, 252n35
Smith, Stephen A., 206–7, 209, 262n85

Smith, Tommie, 97, 128
SMU (Southern Methodist University) football team, 116, 144, 149
Society for American Baseball Research, 196
Sorkin, Aaron, 171
Sotomayor, Sonia, 150
Soul on Ice (Cleaver), 97
Souls of Black Folk, The (Du Bois), 216
Sound of Music, The, 110
South Park, 205
Southern Christian Leadership Conference, 89
Spahn, Warren, 54
Sperber, Murray, 121
Spinks, Leon, 87, 104
sports analytics
  as antilabor, 200–3
  on fan blogs, 203
  Ivy League graduates, 199, 201–2
  James, Bill, 196–98
  in *Moneyball* (M. Lewis), 187–88, 198–201, 210–11
  NFL running backs, 183
  of Oakland Athletics, 198–201
  praise for, 202
  Sports Gene, The (D. Epstein), 37, 45–47. *See also* genetics
  Sports Illustrated, 17, 24, 88–89, 176. *See also* sportswriting
sports intellectuals, 69–70, 93–94, 114
sports management, 17, 170–71, 185, 201. *See also* McCormack, Mark
sports norming, 216, 221
SportsCenter, 164, 166
SportsNight (ESPN2), 173
sportswriting, 71–72, 88–89
  investigative, 147–48
  prestige of, 17, 92–93, 245–46n39, 246n40
  See also *Sports Illustrated*
St. Clair Drake, 87
St. Louis, Brett, 26
Stallone, Sylvester, 112–14
Stargell, Willie, 59, 73
Staub, Michael, 215, 272n13
Staurowsky, Ellen, 250n6
Stewart, Jonathan, 209
Stewart, Kordell, 176
Stinson, Wade, 133–34
Story of Negro League Baseball, The (Brashler), 80–81
Strat-O-Matic, 189–90, 194–95, 207, 211

student-athlete
  affirmative action, 134, 144, 149–51, 251n116, 256n116
  amateur contrasted with, 121, 126, 133, 139
  as class status, 127
  as gift recipient, 119, 122
  NCAA invention of, 117–18, 124–27
  reracialization of, 129, 131–32, 134–35
  as subsidizing amateur, 118–19, 135
  as white, 126–27, 129, 135
  See also amateur; Christian, Ivory; NCAA (National Collegiate Athletic Association)
Students for Fair Admissions v. Harvard, 120, 144, 150. *See also* affirmative action
Sullivan, John L., 109
Super Fight, The, 110–13, 112
Swank, David, 130–31, 140
Sweet Science, The (Liebling), 92
Swimsuit Issue (*Sports Illustrated*), 88, 177, 180

Taboo (Entine), 40–41, 46, 235n75. *See also* genetics
Tagliabue, Paul, 153
talent. *See* giftedness
Talk2, 258n11
Tanner, James, 233n45
Tarahumara people (northern Mexico), 2, 48–51
"Target" (L. Bell), 185
Taurasi, Diana, 220
TCU (Texas Christian University), 121–22, 124, 133
  Christian at, 116–17, 119, 121–22, 127, 149
  teaching *Friday Night Lights* (Bissinger) at, 149–51
Telander, Rick, 148–49
Tempels, Placide, 102
Terrell, Ernie, 87
Teslow, Tracy, 233n31
Tewanima, Lewis, 2
"That Was Pugilism" (J. Lardner), 91
Theismann, Joe, 152–53, 155–57
Thelin, John, 127, 251n20, 253n49
Thomas, Donald, 46–47
Thompson, Hunter S., 108
Thompson, John, 18, 20, 139–40, 174–75
Thomson, Rose, 36

Thorpe, Jim, 2
Those Guys Have All the Fun (J. Miller and Shales), 163
Thrilla in Manila (Ali–Frazier III), 160
Tirico, Mike, 153, 156
Title IX, 12, 128, 147
  Civil Rights Act of 1964 as model for, 137
  at HBCUs (historically Black colleges and universities), 137
  NCAA resistance to, 136–37, 140
To Kill a Mockingbird (film), 105
Tomlin, Mike, 218
trans athletes, 179–80
  barring of, 9, 27, 221, 273n36
Travers, 273n36
Trimbur, Lucia, 228n50, 249n106, 273n32
Troutman Robbins, Stephanie, 259n15
True, Micah, 51
Trujillo, Rafael, 66
Turner, Ted, 164, 176
Tygiel, Jules, 79, 192–93, 242n103

Udall, Mo, 145–46
UFC (Ultimate Fighting Championship), 90, 178–79
Underwood, John, 132–33, 135, 145
United Auto Workers, 30
Universal Baseball Association, Inc., J. Henry Waugh, Prop., The (Coover), 188–89, 211
University of Alabama football team, 96
University of Maryland (UMD), 141, 146
University of Washington (UW), 118, 130
Univision, 62
Unlawful Internet Gambling Enforcement Act (UIGEA), 204–6
Unmaking the Public University (C. Newfield), 121
Unrelated Business Income Tax, 124
Unsportsmanlike Conduct (Byers), 125
US Olympic Track and Field Trials, 1988, 7–8
USA Track and Field (USATF), 45

Vaccaro, Sonny, 172–73
Valenzuela, Fernando, 56
Varsity Blues scandal, 150, 257n133
Versalles, Zoilo, 77
Vick, Michael, 153–57, 154, 181
Villarosa, Linda, 35–36
Viva Baseball! (Regalado), 238n18
Vogan, Travis, 157, 177, 249n113, 258n13

Vora, Kalindi, 203
Voting Rights Act of 1965, 12

Waggoner, Glen, 191, 193, 204
Walcott, Joe, 94
Walker, Eric, 198–99
Walker, Sam, 189
war on crime, 90, 101, 107, 114, 228n37, 244n21
war on drugs, 9, 90, 101, 107, 114, 143
Ward, Geoffrey, 248n101
Watson, Deshaun, 154, 170
Watterson, John, 139, 141, 251n16
Weapons of Math Destruction (O'Neil), 202
Weathers, Carl, 113
Webber, Chris, 172–73
Weiss, George, 64
Weiss, Pierre, 41–42
Wells, Willie, 80
Weltfish, Gene, 30–31
Wepner, Chuck, 113
"What Is Love" (Haddaway), 185
What They Don't Teach You at Harvard Business School (McCormack), 14–16
When in Doubt, Fire the Manager (Dark), 77
White, Derrick, 138
White, Sol, 61, 81, 239n33
white dope (boxing), 91–93, 103–4, 108
White Men Can't Jump, 25
"White Men Can't Run" (Burfoot), 34–35, 52
"White Negro, The" (Mailer), 98–99, 102
Whitfield, Malvin G., 29
Wideman, John Edgar, 117
Wilbon, Michael, 175–76
Will, George, 158, 214
Willard, Jess, 91, 93, 107, 246n43
Williams, Billy Dee, 82

Williams, Ken, 202
Williams, Serena, 13, 16, 179
Williams, Venus, 13, 16
Willis, William, 51
Wilson, A'ja, 220
Wilson, David, 244n21
Wilson, Earl, 77
Wilson, Russell, 154
Winant, Howard, 4
Winslow, Sarah, 192
Witherspoon, Tim, 90
WNBA (Women's National Basketball Association), 178, 220–21
Wolfe, Thomas, 92
Wonderlic test, 167, 217
Woods, Tiger, 13
Woodward, Bob, 148
Workmen's Compensation Act, 124
World Anti-Doping Agency, 39
World Athletics. *See* IAAF (International Association of Athletics Federations)
World Athletics Championships, 23, 39, 41–42, 42, 48
World Series of Poker, 204
Woroner, Murry, 109–12
Wright, Richard, 85–87, 98, 115

X, Malcolm, 95–96
X Games, 39, 156

Yardley, Jonathan, 143
"Yesternow" (M. Davis), 106
You Know Me Al (R. Lardner), 92
Young, Dick, 67–68, 108
Young, Doc, 78–79, 111
Young, George, 167, 217–18
Yzaguirre, Raul, 63

Zirin, Dave, 272n17

For EU product safety concerns, contact us at Calle de José Abascal, 56–1°, 28003 Madrid, Spain or eugpsr@cambridge.org.

www.ingramcontent.com/pod-product-compliance
Ingram Content Group UK Ltd.
Pitfield, Milton Keynes, MK11 3LW, UK
UKHW021503220625
459949UK00018B/555